PC Magazine® Fighting Spyware, Viruses, and Malware

Ed Tittel

Wiley Publishing, Inc.

PC Magazine® Fighting Spyware, Viruses, and Malware
Published by
Wiley Publishing, Inc.
10475 Crosspoint Boulevard
Indianapolis, IN 46256-5774
www.wiley.com

Published simultaneously in Canada

ISBN: 0-7645-7769-7

Manufactured in the United States of America

10 9 8 7 6 5 4 3 2 1

1B/RW/RS/QU/IN

For general information on our other products and services or to obtain technical support, please contact our Customer Care Department within the U.S. at (800) 762-2974, outside the U.S. at (317) 572-3993 or fax (317) 572-4002.

Wiley also publishes its books in a variety of electronic formats. Some content that appears in print may not be available in electronic books.

Library of Congress Cataloging-in-Publication Data

Tittel, Ed.
PC magazine fighting spyware, viruses and malware / Ed Tittel.
p. cm.
Includes bibliographical references and index.
ISBN 0-7645-7769-7 (paper/website)
1. Computer security. 2. Computer viruses. I. Title.
QA76.9.A25T57 2005
005.8--dc22

2004024100

Credits

EXECUTIVE EDITOR
Chris Webb

CONTRIBUTOR AND PROJECT MANAGER
Dawn Rader

SENIOR DEVELOPMENT EDITOR
Kevin Kent

PRODUCTION EDITOR
Gabrielle Nabi

TECHNICAL EDITOR
Mark Justice Hinton

COPY EDITOR
Kim Cofer

EDITORIAL MANAGER
Mary Beth Wakefield

VICE PRESIDENT & EXECUTIVE GROUP PUBLISHER
Richard Swadley

VICE PRESIDENT AND PUBLISHER
Joseph B. Wikert

PROJECT COORDINATOR
Erin Smith

GRAPHICS AND PRODUCTION SPECIALISTS
Lauren Goddard
Heather Pope

QUALITY CONTROL TECHNICIAN
Amanda Briggs
John Greenough
Jessica Kramer
Carl Pierce

MEDIA DEVELOPMENT SPECIALIST
Kit Malone

PROOFREADING AND INDEXING
TECHBOOKS Production Services

About the Author

Ed Tittel is a full-time writer, trainer, and consultant, and the author of more than 100 computer books. He's been writing, researching, and teaching on Windows security topics since 1996. He's taught security classes for the NetWorld/Interop conference (1997–2002), the Internet Security Conference, a.k.a. TISC (1999–2001), and as an adjunct faculty member at Austin Community College in his hometown, of Austin, Texas. Ed also writes regularly about security topics for numerous TechTarget Web sites and for *Certification Magazine* (where he's a columnist and the Technology Editor). Ed also manages the IT certification guide and topic area at InformIT.com, and writes occasionally on security topics for TechBuilder.org, TechRepublic, and other Web sites.

Ed stumbled into the subject of this book — literally — in 2002 when one of his coworkers complained about a toolbar in Internet Explorer that just wouldn't go away. After repeated attempts to remove the offending item — an adware object that replaced defaults galore, and insinuated itself most cleverly into the Web browser and registry — Ed soon learned about anti-spyware and anti-adware software. From this encounter, an abiding interest in the subject matter was born and continues to this day. An inveterate tinkerer cursed with incurable curiosity, Ed has become something of a connoisseur of spyware, adware, and malware protection tools and techniques. For that reason he really enjoyed writing this book and would also be glad to hear from its readers at `etittel@lanw.com` via e-mail. To get past Ed's spam filter, however, please put **PCMFig:** in the subject line of all e-mails you send to him.

I'd like to dedicate this book to my loving wife, Dina, and thank her not only for her support and encouragement, but also for bringing our beautiful son, Gregory, into this world on 2/6/2004. Nothing I can do or say can ever completely communicate my love, appreciation, and affection, but that doesn't mean I won't keep trying!

Preface

When I read that Microsoft was planning for 100 million downloads of Windows XP Service Pack 2 (SP2) — a new add-on to the company's flagship desktop operating system that is being publicly released just as I finish the initial draft of this book — I already knew that the world of computing was crossing over into a new phase of use and existence. Explaining why will take a little doing, but also leads directly into the motivation and justification for this book.

I started using the Internet seriously in 1987 (and had been a serious CompuServe user since the late 1970s). Never in my wildest dreams did I see the Internet becoming a primary vehicle for software distribution, as well as communications, information gathering, socializing, entertainment, and so forth. Windows XP SP2 weighs in at somewhere between 250 and 266 megabytes in size — nearly half the contents of a typical CD-ROM, and a pretty hefty download for anybody who doesn't have a fast Internet connection.

Yet here is Microsoft, gearing up for 100 million downloads of this release — a staggering 210 *quadrillion* bits worth of data — in two months (note: in late October 2004, Microsoft reported there'd been 106 million copies of SP2 accessed, of which 90 million were downloaded and 26 million distributed on CD). And it's just one of many companies that now routinely use the Internet to deliver software, updates, upgrades, and so forth on a completely routine basis. In fact, Microsoft's recommendation for Windows XP users in need of SP2 was to simply enable the Automatic Update function in the operating system, so that it would show up some morning on the desktop, ready to be installed.

But alas, what works so very well for software and content that users actually want to see, use, or install works equally well for unwanted content and software as well. Pop-up advertisements for everything from college degrees to all kinds of medications to salacious materials routinely dog people's desktops as they visit Web sites, and downloading software from unknown or potentially questionable sources can introduce hidden invaders that can sometimes wreak havoc on the unwary or unsuspecting. Likewise, lots of interesting malicious software — called *malware* throughout this book — has interesting ways of using e-mail attachments, file transfers, or supposed image files to weasel its way into unprotected PCs.

Because everybody uses the Internet these days, everybody must also be prepared to deal with what's out there "in the wild" and be able to protect themselves from the unwanted or the uninvited interlopers that will try to make a home on their systems. That's the real reason why I wrote this book: to explain and explore these dangers, to provide some idea of the kinds of risks or threats they pose, and to describe preventative tools and best practices to help everyone avoid the threats they face on a daily basis, unwitting or otherwise. I also describe how to diagnose potential infections or infestations when unwanted visitors do establish residence on your PC, and how to clean up afterwards, if and when this should happen to you. The threats are real, the risks are tangible, and the consequences of infection can be pretty serious indeed, so a great deal of emphasis is put on preventing or avoiding such trouble.

Who Should Read This Book?

If you own a PC and use the Internet (or AOL, or some other private gateway service), you should probably at least look through this book. If you don't already have and use the kinds of tools described in its pages to deal with spyware, adware, pop-up advertisements, viruses, worms, Trojan horses, and spam, you will probably benefit from buying and reading this book. If you do make that investment, you will learn what you need to know to understand these threats, recognize them should they try to enter your PC, and to clean up after them should they succeed in taking up residence. That said, you will also learn how to fend off such threats and will probably be able to avoid the worst risks altogether and learn how to deal with some of the most persistent pests (which thankfully don't seem to pose the biggest risks or threats) on a routine basis.

If you are already familiar with the topics covered here, you might want to consider buying a copy of this book and passing it on to a friend or relative who also owns a PC and uses the Internet, but who may not know as much as you do. As I talked to experts in PC security in many fields while researching this book, the one comment I heard from them over and over again when I told them what I was up to was something like: "Wow! I have to get a copy of your book for my . . ." (fill in the blank here with something like friend, relative, customer, or other people who turn to more knowledgeable members of their personal networks when they need help with their PCs).

What's in the Book?

This book is divided into five parts:

- In **Part I, "Welcome to the Jungle!,"** I describe the characteristics of the Internet that make it such a fertile breeding ground for unwanted content and software of all kinds. I also describe and define the kinds of unwanted content and software that most PC and Internet users will want to take steps to block, foil, or filter out. This includes spyware, adware, pop-up advertisements, spam, and malicious software — namely viruses, worms, Trojan horses, and so-called *blended threats* (these combine characteristics from more than one category). Along the way, I also explain and explore potential sources of information you can consult to keep up with the ever-changing panoply of threats that are discovered daily on the Internet.
- In **Part II, "How Good PCs Go Bad,"** I explain how unwanted software and content finds its way to PCs, and how it can seek permission or otherwise wangle its way into taking up residence on unprotected machines. I explore the many possible channels through which such items can arrive on a PC, including e-mail, instant messaging applications, file transfers, software downloads, and so forth. Fearing that the worst is at least possible, I also describe and explain the typical symptoms of infestation or infection on a PC, and describe the tools and techniques involved in cleaning up after unwanted software establishes residency on a PC, including sources of help and instructions and ways to make doubly sure that your PC is completely cleaned up at the end of the process.

- **Part III, "The Particles of Protection,"** is the heart and soul of this book. In a series of five chapters, each devoted to a particular type of unwanted software or content, or a particular method or tool for foiling same, I describe what you can do to protect your PC and yourself from potential threats and malign influences. Along the way I tackle personal firewalls, anti-adware and anti-spyware packages, pop-up blockers, anti-virus software, and spam blockers (including spam handling services, standalone or plug-in spam filtering software packages, and spam filtering capabilities built into many modern e-mail packages).
- **Part IV, "Commonsense Rules for Safe Computing,"** addresses specific best practices and ground rules worth following when conducting various kinds of activity on or from the Internet. This includes recommendations for ensuring e-mail safety, safe and secure Web browsing, and general system safety for your PC.
- **Part V, "The Habit of Security,"** addresses matters related to maintaining a safe, secure computing environment on your PC once you've put all the necessary pieces and protections in place. It describes and explains a working routine to help maintain security and keep protections up-to-date, and it also explores how you can keep up with current security events and threat alerts, and how you might react should something appear to pose a genuine threat to your PC and its contents. This includes protective and preventive measures of all kinds, as well as best practices to make sure you don't let things slip and therefore become vulnerable.

After having read this book, you should be prepared to face and avoid the threats and exposures that Internet access can pose for any PC. In particular, you should understand what kinds of preventive measures to take, what kinds of protective software to install and use, and have a pretty good idea of where to find and how to install and use the various pieces and parts that go into securing a system. You should thus be able to avoid most sources of trouble online, and be ready to deal with (or sidestep) items that by hook or by crook (by crook, mostly) come calling at your PC's virtual threshold.

For More Information

You can find links to many of the references in this book by pointing your browser at `www.wiley.com/go/pcmag`. Once there, find the links to the book's references by selecting the companion site for this book, or explore some of the other great *PC Magazine* titles available.

Acknowledgments

Ed Tittel — I've been writing professionally for nearly 20 years now, and wrote my first book nearly 15 years ago. Although I've lost exact count, I know I've worked as an author for more than 120 books and have been involved in as many as 200 book projects altogether. During those years and through all those titles, I've had many occasions to appreciate and thank the many people who go into helping to create these books. This has been an extraordinary project for me, because I got the chance to dig into and learn about topics that are not only interesting but incredibly important to those who want to ensure a safe and secure computing experience for themselves and often for their families as well. Thus, my thanks and appreciation go to many people who contributed to this book in some way or another, including:

- My family — My most fervent thanks go to my lovely wife, Dina, who came all the way from Kyrgyzstan to make a home here with me in Austin, Texas. She not only came a long way to be here, she also gave me the best gift of my entire life: my wonderful son, Gregory, born in February 2004. Thanks also for her patience and support in holding up some of my end of the bargain while I was far too busy finishing up this book.
- My friends, colleagues, and posse at LANWrights (a division of Thomson NetG), with some of whom I've worked for nearly 10 years now — Dawn Rader, my project manager and contributor comes in for most of my thanks and appreciation for her many contributions to this book, large and small, but I'd also like to thank Mary Burmeister and Kim Lindros for their many contributions to the quality and character of my working and personal life.
- The entire crew at Wiley — This includes the executives and staff with whom I've worked for over 10 years now — especially Mary Bednarek, Andy Cummings, Joe Wikert, Bob Woerner, and many others. I'd like to single out executive editor Chris Webb for special treatment, because this book is as much a product of his vision and understanding of what PC users want as it is mine, and because he's such a consummate techie at heart (he's the first editor I've ever worked with who told me to go ahead and install a new software component because he'd already tried it and it worked just fine — to his great credit, he was right). Special thanks also to development editor Kevin Kent, who combined a practical sense of timing, requirements, and coverage with the flexibility to deal with the minor bumps and curves in the road of life. I also want to thank the copy editor and technical editor, Kim Cofer and Mark Justice Hinton, for their insightful and helpful input on the work and their many suggestions for ways that could and did improve the coverage. Thanks also to the folks involved in this book's production, proofreading, and indexing as well.
- Though many could — and have — argued that Microsoft is responsible for much of the mess that we find ourselves in today, particularly where spyware, adware, pop-ups, and Web browser vulnerabilities are concerned, I'm much more inclined to be grateful for the results that are finally starting to emerge in tangible form with Windows XP SP2 from their "trustworthy computing" initiative. Although they and the rest of the PC software industry

still have a long way to go before safety and security come with reasonable guarantees, they've made tremendous strides with their security philosophy and out-of-the-box defaults with Windows XP SP2.

- Finally, I'd like to thank the many vendor and industry figures and representatives who helped me research, find materials, software, or resources for this book. This includes Larry Leonard (BHODemon), Matt Otepka (104 Degrees West, PR company for Webroot), Sherri Walkenhorst and the rest of the crew at Connect Public Relations, especially Cory Edwards (Symantec/Norton), Gabriela Toma (BitDefender tech support), Jim Maurer (PopupCheck.com and AuditMyPC.com), Sergei Kaul (Popup-killer-review.com), Christine Stevenson and Nicholas Podrasky (Webroot), and Ken Shaurette (a principal at MPC Security Solutions, who graciously shared his strategies and tool selections with me, in response to articles related to this book). I'm sure there were many others who helped me while I was working on this project, but these are the only names I can find in my e-mail records, so please accept my thanks and my gratitude if I overlooked you by oversight or omission.

Dawn Rader—As always, I'd like to thank Ed Tittel, first and foremost, for not only allowing me to participate in this book, but also for the nearly 11 years of working together and great camaraderie. I also want to thank Kim Lindros and Mary Burmeister for helping me pick up the slack when workloads were hectic—there's no better group of coworkers and friends in the world! Thanks to the team at Wiley for seeing this important book through to completion. To all my friends and family: Thank you for always being there with love, support, and kindness when I need you. Finally, to John Davidson: Your strength, encouragement, and love are the greatest gifts I've ever received. Thank you for being such a good man.

Contents

Part IV Commonsense Rules for Safe Computing

Part V The Habit of Security

Part I

Welcome to the Jungle!

IN THIS PART:

Part I describes and explores the sometimes forbidding, often scary, and inscrutable landscape known as the Internet. This is where those who go online are likely to encounter all kinds of things they can probably live without, including spyware, adware, viruses, worms, Trojans, and other malware. As you work through Part I, you'll learn what kinds of potentially bad things lurk out there, why they're worth avoiding, and how to recognize their effects.

Chapter 1

Unwelcome Intruders Seeking Entry

To some extent, it's reasonable to view the Internet as "the ultimate jungle" of lore and story: deep, dark, and full of dangerous denizens. For PC users, this means that any activities involving a trip into the wild — that is, onto the Internet — carries with it the risks of infection, compromise, or attack that prudent visitors to real jungles usually take steps to avoid. Much of this book talks about what's involved in being prudent, how to limit or eliminate chances of compromise, and what kinds of Internet attacks or other hazards are best avoided whenever possible.

It's a Jungle Out There!

These days, anybody who goes online has a chance to experience the wild frontier. This doesn't require leaving home, or even walking any further than to wherever you keep your computer. But once you turn it on, fire up a Web browser or e-mail program, and start digging into the unbelievable variety that the Internet has to offer, you're also exposing your computer to an assortment of hazards that can vary all the way from merely annoying to potentially catastrophic in terms of what such hazards can do to your machine. All kinds of risks and exposures lurk in waiting for the unwarned or unwary, and require only that you visit a certain Web page or open a certain e-mail attachment to inflict themselves upon you — or at least, upon your computer and its contents.

Caution

Any time something unknown or uncertain comes your way, whether a Web site asks if you want to change your default home page setting, pick a new search engine, or add a toolbar to your browser, or you're asked in your e-mail to open an unexpected e-mail attachment, the safe thing to do is "Just Say No!" — that is, you should refuse such proffered changes and avoid opening any e-mail attachments you're not explicitly expecting. Unfortunately, not all threats are kind enough to ask permission before attempting to get familiar with your PC, but if you have the chance to say no, you probably should.

No one can deny that all kinds of unwanted and potentially dangerous threats are out there. The news media routinely report new hazards as they're discovered, and the rates of discovery are going nowhere but up. Whereas it was unheard of for more than 50 or 60 threats to be reported weekly worldwide in the mid to late 1990s, in 2004, the total number of such reports meets or exceeds those numbers on some days. Why is this happening? As the Internet becomes more pervasive, more people use it, and it creates more opportunities for those who may not have your best interests at heart to seek ways to learn more about you, influence or manage your behavior, or simply to mess with your computer (and probably with your sense of security and well-being, too).

The motivations that drive individuals — and even some companies — to try to find covert or unannounced ways to introduce all kinds of software or tracking tools onto your computer are many and varied. Information is worth money to some, whether it be in the form of reselling information about you to others or using that information to sell things to you directly. This helps explain why visiting so many Web sites results in the deposit of all kinds of small, passive data-collection tools, called *cookies* (more about them later), that record information about your activities on the Web, ready to report them to a server the next time you visit a site that knows how to ask for and read that cookie.

Cross-Reference

Not all cookies are inherently evil. Though some collect information about you that you might not want or need them to know, more benign cookies keep track of site-specific activities, or gather information about you that may actually be helpful the next time you visit a site. As you learn in Chapter 3, cookies don't pose the same kinds of threats that other unwanted deposits on your computer do. Later, in Chapters 6 and 7, you learn more about the tools you can use to fend off cookies. But if you notice that your ability to navigate or be recognized on some Web site suffers because its cookie is turned off, you may want to consider turning such a cookie back on (lots more on this later).

Access to consumers is also worth money, along the lines of "another warm body." Because advertisers pay to show you advertisements on the Web, just as they do on radio or TV, this may help you to understand why visiting certain free Web sites produces a seemingly endless series of small windows designed to inform you, educate you, or perhaps just to catch your eye — but ultimately, also designed to sell you something. Many Web sites generate the funding they need to keep operating by selling advertising to all comers, then inserting banners or separate advertising windows — known as pop-ups or pop-up ads — that they show to visitors who pass through their sites. You can see an example of this kind of thing in Figure 1-1.

You may even notice that some Web sites bring strange "invisible" Web pages to your desktop. Figure 1-2 shows the toolbar icon for what's sometimes called a "one-pixel" Web page — that is, a page frame so small you can't see it. Normally, such pages exist only as a way to bring other (unwanted) stuff to your desktop. Usually, they can't be restored, resized, or maximized by right-clicking their toolbar icons. If you try to move the window, you'll see your cursor dragging and dropping nothing visible!

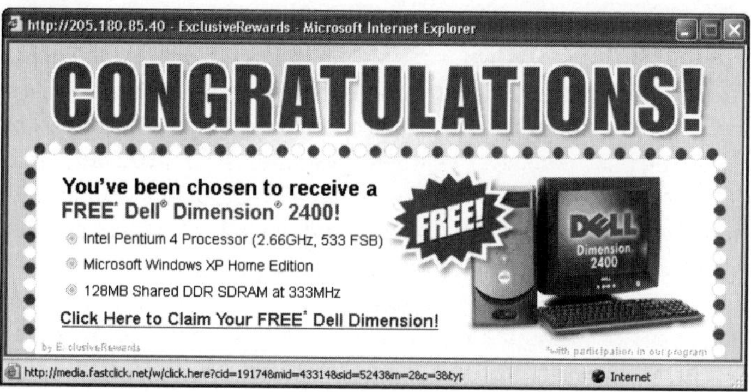

Figure 1-1: Pop-ups jump to the top of your screen, forcing you to close them to keep working on what's underneath. Some are more objectionable than others; all interfere with your desktop.

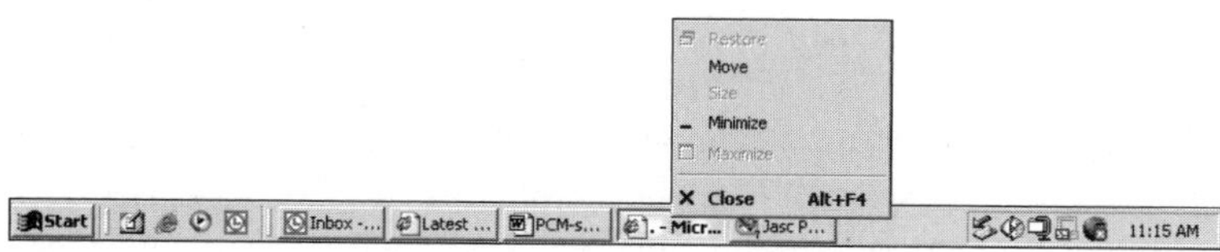

Figure 1-2: A one-pixel Web page shows up on your toolbar (it shows up as a document named period "."), but you can't force it to appear on your desktop. It's there only to open the way for unwanted intrusions or advertisements.

Tip

Because the pop-up menu shown in Figure 1-2 includes a Close control, you can indeed close this unwanted item manually. But it's better to block such items from making a home on your desktop completely—I describe exactly how to do that in Chapter 6.

Some Web sites even try to change the way your Web browser works to turn it to their advantage. If you've ever wondered why your home page has been switched from your favorite starting point on the Internet (perhaps Yahoo! or Google, if you're like many casual Internet users) to some other home page, it might be because you agreed to this change in a dialog box without really realizing the consequences of such an agreement. Some Web sites are reputed to make such changes without even asking, in a sort of home page hijack maneuver.

Other Web sites are still more aggressive with visitors. They don't try to change your home page; instead, they'll request permission to install a toolbar in your Web browser. Besides changing your home page assignment, this also results in the appearance of additional buttons in the control areas

of a browser window. Behind the scenes, it may even change your favorites or bookmarks to preferentially drive you toward sites of their choosing, switch your preferred search engine to their preferred search engine, and all kinds of other things that can be a real pain to figure out, let alone fix. Here again, some Web sites don't even bother to ask your permission: If your computer isn't ready to repel such advances, they'll simply make whatever changes they want and let you deal with the consequences however you can.

As an innocuous example is the Yahoo! toolbar, which you can choose to install at www.yahoo.com if you wnat to see what something like this adds to your browser. In Internet Explorer, toolbars normally appear at the top of the window, just above the Web page display and below the page address. The Yahoo! toolbar, however, is by no means an unwanted item. It's well-behaved about asking install permission but it can give you an idea of what such a browser change might look like.

One of this book's primary goals is to help you recognize these kinds of potential intrusions on your computer, leaving aside for the moment whether or not they pose any real dangers to your computer or your privacy. I also want to explain how such things work, what kinds of traces they leave behind, and how you can clean up after them if you must. Better still, I explain various ways to avoid such unwanted influences and activities on your computer in the hopes that you'll use them in preventive fashion. As you'll see elsewhere in this book (or as you may have or will learn through direct experience some day), it's a lot easier to avoid such trouble than to catch it and have to clean up the aftermath!

In general, however, if unexpected changes occur on your PC, there's a chance that unwanted software may be involved. It's smart to keep your eyes on this kind of thing and to take what steps you can to head them off before they make themselves at home on your computer. In the sections that make up the rest of this chapter, you'll have a chance to see more examples of these things, to understand what they are and how they work, and to appreciate what kinds of symptoms you might notice if one or more of these things take up residence on or try to make their way onto your machine.

Cross-Reference

The rest of this chapter tackles the more benign forms of unwanted software — namely spyware, adware (pop-ups), and spam (unwanted e-mail). Chapter 2 is where I get into the stuff that can sometimes do bad things to your computer, including what's sometimes called *malware* (a contraction of "malicious software"), such as viruses, worms, Trojans, and other members of that unsavory software genre.

Understanding Spyware

To start any discussion of spyware, it's essential to understand what the term means. As the name implies, *spyware* is anything that takes up residence on a computer, usually uninvited, that can report on the activities and preferences of the computer's users, or disclose information about data stored on a computer. In other words, it spies on what the computer is used for and possibly for what it contains, to report on its findings to outsiders when an opportunity presents itself.

Whatis.com provides a slightly more detailed definition of spyware that's interesting to peruse and ponder next:

> Spyware is any technology that aids in gathering information about a person or organization without their knowledge. On the Internet (where it is sometimes called a spybot or tracking software), spyware is programming that is put in someone's computer to secretly gather information about the user and relay it to advertisers or other interested parties. Spyware can get in a computer as a software virus or as the result of installing a new program. Data collecting programs that are installed with the user's knowledge are not considered to be spyware if the user fully understands what data is being collected and with whom it is being shared. However, spyware is often installed without the user's consent, as a drive-by download, or as the result of clicking some option in a deceptive pop-up window.
>
> The cookie is a well-known mechanism for storing information about an Internet user on their own computer. However, the existence of cookies and their use is generally not concealed from users, who can also disallow access to cookie information. Nevertheless, to the extent that a Web site stores information about you in a cookie that you don't know about, the cookie mechanism could be considered a form of spyware.

There's enough material in this lengthy quote from Whatis.com to justify a little follow-up commentary. The term *drive-by download* describes the circumstance in which visiting a Web page causes software to be downloaded and installed on user machines without informing users that this has happened, or without obtaining their prior consent. Please recall also that cookies are passive, mostly textual records that Web sites read and write to help track user history, preferences, and activity. They are covered in more detail in Chapters 7 and 11 of this book.

On the Web

In general, you'll find `www.whatis.com` **a great place to learn about all kinds of computing terminology. Spyware is defined at** `http://searchcrm.techtarget.com/sDefinition/0,,sid11_gci214518,00.html`.

Taking my definition and the Whatis.com definition together, the key points about spyware are as follows:

- Information is gathered without obtaining the user's consent
- It may be relayed to third parties without the user's knowledge
- It may sometimes change the behavior, look, or feel of a PC without either the user's knowledge or consent

The Whatis.com definition mentions viruses as a potential source of spyware; although true, this is a far less common cause than simply visiting certain Web sites that target the unwary or the unprepared. Cookies do indeed deserve mention in this context, because they remain the most widespread and prevalent tool for gathering information about users. But because cookies are easy to turn off or block, they're also relatively easy to deal with. Anti-spyware programs do a great job of this, but privacy controls in most Web browsers can also help you manage cookies quickly and easily. Generally speaking, cookies are not the biggest causes of trouble or concern when it comes to spyware.

In the end, perhaps the Federal Trade Commission's definition of spyware (which you can find at `www.ftc.gov/opa/2004/04/spywaretest.htm`) also bears repeating: Spyware is "software that aids in gathering information about a person or organization without their knowledge and which may send such information to another entity without the consumer's consent, or asserts control over a computer without the consumer's knowledge." The real issue is that something makes changes to your system or gathers and reports information about you without first securing your agreement and consent to do so.

What Qualifies as Spyware?

Microsoft offers some great clues as to what else qualifies as spyware on a Web page entitled "What you can do about spyware and other unwanted software" (see the next On the Web icon for the URL). It makes some valuable points about where spyware comes from and how it behaves, noting that spyware is often picked up when making free downloads (such as free games, tools, utilities, and so forth). It also points out that the information that spyware gathers ranges from fairly innocuous, such as all the Web sites a user visits on a PC, to potentially dangerous, such as account or usernames and the passwords that go with them. Spyware can come from all kinds of sources, such as music- or file-sharing sites, free games from untrusted providers, or tools and utilities from unknown or untrusted sources.

On the Web

Read Microsoft's "What you can do about spyware and other unwanted software" online at `http://www.microsoft.com/athome/security/spyware/spywarewhat.mspx`

Likewise, spyware often travels in company with other software used to display advertisements, also known as adware (the subject of the next section in this chapter, in fact). Sometimes, adware includes spyware components, in that it also tracks user activity, preferences, and behavior, as well as coordinating a ceaseless stream of unwanted pop-ups on your PC's desktop.

Another key concept in deciding whether software on your PC is good or bad hinges on the notion of deception. Deceptive software changes settings or defaults, adds (or removes) components from your PC, and generally manages your system without seeking permission or explaining consequences and outcomes in advance so you can decide whether or not to proceed. Deceptive software often creeps onto systems during the installation of other free software, as with the music, games, tools, or utilities mentioned earlier. It can also be disclosed in long, deliberately obtuse or boring license agreements, which many users agree to without reading deeply or completely (and in that case, some spyware vendors have even been bold enough to claim "informed consent" on the part of hoodwinked users). Sometimes, so-called *active content* is covertly loaded when you visit certain

Web pages (active content basically represents a software-based, program-like capability that gets covertly installed on your machine).

Sometimes, a Web page may ask your permission to add an innocuous-sounding widget to your computer, ostensibly to permit that page to perform some useful function or service. This is when my earlier advice to "Just say No" to unsolicited downloads is worth recalling—and heeding! Likewise, anything that asks you to extend your trust permanently is probably worth denying as well. That means you should avoid clicking the check box in a download that reads "Always trust content from XYZ Corp" unless you're pretty darn sure you really can trust all content from that source (I don't even give Microsoft or Symantec that privilege on my desktops, to be absolutely candid, because I want to be informed and to grant permission before anything shows up there).

Signs of Potential Spyware Infestation

Although other, more subtle signs exist that spyware (or other unwanted software) has invaded your system, the most common and discernible symptoms are as follows:

- **Something new or unexpected shows up**—Whether in your Web browser or on your desktop, it could be anything from a new home or search page, to a toolbar, to a piece of software. Be grateful it's something you can see!
- **An increase in ads, pop-ups, or advertising**—Sometimes, you'll be overwhelmed with ads and it's easy to recognize that something's amiss; at other times, volume may just go up a little, or you'll find that closing one ad provokes another to appear, ad infinitum.
- **Performance slows down noticeably**—If your system starts running sluggishly without a good cause (indexing files, compacting your drives, or other intensive tasks), it may just be that the overhead of recording your actions or delivering oodles of ads are dragging down performance. Worse yet, buggy spyware or adware can make a previously stable system susceptible to crashing.

Among the many potential and unwanted effects of spyware, a little research into news coverage of this topic will document numerous cases of bogged-down systems or Internet access, theft of personal identity or other information, system crashes or instability, and loss of key system files or documents. While some of these are scarier than others, none is welcome news!

Cross-Reference

If your PC starts acting up for no good reason, something may indeed be up to no good on your system. In Chapter 4, you learn more about how to detect and cure spyware, adware, and other infestations that explains how to test and possibly confirm your suspicions, and how to clean up if there's a need.

Even as I'm writing this chapter, the news is full of stories about spyware, adware, and so forth. Scanning relevant headlines, I found items like "One in three PCs hosts spyware or Trojans" and "PCs infested with 30 pieces of spyware" in the recent past. If anything, a review of historical trends in such reporting shows things are getting worse over time, not better.

Understanding Adware and Pop-Ups

If spyware's job is to covertly track and report on user activity or data, *adware's* job is to bring advertising to your desktop — ready, willing, and able to deal with it or not. I want to turn once again to Whatis.com for its take on this term:

> Adware is any software application in which advertising banners are displayed while the program is running. The authors of these applications include additional code that delivers the ads, which can be viewed through pop-up windows or through a bar that appears on a computer screen. The justification for adware is that it helps recover programming development cost and helps to hold down the cost for the user.
>
> Adware has been criticized for occasionally including code that tracks a user's personal information and passes it on to third parties, without the user's authorization or knowledge. This practice has been dubbed spyware and has prompted an outcry from computer security and privacy advocates, including the Electronic Privacy Information Center. (`http://searchsmallbizit.techtarget.com/sDefinition/0,,sid44_gci521293,00.html`)

Here again, you can see a profound tendency for adware and spyware to travel together, if they're not bundled into the same unwanted programs.

In the introduction to this chapter, I discussed the notion of a one-pixel Web page, which creates a running instance of a Web browser on your computer without showing you anything you can see on your desktop. In actuality, it's not that there's nothing there; rather, what's there is just so small you can't really see it. But what these one-pixel windows provide is a constant presence on your computer, thereby creating a launch pad for invoking ad after ad after ad.

Though not everybody objects to all advertisements per se, plenty of unsavory ads — often of an overtly and offensively sexual nature that nobody would want a minor child to see (and which most adults would gladly skip, too) — can pop up on an unprotected desktop. The trick is to avoid adware sites whenever possible, and to know how to escape when ads run amok and just won't stop popping up on your desktop. Only experience can teach the former (but my recommendations on anti-spyware and anti-adware tools will protect you to a large extent, should you choose to follow them).

Using Task Manager to Halt a Pop-up Invasion

If you ever find yourself in a situation in which ads are popping up faster than you can close browser windows with your mouse, here's a trick you can try in the form of a step-by-step example.

Note

For the examples throughout this book, I assume readers are using Microsoft Windows XP, with Service Pack 2 (SP2) or later installed on that machine. Some of the details in step-by-steps will differ if you're using a different version of Windows. It's also worth noting that even though Windows XP SP2 is by no means a perfect operating system, it appears to be the most secure version of Windows Microsoft has ever produced. If you're using an older version of Windows, especially something older than Windows 2000 or Windows Me, it's probably time to think long and hard about upgrading your operating system, and probably your hardware, too, because Windows XP's processing requirements (64MB RAM minimum, 128MB or more RAM recommended, 300 MHz Pentium/Celeron or AMD K6/Athlon/Duron processor or better, 1.5GB or more of free hard disk space, Super VGA [800x600] graphics display and adapter, and keyboard and

Microsoft-compatible mouse) are more than what most older systems include. See `www.microsoft.com/windowsxp/` for more details on Windows XP Home and Professional requirements.

If you click your way through these steps, or find a workable analog on your version of Windows, you can kill your Web browser and thereby bring a pop-up invasion to a screeching halt:

1. Right-click on any open area on your Windows taskbar (by default, it's at the bottom of your screen). This action produces a pop-up menu, as shown in Figure 1-3.

Figure 1-3: Right-clicking on the Windows taskbar produces a pop-up menu from which you can launch Task Manager.

2. On the pop-up menu, select the entry labeled Task Manager . . . .
3. When Windows Task Manager opens, click the Processes tab, if it's not already selected (Figure 1-4 shows Task Manager with the Processes tab selected).

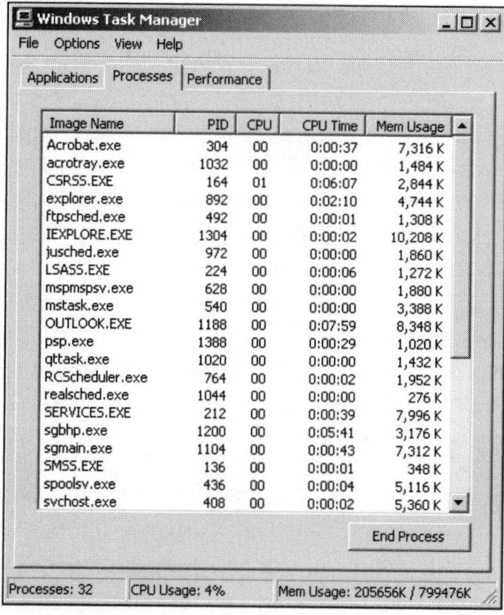

Figure 1-4: The Task Manager display varies by which tab is selected; here, it's the Processes tab, which is the one you want.

4. In the Image Name list, select any line that reads `IEXPLORE.EXE` (or whatever the name for your Web browser's executable process happens to be — for example `mozilla.exe` for Mozilla, `opera.exe` for Opera, and `firefox.exe` for Firefox), and then click the End Process button.
5. Confirm that you do indeed want to end the process by clicking the Yes button on the subsequent screen.

Caution

Clicking the End Process button as directed in the preceding step-by-step list shuts down the process that all open Web browser windows share. If you do this, you'll lose any work you may not yet have saved in whatever browser windows you opened yourself. But this is a sure way to stop an ad invasion, so it's worth knowing. It's strictly an emergency move, but may come in handy some day. Indeed, if it weren't the case that every pop-up that appears on your desktop also creates an application instance in the Task Manager Applications tab view, I would suggest you kill things there instead — but when that view is crammed full of a dozen or more instances of the same thing, with more popping up all the time, desperate moves like the one described here really do make sense.

Of Banners and Pop-Ups

Adware typically brings advertisements to users in one of two forms: banners and pop-ups. Of the two, banners are less objectionable in the way they appear in your Web browser, though their content may be just as unwanted as that in any pop-up.

Banners are advertisements that appear within the normal frame of a Web page. Web site operators sell ads for these spaces, which often occur at the top of most pages, or in areas along the right-hand or left-hand sides of a page, just like magazines sell print ads. As you can always flip the page in a magazine, so can you also scroll away from such ads on a Web site (though some top-of-page banners do use frames to remain in view even so). Figure 1-5 shows a banner on the top of a Web page on a well-behaved Web site: It's labeled on the left-hand side as an advertisement, and you can scroll away from it if you like. Notice the other banner on the lower right, of which you can see only the top edge.

Pop-ups appear in separate browser windows above the Web page you were looking at before they showed up. Normally, you must close the pop-up to return to that page and continue reading, scanning, or whatever else you might have been doing. One or two pop-ups can be annoying; a continuing stream of pop-ups can be overwhelming and infuriating. Figure 1-6 shows a pop-up on an otherwise favorite site where every acronym known to man can be expanded. Another type of ad, called a *pop-under*, appears underneath the open window, only to be discovered later when the covering window is closed. Also, one browser window can deliberately open another window when following a script or executing active content, so not all additional windows are pop-ups or unwanted (there's lots more detail on this subject in Chapter 6, which takes pop-ups as its entire focus).

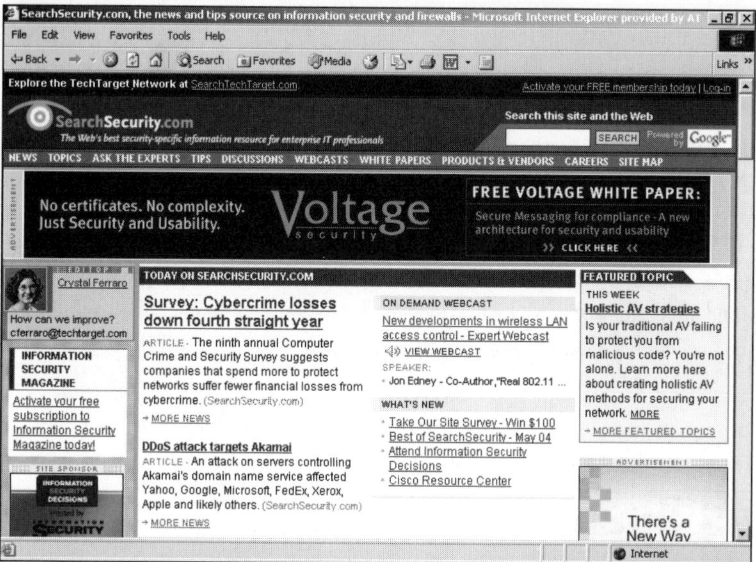

Figure 1-5: Banners appear inside a normal Web page frame, and aren't usually as obnoxious as pop-ups.

Reprinted by permission of Tech Target, Inc.

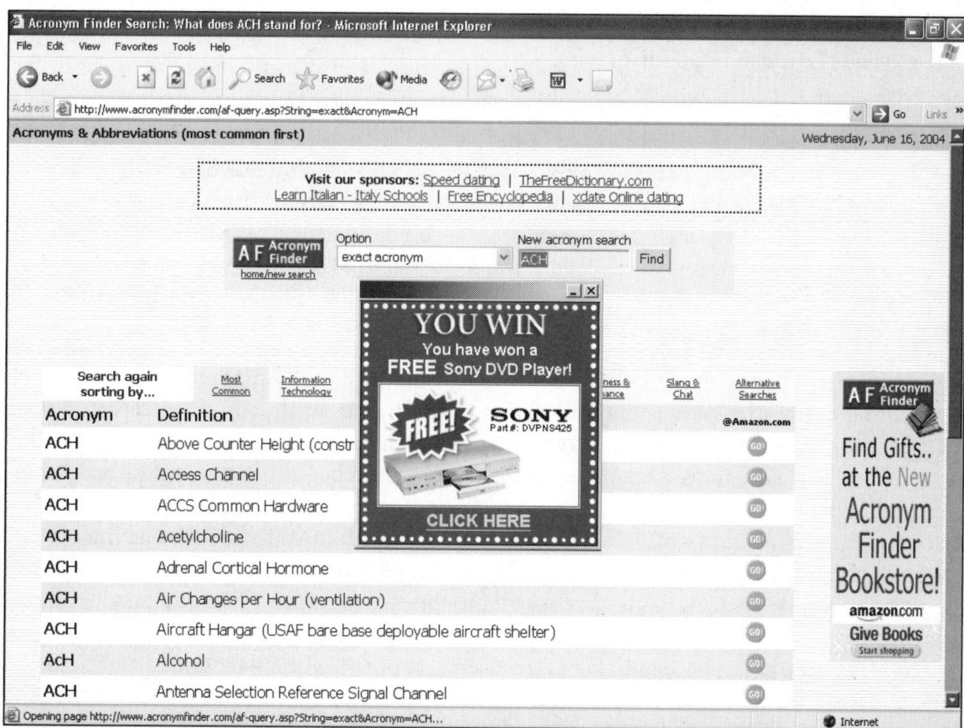

Figure 1-6: The pop-up ad in this figure says you've won a free DVD player! Wanna bet?

Good news for users of Windows XP who install SP2: Not only does the new and improved version of IE 6 include a pop-up blocker that works pretty well (see my discussion of its test results in Chapter 6 for more details), but it's also turned on by default. Thus, once you upgrade (or after you've upgraded) you won't have to put up with such distractions any more unless you actually want to see them.

Cross-Reference

Other kinds of pop-ups besides ads sometimes occur on PCs. These include instant messaging windows, Windows Messenger windows, and other kinds of pop-ups that Windows itself or other applications enable. You learn more about how to recognize and deal with these in Chapters 4 and 6.

Understanding Spam

The exact origins of the term *spam*, as commonly used to identify and denigrate unsolicited e-mail, are a matter of some debate. Most experts tend to mention the now-infamous Monty Python skit in which the word *spam* represents most of what's available on a restaurant menu, wherein the term's sheer repetition becomes thoroughly maddening long before the skit finally ends. Some of the same qualities still adhere to the e-mail variety of spam — in fact, many experts now believe that spam makes up more than 70 percent of all e-mail traffic on the Internet.

Here's the Whatis.com definition for spam:

> Spam is unsolicited e-mail on the Internet. From the sender's point-of-view, it's a form of bulk mail, often to a list obtained from a spambot or to a list obtained by companies that specialize in creating e-mail distribution lists. To the receiver, it usually seems like junk e-mail. It's roughly equivalent to unsolicited telephone marketing calls except that the user pays for part of the message because everyone shares the cost of maintaining the Internet. Spammers typically send a piece of e-mail to a distribution list in the millions, expecting that only a tiny number of readers will respond to their offer. Spam has become a major problem for all Internet users. (`http://searchmobilecomputing.techtarget.com/sDefinition/0,,sid40_gci213031,00.html`)

To help clarify the Whatis.com definition, a *spambot* (a contraction of "spam robot") is a type of software robot that cruises the Web, reading all the pages it can find. As it does, it extracts all e-mail addresses it finds and writes them to a file. Periodically, the spambot's e-mail address file is harvested and used to add to bulk e-mail distribution lists (which often number in the millions of recipients, as the Whatis.com definition indicates).

However the bulk e-mails that send spam obtain their distribution lists, those recipients are almost always united in their distaste for e-mails of that type. But because some miniscule percentage of the population that such e-mail targets apparently bites at whatever's offered, lots of companies — many of them located outside the United States, Canada, and the European Union to get beyond reach of anti-spam laws now in effect in those parts of the world — continue to broadcast spam to the masses.

Spam is also something of a triple-whammy.

- First, by itself spam e-mail is unwanted and causes Internet congestion, consumes e-mail server resources, and generally ticks off a lot of people.
- Second, many forms of spam originate from running malware programs (more on this in Chapter 2) that send e-mail with infected attachments so they can reproduce and keep spreading.

Caution

This helps to explain one of the golden rules of e-mail security: *Never* open an attachment you don't expect to receive, even if it claims to be from a friend or family member.

Numerous clever e-mail-based infections harvest e-mail address books on the computers they infect, then mail themselves to everyone listed therein. To make matters more interesting, this kind of spam often claims to originate from a randomly selected harvested address. Thus, somebody you know (and trust) whose address also appears in a harvested address book can be identified as the sender of an infected e-mail message.

- Third, many e-mail servers with built-in attachment screening capabilities automatically send "warning messages" to senders identified in incoming messages when infection is detected or suspected. This is all well and good when such notification warns a sender about a real infection. But when incoming e-mail uses harvested addresses from innocent third parties, the original spam is doubled when a bogus infection report is sent to somebody who's probably not infected!

Given the astonishing volume and pervasive presence of spam, numerous short-term solutions are possible. Many companies or individuals now route their e-mail through special spam-screening services to clean out the worst of the spam before accepting incoming deliveries. Likewise, most modern e-mail software — including that used on e-mail servers to store and forward messages, and that used on e-mail clients so users can read mail on their desktops — includes all kinds of filters and blocks that can also hunt out and eliminate obvious spam before it shows up (or stays) in somebody's inbox.

The real problem with spam is human ingenuity. It's become a kind of cops-and-robbers game, in that as the good guys come up with more and better ways to identify and block spam from being delivered, the bad guys come up with more and better ways to circumvent identification and sneak into your inbox anyway. In fact, it's the unwanted, covert, and unsolicited nature of spam that permits me to lump it in with spyware and adware, because all of these items find ways to weasel onto computers despite reasonable attempts to keep them away.

Resources

For more discussion of the depth of the problem, you can turn to three good online articles:

Jacques, Robert. "One in three PCs hosts spyware or Trojans." vnunet.com, June 16, 2004, `www.vnunet.com/news/1155923`. A survey of 650,000 consumer PCs turns up 18 million instances of spyware.

Jacques, Robert. "PCs infested with 30 pieces of spyware." vnunet.com, April 16, 2004, `www.vnunet.com/news/1154438`. Most PCs can easily carry as many as 30 pieces of spyware; over 90 percent of machines surveyed show signs of infection.

Thompson, Roger. "We Must Beat Spyware." eweek.com, August 9, 2004.

Additionally, Steve Gibson is a long-time computer wizard who has done a lot of interesting work in the area of computer security including with spyware and adware. His OptOut Web pages are a must-read on this general topic. His free tool is both trustworthy and a real gem: `http://grc.com/optout.htm`.

Summary

As people venture onto the Internet, they soon learn that unwanted, uninvited, and downright sneaky software, messages, and data elements find their way onto their computers. Without taking appropriate preventive measures, and practicing safe computing, it's easy to catch something you'd rather not keep. But when unexpected changes, performance slowdowns, or lots of ads start showing up on a PC, it's time to start wondering if something's up to no good on that machine. In this chapter, you learned about three potential forms of unwanted software or data to which many PCs can fall prey:

- **Spyware** — which generally installs itself on computers unannounced, and gathers data about user activities, Web sites visited, preferences, (and sometimes more).
- **Adware** — which finds ways to make your computer show you lots of advertisements, which can come either in the form of banners (inline text and graphics inside Web pages you visit) or pop-ups (separate Web browser windows that come between you and your work, sometimes in great numbers).
- **Spam** — unsolicited e-mail that can show up in your inbox from bulk e-mailers trying to sell or tell you something you probably don't want to know, or from malware that's trying to reproduce from inside as many inboxes as possible.

In Chapter 2, you learn more about malicious software, or malware, including viruses, worms, Trojans, and other nasties that can not only move in and start using your computer without permission, but that can also wreak havoc on the systems they infect.

Chapter 2

Understanding Malware

When you run into a word that starts with *mal*, it's a literal sign that something is bad. In Latin, the stem *male* usually relates to the identical adverb, which means "badly," that derives from the noun *malus*, which means "bad." Thus, if the term malware rings no bells for you, nor sounds any alarms, think "badware" instead and you'll be on the right track. In the preceding chapter, you learned about some of the more normally benign forms of unwanted software or messages, including spyware, adware, and spam. Although such materials don't normally intend to do bad things, unfortunate or unwanted side effects can sometimes occur from encounters with them (especially when, as can be the case, unwanted e-mail also carries unwanted malware along with it — more on that later).

In this chapter, you learn about unwanted software that's deliberately bad in intent, and sometimes in outcome, for those who cross its path — or more accurately, for those who somehow wind up with malware on their computers. Here, you learn about some of the more malign (there's that *mal* stem again!) denizens that it's far too easy to encounter on or from the Internet these days, including viruses, worms, Trojans, and wicked combinations thereof that go by the not terribly scary names "blended threat" or "hybrid virus." As in the previous chapter, I start with some definitions, explore the threats and exposures that malware can pose to a system and its contents, and talk about needs for proper precautions, best practices, and prevention — but also occasionally, appropriate cures or cleanups.

About Viruses, Worms, Trojans, and More

In general, most experts view the term *malware* as a contraction of the two words "malicious software." By deliberate construction, the word has bad connotations and, likewise, a deservedly bad reputation. Creating the category to which this chapter is devoted, Whatis.com defines malware as follows:

> Malware (for 'malicious software') is programming or files that are developed for the purpose of doing harm. Thus, malware includes computer viruses, worms, and Trojan horses. (`http://searchsecurity.techtarget.com/sDefinition/0,,sid14_gci762187,00.html`)

Actually, I think the psychology of malware is a little less clear-cut than this definition suggests, but I'm not about to argue on behalf of misguided (but sometimes intelligent and gifted) programmers who appear to tackle writing malware like mountain climbers tackle formidable peaks like Mount Everest. The interesting thing about this particular definition is that it introduces a number of important constituent elements — namely viruses, worms, and Trojan horses, which I explore in the sections that follow.

Viruses

One primary characteristic that a piece of software must possess to qualify as a *virus* is a programmed-in urge to reproduce. That is, it must include some mechanism for distributing copies of itself, using any of a variety of mechanisms to spread. Another characteristic common to viruses is that they are covert and do not explicitly advertise their presence or their intentions. This failure to advertise goes hand in hand with another, more general virus characteristic that the reproduction requirement shows in one very specific way — namely, that viruses arrive on systems with their own agendas, and act on their own without any instructions or permission being sought from the users of the machines they occupy. Like real, biological viruses, computer viruses seek to exploit systems for their own purposes and to their own ends. They arrive uninvited, hide in secrecy, and generally work in obscurity.

Whatis.com defines the term *virus* as follows:

> In computers, a virus is a program or programming code that replicates by being copied or initiating its copying to another program, computer boot sector or document. Viruses can be transmitted as attachments to an e-mail note or in a downloaded file, or be present on a diskette or CD. The immediate source of the e-mail note, downloaded file, or diskette you've received is usually unaware that it contains a virus. Some viruses wreak their effect as soon as their code is executed; other viruses lie dormant until circumstances cause their code to be executed by the computer. Some viruses are benign or playful in intent and effect ("Happy Birthday, Ludwig!") and some can be quite harmful, erasing data or causing your hard disk to require reformatting. A virus that replicates itself by resending itself as an e-mail attachment or as part of a network message is known as a worm. (`http://searchsecurity.techtarget.com/sDefinition/0,,sid14_gci213306,00.html`)

Generally speaking, viruses hide within computer files rather than sitting out in the open, in some obvious, visible, and separate form. But viruses must run — that is, a computer must execute the code out of which they're made — to do their dirty work. Until this happens, their ability to do harm is essentially nil. This explains why the most effective technique for fending off viruses is to inspect all files and media that enter a system, looking for signs of potential infection, and refusing to copy any potentially infected files into memory or storage. Once stored, execution becomes possible; if never stored, impossible. Hence, the vital importance of file screening.

Whatis.com's definition of viruses goes on to identify three specific types:

- **File infectors** — Many viruses target files that are likely to be executed in some form or fashion, reasoning well (if sneakily) that it ups their chances to exploit any opportunity to run. This, of course, hinges on a user's decision to execute a file in which a virus is hiding, and explains why ordinary executable files like `.exe` and `.com` are such typical targets for virus infection. But any program file type that Windows can call for execution is likewise susceptible; common ones are listed and briefly described in Table 2-1.

Table 2-1 Common Windows Executable File Types

Extension	*Explanation*
`.bat`	Windows command batch file
`.com`	Specially compiled DOS/Windows binary executable file
`.exe`	Windows standard binary executable file
`.js`	JavaScript language source file
`.mnu`	Associated with menu files for various applications and runtime environments
`.ovl`	Windows or DOS overlay file, usually part of operating system code
`.pif`	Windows program information file
`.prg`	Associated with all kinds of Windows program files, including various databases
`.scr`	Windows screensaver file
`.sys`	Windows data file, also associated with Sysgraph, Sysstat, and SPSS applications
`.vb`	Visual Basic script file
`.vbe`	Visual Basic script file
`.vbs`	Visual Basic for Applications (included in all MS Office components) script file
`.ws`	Windows Script file
`.wsc`	Windows scripting component file
`.wsf`	Windows scripting file (replaces `.js`, `.vbs`, and `.ws` in newer versions of Windows)

For a complete listing of all potentially harmful/executable Windows file extensions, see "Potentially Harmful Extensions" at `www.icdatamaster.com/harmful.html`. This site documents more than 15,000 known file extensions.

- **System or boot-record infectors** — PC media uses special programs that invariably appear in the same location, namely, the boot sector on floppy disks or the master boot record (MBR) on hard disks, to help the computer get up and running as it's started up (unsurprisingly, this is called the *boot process*, or "booting up"). These kinds of viruses can spread only when a PC is booted from infected media (which results in copying the boot sector virus from the startup disk to other disks on the same system). Such viruses are more rare in days when file transfer over the Internet is more common than media exchange, but by no means extinct.

Caution

Once contracted, boot sector viruses can make systems unbootable (unable to start). This requires cleanup, but it's also very helpful to build a set of clean boot diskettes for each system you own (be sure to lock all write protect tabs to prevent them from getting infected, too). You'll have to start the machine to begin cleanup efforts anyway, so keep the clean boot diskettes around in case of emergency. Find all the information about building boot disks you might ever need at `www.bootdisk.com` (add `bootdisk.htm` to the

end of this URL for pointers to Microsoft knowledge base articles about building boot disks for most versions of Windows still in use today)! Personal experience has also taught me that the free (for home use) DOS anti-virus tool F-Prot (`www.f-prot.com`) works very well indeed at rooting out most boot sector viruses. See also the related sidebar "Building an XP Jump Start Floppy" later in this section.

- **Macro viruses** — Today's modern applications — take Microsoft Office as a typical example — often include all kinds of programming language extensions and capabilities as part of what they do. These are called macro languages because they run inside applications that provide all the support they need to execute. Although macro viruses can affect only the applications inside which their code has meaning, users have learned to their dismay that because MS Office components share a common macro language, macro viruses can affect Word, Excel, Outlook (and other components) with equal facility. Until a rash of macro viruses — most notably, the infamous Melissa macro virus and variants that made the rounds in March 1999 — caused Microsoft to rethink its posture, MS Office used to allow immediate execution of all macros inside Word, Excel, and so forth, without warning users or asking their permission. By default today all unsigned macros (those not identified by unforgeable digital signatures) are disabled in Office, and not allowed to run!

Caution

Though they are often more innocuous than other types of viruses, macro viruses are by no means rare or benign: Symantec lists several thousand documented macro viruses at `http://securityresponse.symantec.com`, for example, and some macro viruses delete important system files as part of their operation, necessitating the reinstallation of those system files during post-infection cleanup.

Building an XP Jump Start Floppy

Although Windows XP requires six floppies to build a true set of startup diskettes (which allow you to boot up a computer sans operating system, and get the Windows XP installation process going) you don't need that many to attempt system repairs if your Windows XP system won't boot at some time in the future. Instead, you can easily build a single floppy that essentially bypasses the initial steps in booting your PC from its current *system disk* (which is what Microsoft, for ineffable reasons of its own, calls the disk from which a system begins its initial boot-up) and starts the system from the floppy instead. Thus, it provides a kind of jump start for your system (which is how it got its name). That said, I must warn you that if anything other than the boot information on your hard drive is damaged or missing, the jump start floppy won't get you very far (and may not help at all).

Even so, it's a good idea to build such a floppy and put it into your system toolkit because it can indeed come in very handy from time to time, especially if you're trying to recover from a boot sector virus infection. Here's how to build such a floppy:

1. Take a blank or used floppy and insert it in the floppy drive. Fire up Windows Explorer (Start→All Programs→Accessories→Windows Explorer), and then right-click the icon for the floppy drive. Select Format from the pop-up menu that appears. This produces the Format Floppy window shown in the first sidebar figure. Click Start to format your disk. This step is essential because the floppy must be formatted using the version of Windows it's supposed to boot.

The first step in creating a jump start floppy is to format it properly.

2. Open the system drive on your Windows XP machine (it's usually the C: drive) so you can see the files at the drive root (in the C:\ directory, in other words). The important items here (after the folder listing) are shown in the second sidebar figure.

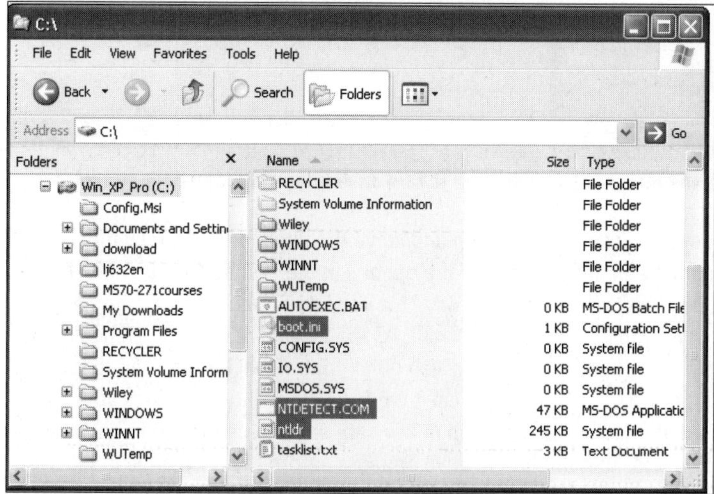

The key files you must copy reside at the root of the system drive (C:\ in this case).

Continued

Building an XP Jump Start Floppy *(Continued)*

3. Copy the following files to the floppy: `NTLDR`, `boot.ini`, `NTDETECT.COM`. If a file named `NTBOOTDD.SYS` appears, copy that one too (this applies only to systems that boot on a SCSI drive for which the BIOS doesn't supply boot information; that's pretty rare nowadays). If you can't see these files, you may need to reconfigure Explorer to show them to you. To do that, click the Tools menu item, then Folder Options. In the resulting Folder Options window, click the View tab, and make sure the radio button next to the setting that reads "Show hidden files and folders" is turned on, as shown in the third sidebar figure. After that you should be able to see and copy the files to your freshly formatted floppy. You can click and drag them, or highlight all three files (hold down the Ctrl key after you click the first one to keep it selected while you select the other two files), then right-click, and use the Copy to item in the pop-up menu to copy them to your floppy drive.

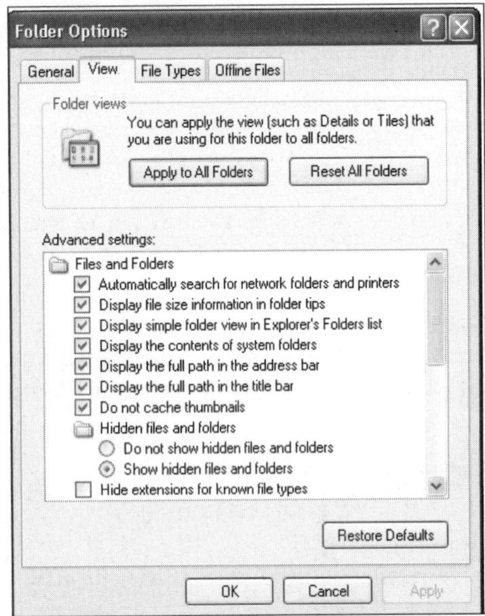

To see NTLDR, NTDETECT.COM, and boot.ini, you may have to turn on display of hidden files and folders.

4. To test your jump start floppy, restart your system and leave the floppy in the floppy drive (click Start → Shut Down, and then select Restart from the options in the "What do you want your computer to do?" pull-down list (be sure to save any files you have open on your machine before you do this, or you may lose the work involved). As the system restarts, you should see it hit the floppy drive briefly (10 seconds or so), at which point control will be returned to the hard disk and booting will continue as usual. If this doesn't work, you may have to check your PC's BIOS settings (which normally requires some kind of key sequence to be pressed right as the system is booting up) to be sure that the floppy drive appears before the hard drive in the system's preconfigured boot order (this is the normal default so it should work for you).

Although this technique is not officially blessed (or documented) by Microsoft, it's handy to build this floppy and keep one of these around for each of your Windows systems.

One key observation about viruses is that they add malicious or unwanted code to existing files, so that infected files include a mix of original material plus the actual code for the virus itself. This means that cleanup tools can often separate the original material from the virus code, and delete only the unwanted virus code as it works. In other cases, it may be necessary to delete the infected file and to replace it with a good, clean, working version of the original. But when a virus is involved, cleanup means the bad stuff is deleted but the good stuff stays behind. Whether or not that good stuff can be reconstituted through careful pruning away of the bad or needs to be replaced depends on the nature of the infection involved.

When categorizing viruses, some experts distinguish boot sector from MBR viruses and treat them as two separate types. You will also occasionally read about a type of virus described as multi-partite. Essentially, it combines the properties of a file infector with those of a system- or boot-record infector in an effective but nasty way. That is, if cleanup repairs infected system or boot records but not infected program files, or program files but not system or boot records, the infection will return to the cleaned-up elements from those not cleaned. Symantec cites four specific viruses as examples of this mixed breed — One_Half, Emperor, Anthrax, and Tequilla — but despite their sophistication none posed serious threats either in terms of damage inflicted or their observed levels of distribution or infection. Rare as they are, you will seldom encounter them.

Unless you're absolutely sure that all files, e-mail attachments, media, and programs that enter your computer are clean and free of viruses — and who can summon that much confidence or assurance nowadays? — prudence dictates that anything that could possibly carry infection be screened before being allowed to take up residence on a system, and that all potential sources of infection be denied that privilege. That's an important job for anti-virus software, which I cover in detail in Chapter 4.

E-MAIL VIRUSES

What earns certain malware designation as an e-mail virus is its chosen method of reproduction. Simply put, viruses that reproduce via e-mail are called *e-mail viruses*. The Whatis.com definition provides some additional detail:

> An e-mail virus is computer code sent to you as an e-mail note attachment which, if activated, will cause some unexpected and usually harmful effect, such as destroying certain files on your hard disk and causing the attachment to be remailed to everyone in your address book. Although not the only kind of computer virus, e-mail viruses are the best known and undoubtedly cause the greatest loss of time and money overall. The best two defenses against e-mail viruses for the individual user are (1) a policy of never opening (for example, double-clicking on) an e-mail attachment unless you know who sent it and what the attachment contains, and (2) installing and using anti-virus software to scan any attachment before you open it. (However, some e-mail viruses may be so new when your receive them that your anti-virus software may not yet be familiar with it.) Business firewall servers also attempt, but not always successfully, to filter out e-mail that may carry a virus attachment. (`http://searchsecurity.techtarget.com/sDefinition/0,,sid14_gci214549,00.html`)

Anti-virus experts distinguish between two types of e-mail viruses depending on how much e-mail they generate. E-mail viruses all tend to employ various methods for harvesting e-mail addresses on machines they infect. Those that send e-mail to a subset of those addresses are called "mailers"; those that send e-mail to all addresses are called "mass mailers." These viruses sometimes differ in their methods for sending e-mail as well. Increasingly, many e-mail viruses include built-in mailing (SMTP) software that lets them send mail without leaving any trace of their activity elsewhere. Some newer e-mail viruses, and most older ones, use e-mail software already installed on the

systems they infect (which can leave traces behind, especially on systems configured to save all sent messages in a Sent Items or similarly named message folder).

The next section moves on to describe and explore the sub-species of malware known as worms.

Worms

Worms seek to infect and replicate without targeting and infecting specific files already present on a computer. They may show up via e-mail, network or instant message software, or other forms of transport and then create more e-mails, messages, or whatever to propagate the same way. Worm activity requires a collection of data or a file to be transported from an infected computer to a potential target for infection, but otherwise worms confine their activities to what they can accomplish inside the applications that move them (often e-mail or messaging software) where they can establish a presence, and run their code. If a virus infects a legitimate file, the virus code can be cleaned out and removed. But since worms generally create and occupy the files that contain their code without using or involving any real, legitimate external data or binary files, the normal cleanup technique for worms is to delete all infected e-mails or messages that provide their containers when worms are quiescent.

One of the most famous worms of all time was also one of the first to be documented. Written in 1988 by Robert Morris, Jr., a graduate computer science student at Cornell College, this program took advantage of bugs in the Unix `sendmail` and `fingerd` programs to spread all over the Internet in a surprisingly short period of time. Many infected servers either crashed or became otherwise unavailable during this event, which became known as "the Internet crash of 1988." Morris was first identified as the author by *The New York Times* and later sentenced to probation, community service, and a $10,000-plus fine. Most estimates of the cost of damage from the worm were in the millions to tens of millions of dollars. Interestingly, this worm wreaked so much havoc because Morris himself made an error in its programming that caused it to spread much more quickly and aggressively than he intended it to. Other worm authors haven't shown such regard for the consequences of their work, but they continue to appear in the wild.

Thousands of documented instances of worms are on record, and several of the most damaging malware attacks reported in the past year have involved worms — most notably Sasser, Welchia, Beagle (or Bagle), and Netsky among them. While they often don't do much damage by way of file deletions, many worms attempt to disable firewalls, anti-virus software, and other security elements by deleting startup Registry keys, terminating active processes, and other similar techniques.

Learning More about Malware Specifics

As you read about malware — especially about specific, named items like the worms called by name in the preceding section — you can easily learn more about them by looking them up. Lots of virus encyclopedias are available online, many of which are worth at least one visit (some you'll return to repeatedly once you get to know them). Here are some well-known favorites:

- Kaspersky Virus Encylopedia/VirusList.com — `www.viruslist.com/eng/viruslist.html`
- Symantec Virus Encylopedia — `http://securityresponse.symantec.com/avcenter/vinfodb.html`
- Trend Micro Virus Encyclopedia — `www.trendmicro.com/vinfo/virusencyclo/`

For a bunch more of such resources, check out the listing of virus databases at the Computer Emergency Readiness Team site at `www.us-cert.gov/other_sources/viruses.html#III`. **Just to get the hang of things, why not try looking up Sasser or Netsky at one or more of these sites?**

Trojan Horses, or Trojans for Short

Nearly everybody knows how the Greek army figured out a way to end the siege of Troy recounted in Homer's *Iliad*: by making the army appear to leave the battlefield, and leaving a monstrous figure of a horse behind as an offering of atonement to Athena. Known forever afterward as the Trojan horse, the wooden figure contained a bevy of soldiers who waited until cover of darkness after the statue was dragged into the city, threw open Troy's gates, and signaled the Greek army (secretly camped nearby) to move in and completely vanquish the Trojans thereafter. The important elements of this story, from a malware perspective, are as follows: something apparently valuable is taken inside a protected space. This something contains a hidden and unwanted menace that attacks, and results in an overthrow of the prevailing system.

In the world of malware, a *Trojan horse*, or more simply a *Trojan*, is a program or file that a user allows or invites onto his or her system, believing that the program or file is normal software, benign, and compliant. In reality, the program or file contains malware that seeks to take over the system or provide a way for an outsider to reach in and assume control. Whatis.com defines the term like this:

> In computers, a Trojan horse is a program in which malicious or harmful code is contained inside apparently harmless programming or data in such a way that it can get control and do its chosen form of damage, such as ruining the file allocation table on your hard disk. In one celebrated case, a Trojan horse was a program that was supposed to find and destroy computer viruses. A Trojan horse may be widely redistributed as part of a computer virus. (`http://searchsecurity.techtarget.com/sDefinition/0,,sid14_gci213221,00.html`)

In many cases Trojan horses install software called a keystroke logger that permits them to capture and store all keyboard activity and mouse clicks. This may not sound dangerous, but in fact, such a Trojan can easily capture account names and passwords, credit card numbers, or bank account information—in fact, anything private a user types at the keyboard while the Trojan is running may be disclosed to presumably malicious third parties as a part of their normal functioning. Look up descriptions of PWSteal.Trojan or PWSteal.Trojan.D for more information on what such malware can do. This also helps explain why the line between spyware (which also captures such information, though not always using keystroke loggers) and Trojan horse software can be pretty blurry.

Definitions versus Real Life: Hybrid Viruses or "Blended Threats"

Defining distinct tribes of malware is all well and good, as in the preceding sections on viruses (and e-mail viruses), worms, and Trojans. But where definitions must often be tightly focused and limit themselves to certain specifics, real life is seldom so obliging. In fact, plenty of malware partakes of characteristics from multiple definitions, which leads to a final, grab-bag category that recognizes this reality. Thus, for example, a recent threat (at least as I write this chapter) on the horizon is

named W32.Netsky.Y@mm. Although it's a worm, it also opens a control channel — known in malware lingo as a *back door* — on port 82 just as a Trojan might, so that an outsider could take control over an infected machine under the right circumstances and control its actions across the Internet.

Some viruses include Trojans; some worms include viruses or Trojans; many malware instances combine characteristics from multiple types of malware within their capabilities. That's why I have to include hybrids or blended threats in any reasonable comprehensive discussion of this genre.

What Can Malware Do?

Recognizing that virus alerts actually document viruses, worms, Trojans, and blended threats or hybrid viruses, perusal of any recent collection of virus alerts will recount a litany of potential horrors. These may be reasonably well described simply by listing the categories that show up routinely under the "Damage" or "Payload" headings in some such alerts:

- **Large scale e-mailing** — If applicable, describes the software's techniques for harvesting and using e-mail addresses for propagation.
- **Deletes files** — If applicable, lists all files that the software attempts to delete. Very often, this list includes key files without which a Windows computer cannot boot or run properly (for example, `boot.ini`, `ntdetect.com`, `ntldr`, and other boot files, or `ntoskrnl.exe` and other key Windows system files).
- **Modifies files** — If applicable, lists all files that the software attempts to change, which may mean addition of Trojans to common executable files or updates to the Windows Registry or other key sources of configuration data. Some malware even attempts to disable anti-virus, anti-spyware, and firewall software in sweeping attempts to open up Windows systems for further exploitation and unauthorized use.
- **Degrades performance** — If applicable, explains what kinds of performance issues may occur on systems or networks affected. For example, the W32.Korgo.F worm merits the following description: "Network propagation routines may degrade overall network performance."
- **Causes system instability** — If applicable, describes the kinds of applications or system errors that might occur, along with other symptoms of pending or potential system or application failure.
- **Releases confidential info** — If applicable, describes what kinds of exposure to confidential data the software allows. For example, the W32.Korgo.F worm's capabilities are described as "Back door functionality allows unauthorized access."
- **Compromises security settings** — If applicable, describes what security settings are altered or downgraded, and what ports opened for unauthorized use. For example, the W32.Netsky.Y worm earns the following language: "Opens a back door on port 82."

That malware's bad behavior can span so many different dimensions is sometimes truly mind-boggling!

Diagnosing Malware: Watching for Changes on Your System

Malware can do all kinds of interesting and unpleasant things to a computer once it takes up residence. But since covert operation (attempts to hide overt traces of activity) and background operation (often not readily visible to those who think they're still in full control over infected machines) are characteristic of malware, how can you tell your computer has caught something? The answer, alas, depends on some sense that things aren't working as they normally do (or should) if you're not confronted with outright system instability or complete failure. Although some instances of malware actually send messages or use pop-ups to announce their presence — for example, the W97M.Jedi macro virus — few types of malware are so brash or helpful.

Some of the same kinds of symptoms of infection that can indicate the presence of spyware and related software can also indicate the presence of malware — namely, appearance of new or unexpected software or behaviors, or otherwise inexplicable performance slowdowns. That's because the computer is doing someone else's bidding and may be busy e-mailing messages, probing networks across the network, or undertaking other activities related to malware's relentless urge to reproduce itself and spread ever further. The first time I ever caught a virus was in a classroom situation in which initial class activities required students to copy Windows files across a network prior to installing a Windows operating system on student machines. A boot sector virus caused file copies to take several hours instead of the hour that was typical at the time, and that's what clued me in that something wicked had come my way!

Unfortunately, malware earns its name through its occasional display of more disturbing or destructive behaviors. From earlier descriptions you know that malware can (and sometimes does) do any or all of a number of nefarious activities. Here, I'll recount some of them again and explain what kinds of consequences can result or what kinds of symptoms such behavior can manifest:

- **Deletes one or more files on a computer** — In the best of situations, this could cause you to go looking for things that aren't there, such as data files or other items that you may notice are gone but that won't keep applications or your computer from working properly. Other symptoms are more serious: applications may become unstable or stop working altogether. Worse yet, Windows itself (or whatever operating system you're using) may likewise become unstable or stop working. Ouch!
- **Inserts additional code into important files** — Typical of the way viruses work, the insertion of extra code (and unexpected background processing activities and tasks related to virus activity) into important or commonly used system or application files can also contribute to system slowdowns, instability, or crashes. To some extent this might reflect a different mindset in the code at work, because virus writers don't usually care if their code is well behaved or not; to some extent it might just reflect a lack of testing, ongoing maintenance, or quality control that's typical for commercial software but seldom practiced for malware.
- **Strange activities manifest** — You might notice your hard drive light is busy a lot when you're not running any programs, that the network is extremely active (or downright congested), or that you start receiving e-mail messages (sometimes hundreds or thousands of

such messages, when a mass mailer goes to work) informing you that you've sent infected messages. Indeed, this could be a result of address spoofing as explained in Chapter 1, but it might also be for real — the only way to be sure what's going on is to start checking for viruses.

- **Strange new things pop up on your system** — This could be something like new folders or files that come out of nowhere, or strange and inexplicable new keys or values showing up in your Windows Registry. Malware always seeks to survive and reproduce, and this often means making extra backup copies of itself in multiple locations on your machine (hence, the appearance of strange files and, sometimes, directories) with calls to those files to reinfect your system (hence, the Registry keys) should that become necessary. In fact, some viruses deliberately exploit back doors or vulnerabilities that other viruses use or create, and themselves look for specific files or Registry keys to knock out their competition (which they then alter or delete to ensure their own continued well-being). Trojans or blended threats often open up new ports on your system to facilitate network activity, sometimes to enable outsiders to exercise remote control and sometimes as part of their attempts to infect other machines.

It's always disconcerting when such things happen, especially since they normally appear as part of an emerging pattern of system slowdown or increasing symptoms of impending failure. That's when it's time to start thinking about potential causes and when a virus scan should always be part of your troubleshooting activities. Indeed, it's sometimes hard to tell when a worsening hard drive failure is causing slowdowns and instability or when those same symptoms are the result of a virus. But you'll never know until you check as many possibilities as you can, and one of them proves to be the culprit.

Note

You'll learn how to scan for viruses, spyware, and other unwanted software later in the book. In fact, you'll have a chance to try out free scans through safe online services or clean downloads for malware, adware, and spyware. This is covered in passing in many other chapters, but is Chapter 4's primary focus. If you've got symptoms to explore, you might want to flip to that chapter right away. Be forewarned, however, that I'll show you how to determine if unwanted software is the cause of your symptoms in the vast majority of cases; what I don't do in this book is to explore all the other potential causes of slowdown, instability, or system failure and how to eliminate them from further consideration. For that purpose, a good general PC troubleshooting, maintenance, or repair book will definitely help you get to the bottom of your troubles if adware, spyware, or malware isn't involved.

On the other hand, I don't think anybody should expose computers to the Internet nowadays without some kind of software protection in place on every computer they use. Among other things — which I cover in detail in Part III of this book — I don't think anybody in his or her right mind should delay any further in installing anti-virus, anti-spyware, and anti-adware programs on their computers, if they don't already have them installed. Once in place, they should be kept current with obsessive vigilance, since new sources of infection are always more likely to be catching than older, better understood ones.

In the next section, you'll learn how malware gets reported to those who must take evasive or protective action to help computer users avoid infection. You'll also learn how alerts and bulletins about new infections are created and how they're broadcast to those concerned about keeping up with or ahead of potential sources of infection.

How Malware Gets Reported, Rated, and Alerted

Although malware shows up in all kinds of places, certain groups and organizations share a particular interest in this kind of software. Hopefully, it makes sense that companies that provide malware protection — usually in the form of anti-virus, anti-spyware, or anti-adware software, or some combination of the three — are keenly interested in any and all new forms of malware that might be discovered. Also, certain clearinghouses for malware information exist that also seek to stay on top of all malware as it's discovered, initially to document its existence, evaluate the kinds of threats it poses, and eventually to describe its behavior, how it may be blocked or prevented from causing infection, and how to clean up after an infection occurs. All of these clearinghouses have some interest in the more general topic of information security, where malware is only one of a large number of recognized potential sources of system attack; some of these clearinghouses focus more specifically on malware (which usually includes viruses, worms, Trojans, and blended threats sometimes described as hybrid viruses) or on spyware and adware, or on all forms of unwanted software just as I do in this book.

Even those individuals, companies, and organizations that put protective measures in place to fend off unwanted software can occasionally be susceptible to brand new forms of such software if it's cleverly engineered and doesn't trigger a defensive block of some kind. In other words, whenever a new type of malware, spyware, or adware appears, or when a variation on an existing type of such software appears that's different enough to slip past defensive measures, somebody inevitably falls victim to that software and gets infected. When that happens, affected individuals or organizations seek to get the word out that something new and wicked has arrived on the digital landscape. There's a specific set of rules for reporting malware, and a series of threat evaluation steps that some alerting groups go through in preparing to get the word out as new malware is discovered, analyzed, and documented.

When a piece of unwanted software of any kind arrives from the Internet, prevailing terminology is that the software is said to be "in the wild," meaning that it's out there on the Internet looking for potential victims. Most forms of malware get rated according to a number of measures of virulence to help those who might have to handle them understand how bad they really are. These include metrics such as the following:

- **Distribution in the wild** — The total number of infections documented, the number of reported sites affected, the geographical distribution of the infection, the amount of work involved in containing or blocking the threat, and the amount of work involved in cleanup or removal all go into weighting this aspect of assessing a malware threat. Usually, analysis of all these contributing factors results in a rating from low through medium to high used to rate how quickly and effectively the software is spreading throughout the Internet community at large.

- **Damage/Exploit/Payload** — This terminology varies, depending on the source of such information, but generally addresses what kinds of exposure to attack or harm can occur on systems if they establish no protection against the malware item under discussion. You'll learn more about how malware gets rated along this particular metric, and in general, later in this chapter.
- **Distribution** — This measures how quickly a threat is able to spread, but also provides clues to aid in its identification. Specific items under this metric usually include description information such as known senders or subject lines for e-mail viruses, sizes of attachments or files where applicable, ports opened or accessed during infection efforts, methods of propagation (e-mail, instant messaging, network messaging, and so forth), and potential targets for infection. Other headings that fall into this category include things like "Method of infection," "Indication of infection," "Installation," "Propagation," and so forth.

Clearinghouses and vendors use these metrics to come up with ratings or rankings for malware, spyware, adware, and so forth. Symantec, for example, rates viruses and other malware on a continuum that goes from "Low" to "High" for each of the three categories in the preceding list and then combines the rankings in each category to come up with an overall threat assessment that falls across a spectrum of five categories, as shown in Table 2-2. Clearinghouses and other vendors use similar approaches, though the details vary, so if you turn to another source, learn as much as you can about their particular rating scheme to help you understand what kind of threat some particular piece of unwanted software can pose.

Table 2-2 Symantec's Overall Risk Assessment Measures

Category	*Verbal Rank*	*Wild*	*Op*	*Damage*	*Op*	*Distribution*
1	Very Low	Low	&	(Low	OR	Low)
2	Low	Low or Moderate	OR	High	OR	High
3	Moderate	High	OR	(High	&	High)
4	Severe	High	&	(High	OR	High)
5	Very Severe	High	&	High	&	High

Understanding how to read Table 2-2 may not be immediately obvious, so here's a verbal recitation of what each entry means as well, by Category number, with some additional explanation:

- **Category 1** — This does not pose a serious threat to users because rankings for all three metrics are low. This indicates low probability of headline coverage, and no reports of the software in the wild (this explains why such software is often called *labware*, because that's where it usually comes from). It also neither does much damage, nor has much potential for widespread infection.

- **Category 2**—This indicates either a virus that is only a low or moderate threat in the wild, and reasonably harmless and easy to contain, or a threat that's not present in the wild with either high damage capability or high likelihood of spreading. It may make headlines, but probably won't.
- **Category 3**—This indicates software that's either highly wild, but is also relatively easy to contain and does little damage, or potentially dangerous or uncontainable software if released into the wild.
- **Category 4**—This is a dangerous threat that's highly wild and either hard to contain or does a lot of damage. This almost always makes headlines and should be countered immediately.
- **Category 5**—This is the only software where all three metrics rate as "High." Normally, if such a threat occurs, e-mail servers are routinely shut down, and all computers should be updated and scanned for infection immediately. Like any other major cataclysm this would probably not just make headlines, but cause severe Internet slowdowns and occasional breakdowns (though not ranked, the Robert Morris Internet worm might have qualified as a Category 5, not because of intentional damage, but because of the number of servers it removed from service).

After following Symantec's alerts and rankings closely for several years, I've observed that Category 1 viruses account for about 90 percent of all listings in their virus encyclopedia. Of the remaining 10 percent, about 6 percent is Category 2, 3 percent Category 3, and 1percent Category 4. I can find no listings of software ranked at Category 5. Over the long term, I see daily average counts for new viruses running between 4 and 5 per day. But long-term numbers don't tell the complete story: the ratio of higher-category viruses to Category 1s is indeed on the upswing. Looking only at the first six months of 2004, for example, those ratios change to 85 percent Category 1, 12 percent Category 2, 2 percent Category 3, and 1 percent Category 4, and daily average frequency bounces from a low of 5 to a high near 8, computed week over week. Malware is not only getting more malign, it's also becoming much more common and frequent! In summarizing Symantec malware reports for various security publications, in fact, I routinely cover only Category 2 and higher (Category 1s are too numerous to mention individually), and focus almost entirely on Category 3 and 4, which is where threats are most palpable and offer the most serious consequences to the unwarned or unwary. Of course, if a Category 5 were ever to appear, it would merit immediate and in-depth coverage as a grave threat indeed.

Other threat rankings tend to be similar, but never exactly the same. Many ratings include values like low, medium or moderate, and high or critical; more than a few also include an extremely high or extremely critical value as well. Simply put, the more extreme the ranking in the direction of cause for concern, the more important it is to investigate further, and possibly to take corrective or protective action.

About Vulnerabilities, Threats, and Exploits

If you're willing to include human fallibility among those failings or weaknesses that malware, spyware, adware, and so forth can use to establish a foothold for infection or installation, then it's perfectly true to say that every known appearance of unwanted software on a system results from vulnerability. Because the term *vulnerability* normally refers to a design flaw, a programming error, or

some kind of inherent weakness in some specific aspect in a software implementation, application, or operating system, it already covers a multitude of frailties. But since some malware, and most spyware and adware requires the user to cooperate by granting permission to install, opening attachments, or installing one thing and getting something else covertly (as with Trojans), it's necessary to add human frailty as a source of vulnerability to come up with a one-size-fits-all designation. Because most security experts agree that human ignorance (if not frailty) is responsible for a majority of security incidents including those having to do with unwanted software, this is very much in keeping with the idea that users must be informed about safe computing practices and ways to protect themselves as part of basic computing education. I'll point out and stress such information in this book at every possible opportunity, in fact.

On any computer system, a *threat* results whenever vulnerabilities persist. Thus, a threat is something like a possibility (if not a promise) that an attack of some kind might occur that uses the vulnerability as the chink in the armor to press that attack forward.

An *exploit* is a threat made real, and usually refers to a documented case in which a vulnerability has been used (or exploited, if you will) to make an attack successful.

Note

Previously, I described a blended threat as something that combines the characteristic forms of attack associated with viruses, worms, or Trojans in a single package. On the heels of this explanation (and applying the terminology defined in this section), it's also a good idea to understand a blended *threat* as something that attempts to *exploit* multiple *vulnerabilities* as part of its characteristic behavior.

Reporting Malware and Other Unwanted Software

Normally, the way the malware side of the equation works is that somebody "catches something" that their current anti-virus software can't handle (this is rare, but it does happen from time to time). When this happens, infected individuals will either contact the vendor(s) from whom they purchased such software, or one of a number of clearinghouses that specialize in handling and disseminating information about documentable exploits. Every potential destination for a report of new unwanted software in the wild has its own specific rules and regulations for reporting such discoveries (however unwelcome they may be); pointers to these are included in the "Where to Go for Malware and Other Alerts" section later in this chapter. What you'll learn here is the general outline of what's involved in making such reports.

But first a proviso: although there are well-documented mechanisms for reporting on malware (meaning viruses, Trojans, worms, and so forth), similar mechanisms are not as well understood when it comes to reporting adware or spyware. Thus, while I can talk about clearinghouses for malware, it's not really appropriate to use the same terminology for spyware and adware because other than a few locations on the Web where some incredibly devoted individuals help to keep track of such things, there's really no credible central reporting or information dissemination authority for such software (I do mention a couple of good such sites in the "Where to Go . . ." section later in this chapter, however).

To begin with, some information gathering is necessary before anyone can report unwanted software. In general, it's important to be able to describe the software as much as is possible (and often, you'll be asked to submit a sample, be it the message, attachment, or whatever provided the source

of the original infection, along with other infected files or outgoing messages as well). Thus, the date and time of the first attack, a description of the method by which it arrived and how it was delivered, and as much about the form and contents of the attack as possible should be included in your initial report. Some vendors, like Symantec or Kaspersky, ask you to send initial e-mail to a special address (`secure@symantec.com`, `newvirus@kaspersky.com`); others document specific procedures for the same purpose (for example, McAfee provides instructions on how to send it a suspected virus that should work equally well for all forms of malware: `http://us.mcafee.com/root/faqs.asp?faq=453`). Of course, vendors assume you're using their software, so they usually want details about that, too!

Tip

If you suspect a machine has become infected with a virus, your first move should be to disconnect it from the Internet or other network connections of any kind (which may ultimately lead to the Internet). That's to stop infection from spreading further, and to isolate the infected machine. You can capture infected files to floppy and compress them into a ZIP or other compressed archive on the infected machine (as long as it continues working well enough to permit such activity, that is) and then use a different machine to transfer files from the floppy to an e-mail message for notification purposes. Be sure to send only to recommended or official addresses, and to label your message a suspected virus report with a potentially infected payload. That way, the recipient can handle it in safe circumstances, and avoid further infection. In fact, you'll normally do this kind of thing after contacting your software vendor, and you'll probably get incredibly detailed instructions from them on how to identify, capture, package, and transmit the file to them. It's a matter for which some care and caution are required, and explains why vendors are only too happy to provide whatever hand-holding their customers think necessary.

Clearinghouses take a different approach to reports. They often distinguish between reporting incidents, which refer to specific sequences of events or occurrences related to an attack, and reporting vulnerabilities, which refer to the bugs, weaknesses, or other shortcomings of specific items of software that allow attacks to occur. Either way, both types of reports are fairly well specified, and most such organizations provide both guidelines and reporting forms for each type. Thus, for example, CERT (a well-known computer security and incident response organization housed at Carnegie-Mellon University in Pittsburgh, Pennsylvania) offers the following forms and guidelines for incident and vulnerability reporting:

- **Incident reporting guidelines**—`www.cert.org/tech_tips/incident_reporting.html`
- **Incident reporting form (online)**—`https://irf.cc.cert.org/`
- **Vulnerability reporting form (online text file)**—`www.cert.org/reporting/vulnerability_form.txt`

Other clearinghouses offer similar support to those seeking to share the bad news in hopes of helping others. Their information is included in Table 2-4 in the "Where to Go . . ." section later in this chapter.

About Malware Reports, Alerts, and Bulletins

Once a clearinghouse or vendor has done sufficient testing and analysis to confirm that what's being reported is heretofore unknown malware and can document its workings, the word on new malware will usually begin to spread. Most anti-virus software vendors are pretty good at responding to new infections in 24 hours or less; seldom will you find that it takes them more than 48 hours not just to get the word out, but also to update their software to fend off such newly discovered attacks (either by eliminating vulnerabilities, denying access to vulnerable parts, or other techniques to repair weaknesses or avoid infection).

Given the pace of new malware discoveries, and the increasing level of their severity, most vendors issue daily virus notifications and downloadable software updates. Most will issue automatic software updates when more dangerous malware is discovered, but also issue automatic updates on a regular (usually weekly) schedule.

What you'll find in a typical virus bulletin, alert, or report usually includes the following ingredients:

- **Some kind of standardized name for the malware** — The Common Vulnerabilities and Exposures (CVE) center at defense contractor MITRE (`www.cve.mitre.org`) has been set up to establish a common naming convention and common names for malware to help make identification consistent across multiple clearinghouses and vendor reports (not all vendors currently support CVE names, though most now routinely include links to CVE documents in their reports, and many are moving to that nomenclature as I write this book). I explain how malware is named in a sidebar entitled "Naming Malware" later in this chapter. Many vendors include as many other names as are known when they write their reports, in the interests of quick identification, recovery, and repair (where needed).
- **Detailed description of the malware** — This includes any or all of e-mail subjects, From addresses, message text, file or attachment names, infection and propagation methods, vulnerabilities exploited, and so forth. Methods of infection are often covered step by step, as are specific changes or updates needed to prevent them. The idea here is to help people recognize symptoms or look for telltale signs of infection, so more information is better than less, and as much such information as is available will usually be provided.
- **Threat or risk assessment** — As discussed earlier in this chapter, most vendors and some clearinghouses rate malware according to their estimation of the threat it poses to those who interact with the Internet. This may not be exactly the same from multiple sources, but will generally provide a pretty good idea about how serious a threat may be, how much damage it can cause, and how fast it can spread.
- **Repair or recovery tools and techniques** — Most vendor reports will include pointers to download removal or recovery tools, when available, but will also include step-by-step instructions for manual repair and recovery if it should not prove possible or feasible to download and use automated tools. This also ends up providing a very detailed description of what parts of a system malware affects, and how those effects can be reversed or repaired.

Once a bulletin, report, or alert is prepared it's made available to the public in several ways:

- Most of the sites that track malware offer opt-in newsletters and e-mail notification services to those who wish to sign up for them. Whenever a new report is created, the word goes out through e-mail to those who've already indicated interest in receiving such information.
- Likewise, vendors and clearinghouses alike maintain Web pages where breaking reports are listed and summaries provided. Those who haven't signed up for e-mail notification can drop in there any time to find the same information by reading current reports, by browsing, or by searching for specific information.
- Finally, anti-virus software updates generally include lists of all forms of malware against which they offer protection as well as new items added since the last update. This data includes links to detailed virus reports available online so users can educate themselves about new malware as they see fit. Because clearinghouses don't usually offer anti-virus or other software to others, this last item doesn't apply to them but otherwise their operations are pretty much the same.

For some examples of this genre, I've picked a moderately serious worm reported on May 1, 2004 called W32.Sasser.B.Worm for which a CVE candidate bulletin is available, as well as numerous vendor virus alerts, bulletins, and reports. Table 2-3 lists sample documents along with URLs and brief descriptions.

Table 2-3 Bulletins, Alerts, and Reports for the Sasser Worm

Organization	***Description***	***URL***
CVE	Candidate vulnerability report CAN-2003-0533	`www.cve.mitre.org/cgi-bin/cvename.cgi?name=CAN-2003-0533`
Symantec	W32.Sasser.B.Worm	`http://securityresponse.symantec.com/avcenter/venc/data/w32.sasser.b.worm.html`
Microsoft	Sasser Virus Alert	`www.microsoft.com/security/incident/sasser.mspx`
Microsoft	Security Bulletin MS04-011	`www.microsoft.com/technet/security/bulletin/MS04-011.mspx`
CERT	W32/Sasser	`www.cert.org/current/archive/2004/05/28/archive.html#sasser`
Kaspersky	W32.Win32.Sasser.b	`www.viruslist.com/eng/viruslist.html?id=1493652`
McAfee	W32/Sasser.worm.b	`http://us.mcafee.com/virusInfo/default.asp?id=description&virus_k=125008`

It's interesting to compare the different ways that different vendors report on viruses like Sasser, and also to compare and contrast the kinds of coverage that clearinghouses like the CVE and CERT provide (which talks primarily about system or software weaknesses, holes, bugs, and so forth that make things vulnerable) versus the kinds of coverage that anti-virus outfits like Symantec, Kaspersky, and McAfee offer (which usually documents the side-effects of the malware and explains how to repair or clean up). Then, too, Microsoft's take on such things is also somewhat different, because it concentrates more on big picture elements, and defers repair and cleanup details to anti-virus vendors.

Naming Malware

When it comes naming malware there's a fixed collection of prefixes and suffixes you'll encounter. Although the order of elements sometimes varies slightly, as does the separator character used (it is normally either a slash "/" or a period "."), what's most different from one source to the next is the root name by which a malware item is identified. By convention, the person who discovers the item gets to choose its name (as a star in a kind of unholy firmament, I guess), but that means timing of discovery is important (since he or she who names first, also names last and best). Because of timing issues, malware names will sometimes change when one vendor's report is pre-empted by another (note, however, that this usually means that although names may change, other details stay more or less the same).

Following are two lists of malware name elements, divided up into prefixes and suffixes (some are so out of date that I skipped them for brevity's sake; for that reason I point to some more comprehensive documents on this subject online at the end of this sidebar). Prefixes usually designate malware application targets, platforms, languages, or types. Suffixes describe malware behaviors, status, types, and detections.

Common Malware Prefixes

- **Macro virus** — Some applications use built-in scripting languages to support simple functions and custom programs; so do macro viruses. The plus side here is that you must run the application and the macro virus to become infected; the minus side is that many users configure applications to execute macros automatically (which greatly increases the odds of infection). Macro virus prefixes include A2KM (Access 2000 macro viruses), A97M (Access 97 macro viruses), O2KM (Office 2000 macro viruses; infect most related applications), O97M (Office 97 macro viruses), OM (Office macro viruses, can infect multiple versions/releases), W2KM (Word 2000 macro viruses), W97M (Word 97 macro viruses), X2KM (Excel 2000 macro viruses), and X97M (Excel 97 macro viruses; can also affect Excel 5.0 and Excel 95).
- **Platform name** — Names the operating system that the virus can infect. Platform virus prefixes include Linux, Palm (Palm OS), UNIX, W32 (32-bit Windows, including Windows 2000, XP, and Server 2003), Win (Windows 3.x), W95 (Windows 95), W98 (Windows 98), and WNT (Windows NT 4.0).
- **Application label** — Where it's not also a macro virus (see the macro virus bullet item for that information) some anti-virus prefixes indicate that viruses are specific to certain applications. These include AOL (Trojan horses specific to AOL online environments; usually steal AOL

passwords), HTML (viruses that target HTML files; usually Web pages), and IRC (viruses that target Internet Relay Chat, an Internet instant messaging protocol and service).

- **Language** — Viruses implemented using specific programming languages or language techniques. Prefixes named for languages include BAT (Batch scripting viruses; affect DOS and Windows), JS (JavaScript viruses; can be invoked on Web pages and in other active content), Java (Java viruses; can be invoked on Web pages, in other active content, and as standalone programs), and VBS (Visual Basic Scripting language, supported in most Microsoft applications and operating systems). Prefixes named for language techniques include HLLC (High Level Language Companion viruses, DOS viruses that create an additional companion file to be spread to other systems), HLLO (High Level Language Overwriting viruses, DOS viruses that overwrite host files with virus files), HLLP (High Level Language Parasitic viruses, DOS viruses that attach themselves to host files), HLLW (High Level Language Worm, a worm compiled using a high-level language like C, C#, Visual Basic, and so forth; usually appears with a platform name prefix as well, as in W32.HLLW.RepeatId).
- **Attack type** — Viruses that implement specific kinds of threats or attacks. These include back door (threats that can allow unauthorized outsiders access to your computer), DDoS (distributed denial of service, a type of attack where multiple machines are taken over, then instructed to saturate a single system or network with traffic, thereby denying legitimate users access), DoS (denial of service, a type of attack where a single system bombards another system or network with traffic, thereby denying legitimate users access), PWSTEAL (a specific type of Trojan that steals passwords), and Trojan or Troj (Trojan horse programs/viruses).

Common Malware Suffixes

- **@m** — This suffix labels a virus or worm as one that replicates using e-mail, but that does so by targeting specific e-mail addresses, or mailing itself only to a limited number of recipients. For example, VBS.Lerki.A@m is a virus written in Visual Basic Script that infects various types of Web-related files and mails itself only to the first address in the Outlook address book.
- **@mm** — This suffix labels a virus or worm as one that replicates using e-mail in a big way, usually by targeting all the e-mail addresses it can find, including entire address books, harvesting addresses from application files on the infected PC, and so forth. W32.Mydoom.Q@mm retrieves all e-mail addresses it can find, including from e-mail address books, Web content files and scripts, database files, and executable code files, and mails to all of them. It creates multiple copies of itself, alters the Windows Registry, and installs and uses a back door Trojan horse.
- **dam** — When malware alters a file in such a way that it can't execute or operate properly, it may acquire this suffix (an abbreviation for "damaged") to indicate it needs replacement or repair. Some files may be corrupted or include leftover remnants of malware code.
- **dr** — Some files act as containers for malware, or are introduced to provide a means to secure entry onto a system for malware. This suffix indicates the file is a dropper for malware, and may contain some kind of malicious payload like a back door, virus, or worm.

Continued

Naming Malware *(Continued)*

- **Family** — Some malware comes in so many varieties (sometimes enough to require two-letter version designators, indicating more than 26 variations on that theme) that it becomes more helpful to speak about this collection as a whole. Typically this is when the Family suffix appears. For example, the Backdoor.Delf.family is a collection of related Trojan horse programs that use keystroke loggers to capture private data.
- **Gen** — This suffix is an abbreviation for the word "generic" and indicates a type of detection that can handle multiple instances of the same type of malware. When family terminology is used to describe threats, there's very often a .gen detection to counter it. For example, the W32.Klez.gen@mm tool is available to counter known variants of the Klez mass mailing worm.
- **Int** — This suffix is an abbreviation for the word "intended" and indicates malware that was designed to work as a virus, worm, or Trojan horse, but which fails to replicate for some reason or another. For example, W97M.Manuiela.Int is a macro worm that infects Microsoft Word documents, but which is unable to propagate thereafter. Because they don't spread much, if at all, they're seldom encountered in the wild.
- **Worm** — Any program that travels around in a separate container of its own making (usually, a file attachment of some kind, or an outright file transfer) that uses some means of network transport to propagate may be called a worm. This includes e-mail attachments, network messaging tools, instant messaging tools, remote procedure calls, and file transport services (like FTP). W32.Beagle.AO@mm is a mass-mailing worm that uses a downloader program to enable copies of itself to be transferred anywhere.

A little judicious thought and some occasional lookup work permits malware names to be pretty informative. The name usually indicates what kind of operating system or application malware targets, and its type (if neither worm nor Trojan, it's a virus). A name may even tell you something about how malware was written and how it behaves or reproduces. Kaspersky's "Virus Naming Practices" (`www.securityfocus.com/infocus/1587`) and Symantec's "Virus Naming Conventions" (`http://securityresponse.symantec.com/avcenter/vnameinfo.html`) also shed interesting light on this subject.

Cross-Reference

Please don't let the number and variety of information sources discussed here and elsewhere in this book overwhelm you. As you'll see in Chapter 14, where I talk about tracking and reacting to bulletins and alerts (when necessary, which is seldom), I recommend that you find one or two sources of information you like, and that relate to your specific desktop configuration. Whenever anything truly noteworthy or scary comes along, it will show up through most if not all of these outlets, so you needn't watch them all. You need attend only to those that speak to you, or to your anti-virus software, personal firewall, anti-spyware/anti-adware software, spam blocking or filtering programs, or other security components you actually use on your PC.

Where to Go for Malware and Other Alerts

Because there are two kinds of sources for malware notifications, users tend to use one or both, along with some interesting supplements. One the one hand, many users pick a brand of anti-virus software (which typically also handles Trojans and worms as well) and rely on updates and notifications from the vendor to keep them up-to-date and out of trouble. On the other hand, various public and governmental (or at least, quasi-government) clearinghouses also track such information and offer notifications of their own. Both sources are best, because only a vendor update for specific software can provide real protection on a computer, but some vendors won't provide notifications until they also have updates or fixes to address them, so clearinghouses can be valuable sources about vulnerabilities, threats, and exploits that may not yet have been fixed, blocked, or otherwise acknowledged.

Table 2-4 lists five top clearinghouses and five top providers of anti-virus (anti-malware, really) software, with some bonus entries (you can decide if they represent plusses or minuses). I apologize in advance if I omitted an entry that somebody thinks should appear here as well. Because there are literally hundreds of anti-virus software vendors and dozens of clearinghouses, I had to draw the line somewhere, and I elected to draw it sooner rather than later. But for that reason, I also urge you to use your favorite search engine or consult your vendor's Web site if you'd like to investigate other alternatives. And remember, you need to pay attention only to those that actually apply to your desktop configuration, or that provide news and information you find especially approachable, intelligible, or useful (and hopefully, all three at once).

Table 2-4 Sources for Malware Bulletins, Alerts, and Reports

Name	*Type*	*Remarks*	*URL*
Microsoft	Bonus	Look for security bulletins and e-mail notifications	`www.microsoft.com/security`
Symantec	Vendor	Security response offers tools and newsletters	`http://securityresponse.symantec.com`
McAfee	Vendor	Sign up for dispatch newsletter	`http://dispatch.mcafee.com/us/default.asp`
CVE	Bonus	Targets common naming and reporting approaches	`www.cve.mitre.org`
CERT	Clearinghouse	Targets vulnerabilities and incidents	`www.cert.org`
VirusList	Clearinghouse	Sign up for mailing list	`www.viruslist.com/eng/maillist.html`
Trend Micro	Vendor	Check security info page regularly	`www.trendmicro.com/vinfo/`
FRISK Software	Vendor	Sign up for e-mail alerts	`http://alerts.f-prot.com/cgi-bin/mf?lang=en`
Panda Software	Vendor	Sign up for virus alerts newsletter	`www.pandasoftware.com/virus_info/`

Continued

Table 2-4 Sources for Malware Bulletins, Alerts, and Reports *(continued)*

Name	***Type***	***Remarks***	***URL***
antivirus online	Clearinghouse	Check for news and information	www.antivirus-online.de/english/bitrtvr.php
Security Focus	Clearinghouse	Check for news and information	www.securityfocus.com/virus
Virus Bulletin	Clearinghouse	Check for news and information	www.virusbtn.com/
Rogue/Suspect Anti-spyware	Clearinghouse(p)	Check for updates	www.spywarewarrior.com/rogue_anti-spyware.htm
Spyware-Guide	Clearinghouse	Maintains comprehensive spyware list	www.spywareguide.com/

(p) Indicates that the Spywarewarrior site is a personal site, run as a set of message forums by volunteers. It's entirely unofficial, but includes lots of useful information and pointers.

Resources

You can turn to the following resources for some further reading on the subjects discussed in this chapter:

Hafner, Katie and John Markoff. *Cyberpunk: Outlaws and Hackers on the Computer Frontier.* Simon & Schuster, 1991. This book concentrates on three famous cases of computer crime; among which is a detailed profile of Robert Morris's Internet Worm (Kevin Mitnick's early exploits and those of the German Chaos Computer Club are also profiled).

Kaspersky. "Computer Virus Classification." www.avp.ch/avpve/classes/classes.stm (accessed on July 15, 2004). An interesting discussion of how to categorize computer viruses by attack profile and internal operation from a group of leading virus and malware researchers.

Skoudis, Ed and Lenny Zeltser. *Malware: Fighting Malicious Code*. Prentice Hall PTR, 2003. As good as a deep technical discussion of malware and techniques for combating same can get, this book is worthwhile for those who really want to master the smallest details of the subject.

Symantec. "What is the difference between viruses, worms, and Trojans?" http://service1.symantec.com/SUPPORT/nav.nsf/docid/1999041209131106 (accessed on July 15, 2004). Symantec's take on distinguishing various types of malware from one another.

Summary

In this chapter, you learned about various types of malware, including viruses, Trojans, and worms. Basically, whereas viruses add themselves inside existing files, worms carry themselves in their own containers, and Trojans come already hidden inside files that purport to (and sometimes do) offer other functions. You also learned about how malware is classified in terms of its assessed threat potential, and how such information gets collected, evaluated, and reported.

In the next chapter, you learn more details about how infections occur and the many devious ways in which unwanted software can seek to hide itself and also keep itself around despite head-on cleanup attempts. Be prepared for numerous surprises along your way down this twisted and convoluted path!

Part II

How Good PCs Go Bad

IN THIS PART:

Part II talks about how unwanted software can make itself at home on so many computers. It explains the various mechanisms that adware, spyware, and malware use to get to your PC's doorstep, and the sometimes sneaky or blatant ways they follow to run on your PC. Given that unwanted visitors or denizens are usually best when removed, it also explains how you can give uninvited guests the boot and close your PC's doors to further infestation or infection.

Chapter 3

Methods of Insertion and Delivery

If you visualize the Internet as a dark dangerous world, full of predators and prey, you won't be too far off the mark. Take it as a given that unwanted software comes knocking on your PC's (metaphorical) front door, and you'll be more wary about anything that seeks entry into your system. If you're not convinced yet, look at your e-mail inbox and see what's there from people you've never heard of. Count the messages in that category with attachments: it's almost sure to be a sizable number! Think of the number of individual Web pages you visit daily, then pause to reflect that any one of them could seek to run software on your computer and you would probably be none the wiser. Think about all the software you download: might an occasional item not be home to a Trojan horse or back door? Who's to know? How can you keep your PC safe and secure when it connects to a dangerous digital universe daily?

In this chapter, you'll learn about the various methods that unwanted software uses to present itself to your PC. You'll also learn about the ways in which it can try (and alas, sometimes succeed) in setting itself up to run on your PC. Like a drink or a pill, unwanted software can only have an effect if you take it in — but whether that happens by malicious design or unhappy accident, once it's been executed unwanted software can indeed cause effects of all kinds! That's why it's important to raise some barriers to entry, and to stay wary and focused as you dig your way through unexpected e-mail, instant messages from unknown senders, decide whether or not to download software from an unknown source, or visit Web sites of uncertain origin.

How Infection or Infestation Occurs

It's really no huge mystery how unwanted software can dump its payload onto your PC. Once it finds a way to grab the CPU and starts executing its commands and instructions, and begins orchestrating its own activities, unwanted software can do just about anything it wants to a computer that's not protected. By arriving in an executable binary form on your PC, unwanted software needs just one more thing to start making things interesting and to start your computer following its agenda and orders, rather than yours — namely, access to your processor and other system resources it seeks to use (memory, disk, network interface, and whatever else it wants).

Of course, this does point to one important characteristic of most unwanted software: it works only on suitable targets. Malware designed to run in a Linux environment in executable form simply

won't work in a Macintosh or Windows environment. It's like an ad campaign that works great in an English-speaking country, but can't make a dent in a German-speaking one. Some forms of malware target specific applications, such as Internet Explorer (IE). If PC users running Opera or Mozilla visit a Web page with malware that targets IE, they won't be affected by that hazard because it's not tailored to work inside their browsers. One of the characteristics that makes macro viruses—which use instructions and code built to run inside specific applications like Microsoft Office components such as Word, Excel, and so forth—so dangerous is that as long as the application works on a specific platform the macro virus probably works, too. (Remember, MS Office runs on many versions of Windows and the Macintosh; plus numerous other office suites read MS Office file formats and interpret those macros as well, including products like OpenOffice or StarOffice for Unix, Linux, and Solaris, among others.)

Once a piece of unwanted software starts running, if it's been engineered right, it can do just about anything it wants to your PC. The real trick is to stop it from running at all (and that's a major subject throughout this entire book). Here, I explain how and why unwanted software is dangerous, and the many ways in which it might seek to enter your system and find a way to run.

More Signs of Infection or Infestation

In earlier chapters, you learned that sluggish performance, occasional instability or crashes, and inexplicable behaviors can be symptoms of infection or infestation arising from unwanted software on a system. Let's take a closer look at some symptoms to help you understand what kinds of things might point to one or more unwanted guests on your PC (these are based on my experiences, along with a story by Neil J. Rubenking for the March 2, 2004, issue of *PC Magazine* entitled "11 Signs of Spyware"):

- Although you're not using your PC to access the Internet, your network interface or modem activity indicator goes crazy, indicating large amounts of Internet communication under way. When this happens, it can sometimes be a sign that unwanted software is running your PC. Take note, however, that automatic update programs for Windows itself, or other software, can provoke Internet activity from time to time as scheduled checks for (and sometimes, downloads of) updates occur. Don't assume that all such activity is necessarily a sign of infection or infestation.
- You open up your long-distance phone bill to discover big charges billed to various 900 number services, many of them international, for calls you're sure neither you nor anybody else in your household made. This can be a sign that a dialer program is on the loose on your PC. Such software is created to use your modem to make somebody else rich, so you'll want to remove it ASAP. You can usually talk the phone company into reducing your bill as well, if not dismissing the charges outright and altogether.
- You use the Internet Explorer "Search" button to go looking for something, and notice that a different search engine pops up to handle your request. Clicking the "Reset Web Settings. . ." button on the Programs tab in Internet Options doesn't change this new setting, either. This is a dead giveaway that unwanted software's alive and well on your machine. See Chapter 4 for some removal recommendations and related resources.

- Whenever you fire up your Web browser (probably IE), a new toolbar appears within its interface. No amount of messing about with the View Toolbars command will keep it out of sight, nor can you figure out how to make it go away. This is another dead giveaway that unwanted software has made a home on your PC; as with the previous item, see Chapter 4 for removal recommendations and related resources.
- Something unexpected shows up in your Favorites list, and even after you delete it, it keeps coming back when you restart your browser. This is a bit more subtle than the two preceding items — default search engines and toolbars are easier to notice — but is every bit as big a warning sign (and equally vexing when you can't make it go away)!
- Your system is sluggish and running noticeably slower than it normally does. You right-click on the Start menu panel to launch Task Manager, and an unfamiliar process shows up on the Processes tab, as depicted in Figure 3-1. A little research on unfamiliar process names, by looking them up in a favorite search engine, for example, is the right way to investigate. In this particular case, my research told me this originated from eFax Messenger Plus, a fax send/receive utility installed deliberately, but it could have easily been something worse. Interestingly enough, killing the `J2GDllCmd.exe` process caused Word to crash on my system, so though deliberately installed, the software struck me as borderline. That's why I removed it from my PC.

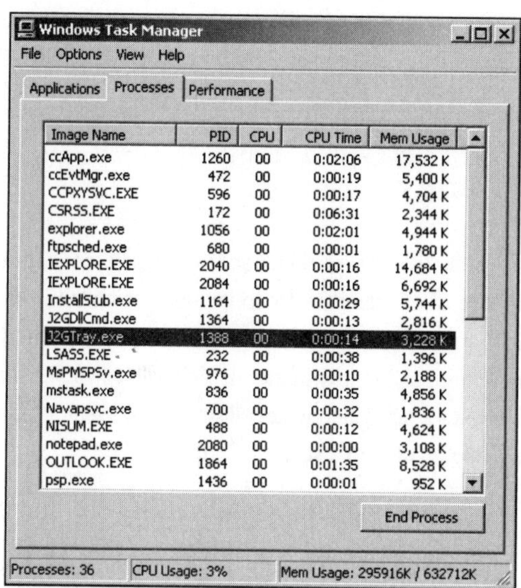

Figure 3-1: Task Manager's Processes tab shows two unfamiliar processes whose names start with J2G (an online search on the process name quickly reveals the source, however).

Note

Count yourself fortunate if you get an obvious indicator that something new is active on your system. Malware goes for outright disguise and often uses the same process names as do legitimate Windows processes (for example, `svchost.exe` is a particular favorite because it's a generic Windows process used to run absolutely essential system and other dynamic link libraries, or DLLs, and normally appears three or more times in the process list. And because you can't kill this process without also killing Windows, it's important to proceed with caution if and when you decide that some instance of `svchost.exe` must go).

- You're bombarded with pop-up advertisements out the wazoo for no good reason. No sooner do you close one, than another one pops up. Some of those ads may even call you by name! This is the most obvious indicator that adware's found a home on your PC; as with earlier items, check Chapter 4 for removal recommendations and related resources.
- You fire off Internet Explorer, only to see that the default home page has changed to some other site. You change it back (Tools → Internet Options → General tab, Home page pane) only to see it change back to the other, unwanted site later on. Your repeated changes just won't stick! As with other unwanted software symptoms, anything that changes a browser default unexpectedly, especially without asking your permission, is a sure sign that something new and potentially unpleasant is loose in your PC.
- Although you're using anti-spyware, anti-virus, and ad-blocking software, it just doesn't seem to be working properly. Sometimes, it doesn't appear to be working at all.

Caution

Certain forms of malware, spyware, and adware include far-searching and -reaching code routines designed to identify and shut down protective software of all kinds. This can include firewalls, VPNs, and other security software as well, not just products that specifically target whatever might have infested your PC. That's why it's a good idea to look for alerts from Windows Security Center (which will tell you right away if a firewall or anti-virus software is turned off) and why it's a good idea to schedule regular system scans for adware, spyware, and malware, as I recommend in Chapter 13 (and elsewhere in this book).

Rubenking saves his most telling observation on spyware for last in his story, and observes that the best (or at least, the most devious) spyware leaves no obvious traces of residence or presence on your PC. He recommends that you scan your machine anyway, and I concur that an absence of obvious symptoms does not necessarily mean that there's nothing lurking on your PC. Sort of a case of no smoke not meaning that there's no fire, you might say. I'm strongly of the opinion that you should scan your systems regularly for all kinds of unwanted software at least once a week, and any time in between should something unusual make you apprehensive. As I wrote this book, I scanned multiple systems multiple times a day—but then, I was courting danger to do the research, too!

In the sections that follow, I review the most common ways in which unwanted software and content makes its way onto a PC, protected or otherwise. These topics are presented in descending order of likelihood or probability, which is why the discussion starts with e-mail attachments (and the related topic, automatic invocation), moves on to talk about file downloads, then about active Web content, and concludes with discussions of infected media, such as floppy disks, removable drives, flash memory devices, and so forth.

Please also note that throughout this book I use the term *infestation* to describe what happens when adware or spyware takes up residence on a PC: That's because it's like ants moving into a household, making themselves at home on top of, around, and in the hidden spaces that surround your belongings. I reserve the term *infection* for malware, because it not only takes up residence on PCs, and it gets inside other files and facilities, but it is also capable of spreading to other PCs from an infected PC (to date, hybrid threats aside, adware and spyware don't normally exhibit infectious behaviors).

E-mail Attachments

Anyone in the world who can find your e-mail address can send you the latest unwanted software simply by constructing an e-mail message for you with the right kind of attachments. My strongly held belief is that worms have become so very popular in the past couple of years simply because they travel so nicely and effectively inside infected e-mails — usually, inside infected e-mail attachments.

That's why so many worms include messages that are designed to persuade or trick the unwarned or unwary to accept and open their attachments. In most cases, opening the attachment executes the unwanted software that triggers infection, and the PC becomes compromised as the payload gets delivered. If the unwanted software does its job properly, it will be deeply embedded in the infected system to make it as difficult to remove as possible. Furthermore, if that unwanted software is malware, it will then start propagating, either by sending more infected e-mails (easy to do, and another great reason why worms are so popular in the malware world), using various network, messaging, or file transfer services, or whatever other means by which it is programmed to spread.

Here again, the trick to avoiding infection is to intercept incoming files (be they outright file transfers or files attached to other things, like e-mail, instant messages, and so forth) and screen them carefully. If they show no signs of infection, it's usually okay to let them in; otherwise, they should be denied entry. That's what anti-virus software does very well, as do most anti-spyware or anti-adware programs with screening and blocking capabilities.

Where things get interesting is when files are packaged in special forms. Early file screening utilities didn't always look deeply enough inside compressed file collections, like those created by programs such as WinZip to squeeze files into smaller packages for faster, more efficient file transfers. Likewise, backup software, e-mail packages, and other applications that manage lots of files also take a kind of "files within files" approach to storing things, and all that has to be screened, too. I found numerous e-mail files with infected attachments in several old Outlook personal folders (`.pst`) files when testing a new anti-virus product recently — a big surprise, considering the PC in question had been scanned weekly by a different, well known, and highly regarded anti-virus product for years! The same thing holds true for non-native archive formats (which not all scanners can handle) such as Macintosh StuffIT archives (`.sit`), Unix gzip (`.gz`) files, and so forth.

Automatic Invocation

To some extent, *automatic invocation* is a lot like active content in that its name indicates that the simple act of moving this kind of material onto your PC can trigger whatever unwanted software it contains. To the extent that HTML-based e-mail is more like a Web page and less like a text message, protecting oneself from active content provides necessary coverage.

Older versions of Outlook would permit active content inside HTML-based e-mail message bodies to execute as soon as the message was highlighted in your Inbox folder, making it appear in the preview pane to the right. The latest version of Outlook 2003 (or the Outlook Express included with Windows XP SP2) won't normally open infected attachments or permit suspect active content to run in the preview pane (known as the "Reading Pane" in Outlook 2003), but you can still force it to open such e-mail if you're willing to disregard its warnings.

That said, here's how you can turn off the preview or reading pane to avoid seeing message content until you actually open a message in its own window:

1. Open Outlook (double-click the shortcut on your desktop, click the icon in the quick launch area of the system tray, or select Start → All Programs → Microsoft Office → Microsoft Office Outlook 2003).
2. Select View → Reading Pane → Off.
3. To exit Outlook, click the X in the upper right-hand corner of the window, or select File → Exit.

The method for Outlook Express is similar, except after opening that program, click View → Layout and uncheck the check box that reads Show preview pane instead.

The bad old days before Microsoft changed its macro execution defaults in Office components may actually provide the best example of how automatic invocation works, and the dangers it presents. Before the Concept virus came along in the mid-1990s and demonstrated the dangers of these settings, most MS Office components were configured by default to execute macros as soon as possible, without warning the user or asking for permission. Figure 3-2 shows Microsoft Word's current default setting, which permits only signed macros from trusted sources to run at all (and by default, no such trusted sources are defined). The conditions that prevailed at the time the Concept virus was loosed corresponded roughly to the low security level setting depicted, at a time when anti-virus software was much scarcer than today (and when it probably didn't check macros at all, either).

Here's how you can check Macro settings in Microsoft Word 2003 (though they are secure by default, it's still nice to know how to get there):

1. Open Microsoft Word 2003 by clicking on a shortcut, or select Start → All Programs → Microsoft Office → Microsoft Office Word 2003.
2. Select Tools → Options.
3. When the Options window opens, click the Security tab.
4. In the Macro Security pane, click the Macro Security button. It shows the default setting, which is High, and means that only signed macros from trusted sources will be allowed to execute (macros from other sources are disabled by default).

The Security window shown in Figure 3-2 shows the security options available for Office macros.

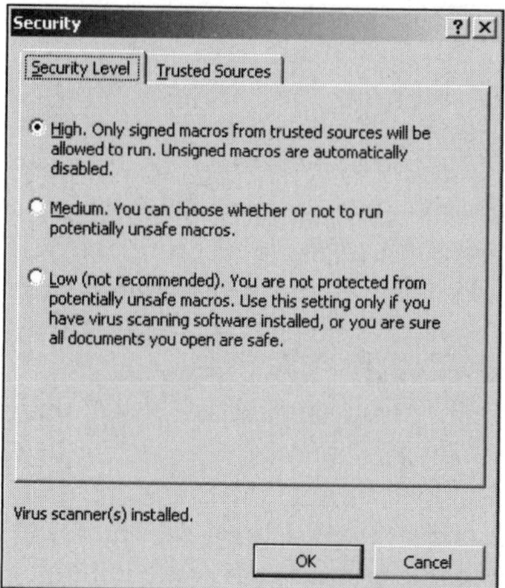

Figure 3-2: Like other modern Microsoft Office components, Word wraps strong security around macros today. When early macro viruses first hit, all executed automatically by default!

Because automatic invocation doesn't happen much any more inside applications, does this mean you don't need to worry about it on your PC? If you disable active content, or switch to some browser other than Internet Explorer for routine Web access, the answer to that question is probably "Yes"—at least, until another example of this kind of behavior is uncovered.

That said, there is a kind of exception to the foregoing statement. There's a large and dangerous class of vulnerabilities called *buffer overflows* (or sometimes, *buffer overruns*, particularly when Microsoft is talking about security issues). A buffer overflow can occur only if code is released that doesn't check to see if input is too long, or that doesn't automatically truncate input to some maximum length. When those precautions are not followed, an input buffer from a program can be completely filled up, and additional input goes directly into protected regions of memory inside the operating system (where random user input should never be allowed). Be that as it may, this kind of vulnerability sometimes allows attackers to execute commands at high levels of privilege and can permit them to take over and remake systems however they please.

If you're willing to consider this as a kind of automatic invocation, then it's by far the most chilling and dangerous type of exploit around. Most experts consider buffer overflows a function of poor software design and incomplete or improper testing, but they're so pervasive (especially in Windows environments) that I had to mention them in this context.

In fact, if you visit the Microsoft Web site and search on *buffer overruns*, you'll find about 100 results in response to that query. Of those results, more than half point to Microsoft Security Bulletins that document specific related vulnerabilities in Microsoft products or software. You'll also find an interesting developer note entitled "Avoiding Buffer Overruns" that explains what kinds of

overruns are most likely and how they can be avoided (see http://msdn.microsoft.com/library/en-us/secbp/security/avoiding_buffer_overruns.asp)—if only Microsoft had followed its own advice from the beginning, what a different world this could be!

File Transfers

When downloading files, you perforce take their contents from wherever they reside and bring them to your machine. Because some such files are intended to be installed—that is, executed within the context of some kind of installation program like InstallShield, Windows Setup, or whatever—you can't help but execute whatever's inside them when you start the installation process on your PC. It's okay to grab files and bring them to your desktop (albeit in a queasy, scary kind of way); what's not okay is when you give some piece of unwanted software permission to run by opening or executing such a file.

That's what makes virus and spyware scanning such an important ingredient to any effective gatekeeper function on a computer. Ideally, you'd like such a scanner to examine the contents of all incoming files (and other data, for that matter, since unwanted code and instructions can hide inside of data just as easily as it can inside executable files) and allow only those that don't contain hidden surprises such as spyware, adware, malware, or other unwanted software to take up residence.

Alas, far too many people go poking around the Internet looking for games, tools, utilities, or other software odds and ends, then bring them home to their computers and install them. All this without thinking: Can I trust the source of the download? What remedies will I have if I catch something? Is the software digitally signed and warranted to be free of unwanted software? All too often, the answer to all of those questions is a resounding "No!"

Of course, you're probably thinking: "How can I get such assurances when what I'm after most often is free software?" Although it's not automatic (some small effort is required), you can find plenty of reputable, reliable sites that routinely and regularly scan all their free downloads to make sure they don't hold any hidden gotchas or unwanted surprises. Table 3-1 lists a handful of the best-known download sites, all of which keep their acts (and their downloads) squeaky clean.

By now, you may be thinking you're exempt from such concerns because you don't download software from the Internet. But even if you only download image files or sound files of some kind, these items too can act as unwitting or unadvertised containers for malware, adware, spyware, and so forth. That helps to explain why all files downloaded from the Internet should be scanned (though admittedly, there is more risk involved in working with files designed to execute on your PC rather than those designed just for viewing or listening because the latter are usually opened within the context of some other program, rather than being executed themselves).

Table 3-1 A Smattering of Reliable Download Sites

Name	*URL*	*Notes*
CNET Downloads.com	www.downloads.com	Outstanding source for all kinds of software
Free Downloads Center	www.freedownloadscenter.com	Popular freeware source
Shareware.com	www.shareware.com	Offers both shareware and freeware

Name	***URL***	***Notes***
The Free Site	`www.thefreesite.com`	Another popular freeware source
Tucows	`www.tucows.com`	The ultimate compilation of Windows software

If you must cruise for free software, images, or sounds, get them from a reliable source. Even so, it's always wise to scan all incoming files and data on your PC for viruses, and to scan regularly for other forms of unwanted software (such as adware or spyware) as well. Be safe, be smart: avoid infection and infestation!

Note

If you follow the recommendations elsewhere in this book — most notably in Chapters 7 (anti-spyware/adware packages) and 8 (anti-virus packages) — all incoming file downloads, e-mail attachments, and removable or transportable media you might access — should be checked for the presence of adware, spyware, and malware anyway.

Active Web Content

Nearly every item that shows up on your PC and may be subject to automatic invocation has something to do with the Web, or at least with Web markup languages and associated code or scripts. In fact, nearly every such item aims squarely at Microsoft's Internet Explorer. Love it or hate it, many security mavens now recommend that users switch to a different browser because of Internet Explorer's many, chronic, and ongoing vulnerabilities and companion exploits (see the sidebar later in this section for a short list of potential alternatives) — at least, whenever possible. That's because certain important services, such as Windows Update or the forthcoming Microsoft Update, both designed for downloading patches, updates, enhancements, and fixes for Microsoft software simply won't work with other Web browsers. Thus, a good approach might be to use "another browser" for everything possible, except where only Internet Explorer will work.

Even Microsoft — along with other luminary security sites like CERT, SANS Internet Storm Center, and Secunia — recommends that Internet Explorer users turn off ActiveX and Scripting in IE to avoid trouble. That's because active Web content basically refers to code or script embedded in Web pages. Without disabling execution of this stuff, any time you download a Web page, your PC could execute whatever code, script, or other instructions it finds inside the document that Internet Explorer reads into your computer. Although turning off active content may cause some Web sites to falter or seem to fail, it's the only sure-fire way to protect yourself from the perils of active content altogether.

I rely on anti-virus, anti-spyware, firewalls, and other ingredients to protect me from unwanted software rather than turning off active content completely for that reason. Nevertheless there are risks involved in following my lead, so that's a decision you must make for yourself.

Tip

Microsoft Knowledge Base Article 154036 is entitled "How to Disable Active Content in Internet Explorer." It provides all the gory details involved in working through the Internet Explorer's security settings to selectively disable various forms of active content, including ActiveX Scripts (which means Microsoft JScript and Visual Basic Scripting Edition), JavaScript and Java applets, ActiveX Controls and Plug-ins, turning off the Java Just-In-Time (JIT) compiler, and turning off Java programs altogether. If you are really interested in tweaking IE security further, consult Knowledge Base Article 174360, "How to Use Security Zones in Internet Explorer" as well. Search for either article by number at `http://support.microsoft.com/default.aspx?scid=fh%3ben-us%3bKBJUMP`. As a handy alternative, you can always try the Knowledge Base search functions at `www.KBAlertz.com` (the site gets its name because you can also sign up for e-mail notification when new Knowledge Base articles appear, a pretty handy service).

What kinds of unwanted software can active content deliver to your PC? Typically, it's more likely to be adware or spyware, rather than other types of malware (though there are some viruses that have been reported delivered through Web page access). Spyware and adware are bad enough by many metrics, including cleanup hassles, vexation factors, and indignation at having unwanted software forced upon one's system. Thus, it's prudent either to turn off active content as described in the aforementioned Microsoft Knowledge Base articles or to switch to another browser except when accessing only official Microsoft (or other usually reliable) Web sites. If you need additional persuasion, consider that the Nimda virus (the prototypical version is named W32.Nimda.A@mm) and the Scob Trojan (documented as JS.Scob.Trojan) are both malware items of sufficiently recent vintage to pose continuing threats, and that both make extensive use of JavaScript to perpetrate their exploits.

If You'd Rather Switch Than Fight . . .

Although there are lots of browsers to choose from should you seek to supplant or supplement Internet Explorer on your Windows desktop, most experts agree that the following represent a reasonable Top 3 (though, as they say on the Internet, YMMV or "your mileage may vary"):

- **Firefox** (`www.mozilla.org/products/firefox/`)—The latest output of the Mozilla project (the original source for Netscape Navigator) with great security, customizability, built-in pop-up blocking, and more.
- **Mozilla** (`www.mozilla.org/products/mozilla1.x/`)—The original (and some would argue superior) IE alternative, also includes newsgroup reader, HTML editor, strong security settings, and broad support for Web standards.
- **Opera** (`www.opera.com/`)—Compact, powerful, secure, with built-in Internet Relay Chat (IRC) client, newsreader, RSS feed support, and more. Built by the guys who created CSS, Opera also supports many XML and CSS standards.

If you'd like to learn more about these alternative browsers and see some screenshots, check out Chapter 11, which devotes itself to methods for practicing Web safety that include selecting and using an alternative browser. You'll also find a list of sites where even more alternatives are documented, though some of these browsers aren't very well known outside their fan bases. I've used Opera as an alternative browser for years, and find it works pretty darn well for sites that don't depend on IE-only capabilities.

Media-Based Infections

As related in Chapter 2, any time you insert media into a computer it can also serve as a source of potential infection. The admonition to screen all incoming files and data applies not just to network or Internet paths, but also to whatever forms of removable media a PC can accommodate. This means everything in this category, including more exotic items like Flash or other memory drives or devices, removable disk drives of all kinds, and tapes or other storage media, as well as floppy disks, CDs, DVDs, and so forth.

You already know from Chapter 2 that some viruses target boot sectors on removable media and activate only when a PC boots up with infected media in some drive. You also know that viruses can infect many types of files (usually executable ones) on removable media and find fresh fields to conquer when those files are opened or executed on other, uninfected machines.

Here again, file screening is an important part of the solution. Indeed, all files should be scanned before they're opened or executed just to make sure they contain no signs of potential trouble. But because of the special nature of boot sector viruses, most anti-virus software takes its scanning capabilities one step further. Each time some removable media is inserted into a computer, the software scans the boot sector before mounting it for read/write access just to make sure it harbors no infections in that area (which is otherwise ignored during normal operations, except when a PC is booting and the BIOS instructs the computer to read boot data from the device that contains that item). If everything checks out, the item will mount and be available to the operating system; if not, it will be blocked from such access to protect the system from potential infection.

The real danger occurs when the PC is booting should an unscanned (or untrusted) disk be present in the machine. Modern Windows operating systems as far back as Windows NT don't rely on the BIOS to perform disk access. If Windows can boot, a boot sector virus can't even infect other media since Windows won't access its code as it performs routine disk operations. Thus the period of vulnerability exists only while the PC is booting before `ntldr` is called to load the operating system, after which the BIOS is no longer involved.

Tip

Modern versions of Windows include utilities for creating boot disks (for Windows NT and Windows 2000, this means creating an ERD, or emergency repair disk; for Windows XP or Windows Server 2003 this means using the Automated System Recovery, or ASR, facility). In any and every case, scan any disk you plan to use to boot a Windows system for infection beforehand (if the target system isn't running, scan it in another machine that is working with suitable anti-virus software also installed).

By Invitation Only

Although this category steps on—or rather, into—some of the territory that others already mentioned in this chapter already occupy, it's one that's well worth mentioning. I alluded to the need for cautious behavior with unwanted or unexpected arrivals on your PC in Chapter 1, with a tongue-in-cheek recital of the old Nancy Reagan anti-drug slogan: "Just Say No!" This observation applies most directly to unexpected e-mail attachments and to downloads of software from unknown or questionable sources.

The idea at work here is that you *must* open an infected file to bring infection into your computer, when those who create unwanted software are too lazy or choose not to build covert means of infection into their wares. Thus, if you get an e-mail with an attachment you're not expecting, if you don't open that attachment, you won't catch anything from it, either. Although the prospect may be painful to contemplate, it's worth remembering that of the few slogans worth having tattooed into one's epidermis, "Never open unexpected or unsolicited files" is probably one of them.

That said, authors of unwanted software are incredibly adept at manipulating their audiences to try and persuade at least a few unwitting accomplices to break this rule, and go ahead and open their suspect (and often, infected) file attachments. I've seen beautifully convincing hoaxes that represent themselves as Microsoft security updates, for example, complete with attachments that readers *must* immediately open and apply to their systems to avoid some fate too horrible to contemplate otherwise. Guess what? The e-mail isn't from Microsoft, and the attachment isn't a security update: it's some kind of unwanted software, and if executed, it's not going to help anybody's security situation even one little bit. In fact, it's virtually guaranteed to make things worse!

Bogus Microsoft Security Updates

There's a great Microsoft Web page entitled "How to Tell if a Microsoft Security-Related Message Is Genuine" (you can read it online, and see some perfectly convincing examples of actual hoaxes at `www.microsoft.com/security/incident/authenticate_mail.mspx`). Among other things, this page delivers good advice on the following questions:

- **Does the message contain attachments?** Microsoft never sends updates via e-mail; neither do other reputable software vendors, because e-mail is too easy to spoof.
- **Is the message digitally signed?** Microsoft uses highly secure digital signatures in e-mail to demonstrate its identity; you won't find this in any hoax because it can't be spoofed.
- **Is the bulletin listed on Microsoft.com?** Anything that comes by e-mail should also be available on the Web site (and in fact, the e-mail should link to the Web version for easy verification). If you're going to download anything, do it from a Web page on the Microsoft site; it's more or less guaranteed (and also digitally signed) to be the real thing.

Keep reading on the aforementioned page; you'll see an example of a bogus security bulletin that was used to distribute the Swen worm back in 2003. Very scary!

The same kind of observations on unexpected attachments also apply to online downloads. If you don't know the company behind the download, and especially if the deal seems too good to be true (such as a terrific tool for free or very little money), it may hide unwanted software within its confines (or the 25-page license might actually mention on page 17 in 6-point type you can barely read that you agree to run and load spyware or adware by downloading and installing the file in question). Thus another security slogan with tattoo potential could be "Never download files unless you're 100 percent sure of what you're getting." Lots of people cheerfully ignore this well-intentioned and sound advice, only to wonder why their systems get infested with unwanted software. Go figure!

Resources

To consult Neil Rubenking's original *PC Magazine* article dated March 2, 2004, "11 Signs of Spyware," please visit `www.pcmag.com/article2/0,1759,1524272,00.asp`.

The Windows Task Manager is a valuable tool in every version of Windows since NT. You can read more about the Windows XP version at `www.microsoft.com/resources/documentation/windows/xp/all/proddocs/en-us/taskman_whats_there_w.mspx`. If you use a different version of Windows, visit `www.microsoft.com/technet/` and search on "Windows <*version*> Task Manager Overview" to read a custom-tailored (and informative) tutorial.

Although it may sometimes appear to be a rat's nest of security problems, Internet Explorer offers lots of ways to manage security settings and to control active content. One of the best overviews of this voluminous and complex topic occurs in a Microsoft Security How-to entitled "Working with Internet Explorer 6 Security Settings." Read it online at `www.microsoft.com/windows/ie/using/howto/security/settings.mspx`.

Exploiting buffer overflows requires a special mindset, lots of patience, and special tools. To approach this from the mindset of the malware author, read "The Tao of Windows Buffer Overflow" at the infamous hacking site "Cult of the Dead Cow" (`www.cultdeadcow.com/cDc_files/cDc-351/`; as far as I know there's no danger in visiting this site, but be warned you do so at your own risk). For a more objective view of the phenomenon see the academic paper "StackGuard: Automatic Adaptive Detection and Prevention of Buffer-Overflow Attacks," by Crispin Cowan, Calton Pu, Dave Maier, Heather Hinton, Jonathan Walpole, Peat Bakke, Steve Beattie, Aaron Grier, PerryWagle, and Qian Zhang, Department of Computer Science and Engineering, Oregon Graduate Institute of Science & Technology, available online at `www.usenix.org/publications/library/proceedings/sec98/cowan.html`.

If you're interested in considering alternative Web browsers to use alongside (or instead of) Internet Explorer, several resources can help you locate and weigh other options:

- Matthew D. Sarrel wrote a nice piece for *PC Magazine* entitled "Time to Find an IE Alternative?" (July 9, 2004) that covers Firefox and Opera (`www.pcmag.com/article2/0,1759,1622109,00.asp`).
- `www.msboycott.com/thealt/alts/internetexplorer.shtml` — One of the less rabid of the legion of "Microsoft alternatives" Web sites, this one does a good job of listing a large number of options with pointers (including ratings or reviews, where available) for and about each one.

Summary

This chapter examined the various ways in which unwanted software can wind up on a PC, and other ways in which it seeks to run and do its dirty work. This included numerous, often invisible, forms of active content in Web pages or other HTML or XML documents. It also included various forms of automatic invocation, either through improper or outmoded security settings, or by inclusion in buffer overruns that are bound to be executed once they occur. I also discussed how any means by which a file or data enters a computer — be it through file transfers, e-mail or other application attachments, or infected media inserted into a PC — also provides potential avenues for infection or infestation. The solution to this problem is at least twofold: first, avoid risky forms of behavior; and second, use screening software to prevent infected files or data from making a home on your PC.

The next chapter explores what happens when infection or infestation occurs and outlines the steps involved in cleaning up the resulting mess. Of course, some such maladies are worse than others and require drastic measures, whereas other infections may be taken care of with relatively little effort or activity. As with other forms of infection or infestation, the cure depends on the malady contracted.

Chapter 4

Detecting and Repairing PC Infestations

Joseph Heller's wonderful, dark novel *Catch-22* raises a fundamental epistemological question in his typically elliptical and irreverent fashion: "How can you tell if you've got flies in your eyes, when you've got flies in your eyes?" Indeed, because much unwanted software goes to great lengths to conceal itself even from those who go looking for it, this is not an easy thing to do. That's why I recommend throughout this book that you obtain, install, and keep various types of screening, blocking, and scanning applications designed to notice unwanted software before it infects your system (that's the screening and blocking part) or find it on your system (even if only in quiescent form) and help you root it out. For obvious reasons, such software is usually called anti-X, where X is some category of unwanted software, such as virus (which usually handles other malware as well), spyware, or adware (and other unwanted stuff).

In fact, some scanning tools not only include means of detecting unwanted software, they include some cleanup abilities, as well. That is, once these tools recognize what kind of unwanted software they're dealing with, they can actually remove such software and put your PC back into a more or less pristine condition. Sometimes, however, more powerful cleanup tools are required. When that's the case, the scanning software will often tell you not just what you need to clean up after, but which tool to get to perform that particular job.

In this chapter, you'll learn how the professionals document what happens when an infection or infestation occurs, and how they perform the analysis, design, and implementation work necessary to figure out how to clean up afterward. Of course, from all that data, it's not terribly difficult to create tools to automate that task—which produces the very tools (or built-in capabilities that get added to scanning software with each new release) that most ordinary mortals use to clean up after malware, adware, spyware, and the rest of this vile software. Therefore, you'll also learn how to find cleanup instructions for specific infections or infestations, what's involved (or at least, what may be involved) in performing typical cleanup tasks manually, and how to use tools designed to simplify and speed up such tasks.

What Can Go Wrong, Occasionally Will

Despite careful application of best and safest computing practices, and application of available preventive measures—which means installing, using, and keeping screeners, blockers, and scanners up to date—some PCs are unlucky enough to get exposed to new or as-yet undocumented sources of infection and infestation. When that happens, such an exposed PC may indeed "catch" something unless the various antisoftware components at work recognize that something potentially dangerous is present and ends up screening or blocking it anyway. This often happens when a virus, Trojan, or worm that's derived from some other known variety comes along, provided it's enough like its sibling or counterpart for the software to recognize it anyway.

But just for grins, assume that something new, undocumented, and virulent comes along and that all software in place doesn't detect its evil design or purpose. If that software somehow gets executed on a PC to which it has gained access, infestation or infection will probably occur. That's when the unlucky PC's user might notice some of the symptoms I've mentioned in previous chapters, such as sluggish performance, unexpected changes to defaults or other program settings, sudden cessation of anti-virus, anti-spyware, or other security software, and so forth. Hypothetical though this discussion may seem, it reflects a grim reality on desktops everywhere, as thousands of machines are infested or infected daily.

When that happens, it's time to scan your system for infection. If you have scanners installed, download the most recent set of updates, and then use them. If they find nothing out of the ordinary or if you don't have any scanners installed, visit at least one online scanner in each category mentioned in Table 4-1 and see if something turns up (look at the URLs to see which companies provide these tools). In the vast majority of cases, something will turn up, and you'll quickly get some idea of what's moved onto your system, along with advice on how to deal with that situation.

Table 4-1 Online Scanners for Malware, Spyware, and Adware

Name	*Category*	*Notes*	*URL*
Virus detection	Malware	Click Check for Security Risks, follow prompts	`http://securityresponse.symantec.com`
Online virus scan	Malware	Follow prompts	`www.bitdefender.com/scan/license.php`
Housecall	Malware	Click Scan Now, follow prompts	`http://housecall.trendmicro.com/`
Pest Scan	Spyware and adware	Click Scan Now, follow prompts	`www.pestscan.com/`
Spy audit	Spyware and adware	Click Find Spyware Now, follow prompts	`www.webroot.com/services/spyaudit.htm`

How the Pros Do It

Let me start by saying that professional malware, spyware, and adware hunters have many advantages that ordinary home or office users do not. This could be a polite way of saying, "Don't try this at home," or it could just help you to understand how they can figure out how to reverse the effects of the many niggling little details involved when unwanted software takes up residence on a PC. Here are some of the things that such professionals have available to them when they start their analyses to detect and document what unwanted software does, and build tools to reverse its effects and remove its presence.

- **Laboratories, full of test machines**—When somebody's desktop or server catches something, it's scary (and potentially traumatic) because these computers have specific uses, contain important data, and provide essential services. A test machine's intended use is to expose it to unwanted software, just to see what happens!
- **Special software for a variety of purposes related to managing test machines**—This includes imaging software that makes it easy to create a pristine, clean installation ready for infection or infestation whenever that's necessary. Generally, a server somewhere maintains a library of disk images designed to be sucked across the network and copied to a disk drive, thereby creating a PC with some operating system, applications, and so forth, ready to be exposed to unwanted software.
- **Special software designed to compare before and after information to report specifically on what's changed (and where possible, exactly what has been changed, added, or deleted)**—TripWire is probably one of the best-known tools in this category. This program is run right after a machine is set up and configured to create a snapshot of the machine's files and other data (think of this as the "before" snapshot). If it's used again right after unwanted software is deliberately introduced on a machine, it starts by making another snapshot of the system (the "after" snapshot). Then, it reports on all files that were added, deleted, or altered as compared to the "before" snapshot. Other tools are necessary to dig into specific Windows subsystems, such as the Windows registry, which is essentially a database of all configuration and device settings for everything in (and running under) Windows on your computer. Some of these, like Registry Watch or Active Registry Monitor, can compare two snapshots and report on what's added, deleted, and changed between the two. When digging into specific files to see what's different—especially important for viruses, which insinuate themselves into other files—some kind of binary, low-level editor is also important. This sort of thing can also help detect various kinds of configuration and default changes that can occur when unwanted software alters applications to do what it wants or to serve its convenience.

Of course, the professionals have some other advantages, too, that can't be overstated. For one thing, they've got a pretty good idea they're dealing with something nasty. This gives them an advantage over most other users, including those who catch things from unwanted software essentially as it's being discovered and documented, because this usually comes as an unpleasant surprise. For another thing, such professionals have investigated the effects of unwanted software before, so they

already have some ideas about what kinds of changes are likely to occur. They already know they should be on the lookout for new files and registry keys, and should also be especially interested in various alterations to program or system defaults, settings, and startup behaviors. Finally, the professionals ultimately don't care what happens to their test machines. They can calmly watch them be destroyed, if that's the outcome from deliberate infection or infestation; they can create new, ready-to-run installations on those machines in a relatively short time. Users whose desktops or servers are dying in front of them often have trouble summoning up that kind of equanimity and poise!

Tip

If you want to play with unwanted software, and really dig into its wily ways and plumb the depths of potential nastiness, do like the pros and get yourself a test machine. Follow my advice for locking down your primary desktop and keep it as safe and secure as possible. When you bring your test machine up for the first time, make a backup or use a utility such as Norton Ghost to take a snapshot of that machine in its pristine state — and for goodness' sake, don't forget to make new snapshots as you add software or make updates to that machine over time. Then you can play to your heart's content, knowing that you can get back to a clean machine, either by restoring your backup or using a clean image to replace an infected test system with a clean, restored one! Now that HUGE USB or FireWire removable disks (160GB and up) retail for under $200, it's affordable and easy to make such snapshots and keep them around for when you need them.

Anatomy of an Infection

Here, you look at a sample set of virus repair instructions to get a sense of what a virus does to a system as it moves in and takes over. The number and levels of detail involved in these instructions should help you understand why only knowledgeable power users or outright Windows experts can tackle this kind of work without a set of marching orders to follow. Simply put, it would take most of us too much time to learn everything necessary to ferret out unwanted software and clean up all signs of its presence to make it worthwhile, given that automated tools and numerous repositories of such instructions make such learning largely unnecessary and that most of us have better things to do with our time. Even so, I'll be sure to mention some tips and tricks that can come in handy for more benign uses (such as when uninstall utilities for commercial software don't completely clean up after the applications they supposedly remove, or when damaged installation logs or other key files prevent such utilities from doing their jobs through no fault of their own).

I'll start with a 10,000-foot view of the potential effects that unwanted software can have on a system, from the standpoint of various traces it leaves behind. For each such item, I'll discuss the system or software components involved, the types of likely traces, the kinds of unwanted software that interact with them, and other information to explain and explore these various areas of concern. After that, I'll point to some specific step-by-step instructions online, and go over how they fit into the various components mentioned on a case-by-case basis. Basically, unwanted software usually does one or more of the types of activities detailed in Table 4-2.

Table 4-2 Activities Performed on System Components by Malware, Spyware, and Adware

Component	*Types of Actions*	*Discussion*
File system	Add new files Delete existing files Modify existing files	All forms of unwanted software can engage in all of these activities, though adware and spyware are less likely to delete files than is malware. When it comes to modifying existing files, viruses are most likely to engage in this behavior, because injection of their own code and payloads into existing files is a hallmark virus feature. Likewise, creating and depositing multiple copies of themselves or their containers is a characteristic of malware that's seldom found in adware or spyware.
Windows registry	Add new keys and values Delete or modify existing keys and values	All forms of unwanted software typically engage in all of these activities, though adware and spyware are less likely to delete or disable security software than is malware. Because interaction with the registry is part of installing any software in a Windows environment, this is virtually a mandatory occurrence for all types of unwanted software.
Windows application (often, Internet Explorer)	Change defaults or configuration settings Add new plug-ins or other code	All forms of unwanted software may interact with one or more applications. Spyware and adware are more likely to add overt, visible elements, such as changed default settings, toolbars, cookies, and so forth. Malware is far more likely to make covert changes or additions to applications that can involve creating new execution threads (to carry out payload instructions), setting up services (SMTP mail, FTP, IRC, and so forth), sending messages, and other activities necessary for propagation and survival.

Continued

Table 4-2 Activities Performed on System Components by Malware, Spyware, and Adware *(continued)*

Component	*Types of Actions*	*Discussion*
Windows runtime environment	Create or alter program controls Stop or start processes Install software	Windows uses special objects called mutexes (short for mutual exclusion objects) to control access to specific program resources, typically to ensure that a shared resource can be used by only one execution thread at a time. Many types of malware create special mutexes that they check for as well, so that multiple instances of the same malware can't run on a Windows computer at the same time. On the process side, many instances of malware look for well-known screening or blocking processes and attempt to terminate them. All types of unwanted software may start processes to handle code execution, though most adware and spyware runs as a thread within an already-active process (often, Internet Explorer). When it comes to installing software, adware and spyware are more likely to take this approach; most viruses bypass normal Windows methods for adding and removing software from a system, as part of their "deep cover."
Windows system calls or application program interfaces (APIs)	Use system facilities to block or hinder repair or recovery activities	Some clever malware invokes special Windows calls (for example, the Sasser worm calls the Windows `AbortSystemShutdown` API to prevent infected machines from shutting down or restarting) to interfere with normal or user-directed activities. Normally, neither spyware nor adware does such things.

Tip

If you believe you've caught something and you're willing to kiss everything goodbye that you've added to or changed in your Windows environment since the last time you booted up your computer, there is a kind of "last-ditch maneuver" you can try to fend off attack. While Windows is first booting up, if you hit the F8 key, you'll see a menu of options, as shown in Figure 4-1. Choose the Last Known Good Configuration option (known to Windows-heads everywhere as the LKGC), and Windows should boot running the version of the registry that existed the last time your system booted — that is, before you got infected, infested, or whatever.

One of my test systems was so fast I never saw the prompt that often flashes on the screen telling you to strike the F8 key to boot into Safe Mode, so it might be smart to hold down the F8 key just as the final items in the pre-Windows boot sequence are ending (which is how I got it to work on that machine myself). If Windows starts to boot anyway, hit Ctrl+Alt+Delete and click the Shut down button to restart again. You DON'T want Windows to boot successfully with the configuration that existed during shutdown because that next complete reboot will enshrine the potentially infected or infested registry on your machine! If you try to reboot and Windows won't respond, you can take a chance on a double last-ditch resort and cycle the power off, wait a minute, then power back up and use the F8 technique just described (but a "rude shut-down" can have serious consequences for any files you might have open at the time, so do this only as a last resort).

Please note also that if you use this technique, you may still have infected files on your system. Although your registry may be clean (until the unwanted software gets another chance to execute), if you don't remove all infected files, you are still subject to infection or infestation.

For more information about Safe Mode booting in Windows XP, see Microsoft Knowledge Base article 315222 (`http://support.microsoft.com/default.aspx?scid=kb;en-us;315222`). For other versions of Windows search the Knowledge Base for similar coverage.

```
Windows Advanced Option Menu
Please select an option:

    Safe Mode
    Safe Mode with Networking
    Safe Mode with Command Prompt

    Enable Boot Logging
    Enable VGA Mode
    Last Known Good Congfiguration (your most recent settings that worked)
    Directory Services Restore Mode (Windows domain controllers only)
    Debugging Mode

    Start Windows Normally
    Reboot

Use the up and down arrow keys to move the highlight to your choice
```

Figure 4-1: The Safe Mode screen for Windows includes the Last Known Good Configuration option, which is what you can try in this case.

How To Clean Out Your System

In general, what's involved in cleanup is restoring deleted stuff as needed, reversing changes, and removing new stuff that unwanted software has introduced. Although this sounds simple, it requires knowing what to work on, how to accomplish the desired tasks, and access to replacement items where necessary. As you take a look at some cleanup instructions in the sections that follow, you'll get a pretty good idea why automated cleanup is both popular and typical (at least for ordinary users) and why manual cleanup is normally an option purely of last resort.

Cleanup #1: Worm W32.Randex.ATX

This Category 2 worm was discovered on June 28, 2004, and, as is typical for most malware, its technical description and cleanup information were published on the following day. It received a Category 2 threat assessment because:

- The number of known infections in the wild was relatively small (less than 50, at one or two sites), resulting in a low ranking on the wild metric.
- It deletes administrative shares, can release confidential information, and installs an Internet Relay Chat (IRC) back door on a computer, resulting in a medium ranking on the damage metric.
- It can target and crack systems with weak administrative passwords, which results in a medium ranking on the distribution metric.

By definition, this combination of metrics translates into Category 2, which makes it moderately threatening but neither terribly damaging nor terribly virulent. Now, I want to describe what W32.Randex.ATX does on those machines it infects. Once it's executed, W32.Randex.ATX performs the following actions:

1. Copies itself to the System folder as a file named `Rpcmon.exe`, using a Windows variable to target that directory. You can easily view all variables defined on your system by opening a command window (Start → Run, type **`cmd.exe`** in the Open field of the Run dialog box) and typing **`set`** at the command line (results are shown in Figure 4-2). A valid way to specify the system folder on any modern Windows version is possible using the string `%SystemRoot%\system32` (if your command window is still open, type **`cd %SystemRoot%\system32`** at the command line and see what happens).

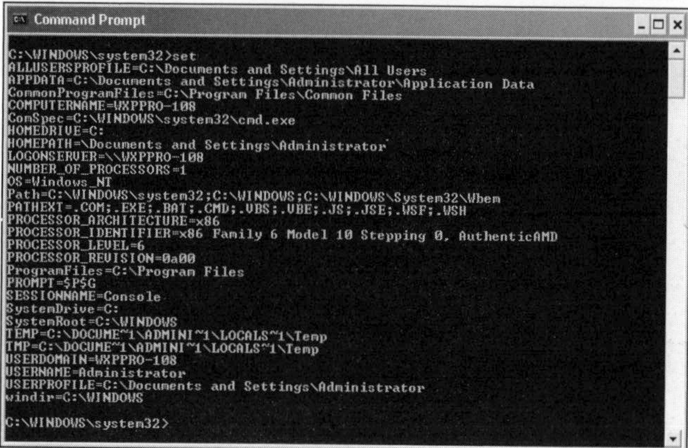

Figure 4-2: Typical system variables and associated values on a Windows XP installation.

2. Adds the value "`Sysmon`" = "`rpcmon.exe`" to various registry keys that are invoked whenever Windows starts up, so as to execute whenever Windows is rebooted. Not coincidentally, this explains why the LKGC technique mentioned earlier in this chapter won't always cure what ails your PC for many instances of unwanted software. Those keys are as follows:

```
HKEY_LOCAL_MACHINE\Software\Microsoft\Windows\CurrentVersion\RunServices
HKEY_LOCAL_MACHINE\Software\Microsoft\Windows\CurrentVersion\Run
HKEY_CURRENT_USER\Software\Microsoft\Windows\CurrentVersion\Run
```

3. Next, the worm creates and executes a file named `%Temp%\Secure.bat`. This is what actually deletes various administrative shares, including `C$`, `D$`, `IPC$`, and `ADMIN$`. These names end with dollar signs so they don't show up in ordinary directory listings; `C$` and `D$` point at the `C:\` and `D:\` drives, `IPC$` is reserved for interprocess communications by Windows; `ADMIN$` is likewise reserved for system administrators. Windows itself and system administrators are normally the only users for these shares, so an ordinary user might not even notice they'd been removed. To see the shares defined on your system, you must log in with administrative privileges and then execute the `net share` command at a command prompt (Figure 4-3 shows the results, which include all shares this worm attempts to delete). If you read the complete Symantec report cited later, you'll note that it uses the term "drop" to describe this action, in keeping with the payload metaphor associated with malware.

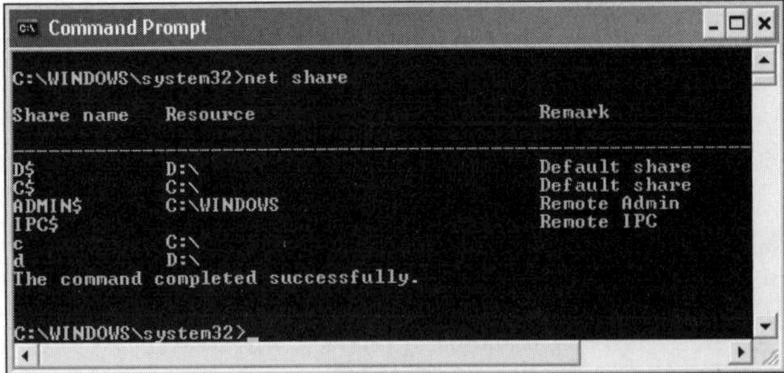

Figure 4-3: W32.Randex.ATX attempts to delete all the capital letter shares that Windows itself creates by default each time it starts up.

4. Starts a keylogger that logs keystrokes to a file named `%SystemRoot%\System32\Ntfvsi.txt`. If retrieved, that file includes any and all account names, passwords, credit card numbers, or other sensitive or confidential data entered after its installation. That's where the confidential information threat comes from in the damage assessment at the beginning of this section.

5. Connects to an IRC server named `batwing.gotdns.com` and listens for further commands (this is the opening of the back door mentioned in the damage assessment at the beginning of the section).

Once installed, some of the actions that this worm can attempt include scanning computers for weak administrative passwords, cracking them, and then copying itself to those machines. It also looks for CD keys for various computer games, which it can send to an IRC channel through its back door. It can mount various forms of denial-of-service attacks against other machines (making infected machines into what are called "zombies" in security jargon, because they attack others mindlessly at somebody else's behest). It even attempts to communicate with Trojans on other machines, and can download updated versions of itself as they become available.

Notice also that these actions provide plenty of ways in which an infection can be identified: one could search for specific registry keys or values, or look for specific files in predictable directories. This is how anti-virus software checks for the presence of infections, among other tests, in fact.

REMOVING W32.RANDEX.ATX

Numerous steps are necessary to remove this worm. Some steps are of a protective nature, to assure a clean and uninfected system after the removal has been completed; others are designed simply to remove the traces of, pointers to, and sources of infection on a Windows PC. As delivered, these instructions presume that you have access to some kind of anti-virus software to help with the cleanup. Otherwise, you'd have to follow the details of a technical malware description item by item and remove all such items to affect a proper cleanup. Here, I presume you can get some help and explain where to find and how to use such help later in this chapter. The instructions here are somewhat more general and high-level so you can apply them using any of the many anti-virus packages available as freeware, shareware, or commercial software nowadays.

A 10,000-foot view of the removal process can be delivered in the form of a relatively short list of activities, as follows:

1. Disable System Restore (applies to Windows XP and Me, but not Windows 2000 or Windows Server 2003).
2. Update virus definitions.
3. Restart the computer in Safe Mode.
4. Run a full system scan and delete all files detected as W32.Randex.ATX.
5. Delete all instances of the `"Sysmon" = "rpcmon.exe"` keys in the registry.

The sections that follow explore each of these activities in more detail. I want to observe at this point that I picked this particular worm to explore with you because most anti-virus vendors did not go to the trouble of building a removal tool for it. Had they done so—and they invariably will for more serious malware—all you'd need to do to clean up the infection would be to download and run the removal tool. It would do the rest of the work required automatically. But because I wanted to give you a feel for what's involved, I picked something that steps through the various processes involved in cleanup, one at a time.

DISABLING SYSTEM RESTORE

Because Windows XP (and Me) includes a built-in check pointing mechanism called System Restore that software programs can invoke (as well as users), most anti-virus experts recommend that this facility be disabled during disinfection processes. This should eliminate any possibility that malware can insert itself into a restore point, thereby avoiding the possibility of reinfection should that restore point ever be used.

Note

Unless it's disabled, Windows does not permit any third-party programs—well-behaved ones, anyway—to modify System Restore. This prohibition also applies to files in the System Restore folder. That explains why it's best to disable this facility to be sure to scan and remove all possible sources of infection, and why this activity is the starting point for the process. Note further that this requirement does not apply to Windows 2000 or Windows Server 2003 systems, which do not include this facility.

To disable or enable System Restore, you must log on with administrative privileges (if you haven't delegated them to any other accounts, log on using the default Administrator account and whatever password goes with it). Turning off System Restore deletes previously defined restore points; you must define new ones after you turn System Restore back on. With all these caveats in mind, here's how to do this:

1. From the Start menu, select All Programs→Accessories→Windows Explorer to launch that program.
2. Right-click My Computer, and then click Properties in the resulting pop-up menu.

3. Click the System Restore tab, and then click the check box to turn off System Restore in the resulting window (this is depicted in Figure 4-4).

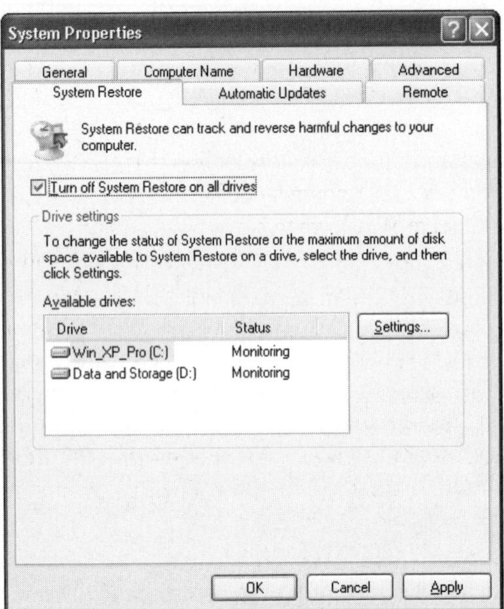

Figure 4-4: Click the check box to disable System Restore on a Windows XP system.

4. Click the Apply button at the bottom of the window to make this change take effect.

5. A warning message appears, as shown in Figure 4-5, that explains what happens if you do this. Because it's necessary, click the Yes button to turn off System Restore.

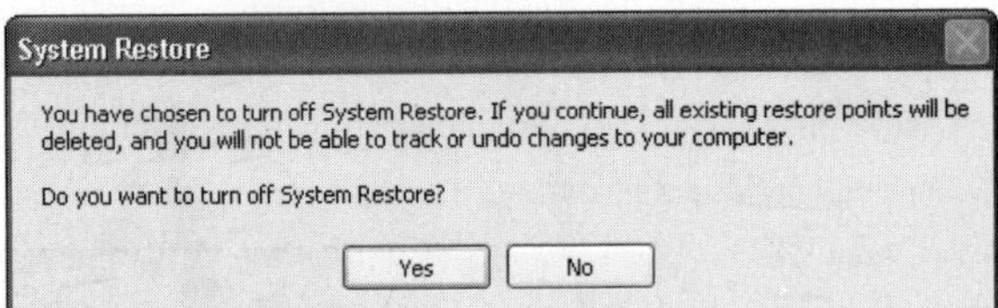

Figure 4-5: Dire warnings notwithstanding, click Yes to turn off System Restore.

6. Click OK to complete the operation.

7. Proceed with the other steps in this section; I'll briefly explain how to turn System Restore back on at the end of the exercise. If you would like to learn more about this facility, how to use it, and how to turn it off and on, please consult the Microsoft Knowledge Base article, "How to: Restore the Operating System to a Previous State in Windows XP," 306084 (`http://support.microsoft.com/default.aspx?scid=kb;EN-US;Q306084`).

Caution

Don't do this "just for fun." If you have numerous restore points already defined (and because many applications create them as part of the installation process, there may be more on your machine than you think), it could take a lot of work to re-create them when you turn System Restore back on!

Curious readers may be interested in understanding how restore points that the System Restore facility manages differ from what happens when the Last Known Good Configuration is used during a reboot. Although the two have the ability to restore Windows to a state it occupied earlier in time, the LKGC goes back only to the last time the machine was rebooted. System Restore, on the other hand, can return to any restore points stored in its database (and therefore can roll back time a long, long way). By the same token, if a usable restore point does not exist in the System Restore database, it can't take your Windows PC anywhere (but most well-behaved software starts installation by taking such a snapshot, and by default Windows XP creates a restore point every 24 hours, or for each 24 hours the machine is turned on, if you don't leave it running all the time). Neither of these techniques does away with files that malware, adware, or spyware may deposit on a PC though (and which therefore remain as potential sources for re-infection), so that's why the other steps in the sequence that follows are necessary.

Tip

If you want to check System Restore settings on your PC, and your keyboard has a WinLogo key (it looks like a little flag waving, and usually sits to the left and right sides of the Alt key (next to the space bar) on keyboards; sometimes it's called the WinKey), simply hold down the WinLogo key and press the E key at the same time. This brings up the System utility from the Control Panel, on which you'll find a System Restore tab you can check. If your keyboard doesn't include a WinLogo key, try Start → Control Panel → System instead. To see a list of WinLogo key sequences and what you can use them for, visit `www.activewin.com/tips/desk_tips_10.shtml`.

UPDATING VIRUS DEFINITIONS

Because I don't know what anti-virus software you're using, I recommend that you investigate how to obtain the most current definitions for your package, download them, and install them. The guiding notion here is that your software should be absolutely as up-to-date as possible so that even if a virus was discovered only yesterday, your software should be able to detect it today. Note further that although Symantec and other vendors do offer automatic update services, they revise those update files only once a week (on Wednesdays, in Symantec's case). You must go to the vendors' Web sites, download their latest anti-virus definitions and update your software manually if you really, really, really want to be completely current (unless it's a Wednesday and you use a Symantec anti-virus product, that is). I'll skip the details on exactly how to do this, because you can get those instructions from the folks who provide you with your anti-virus software anyway. For instance, on the Symantec site, you can find instructions on how to use its LiveUpdate service as well as how (and when) to use manual updates instead (see `http://securityresponse.symantec.com` for details under the

"Virus Definitions" heading). If you use some other vendor's anti-virus software, visit its Web site for similar instructions.

RESTARTING YOUR PC IN SAFE MODE

Figure 4-1 showed the Windows Advanced Option Menu that appears when you press the F8 key while waiting for Windows to start booting up. When you elect to start a Windows machine in Safe Mode, that setting greatly restricts the machine's capabilities. It also creates an ideal environment to look for and remove infections, while making it impossible to spread them any further because, among other things, booting in Safe Mode turns off network access (that's why you should be careful to pick the entry that says "Safe Mode," not the similar-looking one that says "Safe Mode with Networking"). Safe Mode also uses generic display drivers, so don't be too surprised if your desktop and the interfaces you work with look a little different from their usual appearance (screen resolutions will almost always be smaller, which will make everything look bigger as a result).

RUNNING A FULL SYSTEM SCAN

This is where you put your updated anti-virus software to work and instruct it to scan everything that can possibly be infected. This includes any drives or media that can be rewritten, but eliminates most write-once CDs, DVDs, and so forth, from consideration. If you were burning a CD or DVD while an infection occurred, you might want to toss it just on the off chance (a very small one, actually) that it got something catching during the burning process as well. If any infected files turn up and you can instruct the scanner to delete them, please do so; if it won't delete files for you, you must record a complete file specification for each such file (which means you have to know which directory on which drive it lives in, as well as the file name). If that's the case, you'll have to delete those files yourself after the scanner finishes its job, before moving onto the next step. What you're doing here is removing any possible future sources of infection from your system. Because the code that malware executes has to come from somewhere, this should make sure it can be found nowhere on your system.

DELETING REGISTRY ENTRIES

This is where you remove the instructions that execute W32.Randex.ATX as Windows starts up. Any time you make changes to the Windows registry, experts will remind you that a damaged registry can make Windows inoperable, and recommend that you create a backup copy before doing anything. Because you're going to get rid of stuff you don't want anyway, I'll skip those details, but I do provide pointers to some good explanations on how to back up and restore the registry in the "Resources" section at the end of this chapter. If you ever feel like "just playing" with the registry, or feel compelled to attempt more ambitious maneuvers than those I'm about to describe, please do follow that advice beforehand.

Given all these caveats, here's how to perform the task at hand:

1. Click the Start button and select Run from the resulting pop-up menu.
2. Type `regedit` in the Open field of the Run dialog box, and then click OK.
3. When regedit opens the Registry Editor window, click Edit in the top menu bar, and then click Find in the resulting pop-up menu.
4. Type `rpcmon.exe` in the Find window's Find What text field, and then click the Find Next button.

5. Each time the Registry Editor finds the string, it should appear inside a value named Sysmon. To delete each such entry, right-click the value name (it's highlighted in Figure 4-6) and then click Delete in the resulting pop-up menu.

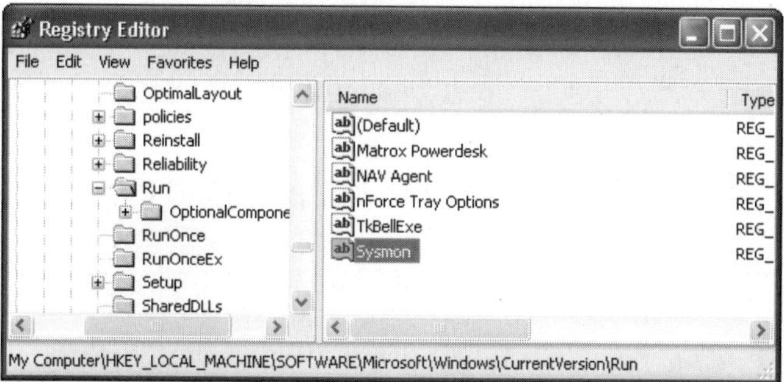

Figure 4-6: Deleting Sysmon in the registry.

6. Repeat the Find command to locate and delete all remaining `rpcmon.exe` values (you can use Ctrl+F to set up your query, then use the F3 function key instead of clicking through the menus if you like; the search value should remain unchanged). You can quit when you click Find Next or F3 and regedit tells you it can't find any more matching entries.
7. Close the Registry Editor by clicking the close button (the red X at the upper right-hand corner of the window) or by clicking the File entry in the menu bar and then clicking Exit on the resulting pop-up menu.

That's all there is to it: It's easy to delete unwanted stuff from the registry as (in this case) when you know the instances of what you seek don't need to be there anyway. Certain other malware writers use commonly occurring strings in the values they add to make it more time-consuming to ferret out and remove their registry additions.

RETURNING TO NORMAL OPERATION

Now that these various tasks have been performed, Windows should be able to return to normal, uninfected operation. This means rebooting the system in normal rather than Safe Mode, performing a final virus scan, and returning to Windows Explorer to turn System Restore back on. You can simply press Ctrl+Alt+Delete to summon the Windows Security window, then click the Shut Down button, select Restart in the Shut Down menu, and click OK; Windows will do the rest.

Tip

If this sort of thing seems tedious, time-consuming, and nit-picky, that's because it is. Remember, we're stepping through this stuff so you can understand in some detail what's involved in cleaning up after spyware, adware, or malware. But that's also why it's well worth your time to scour the major anti-virus or anti-spyware sites I've mentioned for a removal tool — it can do the job faster, safer, and more accurately. I've included these details only so you'll understand and appreciate what virus removal tools do and for that rare case in which you'll have to do it yourself.

When the computer restarts normally, you'll want to perform a final system scan using your antivirus software to make sure no lingering traces or signs of infection are found. If anything untoward turns up, you may have to repeat the process again (hopefully, this means reusing a removal tool, not stepping through a long sequence of system operations like those described in the preceding sections). When you do get a clean bill of health, only one final step remains—namely, restoring System Restore to its normal mode of operation.

Here's what you must do to turn System Restore back on (since you've been there before, I'll skip the screenshots this time):

1. Click the Start button, right-click My Computer, and click Properties in the resulting pop-up menu.
2. Click the System Restore tab.
3. Uncheck the "Turn off System Restore" check box in that pane.
4. Click Apply, and then click OK.

After that, a system formerly infected with W32.Randex.ATX should be restored to its former, uninfected status.

On the Web

For the complete Symantec Security Response report on W32.Randex.ATX, please visit `http://securityresponse.symantec.com/avcenter/venc/data/w32.randex.atx.html`.

Cleanup #2: ABetterInternet

ABetterInternet is adware that was originally discovered in November 2003. It's generally described as fairly benign because it doesn't add many files to a system, nor does it cause large numbers of configuration changes. In fact, if you're lucky, ABetterInternet will deposit an uninstall utility that you can try through the Add/Remove Programs applet in the Control Panel (some reports indicate that if the name ABetterInternet doesn't appear in the list of installed software, it may sometimes show up as WIN 32 BI Application). Those sites that rate adware and spyware uniformly give ABetterInternet pretty low rankings in terms of serious side effects or lingering system changes; despite such low ratings, you can find reports from individuals struggling to keep it off their systems because of some clever startup resurrection maneuvers it makes. This adware is most likely to show up on unprotected systems that have been victims of large numbers of pop-ups or that have downloaded unsafe ActiveX controls.

Technically, ABetterInternet is identified as a type of Internet Explorer Browser Helper Object (BHO), which is nothing more than a small program that runs automatically each time you start that program. In the case of ABetterInternet, the program is often identified as belonging to a class of BHOs that have some tracking and reporting capabilities, but is generally associated with invoking and displaying pop-up ads on PCs where it's running.

Tip

Small software company Definitive Solutions makes a snazzy little item called BHODemon that can show you all the Browser Helper Objects installed in your version of Internet Explorer, and that also rates what it finds. You can even double-click any entry in its listings to see more detailed information about it. Download this donation ware from `www.definitivesolutions.com/bhodemon.htm`; be concerned about anything that shows up that's not listed as benign in the program's Status column. Note: You may have to follow a link from the Definitive Solutions Web site to another Web page for downloads; be prepared! Note that this utility is probably unnecessary on Windows XP systems with SP2, because that version of IE tracks and provides BHO management services (other versions of IE do not).

Although numerous anti-adware tools can remove ABetterInternet automatically, I want to walk you through the work involved in removing this adware to give you a sense of what it does to a system.

REMOVING ABETTERINTERNET

This adware item can introduce any of a number of files, which must be deleted, along with multiple registry keys. Before following the list of steps I'm about to cover, you'll want to boot your Windows machine in Safe Mode to prevent unwanted registry or other changes from occurring automatically during system startup. Because I described this process earlier in this chapter, I won't repeat those steps here except to remind you that you must press the F8 key as Windows begins to boot to gain access to the Windows Advanced Option Menu (depicted in Figure 4-1), where you can then choose the Safe Mode option. Here's what you should do next:

1. Launch the Registry Editor by clicking the Start button. Select the Run entry from the resulting pop-up menu and type **`regedit`** in the Open text field of the Run window. If you press the WinLogo and the R keys simultaneously, that opens the Run window, too.
2. ABetterInternet is also considered a Common Object Model (COM) object, and as such, has an associated universally unique identifier known as a Class ID (abbreviated as CLSID) in the Windows registry. It will be necessary to remove the key associated with this BHO. Search for `CLSID\{000006B1-19B5-414A-849F-2A3C64AW6939}` by pressing Ctrl+F to open the Find window, and then typing in the string exactly as shown. Once found, right-click the entry in the Name column in the right-hand pane and then select Delete from the resulting pop-up menu.
3. That same long ID will also show up in a registry key named `...\Explorer\Browser Helper Objects`, so press F3 to repeat your search (you can edit its contents to remove the `CLSID\` portion of the previous string if you like). This key will show up under the `HKEY_LOCAL_MACHINE\SOFTWARE\Microsoft\Windows\CurrentVersion\Explorer\Browser Helper Objects` subkey.

Note

The Windows registry is divided up into hierarchical data structures called *hives*. These hives are always named the same and have a common set of associated abbreviations. Because I use them throughout the rest of the book, I introduce them here:

HKEY_CLASSES_ROOT	HKCR
HKEY_CURRENT_USER	HKCU
HKEY_LOCAL_MACHINE	HKLM
HKEY_USERS	HKU
HKEY_CURRENT_CONFIG	HKCC

4. Restart your computer in normal mode (Start → Shut Down and choose Restart from the "What do you want the computer to do?" pick list, then click the OK button).
5. Open a command prompt by clicking Start → Run, and then typing **`cmd`** in the Open text field in the Run dialog box. Change your directory location by typing **`cd %windir%`** to navigate to the root Windows directory (on Windows 9x/Me/XP it's usually `C:\Windows`, on Windows NT/2000/2003 it's `C:\WINNT`). Delete any or all of the following files you might find there: `bi.dll`, `host.dll`, `biprep.exe`, `Belt.exe`, or `Belt.ini`. The proper syntax for deleting files at the command line is `del` *`filename.ext`* (for example `del host.dll`). Please also note that files deleted in this way do not show up in the Recycle Bin, so please double-check your spelling before you hit the Enter key and lose that file for good!
6. Launch Windows Internet Explorer by selecting Start → All Programs → Internet Explorer. When the program opens, click Tools on the menu bar and select Internet Options from the resulting pop-up menu. When the Internet Options window opens, click the Programs tab and then click the Reset Web Setting button about halfway down the page. This will restore your default home page and search engine settings.

That's it!

A TALE WITH SOME VARIATIONS

Some spyware/adware databases document more versions of ABetterInternet than the foregoing removal recipe covers. That's okay for an example, because I just wanted to show you what kinds of items must be changed or removed and how to accomplish those tasks. But if you check a really comprehensive listing on ABetterInternet—for example, like that found at `scanspyware.net`—you'd see there might be one or more directories to be searched out and removed, and a great many more potential files or registry keys that might need cleaning out as well. Minute details of what to look for, change, or remove all depend on which version of this adware was present on a specific machine. This underscores the need for good detection and identification tools—like a spyware or adware scanner—that can do the job completely and conclusively. Even when manual removal is required, absolute identification and complete documentation of what should be removed are essential to a successful termination of adware infestation!

Cleanup #3: ClientMan.msdaim

According to most sources, ClientMan is a form of spyware that gathers information about processes active on those machines where it's installed, along with other less desirable forms of behavior. Some sites mention that it occasionally crashes Internet Explorer, others that it attempts to read personal information from various applications and directories. Some versions also redirect searches; others invoke pop-up ads (which would make it a hybrid adware/spyware combination). Whatever it is, most descriptions give it higher threat and hassle factor ratings than ABetterInternet gets. Variants go back as far as March 2003, and most reports indicate it remains active but the most recent reported version is from February 2004.

Like ABetterInternet, ClientMan is also a BHO and is reported to be included noticeably often with file or music sharing software (for example, Grokster). It's also occasionally classified as a Notifier because it can use stealthy means to inform third parties it's been installed on a machine, and as a Trojan because it seeks to add itself to firewall exceptions lists and create back doors on infested systems. At this point, 11 different versions have been identified, which may add anywhere from 2 to 38 objects to an infested machine (depending on the version). As with ABetterInternet, many anti-spyware tools can remove ClientMan automatically. Here, I'll take a look at a manual removal of middling complexity, to show you the kinds of elements involved.

Tip

Here again, if you're lucky, you might find an entry for ClientMan in the Add/Remove Programs applet in the Control Panel. If that's the case, there's no harm in trying an automated uninstaller before stepping through the process of manual removal outlined in the steps that follow. It never hurts to look!

1. Reboot your computer in Safe Mode.
2. Launch the Registry Editor (Start → Run, and then type **`regedit`** in the Open text field of the dialog box).
3. Delete the key named `HKLM\SOFTWARE\Classes\CLSID\{0BA1C6EB-D062-4E3.7-9DB5-B07743.2763.24}` (use Ctrl+F to open the Find window, type the key exactly as specified; right-click the object name, and then select Delete from the resulting pop-up menu).
4. Delete the `HKLM\SOFTWARE\Microsoft\Windows\CurrentVersion\Explorer\Browser Helper Objects\ {0BA1C6EB-D062-4E37-9DB5-B07743276324}` key (use Ctrl+F to open the Find Window, and then type the key exactly as specified, except without embedded spaces outside `Browser Helper Objects`).
5. Click the X box in the upper right-hand corner of the Registry Editor window or click the File entry in the menu bar, and then click Exit in the resulting pop-up menu. Either way, you'll close `regedit`.
6. Reboot your computer normally.

7. Launch a command prompt window (Start → Run, and then type **cmd** in the Open text field of the Run dialog box). Type **del %ProgramFiles%\clientman\run\dnsrep117d78e0.dll** (this removes an automatic startup file).

8. Type **cd %SystemRoot%** (this symbol equates to the location for Windows systems files, and is `C:\Windows` for Windows 9x/Me/XP and `C:\WINNT` for Windows NT, 2000, and Server 2003). Type **del <filename>**, where you replace *filename* with all of the following to delete possible sources of re-infestation: `MSDAIM.DLL`, `msdlgk.dll`, `msglji.dll`, `dsnrep117d78e0.dll`, and `MSMDLD.DLL`.

ANOTHER TALE, BUT STILL MORE VARIATIONS

As with the ABetterInternet adware item discussed in the previous removal recipe, if you look up ClientMan in various spyware databases, you'll find many more potentially infected files, several potential directories the software could set up, and a great many more potential registry settings to investigate. Here again, I urge you to use a good spyware scanner to help you identify exactly which version has infested your machine, and then follow explicit instructions for the removal of whatever version was actually present. Although the details will vary across the known versions of ClientMan, the type and nature of the cleanup activities involved stays the same: Boot in Safe Mode, remove various registry entries, reboot, and then remove various files. That's pretty much the ordinary drill for getting rid of most unwanted software. The trick, of course, is in identifying exactly what must go or change!

Where To Go for Help and Instruction

As I've said repeatedly throughout this chapter, if you can find a tool to automate cleanup for you, it's probably faster, easier (and safer, because registry changes can cause pretty severe problems of their own if misdirected or misapplied) to use one than to do things manually. That said, you'll find the same folks who provide most anti-virus and anti-spyware/anti-adware software also provide separate removal tools (until they can integrate them with their scanners). They also normally provide plenty of information to explain to you what unwanted software does to your system, and what specific actions cleanup or removal tools take on your behalf.

Thus, if you're already using a specific scanner, it should be able to tell you what it thinks it has found on your machine (or much better, what kinds of things it's blocking from obtaining entry to your machine). You can always visit the vendor's Web site to get more information about the specific item being reported, if you want to get their perspective on things. You can also use your favorite search engine to look up other items of information — many of which will show up on other vendor or software developer sites devoted to the care and feeding of such tools — by searching on the name of the unwanted software item of current interest to you (likewise, if you can identify specific files or registry keys associated with that software, they provide additional search points as well).

All this said — with the additional caveat that I'll provide pointers galore to makers of anti-virus, anti-spyware, anti-spam, plus anti-adware and pop-up blocker software in the next part of this book (particularly in Chapters 6 through 9, which cover those very types of software as their primary focus), I've also found some sites to be particularly helpful when it comes to looking up information about unwanted software. These are summarized in Table 4-3, with pointers to helpful URLs.

Table 4-3 Unwanted Software Listings with Removal Details and Helpful Info

Name	*Type(s)*	*URL (Notes)*
PestPatrol	ASVTWO	`http://pestpatrol.com/pestinfo/`
Virus database	ASVTWO	`http://securityresponse.symantec.com/avcenter/vinfodb.html`
ScanSpyware	ASVTWO	`www.scanspyware.net/` (check "Parasites" list)
Online Encyclopedia	ASO	`www.kephyr.com/spywarescanner/library/index.phtml`

A = Adware, S = Spyware, V = Virus, T = Trojan, W = Worm, O = Other

The key to the process is proper identification, because removal details are routinely made part of explaining what unwanted software does and how it works. You've seen this to a large extent in the cleanup case studies earlier in this chapter; as you see more such information on the Web and through your scanning tools, it should become pretty routine!

Is Your PC Clean?

Once you've started using scanning, blocking, and removal tools, the only way to be sure a system is clean — or at least, as clean as the most current scans can report — is to download the latest scanner updates, then check your system again just to make sure any and all traces of unwanted software have been scoured away. Although it can be time-consuming (30 to 45 minutes per machine was typical for my test and production machines as I wrote this book), it's worth the extra time and effort to check one last time to make completely sure a system is clean before declaring victory and returning to what passes for normal work or play on your systems. This entails obtaining and using enough scanning tools — including anti-virus and other malware, plus one or more anti-spyware/anti-adware products — to clean up all potential sources of infection and infestation (on the other hand, you can try a security suite product like Norton Internet Security Suite 2005, or other products mentioned in Appendix A of this book, which cover all these bases with varying degrees of success). Always start by downloading the latest updates, and run a complete system scan on all hard drives and removable media in your system (commercial CDs or DVDs are probably safe, but if you've eliminated everything else you may find yourself in the uncomfortable situation of having to let a vendor know its media may be infected). Only when all your scans come up clean can you safely assume your PC is clean.

Tip

Once you've cleaned up your PC, it's up to you to keep it that way. The best way to do this is to obtain scanners that update themselves automatically on a regular schedule. Indeed, it's cheaper (and perhaps even free) to update and scan on your own initiative, but the costs of forgetfulness or laziness can be greater than you may want to pay. Consider that carefully before you decide to take the cheapest way out of your scanning, blocking, and removal needs for anti-virus, anti-spyware, anti-adware, and pop-up blockers!

Hoaxes

What looks like a software virus (or spyware or adware), spreads like a virus, and certainly causes the same kind of alarm that real malware can? Answer: a hoax. That's the little-understood genre of unwanted information about supposedly unwanted software, which may sometimes be called a virus hoax, a spyware hoax, or what have you.

Although it spreads like a worm, what defines a hoax as such is that it's completely human-generated and propagated. In fact, a hoax consists of a false rumor about some supposed danger of infection or infestation. It relies on quoting authoritative (but anonymous or unnamed) sources, relies on unthinking panic in its recipients, and always encourages those recipients to spread the news to family, friends, coworkers, and anybody else they know. In fact, because official sources of virus information rely on opt-in newsletters, Web site postings, alerts, bulletins, and other mechanisms you've already learned about, it's smart to be suspicious of any warning that asks you to participate in spreading news about infection or infestation.

As you'll learn if you investigate hoaxes further, spreading news about malware, spyware, adware, and so forth is best handled through official channels. There's no need for other people to get involved, including you! By forwarding such messages, you're only allowing the hoax to propagate, and inflicting its major impacts on others: time wasted reading and dealing with something bogus and consumption of bandwidth to ferry messages with no real import or value!

Some security mavens view hoaxes as a form of what some hackers call *social engineering*. This is a technique whereby somebody impersonates a figure of authority (or quotes some made-up figure of authority) to persuade, encourage, or convince people to divulge information or perform actions they shouldn't share or do without proper authorization and interaction. Other classic examples of social engineering include calling into reception desks to ask for names, phone numbers, or e-mail addresses of employees (often important steps in impersonating others to seek access to systems or networks), or calling into IT operations to request passwords (or to ask to have certain passwords reset). Social engineering is a powerful technique because it relies on people's desire to help others, often to the detriment of security policies and rules — it's also at the heart of e-mail attempts to steal financial and identity data called "phishing attacks" that you'll read more about in Chapters 9 and 10.

When it comes to hoaxes, one of the best resources around on this topic is available at Vmyths.com (`www.vmyths.com`). Be sure to check it out; it also has a nice collection of newsletters as well. Your takeaway from this brief discussion should be a reminder that when it comes to spreading the news about the dangers of malware, spyware, adware, or whateverware, your help (and e-mail) aren't necessary!

Resources

The Virus Bulletin is a well-known and respected source of vendor-neutral anti-virus and virus information. It posts regular news, produces a magazine, and offers a terrific collection of information and tutorials on all kinds of virus-related subjects. Visit its Web site at `www.virusbtn.com/`. Also be sure to check out its short but interesting collection of tutorials at `www.virusbtn.com/support/tutorials/`.

Table 4-1 includes pointers to various online scanners for malware, spyware, and adware. Many vendors (including most of those mentioned in the table) also offer free or evaluation copies of their software for download and local use on PCs (and other platforms). These tools can get you started with investigation and cleanup, but they by no means exhaust all the possibilities or options available. Be sure to look further in Chapters 6 through 9, which deal with scanning, blocking, and removal software of many kinds, for many more pointers to tools and utilities.

According to Windows registry guru Jerry Honeycutt, author of the Microsoft Press book *The Windows XP Registry Guide* (Microsoft Press 2002), nothing beats taking Windows registry snapshots with regedit, then using Keith Devens' WinDiff (a utility that can compare two Windows files and list everything that's different between the two—available for download at `www.keithdevens.com/files/windiff/`) to figure out what's different. My own research tells me that Registry Watch (`www.easydesksoftware.com/regwatch.htm`) and Active Registry Monitor (`www.protect-me.com/arm/`) also do this job rather nicely, if you want to start watching how things change before and after you install software. By the way, Jerry also recommends using System Restore and taking your system back to a checkpoint taken before infection occurs as another good way to escape from the clutches of unwanted software. As long as you take regular checkpoints, this should work pretty well!

When it comes to backing up and restoring the Windows registry, you'll find a Microsoft Knowledge Base article and a third-party piece quite helpful in this regard. The KB article is numbered 322756, entitled "How to back up, edit, and restore the registry in Windows XP and Windows Server 2003" (`http://support.microsoft.com/default.aspx?kbid=322756`): it's detailed, thorough, and includes lots of tips and examples you can follow. The other piece comes from a group of gurus that Microsoft identifies as Most Valuable Professionals (known as MVPs, of course); it's entitled "How to backup the Windows XP Registry" (`www.mvps.org/sramesh2k/registry.htm`). It provides some really useful information not mentioned in the KB article. When saving registry data, you'll often write entire hives or keys to specially formatted `.reg` files. Because these are executable files, you may find them blocked if you try to send them as e-mail or instant messaging attachments, so be warned that they're (quite properly) viewed in many quarters as sources of potential danger themselves.

Symantec's Norton Ghost (`www.symantec.com/sabu/ghost/ghost_personal/`) and its companion product Symantec Drive Image 7.0 Backup (`www.powerquest.com/driveimage/`) can take drive snapshots and use them for backup and restore operations. I'm pretty impressed with InaQuick (IQ), which works kind of like an in-place imaging utility (see my review of this product at `www.techbuilder.org/article.htm?ArticleID=48639`).

Bryan Consulting has put together a pretty good set of links on virus (and other unwanted software) hoaxes on a Web page entitled "Virus Hoaxes and Urban Legends" (`www.bryanconsulting.com/stories/storyReader$65`). It includes information from major anti-virus vendors Symantec, McAfee, and F-Secure, along with some interesting pointers on how to evaluate the credibility of information sources online.

Summary

This chapter took a long hard look at the kinds of system components that can be changed, removed, or added when unwanted software takes up residence on a Windows PC. I talked about various methods for conducting post-infection or infestation cleanups stressing various techniques (booting in Safe Mode, turning off System Restore, and so on) that can help to keep a lid on a poten-

tially dangerous or infectious system during various mopping up phases. Along the way, I looked in detail at what's involved in cleaning up some recent and at least mildly vexing malware (the Worm W32.Randex.ATX), adware (ABetterInternet), and spyware (ClientMan). This involved looking at the effects of these various software items, and a step-by-step walkthrough of what manual cleanup for each one might entail. I also discussed various sources for information and instructions online for conducting such activities, while stressing how very preferable it is to find (and use) an automated tool to do this sort of thing for you whenever possible. The chapter concluded with a quick listing of some good online information resources for malware, adware, spyware, and so forth, where the providers not only offer good technical descriptions of actions and effects, but also very likely talk visitors through details of the removal process (even if it is automated).

This concludes Part II of this book. Chapter 5 begins Part III, wherein I look at all the various software elements involved in protecting a Windows system from unwanted software (and other malignant influences) of all kinds. In fact, Chapter 5's focus is on firewalls, those software elements whose job it is to get between individual systems or private networks and the wild and wooly Internet, shielding the good guys from the bad buys as much as possible. Chapters 6 through 9 deal with pop-up and adware blockers (Chapter 6), anti-spyware programs (Chapter 7), anti-virus software (Chapter 8), and spam blockers and filters (Chapter 9). Buckle up! This is where things start to get really interesting!

Part III

The Particles of Protection

IN THIS PART:

Part III turns the tables on the previous part and talks about the various tools available to help stymie pop-ups, adware, spyware, malware, spam, and other unwanted software and content. In fact, all but one of the chapters in this part tackles one such type of unwanted software or content and reviews the software options available to help you identify it, fend it off, and get rid of it and clean up after it when necessary. The first chapter in this part (Chapter 5) deals with a highly recommended (some would say essential) element in PC defense—namely, a firewall. Because the emphasis in this book is on protecting individual systems or small networks, the coverage concentrates on personal firewalls and software designed to help protect individual systems from unwanted software and content. Although that's the emphasis you'll see in the chapters that follow, please be aware that centrally managed, enterprise-class alternatives are available to businesses or organizations that want to tackle unwanted software or content for all their users and systems on a larger scale.

Chapter 5

Personal Firewalls

People sometimes wonder why Microsoft receives so much negative publicity on security matters. These days, it seems that hardly a week goes by without one or more news items dealing with the discovery of a new vulnerability, the depredations caused by some new exploit, or the generally lousy perceived state of security in the Windows operating system, the Internet Explorer browser, or some other Windows-based application, service, or platform. Are things really as bad as they sometimes seem?

Before I answer that question, I'll point out several major factors outside Microsoft's control that help to explain these circumstances. First, most experts estimate that somewhere between 90 and 95 percent of the world's desktops run Windows, and an increasingly large percentage of the world's servers do as well (estimates vary more widely here, depending on how you define the term server, but most such estimates tend to fall somewhere between 25 and 35 percent). Thus, one simple-minded explanation for the regular announcement of vulnerabilities and the discovery of exploits has to do with where the action is. Because so many machines run Windows, it makes sense for those who create and promulgate unwanted software and content to target the biggest possible population so as to maximize their opportunities for success (however they might define what "success" means for them).

Other, less statistical factors are also at work. The very foundation of the protocols and services that make the Internet work sits on top of what security experts like to call an optimistic security model. Whereas a pessimistic security model might be succinctly stated as a variation on Murphy's Law — "What can go wrong, will. Plan for disaster, attack, and failures of all kinds." — an optimistic security model echoes Dr. Pangloss's hopeful outlook as expressed in Voltaire's *Candide*: "This is the best of all possible worlds, so we don't even need to THINK about security." Because of inherent flaws in the very mechanisms that transport data and communications on the Internet, discovery of vulnerabilities and their subsequent exploits is something that any software that touches that environment must endure and deal with as problems arise. This part of the equation is not Microsoft's fault, and explains why other operating systems and applications are also subject to vulnerability and occasional exploit.

But prudence dictates that businesses should anticipate and head off trouble whenever possible, and plan to deal with failure as well as success in many different dimensions. This is where Microsoft comes in for some well-recognized slams, and where the company has been doing everything it can to reinvent itself to change its security outlook from optimistic to pessimistic. (Although perhaps it's more accurate to say that the outlook is changing from one of "security is an add-on; we'll deal with it later" to "security is a basic requirement that should apply to all stages of the software life cycle, from design, to testing, to commercial release, and to all subsequent updates and maintenance

thereafter.") In 2003, Bill Gates launched what Microsoft calls the "Trustworthy Computing Initiative" to address these very issues and to try to get all of its products to include strong, effective security as essential ingredients in their make-up, along with ease of use, marketability, and of course, the features and functions it delivers.

By now, you're probably wondering: "What does all this have to do with firewalls?" Glad you asked! As a key part of promoting its Trustworthy Computing Initiative, Microsoft has substantially boosted security education, information content, and related advice to its customers. You'll now find this kind of stuff all over Microsoft's Web site, in everything from product information, to how-to's, to the many articles, training materials, and technical documentation the company offers to all visitors. Turns out that a cornerstone of its end user education is a collection of Web pages under the title "Protect your PC."

On the Web

You can check out all of the "Protect your PC" information online at `www.microsoft.com/athome/security/protect/`. It's pretty interesting and worth the visit!

The three primary points of this advice can be briefly stated (and in fact are, in these very terms, on the home page just cited) as:

- Use an Internet firewall
- Get computer updates
- Use up-to-date anti-virus software

In fact, Microsoft is not alone in dispensing this advice, nor do I take issue with it (except perhaps to observe that given the many kinds of unwanted software and content PCs can pick up on the Internet, I think it fails only in not going far enough). To those three valuable and appropriate bits of advice, I'd also add:

- Use a pop-up blocker
- Use anti-spyware/adware software
- Take steps to eliminate spam
- Perform regular scans to identify and clean up unwanted software and content on your PC

After I explain what a firewall is and what a firewall does, you shouldn't have any trouble understanding why firewalls are important when it comes to establishing proper defenses against unwanted software and content. I also think this explains why Microsoft has decided to enable its Internet Connection Firewall by default—it's been a built-in component in Windows XP since its original release in 2001, but is renamed to Windows Firewall and turned on in Windows XP Service

Pack 2 (SP2). That's because turning on the firewall means users gain an added and important level of protection from many potential sources of attack automatically. This is in keeping with the Trustworthy Computing Initiative, and in Microsoft's gradual shift from shipping products with optimistic security settings and defaults to more pessimistic ones.

What Is a Firewall?

Before I wax eloquent and occasionally profane on what firewalls do for systems and networks, I want to start with the absolutely essential job that structural firewalls perform. In the building and engineering trades, firewalls are important design components in structures and vehicles whose job is to halt or retard the spread of fire from one part or area to another part or area. Thus, in a building, a firewall might be constructed between floors in a multi-story structure, or perhaps inside the common walls and surfaces where two wings adjoin. Should one part of the structure catch fire, the firewall's job is to at least slow its spread, if not to stop it from spreading altogether. Likewise, in an automobile or truck, the most common place for a firewall is between the engine compartment (where highly combustible fuels burn at high temperatures) and the passenger compartment (where temperatures over 100 degrees Fahrenheit are usually judged to be extremely uncomfortable, if not downright intolerable). For small engine fires, the firewall can stop the spread and keep the passenger compartment from igniting; for larger fires, its job is to give the passengers enough time to get out of the car before their immediate surroundings are also set ablaze. Keep these characteristics in mind as you read about Internet firewalls; the metaphor may be stretched somewhat in the translation to the computing world, but it still applies!

A simple explanation of an Internet firewall—or in more generic terms, a network firewall—retains the notion of a barrier that's so important in physical firewalls in buildings or vehicles. What's different in this case is that an Internet firewall's real job is to inspect items that seek to pass through it. An Internet firewall screens traffic that shows up at some interface. It should deny transit to anything recognizably malign, unwanted, inappropriate, or even suspicious, while allowing at least some benign information through. This basic structure requires a device of some kind with at least one connection through which incoming traffic can come from "the outside" to a computer or a network on "the inside." Two different scenarios are depicted in Figure 5-1. They show the two most common situations in which personal firewalls occur. Basically, in the minimal case, a personal firewall simply sits between a single PC and an Internet connection; in the other case, a personal firewall sits between an Internet connection on the outside, with two or more (and seldom more than half a dozen) PCs or other devices on the inside. But lots of bigger, heavier-duty firewalls are in use in companies, organizations, and institutions of all kinds. These commonly guard Internet links for anywhere from a handful to thousands of PCs and other devices, so if you want to understand how industrial-strength firewalls work, they resemble the kind shown in Figure 5-1, where they sit between the Internet and an "inside network," albeit on a much larger scale.

Thus, in conceptual terms, a firewall's most important task is to protect what's on the inside from what's on the outside. What's on the inside could be a single PC (the most common circumstance when a personal firewall is used), or it could be a small network (usually no more than a handful of computers).

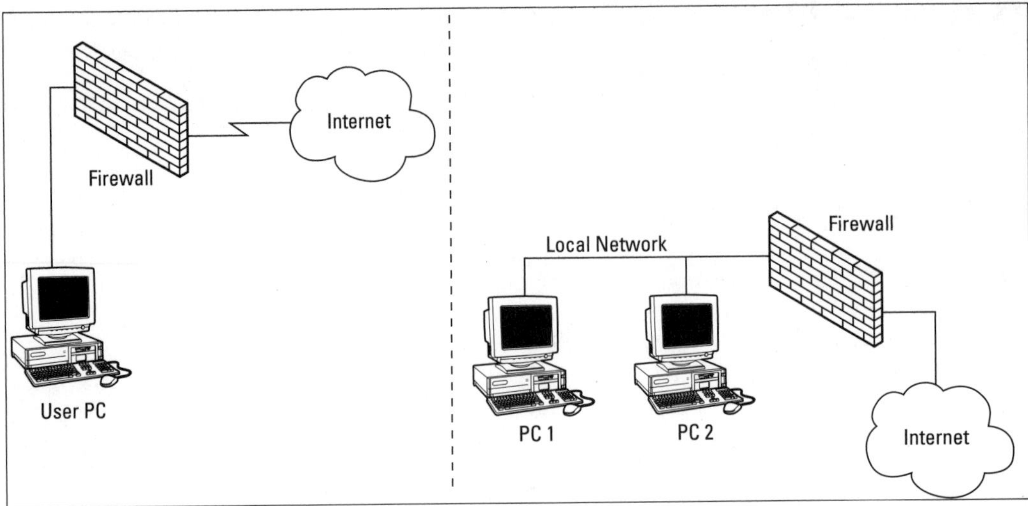

Figure 5-1: Firewalls usually sit between a single PC and an Internet connection (left-hand side), or between an Internet connection and an internal network of some kind.

Recall, however that a firewall works by screening traffic. This means it can inspect and act on outbound traffic, as well as inbound traffic. In some family computing situations, parents or other responsible parties find that a firewall's ability to block access to certain Web sites for certain users provides an added layer of protection and comfort. Likewise, if they know what they're doing, they may even choose to prevent certain kinds of communication from entering or leaving the PC (or PCs) under their control — more on this later. To impose these kinds of controls when firewalls don't deliver them explicitly, many families install Web site or content screening software on some PCs to protect sensitive eyes from unwanted or inappropriate content. This explains the popularity of software programs such as Net Nanny, Cyber Sentinel, CYBERsitter, and so forth. In reality, this kind of software also acts as a kind of content firewall, in that it prevents access to predefined lists of content providers known to offer materials inappropriate for children, and screens content access requests to look for signs of attempts to access other such content, which it also blocks.

But to understand important details in how a firewall works, it's first necessary to understand the communications rules and formats that the Internet uses — called Internet protocols — so that's what I tackle in the next section.

Note

The next series of sections in this chapter contains technical coverage about the rules governing networked communications, message formats, network services, and a whole lot more that make the Internet work. Known collectively as the Transmission Control Protocol/Internet Protocol (TCP/IP) protocol suite, it's essential subject matter for those who want to understand how firewalls work, what they do, and why they're so important. If you know this stuff already, feel free to skip ahead to the "Top Personal Firewall Picks" section; if not, please read the next sections over — they'll really help your understanding of and appreciation for what's covered later in the chapter.

What Is TCP/IP and How Does It Relate to Firewalls?

This section focuses on a group of networking protocols and related services that not only make the Internet work, but that also make firewalls and related technologies necessary. I'm talking about something called Transmission Control Protocol/Internet Protocol (TCP/IP). Along the way, I explain the terms *protocol* and *service*, as fundamental concepts. I also describe the most important pieces and parts in the hundreds (if not thousands) of elements that make up TCP/IP. Most importantly, I explain what it is about how TCP/IP works and behaves that makes firewalls essential to monitor any connection to the Internet, be it to permit a single PC or a network of computers to surf the Web, send and receive e-mail, and do all the other things that people and computers do online together.

It's not at all inaccurate to describe TCP/IP as the collection of networking protocols and services that make the Internet run. But all this means is that unless you understand what a protocol is, what it does, and how it operates, and likewise for a service, TCP/IP remains total gibberish. Never fear: I start the demystification process in the next section.

ABOUT PROTOCOLS AND SERVICES

I want to start with a definition. A *protocol* is a collection of rules that describe valid sequences of and formats for messages that a sender may direct to a receiver (or to multiple receivers, as the case may sometimes be). Simply put, a protocol describes the kinds of communication that can occur between a sender and a receiver, specifies what order those messages should or must follow, and lays down rules to delineate the formats that such communications should use.

I've described TCP/IP already as a group or a collection of protocols. In general networking terms, any group of related protocols may be called a *protocol suite*, particularly in light of certain interdependencies or relationships that exist among and between its members. Thus, when you talk abstractly about TCP/IP as a set of rules, formats, and so forth, it's appropriate to refer to the TCP/IP protocol suite.

But it's sometimes necessary to talk about how one or more TCP/IP protocols operate on a specific computer running some specific operating system with a particular type of Internet connection, and so forth and so on. In this situation, it's typical to describe that group of protocols as a *protocol stack*. This helps emphasize the existence of a layered, interdependent set of software components that actually implement these protocols on a particular device or computer. Protocol stacks are often associated with operating systems nowadays, so you might hear somebody compare and contrast the Windows 95 TCP/IP stack with the Windows XP stack, or even with the Mac OS or OSX Panther stack.

The notion of a service exists for a different purpose: Rather than describing what a protocol is, in TCP/IP terms, a *service* defines what a protocol can do. This helps explain a common correspondence between protocol names and the services they deliver. Thus, an e-mail protocol supports methods for storing and forwarding messages, which means it enables an e-mail server to direct e-mail to some recipient, to understand local and remote e-mail addresses, to store e-mail messages for local recipients, or to forward or send messages destined for remote recipients to other e-mail servers, and so on. This means an e-mail delivery service really works much like a two-way message transfer system. Local messages can be held for user pick-up, remote messages can be shipped to other servers where the remote recipient's e-mail is stored, or the messages can be forwarded to some other server, and so forth.

THE KEYS TO TCP/IP

Work on TCP/IP started in the mid-1970s, and it's been in steady (and increasing) use since the early 1980s. Today, in fact, TCP/IP supports many hundreds of different protocols and services, used for things such as:

- Identifying servers (domain names and addresses) and users (e-mail names and addresses)
- Enabling a wide variety of networking technologies to access the Internet (telephones and modems, all kinds of wired and wireless network media, among others)
- Providing all kinds of ways to interact and exchange information (e-mail, Web sites, voice communications, video conferencing, and lots, lots more)

It's not important to understand all the underlying details right now, but you should get the idea that TCP/IP makes it possible to do lots of different things on a network, including anything you might have used a network for yourself.

The name TCP/IP is based on two individual protocols that provide some of this protocol suite's most basic and important capabilities:

- **TCP** is an abbreviation for **Transmission Control Protocol**; it provides reliable, robust delivery when sending information or messages from a sender to a receiver. TCP also provides sequencing services, so it can take big pieces of data, break them into lots of small pieces to be sent across a network, keep track of all the small pieces as they arrive (or fail to arrive) at the receiving end, and then make sure all small pieces get delivered and reassembled in the correct order. If the delivery and reassembly does not succeed, TCP can inform a recipient that the data transfer failed. This explains why TCP enables so many named Internet services, such as e-mail, file transfer, and Web access.
- **IP** is an abbreviation for **Internet Protocol**; it defines how to address and route data packages to get them from a sender to a receiver. IP is an essential element in TCP/IP, because nearly every kind of Internet communication uses IP to move and direct data. By contrast, even though TCP transports data for lots of TCP/IP services, it does not transport data for every TCP/IP service; IP ferries nearly every Internet communication with only a very few exceptions.

Despite the many hundreds of other protocols and services that also belong to the TCP/IP suite, IP and TCP are important enough to name the whole shebang. Poets call this kind of naming mechanism *synecdoche*, where a part of something stands for the whole — in this case, two very important parts! Formal specifications for TCP/IP protocols are stated in the form of documents known as *RFCs* (Requests for Comments). Although this may sound a little tentative or wishy-washy, RFCs describe and govern existing and proposed TCP/IP protocols and services. To see the entire collection of RFCs, or to inspect the most current list of "Internet Official Protocol Standards," look for the highest numbered RFC that ends with the digits "00." As I write this chapter, that's RFC 3000.

On the Web

You can find RFCs at many locations online (for example, visit your favorite search engine and search on "RFC 3000"). You can read RFC 3000 online at `www.cis.ohio-state.edu/cgi-bin/rfc/rfc3000.html`. There's an index of RFCs and related materials at that same Web site at `www.cis.ohio-state.edu/cs/Services/rfc/index.html`.

RELATING INTERNET FIREWALLS TO TCP/IP

At the outset of this chapter, I explained that the Internet protocols themselves — by which, of course, I meant TCP/IP — were designed following an optimistic security model. In fact, TCP/IP was designed and implemented in an academic laboratory setting, more or less as an experiment to see if something like it could be done. Alas, none of those original designers had the slightest clue about the global importance and reach that TCP/IP would one day attain. That explains why core TCP/IP protocols act as if they can trust users to be on their best behavior, and assume they won't try to bypass or ignore its relatively simple and straightforward security measures.

In its earliest years of use, TCP/IP was kind of a hobbyhorse for a small and clannish bunch of highly educated and motivated researchers. Under those circumstances, an optimistic security model didn't work at all badly. But today TCP/IP is ubiquitous and global; you can't count on the educated and informed understanding of users, nor on their good intentions or goodwill. Because TCP/IP's underlying fundamentals haven't changed since the old days, protective elements such as firewalls are needed to stand guard between "safe" inside systems or networks and "unsafe" public systems and networks. Likewise, numerous enhancements to older core services and additions of new protocols and services have occurred to up TCP/IP's security model to somewhere between "guardedly optimistic" and "downright pessimistic."

Note

The most widely used version of TCP/IP is called IPv4. It embodies an optimistic security model. A new version of TCP/IP, known as IPv6, is largely sketched out, but still in development. Although it is used in some networks and for some parts of the Internet, most experts don't believe IPv6 will service a significant proportion of the global Internet until some time between 2010 and 2015. IPv6 seeks to learn from recent history and embodies a pessimistic security model. Thus, as the world switches over to IPv6 slowly but surely, far fewer security bolt-ons, add-ons, or enhancements should be necessary to maintain proper security. My guess is that firewalls will still be around, though, and still perceived as necessary!

A LOOK INSIDE THE TCP/IP STACK

As you may recall, you use the term *TCP/IP stack* to identify a collection of software components and elements that make TCP/IP protocols and services work on a particular computer. In this connection, you should also understand that TCP/IP protocols (and related services) also organize themselves into various layers to represent and embody a hierarchical networking model. Thus, lower

layers support upper layers, and protocols and services at lower layers provide essential functions for protocols and services at higher layers. If it helps your understanding, you might say layering explains how TCP/IP earned its designation. As individual, lower-layer protocols, both TCP and IP (and their related services) support a lot of important higher-layer protocols (and related services)—things that users really care about. In most cases, therefore, using a TCP/IP stack means operating various interlinked and interdependent software components that correspond somewhat to actual protocols and services in use. It also involves software drivers to permit a PC to communicate with network interfaces, such as a telephone or cable modem, a network interface card for wired or wireless media, or whatever else is needed to access the Internet.

In fact, the TCP/IP protocol suite is divided into four layers, and it's helpful to understand what each layer does and how it relates to adjacent layers. This matches a formal networking model for TCP/IP that's sometimes called the DARPA model (DARPA is the Defense Advanced Research Projects Agency, the original U.S. government agency that funded the development of TCP/IP). It's also known as the TCP/IP networking model. Figure 5-2 depicts the TCP/IP networking model, whereas Table 5-1 lists some common TCP/IP protocols associated with each layer.

Application layer
Transport layer
Internet layer
Network Access layer

Figure 5-2: The TCP/IP networking model is divided into four interconnected layers.

Working from the bottom of Figure 5-2 up, I describe each of the four layers of the TCP/IP networking model (although each layer's name starts with TCP/IP, you'll often hear it referenced without that preamble so that, for example, the TCP/IP Network Access layer and the Network Access layer are used interchangeably):

- **TCP/IP Network Access layer**—Some references call this the Network Interface layer. Either way, it's the layer in which networking hardware, interface cards, and communications technologies like Ethernet or Token Ring are at work. It's also the layer at which specific connection-management or wide area network (WAN) protocols come into play. Think of it as the layer where cables, interfaces, and hardware connections to computers and other devices work.
- **TCP/IP Internet layer**—This layer is where addressing and routing between computers on the Internet is handled. This layer also allows multiple networks to interconnect, and it supports global naming and addressing schemes that make the world-wide public Internet

work. At this layer, networking concepts of "here" (the origination point for communication) and "there" (the destination point for communication) operate, and the routing needed to get from "here" to "there" is managed.

- **TCP/IP Transport layer** — Sometimes called the Host-to-Host layer, this layer handles everything necessary to transfer data from one computer to another. This means taking data items of arbitrary size, segmenting them into an identifiable sequences of smaller messages suitable for network transmission, and managing their delivery from sender to receiver. Reliability and robustness means that delivery is tracked, failed transmissions retried, and received messages reassembled to match their original order. Persistent failures may result in error messages, depending on the actual protocol in use.
- **TCP/IP Application layer** — Sometimes called the Process layer, this is where a protocol stack hooks up with applications or processes on a host machine. That's why this layer deals with user interfaces and services capabilities. It's also the layer where recognizable services such as e-mail, Web access, file transfer, and other activities operate. In fact, the Application layer determines the types of functions and behaviors that TCP/IP provides to its users.

Table 5-1 Where Common Protocols Fit into the TCP/IP Networking Model

Name	*Acronym*	*Explanation*
Network Access Layer		
Point-to-Point Tunneling Protocol	PPTP	Serial line connection protocol (widely used with telephone modems in most modern operating systems and devices)
PPP over Ethernet	PPPoE	Newer serial line connection protocol (designed for use with broadband connections like cable modem or DSL)
X.25	X.25	European ITU WAN protocol (widely used for low- or medium-bandwidth telephone modems outside the U.S.)
Internet Layer		
Address Resolution Protocol	ARP	Converts numeric IP addresses to hardware addresses
Border Gateway Protocol	BGP	Newer, exterior routing protocol (used to interconnect multiple routing domains or Internet backbones)
Internet Control Message Protocol	ICMP	Manages and monitors IP routing and network activity
Internet Protocol	IP	Routes packets from sender to receiver

Continued

Table 5-1 Where Common Protocols Fit into the TCP/IP Networking Model *(continued)*

Name	*Acronym*	*Explanation*
Internet Layer		
Open Shortest Path First	OSPF	Newer, interior routing protocol used inside large private networks or routing domains
Packet Internetwork Groper	PING	Checks access to and performance in reaching specific network locations (service based on ICMP)
Routing Information Protocol	RIP	Old-fashioned, basic IP routing protocol
Transport Layer		
Transmission Control Protocol	TCP	Reliable, connection-oriented transport protocol
User Datagram Protocol	UDP	Unreliable, connectionless transport protocol
Application Layer		
File Transfer Protocol	FTP	Remote file access and transfer services
Hypertext Transfer Protocol	HTTP	Supports Web access
Network News Transport Protocol	NNTP	Supports Internet newsgroup access
Simple Mail Transfer Protocol	SMTP	Supports e-mail delivery from sender to receiver

Personal firewalls focus their activities and capabilities at the Internet and Transport layers; more advanced firewalls cover these layers, but can also operate at the Application layer to some extent or another. You'll understand this distinction a little later in this chapter when I talk about the kinds of things that firewalls do, and what capabilities they require to do them in the section titled "Top Personal Firewall Picks." But first, I want to explore the basics of IP addressing and domain names — not coincidentally, that's the topic of the next section.

UNDERSTANDING BASIC IP ADDRESSING

Now that you know that a key function of the Internet layer in the TCP/IP networking model deals with identifying individual devices, and figuring out how to move data from here to there, you can appreciate the importance of names and addresses for TCP/IP. Essentially they're what make things work, and what enables hundreds of millions of individual devices to recognize and communicate with one another. I want to dig into how the most widely used version of IP — namely IPv4 — handles addressing. For this book, it suffices to say that IPv6 was designed with much bigger and more flexible addressing capabilities to increase the size of the IP address space (which sets the upper limit on how many devices can interact and identify each other) by an astonishing number (at least 10^{40}, depending on how final addressing implementations shake out).

IP uses three different kinds of related addresses, depending on how those addresses are intended to be understood and used:

- **Symbolic names** — Also known as Internet domain names, these are meant primarily for human consumption and use. Such names take the form of `www.microsoft.com` or `etittel@lanw.com`. But if it is to actually be used on the Internet (or any other TCP/IP-based network), any domain name must match up with at least one unique numeric IP address. When it comes to their Internet uses, domain names exist to link to numeric IP addresses. A very special TCP/IP service known as the domain name system (DNS) exists to translate symbolic names to numeric IP addresses (though it can also go the other way, and do lots of other interesting things, too).
- **Logical numeric (IP) address** — For IPv4, this is a string of four numbers, separated by dots: for example, 10.6.120.78 or 172.16.1.33. Each number must take a decimal value of 255 or less, since each number can be up to only 8 bits ($2^8 = 256$, so the largest 8-bit number is 255). Most of the time 8-bit numbers are called *bytes*, but TCP/IP experts like to call them *octets*, which is just a fancier synonym. Numeric IP addresses usually appear in what's called *dotted decimal* form, which is four decimal numbers, separated by dots or periods. This is the address that the IP protocol uses to identify all hosts and interfaces on the Internet. It's a logical address because it's not part of how hardware is made or built (this is a good thing, because changing IP addresses — a sometimes tedious exercise that goes by the name of renumbering — requires changes only to software configuration files).
- **Physical numeric (MAC) address** — Network interfaces are endowed with 6-byte numeric addresses during manufacturing. This address is called a Media Access Control (MAC) layer address. The first 3 bytes identify an interface's manufacturer and the second 3 bytes represent a unique counter. It's designed to make it impossible for two physical interfaces to share a single physical address. In the TCP/IP suite, the Address Resolution Protocol (ARP) is used to translate numeric IP addresses to MAC addresses; the Reverse ARP (RARP) goes from MAC addresses to numeric IP addresses. This address operates at the Network Access layer, because it identifies specific hardware components attached to a network. It's important to identify sender and receiver only when two computers on the same network are actually exchanging data or messages with one another.

If you can remember that IP addresses link to domain names for humans to use, and that IP addresses also link to MAC addresses to identify specific network interfaces, you've understood the motivation for this whole scheme.

If your PC is connected to a TCP/IP network, or straight to the Internet, there's an IP address at work somewhere in there. A simple trip to the command line will show you the most basic information about that IP address. Here's how:

1. Open a command window. You can try holding down the WinLogo key and pressing the R key (if your keyboard is so equipped), or you can click the Start menu and then click Run in the resulting pop-up menu. Either way, type **`cmd`** (or **`cmd.exe`**) into the Open text field of the Run dialog box and then click OK to open the command window itself.

2. When the command prompt appears, type **ipconfig** and then press Enter. You'll see a display much like the following (but details will differ for reasons I explain in the section that follows).

```
Windows IP Configuration

Ethernet adapter LANW LAN connection:

        Connection-specific DNS Suffix  . :
        IP Address. . . . . . . . . . . . : 172.16.1.10
        Subnet Mask . . . . . . . . . . . : 255.255.255
        Default Gateway . . . . . . . . . : 172.16.1.17
```

3. Type **exit** at the command prompt and then press the Enter key to close the command window.

The salient points to take away from this exercise include the notion that each computer has at least one IP address, and that an address to reach other networks (often, but not always to get to the Internet) is what the Default Gateway provides. The rest of the details will be covered very soon.

ANATOMY OF AN IP ADDRESS

Using dotted-quad notation (four numbers, separated by periods, each number between 0 and 255, of the form *x.x.x.x*), logical IP numeric addresses hide a wealth of structural details. When initially released, IP addresses were divided into five classes, labeled Class A through Class E. Classes A, B, and C consumed the bulk of the total IP address space, and classes D and E were reserved for special (D) and experimental (E) use. Although that structure is no longer completely accurate, it's worth understanding anyway, as described in Table 5-2. The key lies in recognizing that all five classes divide the 32 bits in a numeric IP address between a network portion on the left and a host portion on the right, to identify entire networks and individual network interfaces, respectively.

Table 5-2 IP Address Classes A through C

Class	*Map*	*#Nets*	*#Hosts*	*Address Layout*
Class A	*n.h.h.h*	124	16,777,214	0*bbbbbbb.bbbbbbbb.bbbbbbbb.bbbbbbbb*
Class B	*n.n.h.h*	16,366	65,534	10*bbbbbb.bbbbbbbb.bbbbbbbb.bbbbbbbb*
Class C	*n.n.n.h*	2,096,894	254	110*bbbbb.bbbbbbbb.bbbbbbbb.bbbbbbbb*

Here's how to understand Table 5-2. In the Map column, *n* stands for network, and *h* stands for host. In address classes with a smaller number of *n*s, you find a smaller number of networks, but each network has a large number of hosts (Class A, in other words). In address classes with a smaller number of *h*s, you find lots of networks, but each network has only a small number of hosts (Class

C). Smack dab in the middle is Class B, which has a middling number of networks, each with a middling number of hosts. Hardware can identify address classes very quickly because all Class A's begin with a leading zero, Class B's with a 10, Class C's with a 110, D's with 1110, and (you guessed it) Class E's with 11110!

If an IP address shows only zeros in the host portion, that denotes a *network address* (rather than the address for a specific interface on that network). If an IP address shows only ones in the host portion, it denotes a *broadcast address*, to which all devices will listen and respond — IP's answer to the "all points bulletin."

Since about 1993–1994, class-based IP addressing has been replaced by a different addressing scheme that doesn't divide things up purely on 8-bit boundaries. This technique is called Classless Inter-Domain Routing (CIDR, usually pronounced like the fruit drink, cider). This method includes a pair of numbers that explicitly denotes where the boundary between the network and host portions of an address sits. For example, 23/9 means that the 32 bits in the IP address are split so that the first 23 bits cover the network part, and the last 9 bits cover the host part. Because this permits more flexible use of IP addresses, it's helped IPv4 to find a new lease on life while waiting for IPv6 to take over, and a 128-bit address space to enable every square foot of the planet (and then some) to have its own unique Internet address.

There's a special RFC (1918) that allocates space within the A, B, and C address classes for what's called private use. Even though Classes A, B, and C may not be used any more, these reservations remain important. Anybody who wants to can use these private IP addresses inside their network boundaries, but these addresses won't be allowed to identify source or destination addresses for any traffic on the Internet. That's because more than one instance of each such address is possible, and the Internet itself deals only with unique addresses. It can't tolerate duplicates (and when duplicate addresses are detected, all interfaces that share a common address immediately quit working). Private IP addresses are good, because they permit companies or organizations to use them without having to pay for public IP addresses. However, if interfaces (and the computers or other devices to which they're attached) want to access the Internet, they have to use special Network Address Translation (NAT) software to map all private addresses to a public address (absolutely required for the Internet side of any firewall connection in any case). This has to be done before any of that traffic can be readdressed and allowed to traverse the public Internet. Table 5-3 identifies all three private IP address ranges (and I stress this is pretty handy stuff; I use private IP addresses on several of my own networks). In fact, if a Windows XP machine isn't supplied with an IP address or can't find an address server to give it one of its own, it will automatically assign itself a number from the private IP ranges in Class C.

Classes D and E

As described earlier, Classes D and E are reserved for special purposes. Class D supports multicast services, where a single network address can reach all hosts that register to listen on that address. (This explains how modern routers share update information: all listen on specific multicast addresses and download whatever comes to that address.) Class E is reserved purely for experimental use; it's where up-and-coming or not-ready-for-prime-time Internet protocols and services make their first (and sometimes their only) debuts.

Table 5-3 Private IP Addresses as Specified in RFC 1918

Class	*Address Ranges*	*#Nets*
Class A	10.0.0.0–10.255.255.255	1
Class B	172.16.0.0–172.31.255.255	16
Class C	192.68.0.0–192.68.255.255	256

If you'll recall, the command-line exercise earlier in the chapter used the simplest version of the `ipconfig` command. There's a more complete version that can completely document your PC's TCP/IP configuration, which I'll show you now that you can understand more of the information items it contains (and explain others that are important, but which you might not yet understand without some help).

1. Open a command window (press the WinLogo and R keys simultaneously, or click Start and then Run; either way type **`cmd`** into the Open text field of the Run dialog box and then click OK).
2. At the command prompt, type **`ipconfig /all`** and then press the Enter key. A display something like the following should appear:

```
Windows IP Configuration
        Host Name . . . . . . . . . . . . : wxppro-108
        Primary Dns Suffix  . . . . . . . :
        Node Type . . . . . . . . . . . . : Unknown
        IP Routing Enabled. . . . . . . . : No
        WINS Proxy Enabled. . . . . . . . : No

        Physical Address. . . . . . . . . : 00-0C-6E-68-C2-AD

Ethernet adapter LANW LAN connection:
        Connection-specific DNS Suffix  . :
        Description . . . . . . . . . . . : 3Com 3C920B-EMB Integrated Fast
Ethernet Controller
        Physical Address. . . . . . . . . : 00-26-54-0E-9A-EE
        Dhcp Enabled. . . . . . . . . . . : No
        IP Address. . . . . . . . . . . . : 172.16.1.108
        Subnet Mask . . . . . . . . . . . : 255.255.255.0
        Default Gateway . . . . . . . . . : 172.16.1.17
        DNS Servers . . . . . . . . . . . : 24.93.40.62
```

3. To close this window, type **`exit`** at the command prompt and then press Enter.

Note that I edited some white space out of the response just to keep things as compact as possible, but otherwise, it's a faithful reproduction from my test machine. Adding the `/all` switch to the `ipconfig` command basically tells Windows you want to know everything it can tell you about the TCP/IP configuration on the machine you're using. That's why you see so much more information here. Among the interesting pieces of information present are the following entries:

- `Primary Dns Suffix`—Those whose Internet service providers or network operators run their own name services generally provide information about the local domain name here (I don't run a local DNS server on my network, so this shows up blank here).
- `IP Routing Enabled`—On a computer with multiple network interfaces where traffic moves in on one interface and out on another (very commonly the case for a machine attached to the Internet and a local area network, where a firewall should be running) this often reads "Yes." On connections where an external network appliance is used, when lone machines attach to the Internet, or when a PC is connected to a local area network (as is the case with the test PC illustrated here) this reads "No," as shown.
- `WINS Proxy Enabled`—The Windows Internet Naming Service (WINS) is a Microsoft name service that older versions of Windows use to resolve Microsoft and Internet naming schemes. You'll seldom see this set to "Yes" on home machines or networks.
- `Physical Address`—This is the Media Access Control (MAC) layer address burned into firmware on the network interface card you're using to access the network. Ultimately, it identifies one and only one network (and possibly, Internet) connection.
- The Ethernet adapter connection information describes the network interface on the test machine illustrated; it's on a network named `LANW LAN`. Some of the other details repeat what appeared in the simple `ipconfig` listing; others offer new information (I include only those here):
    - `Description`—Reads the first 3 bytes of the MAC layer address to identify the maker and kind of Ethernet interface in use.
    - `Dhcp enabled`—Indicates whether or not the IP address for the interface is furnished by a special IP service called the Dynamic Host Configuration Protocol (DHCP). On networks where DHCP is available, Windows machines need only be configured to obtain address information from a DHCP server, and everything else is handled automatically. Virtually all ISP Internet links use DHCP to make things as easy as possible for all parties involved in making an Internet connection.
    - `IP Address`—Shows the IP address in use for this machine; in this case, it's statically assigned from the Class B private IP range.
    - `Subnet Mask`—This Class B address uses a Class C mask because even 100 nodes is more than this network will ever support.
    - `DNS Servers`—The first of a set of domain name system (DNS) addresses where the computer can request that symbolic names like `www.microsoft.com` be translated into numeric IP addresses like 207.46.156.252 (this service lets people use names that make sense to them, and computers translate those names into addresses that make sense to them).

A QUICK PEEK INSIDE IP

Protocols define rules and formats for messages used to exchange information, make and reply to requests for service, and all kinds of other network communications. Because most messages travel inside IP packets at the Internet layer, the rules that govern IP also govern the primary characteristics of TCP/IP communication. This is important because firewalls pay close attention to certain fields in the first 64 bytes of an IP packet, which follows a standard layout called an "IP header." Although I don't describe all of these fields (because they seldom provide data that firewalls act upon), Figure 5-3 depicts a complete IP header layout. I put a grey background behind those field names that firewalls attend to most, so you can immediately see which ones can be important. (These appear in italic font in the bulleted list that follows the figure, as well.)

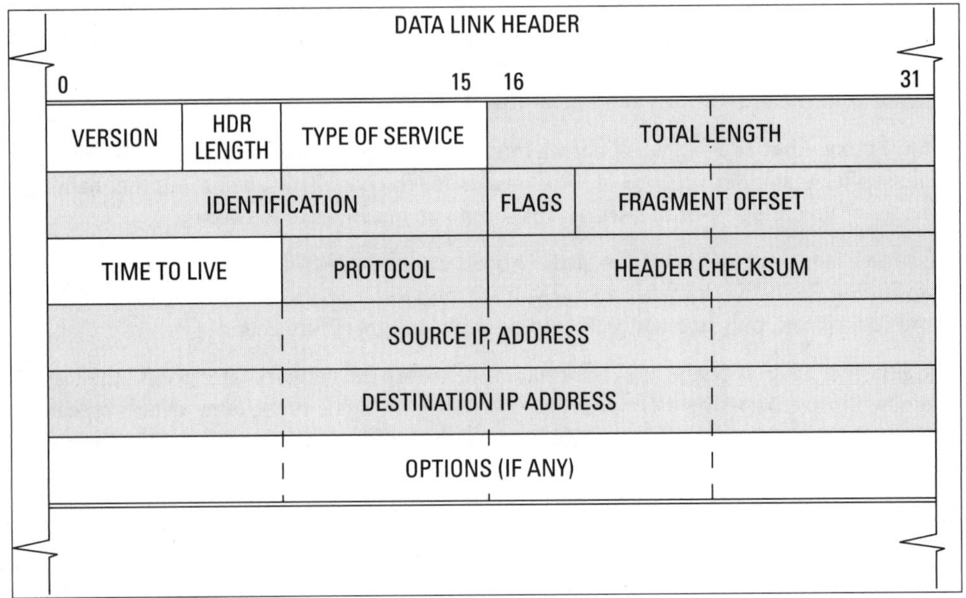

Figure 5-3: Firewalls look closely at IP headers to decide what to do with them as they attempt to "pass through."

- **Version** — Identifies IP version in use as either 4 (IPv4) or 6 (IPv6); here, I cover only IPv4.
- **Header length** — Specifies IP header length in bytes, divided by 4 (all IP headers must have lengths divisible by 4, so this reduces length data by 2 bits).
- **Type of Service (TOS)** — Here, bits 1 through 3 define precedence, which routers use to prioritize traffic. Bits 4 through 7 contain the actual TOS value, used to specify general routing characteristics (RFC 1349 has the details).
- ***Total length*** — Specifies the actual packet length, which includes the true size of the IP header, plus anything in the data portion of the packet (called the payload). This value does not include padding (extra unused bytes added to meet minimum length requirements for short packets).

- ***Identification***—A unique identifier used to reassemble fragments when an IP packet must be divided into smaller pieces (called fragmentation) between sender and receiver.
- ***Flags***—Three bits for packet fragmentation data. Bit 1 is always 0. If bit 2 is 0, the packet may be fragmented in transit; if it's 1, no fragmentation is allowed. If bit 3 is 0, it's the last fragment in a series; if it's 1, additional fragments follow.
- ***Fragment offset***—When IP packets traverse networks that can't carry them because they're too big, they are divided into smaller fragments. Fragment offset describes where to put a fragment to reconstitute the original IP packet. Certain network attacks deliberately misuse offset values to try to break IP stacks; firewalls can track such values, do the math, and deny packets with illegal or invalid offset values.
- ***Protocol***—This identifies which protocol resides inside an IP packet's payload. Firewalls watch this closely, because they often allow or deny traffic based on this value.
- ***Header checksum***—Used to check integrity of an IP header. The checksum is calculated and written inside the IP packet before it's sent and then recalculated upon receipt. Both values must agree or the IP packet is discarded.
- ***Source IP address***—The sender's reported IP address; firewalls can use this to allow or deny traffic.
- ***Destination IP address***—The recipient's IP address; firewalls can also use this to allow or deny traffic.

Because firewalls can inspect and act on IP header values quickly and easily, this provides a foundation for much of what firewalls do. Of all the fields mentioned, source and destination addresses and protocol field values probably get the most attention of all. But firewalls can also act on information in an IP packet's payload, as you learn in the next section.

TRANSPORT AND APPLICATION LAYER PROTOCOLS

If you could somehow look inside the wires and cables that are used to carry Internet traffic, you'd see a huge number of IP packets traveling to and fro in a ceaseless stream. Look further inside the IP packets, and you'd find mostly TCP and UDP packets in use to transport data from senders to receivers. Inside those TCP and UDP packets, you'd find Application layer payloads for services such as network news, Web access, file transfer, e-mail, and so on.

There's actually a technical field in networking called protocol analysis that does just that, but you don't need to care about that level of detail in understanding what firewalls do. All you need to care about is that those TCP and UDP packets (especially their headers) carry information of great interest to firewalls, and that occasionally firewalls can look even further inside to look at Application layer headers and data as well.

But the deeper a firewall is asked to look inside the packets it should approve or deny transit, the longer it takes to grant or deny such permission. Packets can arrive at firewalls at astonishing rates sometimes, so it's important to realize that more complex inspection or filtering techniques can sometimes slow things down. This also explains why firewalls work best at the "edges" of the Internet, between links to public carriers and service providers and private systems or networks. As you get closer to the core or backbone of the Internet, traffic comes and goes so quickly that routers have time only to look at IP headers, and not much else, as traffic screams past.

Firewalls don't have to deal with that kind of volume, though for larger networks arrival and departure rates can still be pretty high. In fact, this explains one key difference between personal firewalls and other, more capable firewalls: Personal firewalls don't need to deal with very high traffic volumes because they normally service only one or up to a handful of computers, whereas other firewalls may deal with tens, hundreds, or thousands of computers astride Internet connections with much higher bandwidth. Table 5-4 briefly summarizes the key information that firewalls look for at the Transport and Application layers (and please recall that each Application layer protocol has its own associated message types and layouts that firewalls can inspect and track to some extent or another).

Table 5-4 What Firewalls Inspect at Transport and Application Layers

Transport Layer	
Field Name	***Explanation***
Source port	A number between 0 and 65,535 that identifies the application or process that sent this UDP or TCP packet. A major focus for firewall behavior, port numbers are covered in the next section.
Destination port	Identifies a receiving application or process to which the packet is sent, for both UDP and TCP. When attempts to access unwanted, unused, or suspicious port numbers occur, firewalls may block traffic based on the destination port.
TCP sequence number	A number that identifies each individual TCP packet, called a *segment*, used to reassemble incoming packets upon reception, but can be deliberately manipulated in some forms of attack. Some firewalls check for invalid numbers and discard offending packets.
TCP data offset	States where in the reassembled application message payload data should be placed. As with sequence numbers, some firewalls check for invalid offsets and discard offending packets.
TCP flags	TCP goes through a predetermined sequence of initial packet exchanges between sender and receiver to establish a working connection. Some attacks start this sequence, and then leave it hanging; others flood recipients with initial packets. Many routers and firewalls look for and drop incoming packets that match known attack profiles.
Application Layer	
Field Name/Type	***Explanation***
Message type	Within most application protocols, packets have an associated type (request, reply, and error messages are pretty common types). Some firewalls scan for suspicious patterns of message types to block potential attacks.

Application Layer	
Field Name/Type	***Explanation***
Source domain name	Many Application layer protocols include domain names. These can be compared to originating IP addresses in what's called a reverse DNS lookup (which translates an IP address into a domain name instead of the other way around) to make sure both values are linked. A common attack signature called *spoofing* occurs when a false source address or domain name is supplied; firewalls check this on incoming traffic.
Command content	Most TCP/IP application protocols use specific request and reply messages or commands to provide a service. Some firewalls read the syntax of specific incoming messages, and then allow or deny them based on their potential impact. This is as deep into packet structure as sophisticated firewalls ever go.

MORE ABOUT TCP AND UDP PORT NUMBERS

Table 5-4 mentions sending and receiving *port numbers*; such numbers identify both senders and receivers of UDP and TCP packets. They identify the sending and receiving application or process where the packet originated (*source port*) and where it's going (*destination port*). Port numbers are 16-bit integers with values from 0 to 65,535. Port numbers are organized into three ranges of values:

- **Well-known port numbers (0–1,023)**—Well-known port numbers correspond to various TCP/IP core services that systems offer; for that reason, they're also sometimes called "service port numbers" or simply "service ports." These numbers typically identify well-known services such as FTP (ports 20 for data transfer and 21 for command and control information), SMTP (port 25), HTTP (port 80), POP3 (port 110), and so forth. Initial requests for service are sent to well-known port addresses, but when a service connection is established, both clients (sends service request to well-known port with dynamic port where it will accept replies) and servers (answers on well-known port, replies with new port address, and then sends service replies) use dynamic port numbers while that connection remains open. A hand-off from the well-known address to a dynamic address occurs as quickly as possible, so that other requests arriving at the well-known port address can be serviced as needed.
- **Registered port numbers (1,024–49,151)**—Registered port numbers correspond to specific industry applications or processes. Thus port 1188, for example, is associated with HP's Web administration services. Despite existing registrations, certain TCP/IP implementations use port numbers 1024 through 5000 as temporary, dynamic port numbers (see next bullet). If a client makes a request to a registered port number, a hand-off to a dynamic port number will also occur immediately thereafter.
- **Dynamic port numbers (49,152–65,535)**—Dynamic ports are used only while a temporary connection between a sender and a receiver remains active. Once closed, they're discarded so they can be re-used as needed.

If a service can work with either TCP or UDP, the port numbers for each transport will often be identical, but not always (however, this correspondence is more like a rule than an anomaly). Many attackers begin their reconnaissance of systems or networks under consideration for attack by scanning port numbers on Internet interfaces—thus, one of a firewall's most important jobs is not to respond when unwanted callers come a-scanning! I talk more about this in the next section.

Right now, you can take a look at the ports that are open on your Windows machine by using yet another command-line IP utility. It's called `netstat`, and it displays TCP/IP protocol statistics and current TCP/IP network connections. This utility can also show port numbers for active connections (those in use as you run the command) and listening ports (port numbers for which TCP or UDP is ready to respond to requests or replies) on your PC. Such information can be informative and interesting. Here's how to see what's up on your machine:

1. Open a command window (press the WinLogo and R keys simultaneously, or click Start and then Run; then type **cmd** into the Open text field of the Run dialog box and click OK).
2. At the command prompt, type **netstat -an** and then press the Enter key. (`-a` tells `netstat` to list all connections and listening ports; `-n` tells `netstat` to display addresses and port numbers in numerical form; `-an` tells `netstat` to do both at the same time.) The resulting output should resemble the following (but details will vary widely, according to what's installed and running on your PC):

```
C:\>netstat -an

Active Connections

  Proto  Local Address          Foreign Address        State
  TCP    0.0.0.0:135            0.0.0.0:0              LISTENING
  TCP    0.0.0.0:445            0.0.0.0:0              LISTENING
  TCP    172.16.1.108:139       0.0.0.0:0              LISTENING
  TCP    172.16.1.108:1036      216.58.162.100:80      CLOSE_WAIT
  TCP    172.16.1.108:1039      216.150.206.248:80     CLOSE_WAIT
  UDP    0.0.0.0:445            *:*
  UDP    0.0.0.0:500            *:*
  UDP    0.0.0.0:1028           *:*
  UDP    0.0.0.0:4500           *:*
  UDP    127.0.0.1:123          *:*
  UDP    172.16.1.108:123       *:*
  UDP    172.16.1.108:137       *:*
  UDP    172.16.1.108:138       *:*
```

Understanding this output takes a little detective work, but is worth the exercise. Many of the ports shown in the listing are dangerous to expose to the Internet, but safe as long as they're restricted only to a local area network. On a standalone PC, the range of port addresses from 135 to 139 (a range associated with Microsoft NetBIOS) are unlikely to appear; if they do, it's profound cause for concern. Port 445 is associated with Microsoft directory services, and port 500 with the Internet Security Association and Key Management Protocol (ISAKMP); these needn't be exposed to the Internet under most circumstances. Ports 1028 and 4500 are temporary UDP ports used for file transfer with another machine on my local network. Again, they needn't be open for general Internet access unless you're running some kind of application that warrants their presence. Port 123 is associated with the Network Time Protocol, used to synchronize my local system clocks with the time server at Texas A&M University; if you don't use a time service you shouldn't see this active, either. Finally, ports 1036 and 1039 are associated with specific IP addresses at Webroot.com, in conjunction with my use of the Spy Sweeper software. In this case, open ports were purely local with no Internet access, except for 1036 and 1039 as noted.

On the Web

You can find a complete list of assigned port numbers with additional discussion of well-known, registered, and dynamic port numbers at the Internet Assigned Numbers Authority's (IANA's) Web page at: `www.iana.org/assignments/port-numbers`.

How a Firewall Looks at TCP/IP — Literally!

The short phrase "packet inspection" describes exactly what a firewall does. That said, packet inspection covers many types of examination starting at the IP packet level, continuing through to UDP and TCP transport payloads, and sometimes extends all the way into the headers (and on some occasions, even the payloads) of Application-layer packets. Firewalls inspect this information carefully to look for illegal, unwanted, or potentially dangerous IP addresses, protocols, port numbers, or patterns of activity. Firewalls can be configured to block all unused protocols and to protect your ports. Some firewalls attempt to block all traffic that might indicate that an attack is either imminent or under way. Other firewalls can block access to certain domain names for outgoing traffic, either to enact workplace acceptable use policies or to offer families a means to block access to inappropriate or prurient materials.

But all this capability hinges on a firewall's ability to look inside the traffic passing through it, and then to apply a set of rules as to what's allowed to pass through and what's not. Firewalls also work very well to protect systems and networks from scans and other attempts to snoop, attack, and even penetrate them. Kind of makes packet inspection sound a bit less dull and boring, doesn't it?

The section that follows takes a look at some top personal firewall picks, and explains what makes them so common, popular, or both. After that, I walk you through a firewall installation and then explore some scanning tools you can use to check your system's (and firewall's) security. It's time to put all this newfound TCP/IP knowledge to work!

Top Personal Firewall Picks

Before exploring some of your firewall options, it's important to understand what you need (and don't need) a firewall to do for you. You do need a firewall to help protect your system from unwanted access, and it's a good thing if a firewall helps your system keep a low profile (or no profile) in the sense that it won't show much (or anything) to those who might attempt to scan it. If you stop to think that a firewall works by denying some traffic the rights of transit, it should make sense

that you don't want a firewall to block access to things you need or want to visit, even though you do want it to block things you don't need or don't want.

Getting a firewall configuration can be something of a "Goldilocks chore" in that it may take a few oscillations between too much and not enough protection before you finally determine what's just right for your needs and your situation. I've installed firewalls on small local networks, only to realize shortly thereafter that although they did indeed render the network invisible to scans from the Internet, they also turned off the ability to exchange files between systems on the local network, and made users unable to use a network-attached printer for output. Because the users needed both of those capabilities very much, I had to work my way through documentation and configuration settings until things were working the way I wanted them to, but I still had the kind of protection I wanted a firewall for in the first place.

Pondering the XP Default — Internet Connection Firewall/Windows Firewall

Outside the top firewall picks I'm about to explore, there's a default option that Windows XP owners should consider: Windows XP, in both Home and Professional editions, includes a built-in firewall. Until Microsoft released Service Pack 2 (SP2) for Windows XP, this facility was known as the Internet Connection Firewall (ICF). Starting with the introduction of SP2, it's known as the Windows Firewall. Prior to SP2, the firewall was installed as part of the Windows XP installation process but was disabled by default. Because one of the primary motivations behind what's new inside SP2 is to improve security, and it's a truism that any firewall is better than no firewall, it should come as no surprise that Windows Firewall is turned on by default when you install Windows XP SP2. But what does this buy you?

Most experts are unanimous in their belief that although ICF is better than nothing; most other firewall options offer more explicit (and sometimes more accessible) controls than ICF. Many also agree that these other options provide more or better protection than ICF — and it's not just a case of getting what you pay for — other free firewall options are available that beat ICF when standard external security scans are compared side-by-side. But Windows Firewall seems to be a different story: When I applied a battery of basic and more extended security scans (more on these later in the chapter) to Windows Firewall, it did not perform significantly worse than either of the top-rated personal firewalls covered later in this chapter. To me, this makes default "out of the box" security for Windows XP SP2 not only safer than any prior release of Windows to date, but it also makes Windows Firewall an acceptable firewall option for most users! On the other hand, experts are unanimous in noting that while Windows Firewall does a fine job of screening incoming traffic, it does nothing to screen or groom outgoing traffic (which most other firewalls do nicely, including those mentioned later in this chapter).

That said, I want to take a look at Windows Firewall from Windows XP SP2. It's fairly simple and offers acceptable protection by default. Windows Firewall is accessible through Control Panel. It includes three panes that provide access to a fairly broad range of controls; there are also 15 Group Policy Objects related to Windows Firewall that offer additional controls as well.

To explore Windows Firewall on a Windows XP machine with SP2 installed, click Start → Control Panel → Windows Firewall. This produces a window onscreen like the one shown in Figure 5-4, which shows the General tab in the Windows Firewall Control Panel applet (and which, of course, also shows that the firewall has been turned on by default as well). On the tab, the only other options are to turn off the firewall (which I concur with Microsoft is not a good idea unless you plan to install another firewall, or know you're protected by another firewall — if, for example, this is not the

computer that's hooked directly to the Internet, but the machine that is connected to the Internet does have a firewall with up-to-date software installed). The "Don't allow exceptions" check box is a way to temporarily increase security when you leave your home connection for something more public — the premier example of this would be when using wireless networking at a hot spot in a restaurant, an airport, or some other public place.

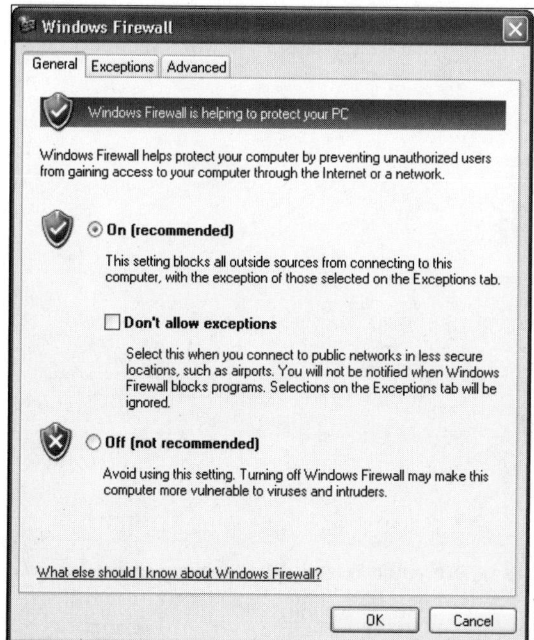

Figure 5-4: The General tab comes up by default in Windows Firewall.

The Exceptions tab is where you tell Windows Firewall what kinds of things can go on without requiring the firewall's attention or mediation. The idea is that the firewall scans everything coming off the Internet (or traveling across the local network) except what appears on this pane. Notice that by default (the checked selections shown in the Programs and Services pane in Figure 5-5) Windows Firewall allows file and printer sharing to occur (which means you should be able to access your printer and disk drives on other nearby computers without difficulty) and that it also allows traffic related to Remote Assistance (which is a Microsoft facility to allow somebody to inspect and operate your computer remotely, presumably with your permission or by your invitation). You can add additional programs that require network assistance by clicking the Add Program button and selecting from a pick list there. You can also manage port definitions that the firewall will permit to be used (outgoing) or accessed (incoming) here. Use the Edit button to see ports for which exceptions have already been defined. You'll find that local subnet access for otherwise dangerous ports associated with NetBIOS (ports 137, 138, and 139) and with Server Message Block file transfers and Active Directory (port 445) are also defined by default. As long as the Internet is blocked from access to these (and other ports) — and it most surely is — you're okay.

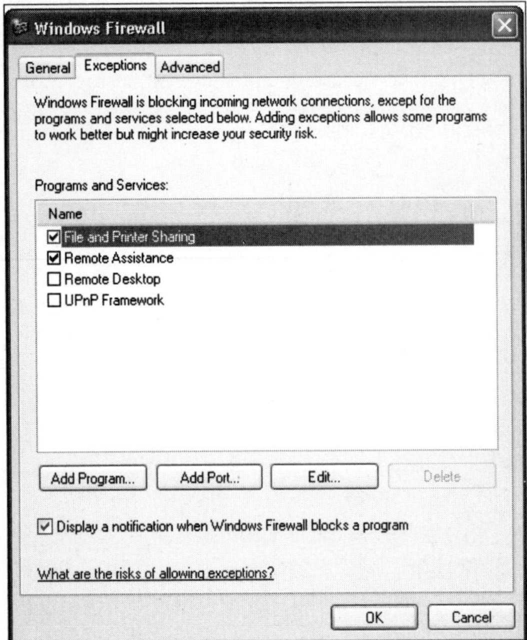

Figure 5-5: The Exceptions tab shows what the firewall will tolerate; anything not listed here is blocked by default.

The Advanced tab is shown in Figure 5-6. This is where you'd come to handle any of the following tasks:

- Manage multiple network connections individually (in the Network Connection Setting pane).
- Turn security logging on or off and manage the level of detail written to security logs when it's turned on (the Security Logging pane).
- Determine what kinds of responses to specific Internet Control Message Protocol (ICMP) messages this machine will provide. By default, a computer with Windows Firewall installed responds only to pings with minimal detail. Unless you're troubleshooting an Internet connection with somebody's help — in which case they'll tell you what to turn on, and you should turn it off when they're finished helping — you should not need to change any of these settings.
- Restore the Windows Firewall to the defaults described throughout here by clicking the Restore Defaults button (in the Default Settings pane).

Caution

This deletes any customization or changes you made after installing Windows XP, so it may be smart to visit each window and sub-window and record all settings before returning Windows Firewall to "fresh from the factory" settings.

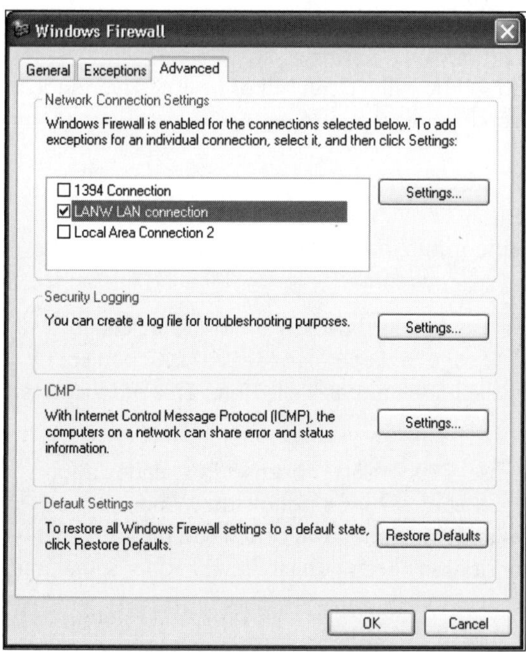

Figure 5-6: The Advanced tab shows additional settings for Windows Firewall.

The other controls that manage the Windows Firewall require access to Group Policy Objects, and manipulation of Group Policy at the right level (local computer, workgroup, domain, and so forth). This takes us outside the scope of this book, but if you check the resources at the end of this chapter, you'll find a pointer to a Microsoft white paper that explains why you might want to do this, and how you can get it done.

Top Firewall Picks

Although there are lots of other candidates for consideration — see the "Resources" section at the end of this chapter for pointers to a relatively recent *PC Magazine* comparative review (November 2003) and to the Home PC Firewall Guide (my favorite source of firewall information in particular, and personal PC security information in general) — I concentrate on two products here that win

everybody's accolades, beyond the Microsoft Windows Firewall that comes built into Windows XP SP2 (and don't hesitate to give them my personal endorsement, either, since I use both products myself):

- Norton Personal Firewall 2005 (`www.symantec.com`; search on product name)
- ZoneAlarm Pro 5.0 (`www.zonealarm.com`; pointers on the home page)

Both Norton and ZoneAlarm firewalls earned Editor's Choice status in *PC Magazine*'s November 2003 comparative review, and also get top rankings at the Home PC Firewall Guide. As I write this chapter, the Windows Firewall platform hasn't been available long enough to get rated or for comparisons with other firewalls to be available. That said, my own testing against online security scans routinely used to test and rate firewalls gives Windows Firewall a clean bill of health. Beyond these options, other worthwhile choices I've used with good results that also get recommendations from full-time security professionals include:

- **Kerio Personal Firewall** — Free for home use, $39 for business use. Visit `www.kerio.com/us/kerio.html` to see vendor info, but also check out links to reviews at the Home PC Firewall Guide.
- **Sygate Personal Firewall** — Free for home use, $20 for business use of plain version, $40 for business use of Pro version. Visit `http://soho.sygate.com/default.htm` to see vendor info, but check out Home PC Firewall Guide links as well. Note: This product was a *PC Magazine* Editor's Choice in 2002.
- **Tiny Firewall 6.0** — $49 for a desktop license, $79 for server license. For vendor information, visit `www.tinysoftware.com/home/tiny2?la=EN` (follow the Windows Firewall menus to read more about features and functions). I've gotten several strong personal recommendations for this firewall, but it hasn't been publicly reviewed for some time now (not since 2001, in fact, as far as I can determine).

The sections that follow look at ZoneAlarm Pro and Norton Internet Firewall in more detail, and compare and contrast them with Windows Firewall as well.

ZONEALARM PRO 5.0

ZoneAlarm Pro is commercial software that costs $39.95 to buy, including one year of automatic updates and support (it costs $19.95 a year for access to automatic updates and technical support). Although Zone Labs is now a part of Check Point Software Technologies, the organization has been involved with personal firewalls since the late 1990s (the company's first personal firewalls appeared in 1999). ZoneAlarm is a free version of ZoneAlarm Pro that's also available on the company's Web site (it's quite similar to ZoneAlarm Pro, except that it doesn't do automatic program screening, nor does it offer as much low-level security control).

One of the most important services any firewall can provide is depicted in Figure 5-7. This shows an alert that ZoneAlarm issued as I was performing a security scan from a Web site against my test machine, indicating its attempt to make an FTP (File Transfer Protocol) connection. Not only does this indicate what kind of activity is under way, it shows the dynamic TCP/IP port number in use (8279) and provides the domain name (`security.symantec.com`) and the IP address (206.204.10.210) from which the attempt originates.

Note

It's a typical firewall feature to be notified when an external attempt to access a machine occurs. But in most cases, users elect to suppress such notifications and simply allow the firewall to write them to a log file for later review. Firewalls also notify users when programs attempt to access the Internet as well, but in that case, it's smart to leave those alerts turned on, so you can approve valid or wanted access requests while denying invalid or unwanted requests.

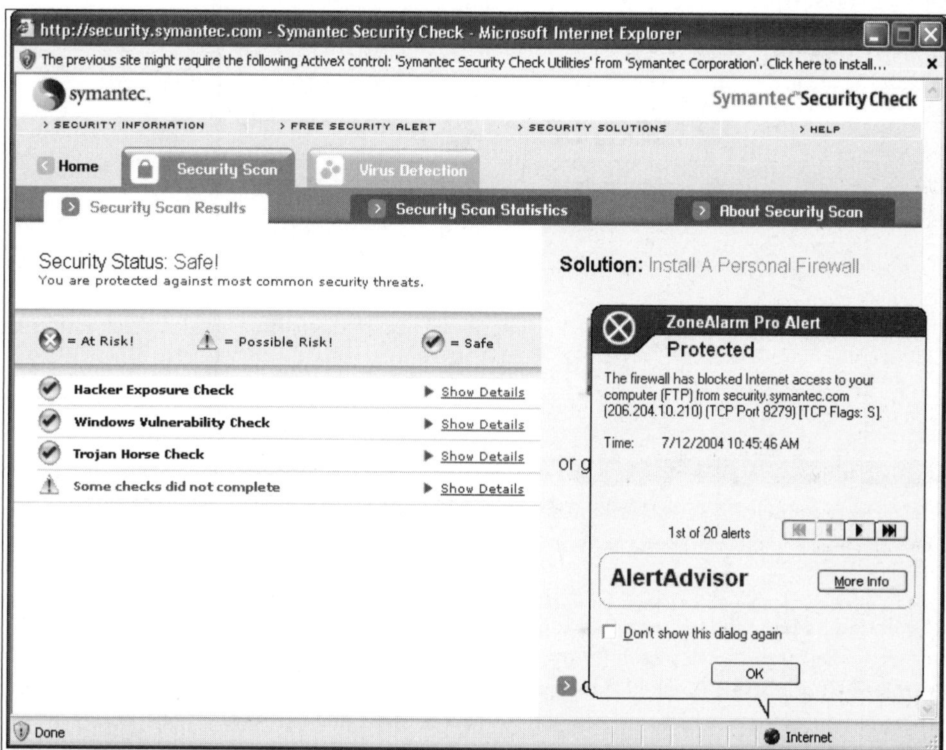

Figure 5-7: ZoneAlarm (both Pro and plain versions) issues alerts when external connection attempts (or port probes) occur. Many users elect to turn these off, preferring to access log files at their leisure to see such data instead.

A quick peek at ZoneAlarm Pro's Overview page shows the overall scope of the program (see Figure 5-8). By default, the Status pane is on top and shows the status of the software's capabilities, including blocked attempts at inbound access, the number of programs approved for Internet access (all other programs are blocked, but also alerted, so that users give the software a chance to "learn" over time what programs can access the Internet and what programs can't), and e-mail and anti-virus status. Notice also that the update status of the firewall software itself is reported on the far right, along with easy access to a tutorial and the vendor's Web site.

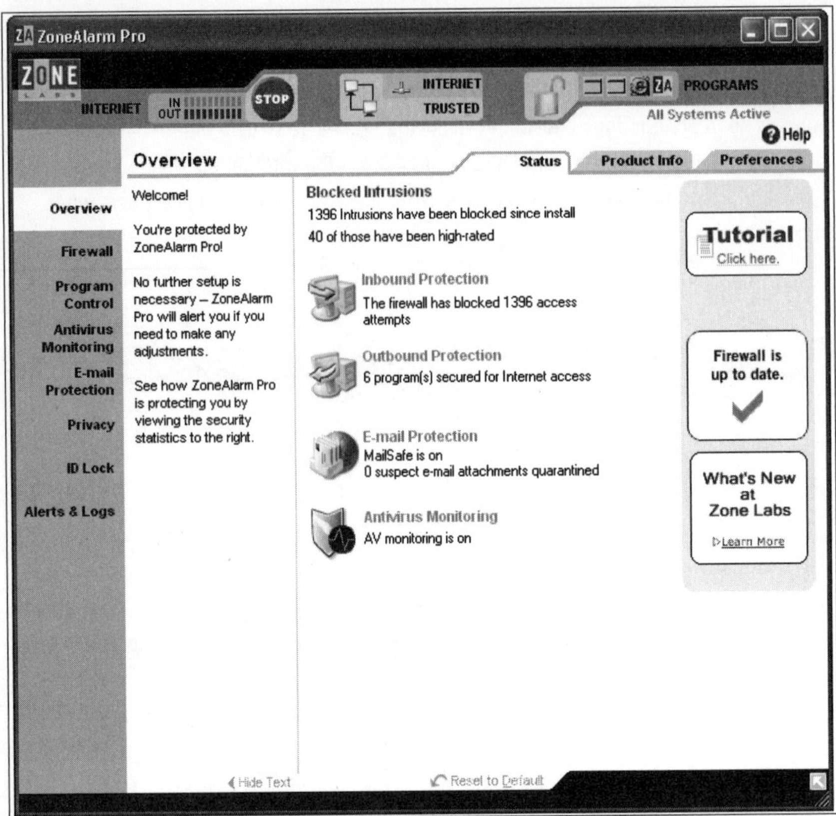

Figure 5-8: The Overview page for ZoneAlarm Pro shows overall program and update status, and provides access to other firewall controls.

The Firewall item's Main tab is depicted in Figure 5-9. This is where you manage security settings for the Internet (called the Internet Zone), any local networks to which your PC may be attached (called the Trusted Zone), and a Blocked Zone (which represents IP addresses in various forms from individual hosts to entire networks to be allowed no access through the firewall). The Zones tab is where you define individual IP addresses or address ranges to assign to the three zones that ZoneAlarm recognizes (Trusted, Internet, and Blocked). In general, if you have a local network, other computers on that network should be represented in some way in the Trusted Zone. This allows them to access files and printers and do other things that network peers are normally allowed to do without restriction. The Internet Zone is allowed considerably less latitude (its access is controlled by Internet Zone Security settings, as shown in Figure 5-9. By default, things are locked down pretty tightly — as they should be). Trusted Zone Security is set up for normal Windows networking requirements and works nicely (you can investigate how these two zones are defined by default by clicking the Custom button in either pane and looking at what's already set in both places). Blocked Zones have no controls because they're completely fenced off. The Advanced button on the bottom of the window provides controls for Internet Connection Sharing or Network Address Translation use and services, as well as more complex controls for general and network settings. In most cases, you shouldn't have to change any defaults here.

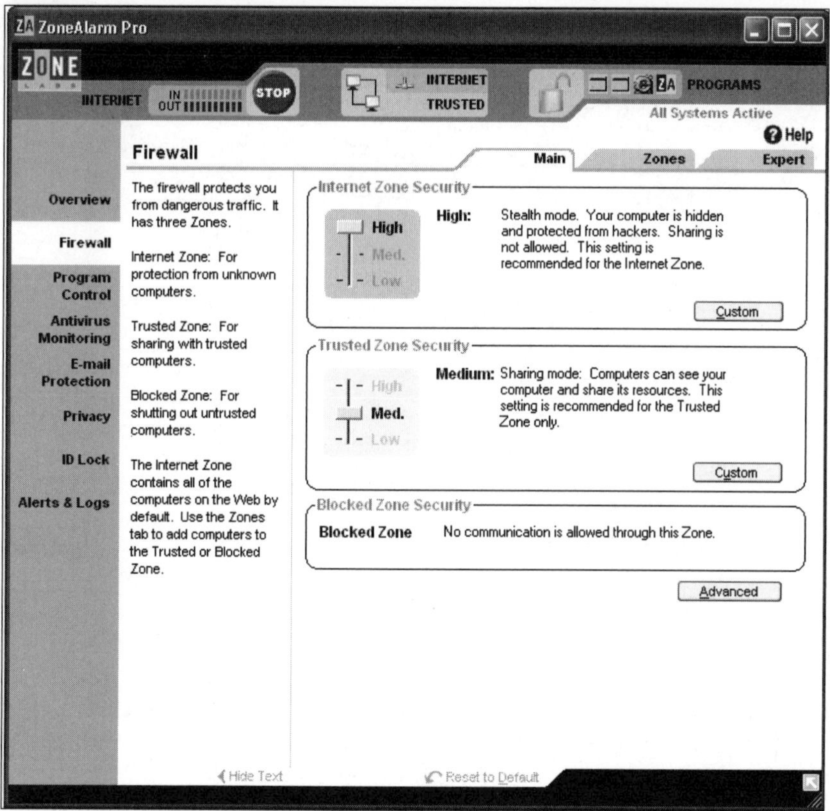

Figure 5-9: The Firewall window provides various types and levels of security control, but is easy to understand and manage.

As you begin working with ZoneAlarm—as is typical for other firewalls—as programs try to access the network, the firewall alerts you and asks you to grant or deny permission. If you're not sure, the alert window provides a hyperlink back to the Zone Alarm Web site that can give you advice on whether or not to grant such access. In most cases, if the request shows a target on a local network or a special address like 0.0.0.0 or 127.0.0.1 (also known as the loopback address, a way for computers to access themselves through an Internet interface), it's okay to grant permission. Otherwise, if you're not sure what to do, access the Zone Alarm information online. If you're still unsure after that, it's always safer to deny access to something unknown than to allow it. Figure 5-10 depicts the Program Control window for ZoneAlarm Pro. The Access settings indicate whether the program can access the Trusted or Internet Zones with a green check mark, denies access with a red X, and prompts the user for permission each time access is requested with a blue question mark. By default, permission is requested. The safest setting is to deny access, and that's very often what should be selected for server-level access (because few end-user applications act as servers this should cause no trouble).

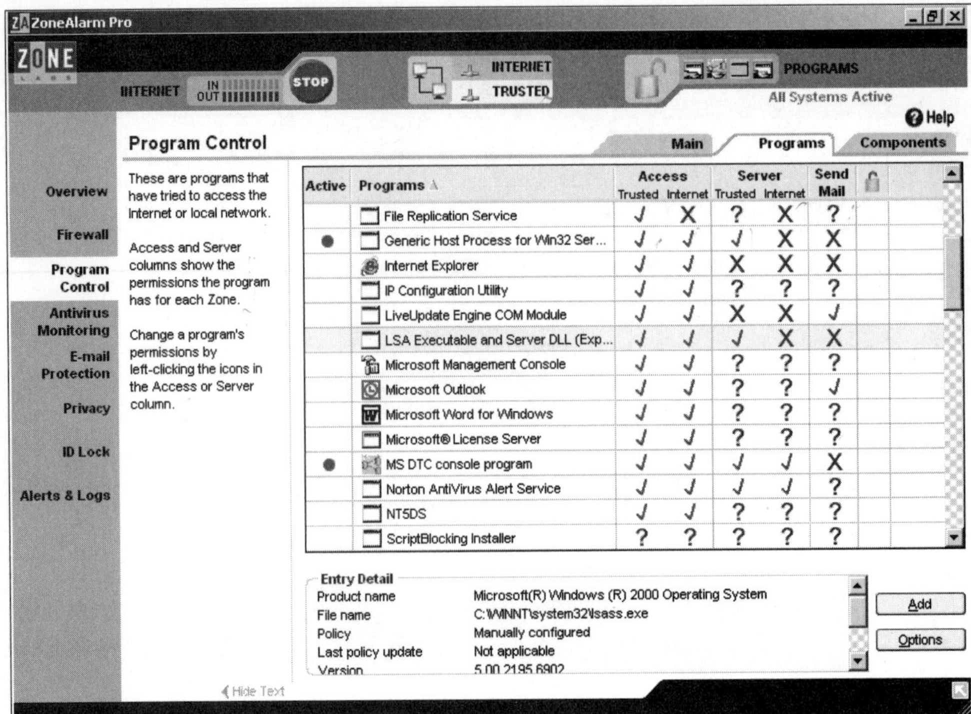

Figure 5-10: ZoneAlarm Pro's Program Control window lets you manage client- and server-side access, as well as a program's permission to emit e-mail.

All in all, ZoneAlarm Pro is easy to install, configure, and manage. Left to its own defaults, it provides protection as good as or better than Windows Firewall. It was not set up to turn off Windows Firewall during installation, but did re-enable Windows Firewall during the uninstallation process. Highly recommended.

NORTON PERSONAL FIREWALL 2004

Norton Personal Firewall 2004 is commercial software like ZoneAlarm Pro. Although it costs $49.95 ($10 more than Zone Alarm Pro), annual subscription service is also $19.95 after the first year runs out. As with all other security software, I strongly urge all users to pay for subscription or update services when they're part of a vendor's offerings, simply because they make automatic updates possible. If the computer has to remember to download updates or fixes, it will; humans aren't always that reliable, despite their best intentions. Thus, if you can opt for automatic update services, they're well worth paying for, given the extra protection and comfort they deliver.

Norton Personal Firewall information shows up in the context of Norton Internet Security in the screen shots that follow, within Personal Firewall display areas. Figure 5-11, for example, tracks

attack information, counts intrusion attempts, and provides an IP address for whichever attacker has probed your system most often.

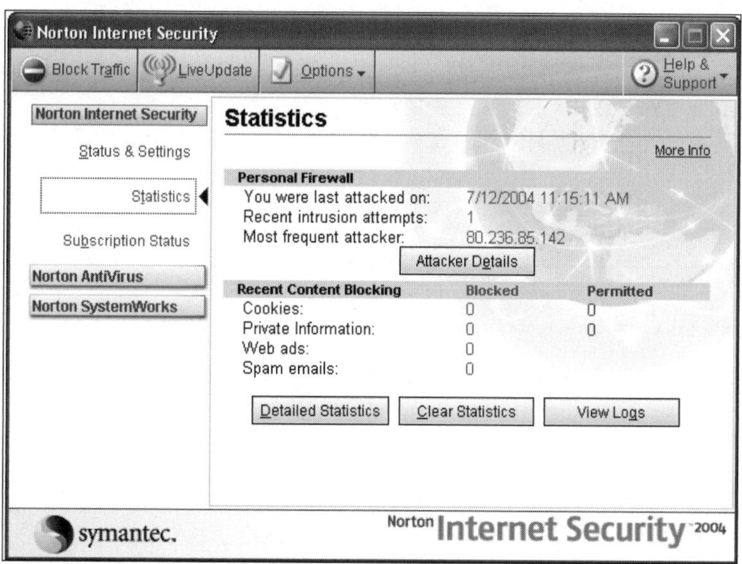

Figure 5-11: Norton Personal Firewall statistics summarize log information for easy perusal.

Access to Personal Firewall configuration and controls shown in Figures 5-12 and 5-13 is easy. Click the Status and Settings item (just above the Statistics item highlighted in Figure 5-11), click Personal Firewall, and then click the Configure button on the right. Figure 5-12 provides access to basic security settings for the firewall, where medium-level security applies by default (somewhat different from ZoneAlarm Pro, in that it continues to allow Java and ActiveX controls to remain active). For most users, however, this setting should be fine and gave a clean bill of health from all of the various security scans I tried.

Norton's automatic program controls are turned on in Figure 5-13 (again, by default). This lets the software decide what to do with programs that attempt to access the Internet, and my experience is that it does a pretty darn good job. This involves less lookup and user activity than ZoneAlarm Pro requires, and may appeal to those who are looking for firewall software to do its job quietly and effectively without a lot of need for user input. Here again, this is something that ordinary users shouldn't need to mess with much, if at all. The Networking control lets you establish what goes into Trusted or Restricted (same as Zone Alarm Pro's Blocked) Zones using domain names, individual IP addresses or address ranges, or IP network addresses and associated subnet masks (these are numbers that put a 1 in every bit of the network portion of an IP address, and are used to block off the network part of addresses, to concentrate on host addresses, on local networks).

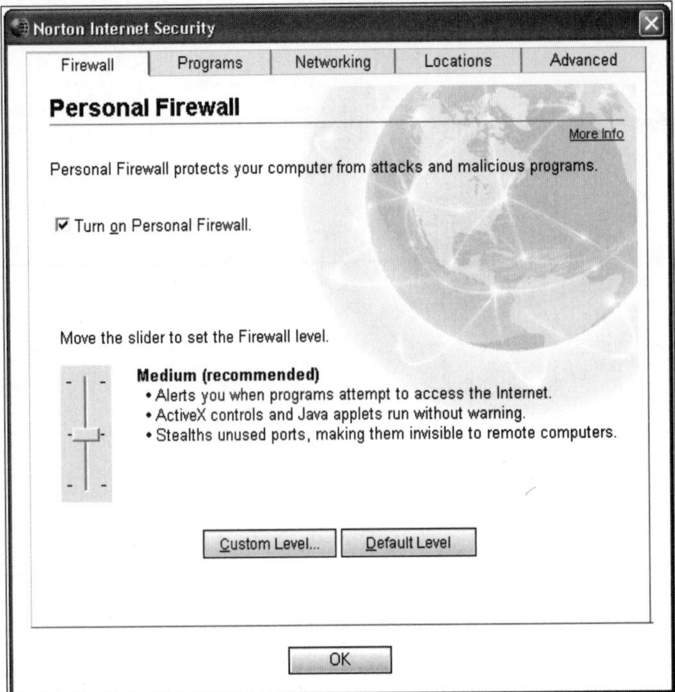

Figure 5-12: Although defaults are a little looser on active Web content than ZoneAlarm, Norton Personal Firewall still does the job pretty nicely.

On the plus side, Norton is a bit more automatic and simple than ZoneAlarm Pro, but doesn't provide as much detailed security control (and also costs $10 more to buy). For some, this is a plus; for others, a minus. Either way, the program works very well and also comes highly recommended. Those also interested in the award-winning Norton AntiSpam and the company's highly rated antivirus software might want to consider springing $69.95 for the Norton Internet Security 2005 suite instead. Although it costs more than any single component, because it includes nearly everything you'll need to secure your PC (except perhaps anti-spyware/anti-adware, but even that is being added to the suite as I'm writing this chapter) it's a great value for the money.

Cross-Reference

See Appendix A for more information on the Norton Internet Security 2005 suite and other security suites.

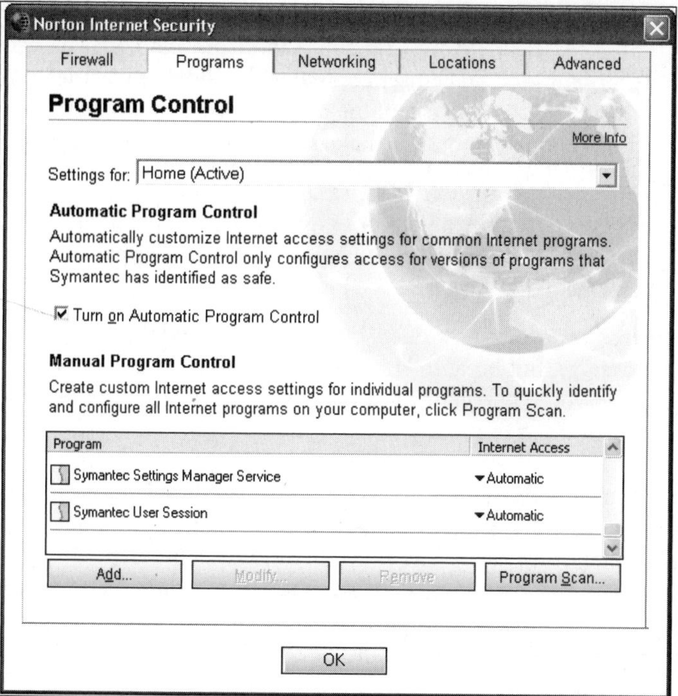

Figure 5-13: Program controls are a bit simpler in Norton Personal Firewall than in ZoneAlarm Pro, and generally do a great job of managing access in your best interests.

Installing and Using a Personal Firewall

One big advantage for Windows Firewall is that there's no work at all involved in installation: that happens automatically when SP2 is installed. But the task isn't too much more difficult for either ZoneAlarm Pro or Norton Personal Firewall. ZoneAlarm takes you through a series of questions, Norton Personal Firewall steps you through a similar series of selections, but neither takes more than 5 minutes, nor does either one involve too much rocket science.

ZoneAlarm Pro's series of questions is illuminating and interesting, so let's step through it as a guide to the kinds of things involved in setting up a personal firewall:

- **How do you connect to the Internet?** Available pull-down options are dial-up, DSL, cable, wireless, or T1. This helps the software identify what kind of connection you're using, and what low-level protocols are likely to be in use. Because I use cable modems, I took that choice when setting up my copies of the software.

- **What type of computer did you purchase ZoneAlarm Pro to protect?** Available pull-down options are Family PC, Single User PC, Work Computer, and Home Laptop. This lets individuals set up controls for multi- or single-user computers, to indicate whether they're for private or professional use, and to indicate if the machine will stay where it is, or if it might leave this connection (Home Laptop). To make sure multi-user features were installed, I chose Family PC.
- **Is your PC connected to other computers by a network?** Available pull-down options are No, Yes (Home), and Yes (Corporate). I chose No, but have also worked extensively with the software on a local home network as well.
- **Do you use anti-virus software?** Zone Labs now offers bundles that include anti-virus protection as well as firewall coverage. But because I'm examining anti-virus stuff separately, I chose Yes, so the software would know it had to work with a different third-party package.

Total time in initial installation went by very quickly. Later on, you can always go back and change settings, add new computers (or network address ranges) to accommodate in-home networks, and so forth. The only regular interaction you'll have with the software after that — typical for most firewalls (except those that have applicable automatic features) — is to be informed when a program attempts Internet or network access for the first time, so you can explicitly approve or deny such access on a one-shot or ongoing basis. Windows Firewall and ZoneAlarm Pro do this, but Norton Personal Firewall does this only if you turn off automatic program handling and force the firewall into manual response mode.

Checking Your Work

Suppose you've decided that following Microsoft's and my advice is worthwhile and have gone ahead and installed a firewall on your computer. That work behind you, how can you be sure it's doing its job properly? Easy! Lots of online security scanning services are available (some free, some for a fee) that can tell you whether your computer is adequately protected. Any time you change something security related on your PC — and installing, updating, or configuring a firewall definitely counts in this regard — you should scan your machine as a way to check your work before moving on to other tasks.

Fortunately, this doesn't have to take a lot of time or effort, and it can raise your comfort level quite a lot. It's also a handy item to keep in your favorites list or bookmarks when friends or family come looking for PC advice. In many cases, these tools will tell them if they've got anything to be concerned about, security-wise. They can make your job of helping out easier by showing them how to better take care of themselves and, if necessary, helping you narrow your focus for concern right from the get-go.

Table 5-5 names four truly outstanding sites for Web-based security scans, all of which offer reasonably effective free scans to the public (and two of which offer comprehensive, completely thorough scans for $10). In addition to using one or more of these to scan your PC whenever you make security changes, I also recommend scanning your system once a month just to make sure everything is okay. I refer to this practice as the Inverse Golden Rule, otherwise known as "Do unto yourself, before others can do unto you!"

Table 5-5 Online Security Scanners

Name	*Notes*	*URL*
Steve Gibson Research	ShieldsUP!*	`http://grc.com`
Symantec Security Check	Offers AV and * security check	`http://securityresponse.symantec.com`
HackerWhacker	Free Tools: click Run Test button+	`http://omega.hackerwhacker.com/freetools.php`
Security Space	Click Security Audit, select Single Test^	`www.securityspace.com`

* Described in more detail next.

+ HackerWhacker offers a one-week membership, with complete access to all scans, for $9.99.

^ Security Space offers a year's worth of end-user scans for a paltry $9.95; a great deal!

I checked all the firewalls covered in some detail in this chapter against the free scans available at all four sites; all achieved pretty good results or passed those reviews with flying colors. Two of these sites are worth a little more discussion, if only to tell you what you'll find (and what to do when you get there):

- When you visit Gibson Research, click the ShieldsUP! button on the home page. This takes you to a front page that shows you what his site can determine about your IP address and domain name. After that, you'll see a menu of test options you can run against your PC. I strongly recommend that you use the File Sharing, Common Ports, and All Service Ports tests; if you come back with less than a clean bill of health, Gibson is very generous with his remediation advice to help you fix anything amiss that might pop up. Definitely worth a visit. For a purely Windows-based (Windows Firewall) installation, using a Windows XP SP2 machine as an Internet gateway, I had to use the Network Setup Wizard to share that machine's Internet connection with other computers on the network. This required an additional security tuning step to get a perfect bill of health from Gibson's site. If this situation applies to you, see the "Using Windows XP SP2 for Your Internet Gateway" sidebar for details.
- When you visit the Symantec Security Response center, halfway down that page you'll want to select a graphical button that reads "check for security risks." This spawns another window that gives you options to run either a security scan or an anti-virus scan (I think you know which one you should pick here). Also worth a visit.

The bottom line is that you should make regular security scans part of your overall security routine (more on this in Part V of this book). If you don't like any of the options I've just mentioned, don't worry — visit your favorite search engine and search on "free security scan" or "free online security scan" and you'll find lots more options I didn't have room to cover here!

Using Windows XP SP2 for Your Internet Gateway

If you want to share an Internet connection from a Windows XP SP2 machine with other computers on a local network, you must use the Network Setup Wizard to share that connection with those other machines. To do this, click Start → My Network Places and then select the entry that reads "Set up a home or small office network" under the Network Tasks heading in that window. As you work with the Network Setup Wizard, it guides you through a number of steps involved in setting up a shared Internet connection through your XP machine. By default, however, this wizard configures the gateway machine to respond to incoming pings from the Internet (Start → Control Panel → Security Center → Windows Firewall, click the Advanced tab, and then click the Settings button in the ICMP pane) as shown in first sidebar figure. This setting is actually worded "Allow incoming echo request," but for all practical purposes that means "respond to incoming pings."

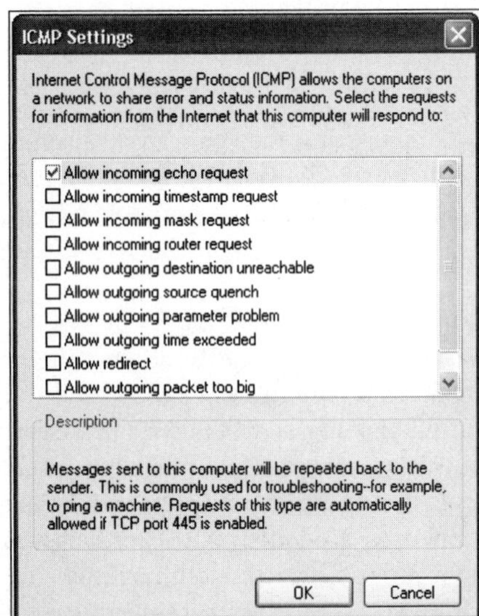

By default, even the Network Setup Wizard configures the Internet side of the gateway machine to respond to incoming pings.

Why does this matter? Gibson and other security experts believe that any response at all to network scanning alerts potential attackers to the existence of your machine and invites further scrutiny and possible attack. Turning off incoming ICMP echo requests is the only way to get a perfect bill of health on Gibson's (and other) network security scans. As it happens, when TCP port 445 is turned on, the Windows Firewall is automatically configured to accept incoming pings, even if that port is turned on only for the local subnet. Thus, to turn off this automatic feature, I had to go to the Exceptions tab in Windows Firewall, double-click File and Printer Sharing, and then unclick the check box next to TCP 445 in that display, as shown in the second sidebar figure. Although it's not obvious — and some Windows Firewall documentation claims otherwise — leaving port 445 turned on even on the local subnet also enables incoming ICMP echo requests on all interfaces on the Internet gateway machine.

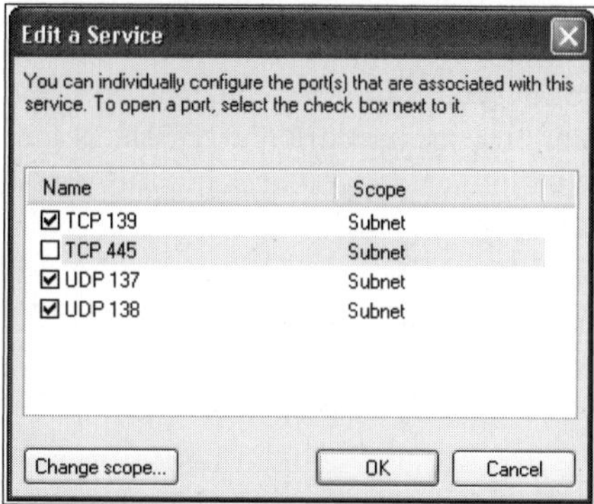

Unclicking TCP 445 on the Edit a Service window for File and Printer sharing disables incoming echo requests.

There is a potential fly in the ointment here, too: If you need to run Active Directory or any other service that absolutely requires TCP port 445 on your local network, you'll have to live with responding to pings from the Internet — that, or use a different firewall on your Windows XP machine (ZoneAlarm Pro and Norton Personal Firewall don't have this problem).

Running Multiple Firewalls

This is a section that occurs in each chapter in Part III of this book; it addresses the question of running more than one program of the same type on a single PC. Because this is the firewall chapter, I'm answering the question "Should you run more than one firewall on a single PC?"

Interestingly, the various firewall vendors whose products I tested seemed to agree by their behavior with my answer to that question — namely: "No!" Although ZoneAlarm Pro didn't disable Windows Firewall during its installation (though I did so shortly thereafter), it did re-enable the software after it was uninstalled. Norton Personal Firewall handled both ends of things perfectly; it turned off Windows Firewall during installation, and turned it back on during uninstallation.

Because firewalls basically inspect all incoming (and sometimes, outgoing) traffic on one or more network interfaces, you don't want more than one program arrogating this privilege to itself. Aside from the issue of primacy (who goes first?), the issue of how to handle and manage problems that both packages discover, one after the other, can also be dicey. Suffice it to say that using one program is enough, but that two can cause system crashes and instability in the worst case imaginable and slow down system performance in the best case. This observation turns out to apply to many kinds of security software that watches traffic or system activity in real time, and can step in to interfere with things (in a helpful way, of course) if something untoward or unwanted is discovered.

This is a case where too much of a good thing is not itself a good thing, so please — use only one firewall per PC!

Other Paths to Firewall Bliss

Those who sign up with their Internet service providers for home networks often get an appliance out of the deal — a network appliance, that is. Built to combine the roles of network hub (sometimes wired, sometimes wireless), cable or DSL modem, and so forth, these devices provide an easy way for home users to hook up multiple computers (and other devices) to interact with each other and the Internet. Very often, these network appliances also include security functions, such as a firewall. If that's the case, you can run security scans from a computer on your network and test the abilities of that firewall by seeing how well it protects the machines behind it from potential Internet threats. But if you've got such a firewall in place and it's doing an adequate job, there's no need to add more elsewhere on your network (although some security mavens do take a different stand and recommend protecting individual systems, each with its own independent firewall, I'm not a member of that school).

That said, there is at least one exception to this statement. If you use a laptop at home and take it elsewhere with you, particularly if you use it on public networks (wired or wireless, it really doesn't matter all that much), you'll probably want to install a firewall on that machine. You can set up multiple hardware profiles in Windows XP so that when you boot up at home, your firewall is turned off, but when you boot up away from home, it comes on to do its job of protecting you when you're outside that umbrella.

Some security experts argue that it's best to put security functions on a separate box on the network boundary. By using it for nothing else, you can shut down all unnecessary services, close all unused ports, and harden that system against attack much more than if you also want to use it for a desktop machine. In fact, even if you have only one machine at home, it might make sense to use a network appliance with security (and firewall) capabilities to offload those functions from your desktop. It's probably not a good idea to buy a second computer just to use for a firewall: That's because network appliances are much cheaper, and you can leave the work involved in hardening and maintaining the system to others, in most cases.

Resources

For a sense of how Microsoft fares in vulnerability reports and assessments, third-party sites are a good place to turn for evidence. Secunia is a security company that specializes in researching, issuing, and managing security advisories. It also supports a search engine against its advisory database, so a visit to `http://secunia.com/advisories/` to search against that database can be pretty illuminating. Try a specific version of Windows or Windows Internet Explorer to get a sense of what drives many consumers' concerns about Microsoft.

Microsoft's Trustworthy Computing Initiative, though slow in coming and not always easy to see at work, is nevertheless worth further reading and investigation. Learn more about it at `www.microsoft.com/mscorp/twc/`. To learn more about Windows XP SP2 visit `www.microsoft.com` and search on "Windows XP SP2" to get the most current information.

TCP/IP is a subject that Internet users can spend a lifetime learning about (I leave to you to decide whether or not your interest carries anywhere near that far). One of the best overall introductions to the subject I know of is Douglas E. Comer's *Internetworking with TCP/IP: Principles, Protocols, and*

Architecture, Volume 1, 4th edition (Pearson Education, 2000). The *TCP/IP Bible* by Rod Scrimger, et al. (Wiley, 2001) is also a pretty good starting point for this subject.

Microsoft's Internet Connection Firewall and Windows Firewall are copiously documented on TechNet (visit `www.technet.com`, then search on either product name). One helpful Internet Connection Firewall document is the "Internet Connection Firewall overview" (`www.microsoft.com/WINDOWSXP/home/using/productdoc/en/hnw_understanding_firewall.asp`).

The two best sources of comparative firewall information I know of — but be warned, they don't take Windows XP SP2 Windows Firewall into consideration — are the *PC Magazine* firewall review from November 2003 (`www.pcmag.com/article2/0,1759,1370707,00.asp`) and the reviews pointers and ratings at the Home PC Firewall Guide (`www.firewallguide.com/software.htm`). Be sure to check them out, especially for newer information on Windows Firewall.

The Zone Labs Web site at `www.zonelabs.com` includes security advisories, technical notes, and technical support information, all on the company's Service and Support page. This site provides a wealth of anti-virus information, along with tutorials, newsletters, and increasing adware and spyware alerts and coverage. Symantec's Security Response Center (`http://securityresponse.symantec.com`) is also well worth a visit.

If you'd like to check out more security scanning/checking services on the Web, above and beyond those mentioned in the main body of this chapter, I also recommend `www.AuditMyPC.com`. The intrepid and well-informed technical editor for this book, Mark Justice Hinton, also suggested `www.pcflank.com` and `www.pcpitstop.com`, as well. Both sites were new to me until he recommended them, but a quick visit convinced me that they're pretty useful, and worthy of inclusion here.

To learn more about security appliances, see Dawn Kawamoto's CNET story "Security-appliance market sees gains" (`http://news.com.com/2100-7355-5079045.html`). Written in September 2003, it's a bit dated but still identifies key industry players — great choices when looking for potential purchases — and market activity. If you want to acquire such a device for yourself, talk first to your Internet service provider (mine, for example, is Time-Warner's Road Runner division, and it offers interested customers a nice security appliance in my area for an additional $5 a month; it includes a router, a hub [in either wired or wireless versions], NAT/PAT services, and a firewall — all updated and managed by the company as part of its monthly service charges).

Summary

This chapter took a long, hard look at what firewalls do and how they work. I tried to explain why firewalls are so necessary an ingredient when securing an Internet connection nowadays. Then I dug into some leading software firewall choices, including the Windows Firewall introduced with Microsoft Windows XP SP2, ZoneAlarm Pro, and Norton Personal Firewall, looking at their various features and functions. I also discussed how you can check your system security (with or without a firewall, though I warn you in advance you probably won't like what you see without one), and why it's not a good idea to run multiple firewalls on any single PC.

The next chapter turns to a somewhat lighter subject — namely, pop-up windows and tools and techniques you can use to block them. This effort requires a whole lot less learning and activity, and can produce immediate results (or relief, if you're inundated). Please read on for the whole fascinating pop-up parade!

Chapter 6

Pop-Up Blockers

Have you ever been surfing the Web, and suddenly found yourself closing one or more browser windows that pop up, seemingly out of nowhere? Ever clicked a link to visit one page, only to have multiple windows open in response? Run your cursor over a graphic and watched another window blossom? The causes are many, the effects are legion, but everybody's been the victim of at least one pop-up window.

Fortunately, although there are many sources from whence pop-ups originate, an increasing number of solutions are available to help you block them from view (or in some cases, to help you block those you don't want to see, while letting those you do want to see still appear). While researching this chapter, I talked to several Web professionals who opined that, although the numbers of advertisers who use pop-ups is still pretty large, even they are aware that sufficient means to block this channel means that they won't be reaching as many targets in the future as they've been able to reach in the past.

That said, other experts believe that as software finds more and better ways to block pop-ups, clever programmers who create Web pages will figure out more and better new (and unknown) ways to keep them coming at you (at least, for a little while). This kind of cops-and-robbers mentality characterizes other sectors of the unwanted software and content worlds, so why shouldn't it work for pop-ups as well?

Caution

It's not just sleazeballs and panderers whose Web sites include pop-up ads. Some entirely reputable and otherwise completely positive presences on the Web sell pop-up ads to generate revenue to support their services — one of my favorites (a must-have entry in your favorites or bookmarks if you work anywhere around hi-tech), for example, is `www.acronymfinder.com`, a handy lookup tool that can help you turn alphabet soup into something more intelligible in most cases (see Figure 6-1).

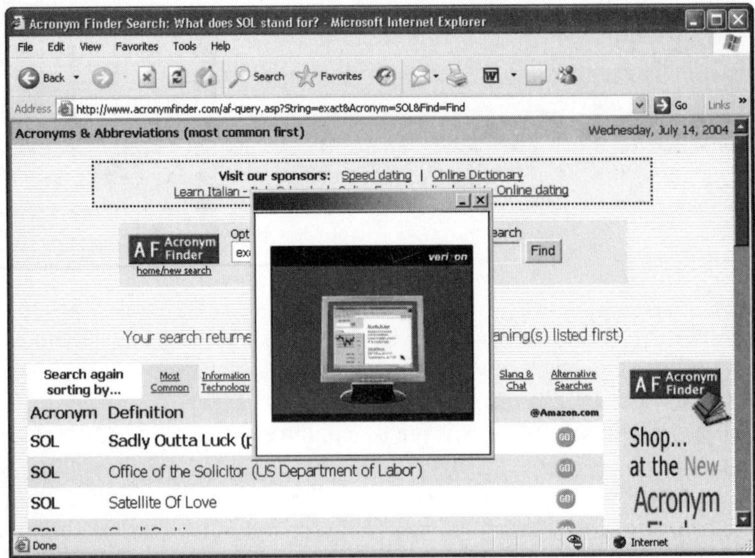

Figure 6-1: An innocuous example of the genre, this is the opening screen for an animated Verizon DSL ad. Without protection from some kind of ad-blocker, readers had better ponder the acronym being expanded.

What Is a Pop-Up?

I've characterized a pop-up as an uninvited or unsolicited browser window that shows up on your desktop, but that's really just scratching the surface of the term. Pop-ups can appear above your browser window and become active, so that you have to do something to return to your original focus. Pop-ups can appear underneath your browser window (though they're more correctly called pop-unders in that case). They can also show up in complete browser windows with a full set of controls and interface widgets, or they can show up inside a frame that offers no ready means of access for you to shut them down. Such windows can be of fixed size (usually designed to frame an advertisement or other graphic), or they can be resizable (just like a regular browser window you open deliberately).

Whatis.com defines a pop-up as follows:

> A pop-up is a graphical user interface (GUI) display area, usually a small window, that suddenly appears ("pops up") in the foreground of the visual interface. Pop-ups can be initiated by a single or double mouse click or rollover (sometimes called a mouseover), and also possibly by voice command or can simply be timed to occur. A pop-up window must be smaller than the background window or interface; otherwise, it's a replacement interface. On the World Wide Web, JavaScript (and less commonly, Java applets) are used to create interactive effects including pop-up and full overlay windows. A menu or taskbar pull-down can be considered a form of pop-up. So can the little message box you get when you move your mouse over taskbars in many PC applications. (`http://whatis.techtarget.com/definition/0,,sid9_gci212806,00.html`)

This definition agrees with what I've talked about so far, but it lacks some specificity to help us understand the term as a form of unwanted software, often including unwanted content. In fact, one of the pop-up experts I talked to, Jim Maurer, who built and now runs the Web site PopUpCheck.com, said he first became aware of pop-ups as a potential problem when a coworker complained about windows filled with sexually explicit images appearing on her desktop machine at work. Indeed those who program pop-ups to occur can fill them with whatever they choose—which definitely raises the prospect of subjecting viewers to unwanted content. But it's because those pop-ups also appear without requiring user solicitation or approval that they really qualify as unwanted.

Thus, Whatis.com's definition for the term *pop-up ad* is also both relevant and interesting in this context:

> A pop-up ad is a pop-up window used for advertising. When the program is initiated by some user action, such as a mouse click or a mouseover, a window containing an offer for some product or service appears in the foreground of the visual interface. Like all pop-ups, a pop-up ad is smaller than the background interface—windows that fill the user interface are called replacement interfaces—and usually resembles a small browser window with only the close, minimize, and maximize options at the top. A variation on the pop-up ad, the pop-under, is a window that loads behind the Web page that you're viewing, only to appear when you leave that Web site. (`http://whatis.techtarget.com/definition/0,,sid9_gci891896,00.html`)

The definition goes on to mention that pop-up ads are unpopular with the average surfer, and that numerous products can disable them—in fact, such software is the focus for this chapter.

Next, Whatis.com's pop-up ad definition keys in on a critical point about pop-up blockers:

> One thing to look for in such a program is the ability to differentiate between user-initiated pop-up windows and others, because many other applications (such as Webcasts, for example) make use of pop-up windows. If a pop-up stopper utility can't tell the difference between a pop-up window that the user has requested and an unsought pop-up ad, the program may cause more problems for the user than it solves.

This observation is important because it indicates why there's a legitimate need for pop-up blockers—namely, like a firewall, to block unwanted or malicious stuff, while letting the good (or wanted) stuff through. Blocking all pop-ups is relatively easy, but it does nullify some Web pages and Web applications that use pop-ups for positive, beneficial purposes.

In this chapter, I use the term *pop-up* to describe a form of unwanted software and content that is associated with Web pages or other documents that use markup languages like HTML or XML. By Whatis.com's definition, this is really a pop-up ad, but I should be able to keep that distinction clear (and absolve other entirely benign forms of pop-ups routinely built into well-behaved windows and other GUI applications) throughout this chapter. I do this in part for brevity's sake, but also because this use of the term *pop-up* (without the trailing ad or advertisement) is also the norm when talking about unwanted software and content in general. Thus, the software used to control these beasts—or whatever you want to call them—is known as a *pop-up blocker*, not often as a *pop-up ad blocker*. Nevertheless, this part of the discussion of unwanted software falls under the general heading of unwanted advertisements, for the most obvious and banal of reasons.

Tip

If you're running Windows XP SP2 (or later) you may be wondering what this fuss is all about. That's because a pop-up blocker comes built into the version of Internet Explorer included with that release, and it's turned on by default. Because this tool also does a darn fine job, if you're using this software, you may not see too many (or any) pop-ups. If so, feel free to zip through (or skip over) this chapter. If you're not running Windows XP SP2 (or later), you might ask yourself "Why not?"

How Do Pop-Ups Work?

"What makes pop-ups occur?" is also an interesting question. Generally speaking, pop-ups occur when active content on a Web page instructs your Web browser to open some page (or even, to access some other Web site in a separate window) without soliciting your input or permission, or even warning you about what's coming next. The first Whatis.com definition for a general pop-up mentions that JavaScript is often a culprit, but that Java applets can also cause pop-ups. In fact, ActiveX, Java Server Pages (JSP), PHP: Hypertext Preprocessor (PHP), Active Server Pages (ASP), and other kinds of active content — code for programs that executes as the Web page document is read, basically — can also cause pop-ups to occur.

Pop-up expert and pop-up blocker advocate Sergei Kaul provides an interesting taxonomy of pop-ups on his Web site (`www.popup-killer-review.com`). He identifies four different kinds of pop-ups that pop-up blockers must attempt to recognize and disable, if they're to work properly:

- **Ordinary windows** — These open when the Web browser executes the JavaScript `window.open()` operator and then load that window's content from the Internet. Web browsers recognize that this instruction is being processed and signal an event to denote the opening of a new window. Pop-up blockers disable such operations routinely because it's easy for them to tell that no corresponding mouse click or user interaction preceded this event, making it easy to recognize something unwanted. They'll either deny the attempt to open the window, or shut it so fast it never shows up onscreen.
- **Synthesized windows** — This starts the same way as the preceding item with the invocation of the JavaScript `window.open()` operator, but instead of reading content from the Internet, additional JavaScript instructions in the script construct that content on the spot. This allows pop-up blockers to be aware that something unsolicited is underway, because a window is indeed opened. But a simple-minded approach of blocking incoming content from the Internet into that window won't work, because there's nothing incoming to block. To work correctly, the pop-up blocker must either deny the attempt to open the window, or shut it so quickly thereafter that the user never knows it was there.
- **Modeless dialog windows** — These open in response to the JavaScript `window.showModelessDialog()` operator. These windows look and act pretty much the same as ordinary browser windows, but they don't trigger the same window-open event that lets

pop-up blockers deal with the other kinds of pop-ups already mentioned. To recognize this kind of window, a pop-up blocker has to parse incoming scripts and other active content to look for (and deny) attempts to execute such calls. (Note: Figure 6-1 is an example of this type of pop-up, as quick inspection of the source for the home page, `www.acronymfinder.com`, will confirm.)

- **Unfathered windows** — These are opened by some application other than the Web browser, so even if they're browser windows (and think about how Outlook and other applications can display HTML, open browser windows, and so forth, before objecting too strenuously to this apparently outrageous statement), they won't trigger an event that a browser-based pop-up blocker can catch. Kaul mentions adware application Gator in this context, which has the ability to scan user browser activity, then issue its own window-opening commands to deliver infamous pop-under ads to follow suit.

On the Web

If you visit `www.popup-killer-review.com`, you can turn off any pop-up blockers you might have installed for the duration of your visit and run Kaul's tests to see examples of each of the kinds mentioned here, in various forms. Please remember to turn your blocker back on when you leave, though! Details on how to do this for the built-in IE blocker appear later in this chapter, in the section entitled "Pondering the XP Default."

Blocking Pop-Ups with Software

Because lots of different ways exist for pop-ups to show up on your desktop, it takes pretty capable software to separate the good, desirable pop-ups from the bad, undesirable ones. Although some software may wrongfully identify benign windows and block them (a faulty recognition called a false positive, in that it identifies something incorrectly and errs by denying the appearance of something benign, rather than a false negative, which fails to recognize something malign, and lets it through anyway), most people are willing to tolerate a small amount of over-zealousness in exchange for software that succeeds in eliminating the stuff they don't want.

Kaul breaks his classification of pop-up blockers into categories as well (and uses that classification to rate more than 100 different pop-up blockers on his Web site). His terminology is a little more colorful, as you'll note further when you read his classifications or visit his site — his term for this whole class of software is pop-up killer, in fact, rather than pop-up blocker. Colorful or otherwise, his software categories are:

- **Intelligent pop-up blockers** — These use internal rules and programming to separate pop-ups from real, useful windows. They block the pop-ups and let the real windows through automatically. On the plus side, they do the best job out-of-the-box in helping you block pop-up ads from appearing. On the minus side, they tend to be the most expensive blockers around, and if they make a false positive identification the window won't be

allowed to appear unless you interact with the program to issue a manual override (usually, through some kind of exception list).

- **Trainable pop-up blockers** — As you encounter pop-up windows, you tell the software which ones are good and which ones are bad. On the plus side, once this software learns to recognize the bad pop-ups you won't see them anymore. On the minus side, every time this software encounters a new pop-up you have to identify it as good or bad. If you're willing to spend the time and expend the effort, these programs handle things exactly the way you want them to, once you classify each new pop-up properly.
- **Serial pop-up blockers** — This software stops all new windows from opening, whether they're pop-ups or real, useful windows. Although this approach works, it can make some sites unpleasant to visit. It may disable some key interface capabilities (for example, I couldn't make JavaScript-based page transitions on the Novell site to jump from a graphic with hot spots to corresponding Web pages when all pop-ups were blocked) on Web sites. Such software may even make some Web-based applications unusable (the Whatis.com definition mentions that Web chats may not work properly or at all, because part of their business is finding sponsors for and inviting site members to such chats).

Caution

The same issues with unusability or disabled capabilities that blocking all pop-ups can cause can also occur if you configure Internet Explorer to block all active content from executing (this means .NET Framework components, ActiveX controls, the Microsoft VM (used with Java), Active Scripting, Scripting of Java Applets, JavaScript, and so forth, within the Tools → Internet Options window on the Security tab). For example, when I visit my Yahoo! Mail account using Opera (where I keep JavaScript turned off deliberately), I sometimes can't read messages with attachments, because a JavaScript must run to get me to those e-mails. Likewise, when following what looks like a hyperlink on some Web pages (but really invokes a JavaScript to follow an apparent hyperlink), you might get nowhere if JavaScript is turned off!

- **Pop-up killing browsers** — Some modern Web browsers such as Firefox, Mozilla, Netscape Navigator, and Opera all offer built-in pop-up blockers. Kaul gives the first three just mentioned pretty high marks in this department, in fact (and Opera is by no means among the worst-rated items in his lists).

On the Web

Sergei Kaul's Pop-up Killer Web site is chock-full of fascinating information, discussion, and additional details on pop-ups: how they occur, how they're made, and how to deal with them. He also offers the most comprehensive list of pop-up blockers I've seen anywhere, including all my favorite toolbars. If you're persistent, you can dig your way through the whole site at `www.popup-killer-review.com` in about an hour. Give it a try!

My recommendation is that you concentrate on the intelligent pop-up blocker category, unless you're considering adding another browser to your desktop software mix. In that case, you may want to look at Kaul's ratings of the pop-up handling capabilities of the various browsers he covers as well. I also believe you'll find Jim Maurer's PopUpCheck.com Web site of great interest in the selection process as well: His explanations of his tests, and his reporting of test results is a little easier to follow than Kaul's. He also covers a much larger range of cases in his testing, and explains them more approachably. That said, his ratings seem to corroborate those on Kaul's more exhaustive list of pop-up blocker software where coverage for the two sites overlaps. Also, Maurer offers a Top 10 ranking for free pop-up blockers on his site that's definitely worth investigating (and comparing with Kaul's ratings as well). Later on in this chapter, you'll have a chance to try some of these tests on your PC and see how it fares.

On the Web

Jim Maurer's PopUpCheck.com site offers descriptions of 18 tests you can perform to check your browser's ability to block pop-ups. His standard pop-up test covers nine of those items, his miscellaneous pop-up tests cover another four, and his advanced pop-up tests cover the rest. Depending on how much time you've got on your hands, and how much this sort of thing really interests you, try as many as you like. You'll find them all available through his home page at `www.popupcheck.com`.

I assume that you are strongly interested in blocking pop-ups (if you're not doing so already) because they can be so vexing and irritating. In some work environments, blocking pop-ups may be the only way to honor organizational policies regarding viewing of questionable materials, or materials of a sexual nature, in the workplace. I think it's a pretty good idea at home as well, because not all family members should be exposed to such materials, either. Plus, who needs the aggravation?

But that said, there is a class of pop-ups that's worth learning a little more about, even if your pop-up blocker handles them, too. These are pop-up windows associated with messaging services or applications. They include the Microsoft Messenger service and a facility that's part of the Microsoft command-line `net` commands—specifically `net send`.

Still More Pop-Ups to Block?

The additional items that Jim Maurer describes tests for on his site, PopUpCheck.com, may be worth looking over—at least for those interested in what kinds of things are worth testing for. These items include only those not already mentioned in the preceding section—namely, what Kaul calls ordinary windows, synthesized windows, modeless dialog windows, and unfathered windows. In fact, he describes, illustrates, and tests for 14 additional types of pop-ups. Visit his site to see all these examples. (For most readers, however, this is probably overkill: As long as your blocker keeps pop-ups away, do you really want or care to know about all the different varieties of trigger events or JavaScript types that can cause pop-ups to appear? I didn't think so.)

As far as the Microsoft Messenger service goes, the same Steve Gibson who provided the ShieldsUP! security scan you read about in the previous chapter also provides a great little check and an accompanying utility called "Shoot the Messenger" that you can use to close the open door that his utility might discover. Here's how to try this out on your system:

1. Open your Web browser and visit Gibson's "Shoot the Messenger" page at `www.grc.com/stm/shootthemessenger.htm`.
2. Click the Download now button to copy this small, 22K utility to your computer (I keep a special directory for widgets I call Ziphell on my PC so I can find this stuff later if I want it, and keep such stuff together in one place).
3. Open My Computer and navigate to the directory where you put the file you just downloaded, `shootthemessenger.exe`. Double-click the file name to launch the utility.
4. If you're running Windows XP Service Pack 2 (or have already disabled this service through other means), you'll see a screen that indicates the Messenger Service is disabled, as shown in Figure 6-2. If not, you'll see a warning message (in red on your screen) that reads "Messenger Service is Currently Running!" Just click the Disable Messenger button to turn it off, and you're safe from Messenger pop-ups.

Figure 6-2: If the Messenger Service is disabled, you'll see a window that looks like this. If not, don't worry— it's an easy fix!

5. Click the Exit button to close the utility.

The good news about this maneuver, which stops the Microsoft Messenger Service—if you open the Services control, available through Start→Control Panel→Administrative Tools→Services, you'll see its status is reported as "Disabled" after you run Shoot the Messenger—is that it also stops pop-ups from the `net send` command as well. The bad news is that turning off this service also stops pop-ups from the Windows Alerter service, which can warn you about events or crises on other machines on a network (but isn't really needed for small networks or standalone machines).

Top Pop-Up Blockers

Before I start exploring some leading pop-up blockers, it's important to recognize that there are many commercial software packages to consider, plus lots of very capable freeware. If you do decide to pay for a pop-up blocker, you'll find that most such packages cost $30 or less. Considering that both of the browser add-ins that Kaul and Maurer grant their highest scores and ratings are freeware, I certainly don't think you should spend anything without first trying out what you can get for free. My explorations also concentrate completely on freeware because of the number of free options available, and their excellent performance at the task of blocking unwanted pop-ups.

Selecting a free pop-up blocker also has the added advantage of making it possible for you to try out more than one selection before you settle down with a final choice. When it comes to picking the pop-up blocker that's right for you, I encourage you to find something that looks good to you (and don't be afraid to ignore our top-ranked items and dig into Kaul and Maurer's more comprehensive listings to find something a bit further off the beaten track), try it, and keep using it if you like it and it does the job. Otherwise, uninstall it and repeat that process until you're happy with your selection. Oh, and don't forget to try out the XP default, either — it's brand new to Windows XP SP2 (and not even rated on the Kaul site as I write this, but Maurer gives it his second highest ranking just behind the Google Toolbar).

Pondering the XP Default

A new version of IE is included with Windows XP SP2. Among other things, it includes a built-in pop-up blocker. For brevity let's call this pop-up blocker the IE SP2 pop-up blocker from here on out.

Here's how the IE SP2 pop-up blocker performs against the various tests at the Kaul and Maurer sites. Its test results are pretty darn good, too: It scores 380 out of 400 points on the Maurer tests (simple, miscellaneous, advanced, and capacity, with points off only in the capacity department). As an example, see Figure 6-3 for the Maurer simple pop-up test results. On the Kaul site tests, the IE SP2 pop-up blocker gets a plus (or all the points) for every test except the unfathered window test (which it fails, like many other pop-up blockers do as evidenced by the reports on his site, which give a passing score on this test only to two items). According to Kaul's metrics, this gives it a PKIQ of 100/86, which is the third best score that he reports for all 100-plus pop-up blockers he reviews.

What does this mean? It means that once you install Windows XP SP2 on a PC, you won't need to add an aftermarket pop-up blocker to Internet Explorer unless you're a fussy perfectionist who can tolerate only the best of everything. My own experience working with the built-in pop-up blocker day in and day out is that it works well enough to keep unwanted pop-ups at bay that I really didn't notice any popping up once this software was installed. You can even turn pop-ups back on more or less at will, either temporarily or permanently (and boy, will you notice that you've opened up your system if you surf to any pop-up laden sites).

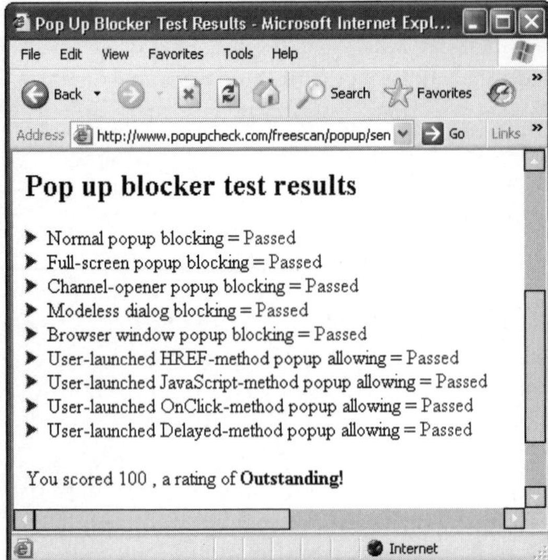

Figure 6-3: The built-in pop-up blocker in the version of Internet Explorer included with Windows XP SP2 scores less than perfectly on only one test at each of the Kaul and Maurer sites.

PopupCheck.com™ is a holding of James Maurer LLC.

The pop-up blocker controls in IE occur in the Tools menu. It's turned on by default, but you can access its controls as shown in Figure 6-4. Notice that there are two cascading menu entries at the far right: one to turn the built-in pop-up blocker on or off, the other to access its settings, as shown in Figure 6-5. Please note that if the pop-up blocker is turned on, you can set it to three different filter levels (working from the bottom up in the pull-down list on display there):

- **Low** — Only pop-ups from secure sites are allowed. Microsoft uses this terminology to mean a Web site you can trust, and provides an article entitled "How to decide if you can trust a Web site" in its Help and Support Center files to explain what it means here in detail. The upshot of the matter is that it allows you to designate sites from which you're willing to accept pop-ups.
- **Medium** — This is the default setting, and the one used to generate the test results reported earlier in this section. It blocks nearly all types of automatic pop-ups, as the Maurer and Kaul test results show pretty clearly. This setting should be adequate for most users.
- **High** — This setting blocks all pop-ups, making it equivalent to what Kaul calls a "serial pop-up killer" in his classification scheme. This is probably overkill for most users, especially for those who visit sites that use pop-ups for beneficial purposes, as so many of them do.

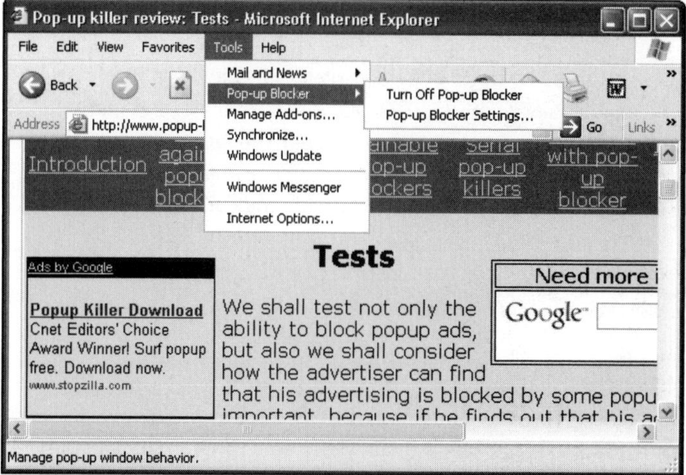

Figure 6-4: Pop-up blocker controls reside within the IE Tools menu, and include an on/off toggle, and an item you can use to access the settings window shown in Figure 6-5.

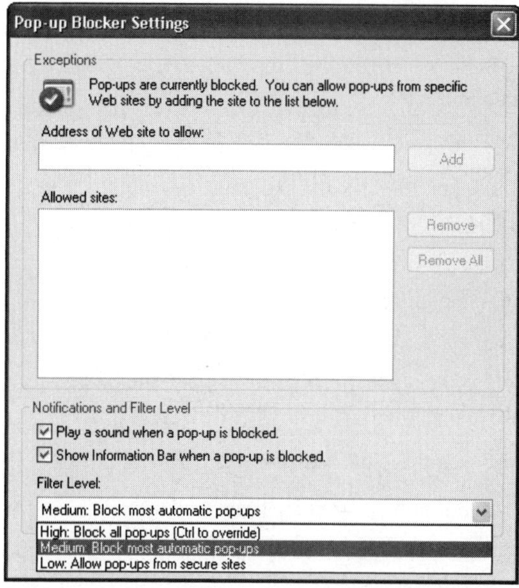

Figure 6-5: The IE pop-up blocker is turned on to the Medium filter level by default, but accepts exclusions at any such level.

Given its overall functionality and ease of access and use, I'd rate this pop-up blocker as good enough for the vast majority of users. But for the benefit of those who can't upgrade to SP2 quickly (or at all, for users of other Windows versions), I also mention other options in the next section as well.

Down and Dirty with IE's Pop-Up Blocker

You can tell when the IE pop-up blocker is turned on by its effects as well as by checking its status through the IE menus and controls. When it blocks a pop-up, IE displays an information bar just above the primary Web page area that tells you a pop-up has been blocked. Likewise, you will also see an international No symbol (a red circle with a diagonal line through it) above a Web page icon at the left of that bar, and in the tray at the bottom of the IE window as well. You can see both of these items in the sidebar figure.

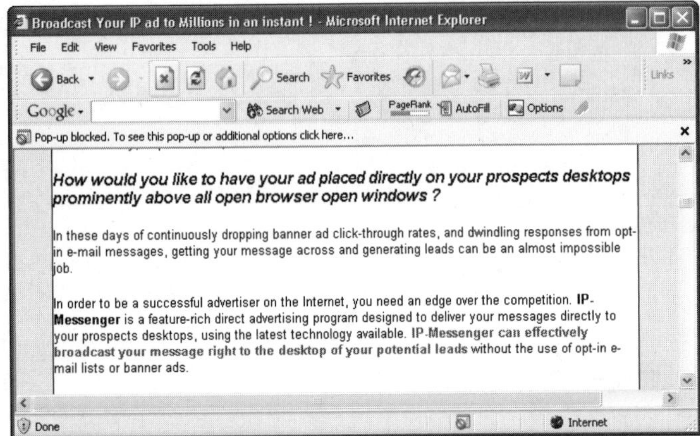

When you visit a site with pop-ups, IE gives two visual notifications that they've been blocked.

If you click on the information bar, it provides pop-up blocker controls just like those available through the Tools → Pop-up Blocker menu item in IE. The following text appears in two pop-up menus that read as follows (with my explanations):

- **Temporarily Allow Pop-ups** — This lets you enable pop-ups from the current site only until you navigate to another Web site.
- **Always Allow Pop-ups from this site** — This lets you disable the blocker on a per-site basis so that you can selectively turn on pop-ups for those sites where you actually want to see them.
- **Settings** — This cascades into a submenu, itself with three entries:
  - **Turn Off Pop-up Blocker** — This turns off the pop-up blocker completely.
  - **Show Information Bar for Pop-ups** — When checked, this turns on the information bar whenever pop-ups are blocked; when unchecked, no information bar will appear.
  - **More Settings** — Opens the Pop-up Blocker Settings window (discussed in the following paragraph).
- **Information Bar Help** — Opens the IE Help utility with all kinds of information bar explanations, descriptions, and answers to common questions.

Please recall that the Pop-Up Blocker Settings window is shown in Figure 6-5. It permits users to identify sites for which the pop-up blocker will be turned off. It also includes notification controls. By default, the information bar is shown when a pop-up is blocked, but this can be combined (or replaced) with a sound notification by checking the appropriate box or boxes in the Notifications and Filter Level pane. I talked about the filter level in the preceding section, so I'll skip further mention of that here, but note also that you can access a FAQ on the IE Pop-up Blocker through this window as well.

Top Pop-Up Blocker Picks

Although there are more than 100 candidates for consideration — check the items listed under all four pop-up blocker categories at the Kaul site — I concentrate on a handful of products here that win high ratings, above and beyond the new pop-up blocker built into Internet Explorer 6.0.5 included in Windows XP SP2:

- **AdBuster** — This free toolbar integrates into Internet Explorer, as another entry into the View→Toolbars menu. It scores 380 on Maurer's tests, just like the IE built-in pop-up blocker, and earns a perfect PKIQ of 100/100 from Kaul. To download this free software, visit `www.gogodata.com/adbuster`. It takes less than a minute to download (285K), and about the same amount of time to install. The toolbar registers with the Add/Remove Programs applet in Control Panel and takes less than 10 seconds to uninstall.
- **Google Toolbar** — This free toolbar integrates into Internet Explorer, as another entry in the View→Toolbars menu. It includes pretty comprehensive pop-up blocking capabilities that score 385 on Maurer's tests (the highest overall score he awards, in fact), and earns a PKIQ of 89/71 from Kaul. To download this free software, visit `http://toolbar.google.com`. It takes less than a minute to download (467K), and about the same amount of time to install. It registers with the Add/Remove Programs applet in Control Panel and takes less than 10 seconds to uninstall. As an added bonus, if you use the Google search engine, you'll get improved access to and controls over its searching capabilities.
- **Window Shades** — This is a separate program that runs in the background and checks on Web page activity as IE tries to open new pages. It can interrogate the user for permission each time a new window is to be opened (whether a benign window or a pop-up) or handle decisions automatically (by turning off that dialog). This tool scores 390 on Maurer's tests, and Kaul doesn't give it a PKIQ because he classifies it as a Trainable pop-up blocker. Download this program from `www.g-m-m.com/`. It takes about a minute to download (972K), and about the same amount of time to install. It includes an uninstall menu item, or you can uninstall using the Add/Remove Programs applet in Control Panel (takes about a minute to uninstall).
- **Pop This!** — An Internet Explorer add-in (shows up in the Tools menu after installation), this tool scores 350 on Maurer's tests and rates an 89/71 PKIQ from Kaul. The file is 1.44MB and takes about a minute to download and about the same amount of time to install. You can download the file from `www.mathies.com/popthis/`. The program registers with the Add/Remove Programs applet in Control Panel and takes about one minute to uninstall.

Of all the options listed here, I hasten to point out that only AdBuster meets or exceeds the IE built-in pop-up blocker on both the Maurer and Kaul tests. That said, the Google Toolbar and Window Shades beat the IE built-in pop-up blocker on Maurer scores. To my way of thinking, this makes the "short list" of alternatives worth messing with pretty short, indeed!

Checking Your Work

If you install a pop-up blocker, use the IE built-in blocker, or are simply curious to see how well or poorly your current configuration deals with pop-ups, I invite you to visit one or more of the sites listed in Table 6-1. Be sure to note which tests your pop-up blocker fails, because you can check posted test results to look for an alternative that beats those ratings. Although the IE built-in pop-up blocker doesn't get perfect scores on any of these sites (it fails four advanced tests on the PopupTest site, and falls prey to its third-party Flash demonstration pages as well), it does the job as well or better than most rated items.

Table 6-1 Online Pop-Up Checking/Testing Sites

Name	*Notes*	*URL*
PopUpCheck	Offers scoring details and some auto-reporting	`www.popupcheck.com`
Pop-up Killer Review	Scoring requires some homework*	`www.popup-killer-review.com`
PopupTest+	Interesting advanced tests	`www.popuptest.com`

* Look for items that earn the same plus/minus designations from Kaul and then grant the corresponding PKIQ (I couldn't find clear scoring instructions).

+ Offers very interesting test battery, but some of his recommended items themselves include adware, so test anything recommended there not also recommended at one or both of the other two test sites.

I tested all the pop-up blockers covered in some detail in this chapter against the free scans available at all three sites; all got nearly perfect scores. Be prepared to spend some time clicking through a bunch of pages and links (it usually takes at least five minutes to finish any complete test battery, longer if you're not using a broadband Internet connection).

I'd urge you to check your Web browser against these test or check sites just to see how your current configuration scores. If you don't like any of the options just mentioned, or don't want to use the IE built-in pop-up blocker, don't worry—Sergei Kaul mentions 116 pop-up blockers in his Web pages, and the other two sites include lots of such listings themselves. You won't be strapped for alternative choices, in any case!

Running Multiple Pop-Up Blockers

This is a section that occurs in each chapter in Part III of this book; it addresses the question of running more than one program of the same type on a single PC. Because this is the pop-up blocker chapter, I'm answering the question: "Should you run more than one pop-up blocker at the same time on a single PC?"

All of the sources I consulted on this topic gave one unanimous answer: "No!" But on a few occasions during my own testing of pop-up blockers, I inadvertently left more than one active while running Internet Explorer without any apparent ill effects.

That said, because pop-up blockers basically inspect all incoming HTTP (the protocol that supports loading and unloading, opening and closing of Web pages) traffic that enters your browser, you don't want more than one program trying to do this job. Aside from the issue of which one goes first, it could be interesting to see what happens if two pop-up blockers disagree when it comes to identifying pop-ups. As with firewalls, using one program is enough, even if two may not immediately cause system crashes or instability. As you learn in other instances of this section in chapters that follow in Part III, running only a single program to do some specific task turns out to be the norm for most kinds of security software that watches traffic or system activity in real time, and can step in to interfere with things (in a helpful way, of course) if something untoward or unwanted is discovered.

This is a case where too much of a good thing may not itself produce the best results, so please — use only one pop-up blocker per PC!

Caution

Remember that the built-in IE pop-up blocker in Windows XP SP2 is turned on by default. If you plan to install some third-party alternative, whatever it may be, turn off the default option first (Tools → Pop-up blocker → Turn Off Pop-up Blocker).

Resources

Understanding pop-up ads means dealing with all kinds of special interests: upstanding businesses that want to use what they perceive to be a legitimate channel for reaching Web surfers, shady outfits that insist on making Web surfers see their content whether relevant or otherwise, and the Web surfers themselves who have to wade through, block out, or close down this stuff when it starts taking over their desktops. For an interesting take from the advertising profession's perspective, see e-media and marketing professional Tessa Wegert's 2002 article "Pop-Up Ads, Part 1: Good? Bad? Ugly?" (`www.clickz.com/experts/media/media_buy/article.php/991121`) and her follow-up piece "Pop-Up Ads, Part 2: Usage Guidelines for Legitimate Marketers" (`www.clickz.com/experts/media/media_buy/article.php/995311`).

As I indicated in the chapter, Sergei Kaul's Web site at www.popup-killer-review.com is a great source of information about how pop-ups are programmed, and shares considerable information about how pop-up blockers do (or should) handle them. He also uses his bank of test pop-ups to rate an astonishing 116 software items that block pop-ups, for everything from IE toolbars or plug-ins, to standalone software, to alternative Web browsers with built-in pop-up blocking functions. Likewise, Jim Maurer's site at www.popupcheck.com is also a good place to learn more about the mechanics of pop-up operation, and nicely documents many types of pop-ups, with his own battery of examples and tests to back things up. Finally, the site at www.popuptest.com also includes many examples and tests, but I wasn't able to get a response from the site's operator to my inquiries, so I can't tell you much more about them here.

If the concept of active Web content remains elusive, some additional reading might be helpful. The Computer Emergency Readiness Team (CERT) offers a short but sweet Cyber Security Tip entitled "Browsing Safely: Understanding Active Content and Cookies" (www.us-cert.gov/cas/tips/ST04-012.html) that's worth a quick read. Microsoft's overview of Active Server Pages also provides helpful descriptions and examples (www.microsoft.com/windows2000/en/server/iis/htm/asp/iiwaabt.htm).

If you're simply interested in learning more about pop-ups, pop-up blockers, and related topics, there's additional information galore to be had online on these topics. I visited the pages of *PC Magazine* and got lots of hits on "pop-up" and "pop-up blocker"; other PC, IT, and information security magazines should provide similar results. Try this technique on your favorite search engine, and expect tens of thousands of hits in reply!

Summary

This chapter looked at the many kinds of pop-up ads that pop-up blockers have to recognize and handle if they're to do their jobs properly. I surveyed the field of relevant products and again observed that the new default option — the built-in pop-up blocker that's now included in the new release of Internet Explorer that's part of Windows XP SP2 — does an entirely credible job of blocking the vast majority of known types of pop-ups. I also looked at a few other products that either meet or exceed the IE built-in pop-up blocker, according to various sets of test results I obtained and discussed. Whatever option you choose, it's pretty clear that some kind of pop-up blocker is an essential ingredient for those who need to surf the Web!

But whereas pop-up ads may subject users to inappropriate or unwanted content, they are usually more annoying than potentially damaging or destructive. That's not the case with spyware, however, which can make changes to desktops that are designed to be hard to reverse, and which can gather private or sensitive information about users that might cause financial damage as well as messing with your PC. The next chapter tackles anti-spyware tools that should help keep this stuff out of PCs (and take them off PCs that might already have picked up a few unnoticed bits and pieces of spyware).

Chapter 7

Anti-Spyware and Anti-Adware Programs

In a recent discussion with Symantec Corporation, I learned that Symantec found itself forced to start dealing with spyware and adware simply because users of Symantec anti-virus programs really couldn't tell the difference between a system infected with malware (virus, Trojan, worm, and so forth) and a system infested with adware or spyware. In fact, I was told that for the past three months, nearly one out of every five calls for help to Symantec ended up involving spyware or adware rather than malware.

Before you feel sorry for those poor ignorant folks who can't tell the difference, stop and think about the most common symptoms. As it happens, some forms of spyware or adware can present the same sorts of telltales that malware can — namely diminished performance, system instability that can be occasional or more constant, mysterious appearance of new processes, Transmission Control Protocol (TCP) or User Datagram Protocol (UDP) ports opened for no apparent reason, and so forth. However, other symptoms of adware or spyware — such as increased pop-up ads, or changes to default home pages or search engines — seldom occur from malware, if ever.

These days, malware experts recognize that certain threats should rightly be called blended, in that they combine virus, worm, and sometimes even Trojan characteristics within a single executable. But in some cases, the same is true for spyware, in that it may include Trojan characteristics (reporting of data gathered or harvested from user machines has to occur somehow, and some such software uses Internet Relay Chat [IRC] or other instant messaging services, or may simply open specific ports to signal its readiness to serve up information on demand; other types are more aggressive and include back doors or clients designed for unadvertised and unauthorized remote access). Likewise, some adware also includes mechanisms to transfer ads to user machines so that they can be displayed even when a PC isn't logged on to the Internet (and boy, can that ever give you a case of the creeps the first time that happens)!

The boundaries between malware, adware, and spyware are getting harder to draw cleanly, so I can't help but observe that Symantec isn't the only vendor with a well-known set of anti-virus tools (not to mention other personal and organizational security offerings) that is taking steps to exclude adware and spyware using its protective shielding — there's an increasing trend among the major players to make anti-spyware/anti-adware part of their offerings, and to include such functionality in their bundled products as covered in Appendix A. But where a sense of urgency and importance in protecting one's PC from malware is pretty well understood and established, protecting oneself against adware, spyware, and other forms of unwanted software and content is really just starting to

take hold. In fact, in a July 2004 report from Trend Micro (makers of PC-Cillin, another well-known anti-virus package with growing anti-spyware and anti-adware coverage) includes this chilling statement: "Reports now show that nearly one in three computers are infected with a Trojan horse or system monitor planted by spyware. These hidden software programs gather and transmit information about a person or organization via the Internet without their knowledge." According to definitions presented earlier in this book, it's hard to say what's spyware and what's malware because of these capabilities — it's really both!

Microsoft's Protect Your PC Web page fails to make this case. Although the company clearly recognizes the importance of patching a PC's operating system (and especially, of keeping up with security updates), strongly recommends the use of a firewall, and stresses use of up-to-date anti-virus software, it omits mention of any need to protect PCs against adware, spyware, spam, and other forms of unwanted software and content. I'd argue that the company's more protective security defaults in Windows XP Service Pack 2 (SP2), along with the pop-up blocker in Internet Explorer (IE) and the more capable Windows Firewall, signify Microsoft's growing sensitivity to such matters. But the company's failure to mention adware or spyware does not mean you needn't worry about its potential impact on your PC, or that you shouldn't add some kind of anti-spyware and anti-adware software to your personal PC security arsenal.

On the Web

Download the Trend Micro Technical Note "Spyware — a Hidden Threat" from `www.trendmicro.com/NR/rdonlyres/B942C2E4-16A1-4AC0-9D42-B208558AE187/11977/WP01Spyware_ForTMWebsite_070204US.pdf`**. (If you don't feel like keying in such a long URL, simply visit** `www.trendmicro.com` **and then use its search engine to look for pages related to spyware.) You can find Microsoft's Protect Your PC home page at** `www.microsoft.com/athome/security/protect/default.aspx`**.**

What Are Spyware and Adware, Really?

You've already seen formal definitions for these terms earlier in this book, but their essence is that both types of software enter a system uninvited and often without soliciting permission. Whereas adware may sometimes claim it's been granted permission because of terms and conditions buried somewhere in fine print in a multipage software license or end user license agreement — you know, the ones where you click "I agree" without necessarily reading all the fine print — most experts agree that claims of full and open disclosure as a result are not credible or terribly ethical. Spyware seldom seeks to cloak itself in respectability, but some kinds of spyware — especially browser cookies designed to profile visitors who return to a Web site — may also be granted user permission through licenses or usage agreements. What's different about spyware as compared to adware is that it gathers information about users so it can report it to a third party. What's different about adware as compared to spyware is that it seeks to create conduits for sending or displaying advertisements (and may also collect user information to better target ad selection based on user preferences, sites visited, items purchased, and so forth) as a primary objective.

How would you classify an item of software with the following characteristics?

- Shows up uninvited, and attempts to foil various potential means of detection (anti-virus, anti-spyware/anti-adware, and sometimes even firewall software). Does everything it can to stay hidden and remain undetected. These are characteristic of spyware, adware, and malware alike.
- Scans all files on the computer on which it resides (especially e-mail messages, documents, text files, and other sources of personal information), harvesting names, addresses, phone numbers, social security numbers, bank account information, credit card numbers and other related data, and so forth. Stores all of this information in some covert manner, possibly encrypted. This is a typical characteristic of more malicious forms of spyware.
- When some time or data collection threshold is passed, opens a "safe" port on the infected computer and uploads all harvested data to a server elsewhere on the Internet. As soon as the upload concludes, the open ports are closed and the software goes back into hiding. Alternatively, the software could create an e-mail message, and then use a client e-mail package to send it or employ its own built-in Simple Mail Transfer Protocol (SMTP) engine. This opens a back door to communicate private, confidential information without a user's knowledge or consent and is characteristic of spyware and some Trojans.

First, it's important to state that, as I write this chapter, no known malware or spyware exhibits this exact collection of characteristics. Security experts also believe that malware is changing from a hobbyist or "mountain climber" mentality (those who do things for fun, or because they can or want to prove they can) to more of a professional criminal mentality. Now that repeated exploits have demonstrated how vulnerable common operating systems and applications can be, professional criminals can't help but recognize serious opportunities to practice identity theft and use that information to steal money from unsuspecting Internet users. Many American households carry $20,000 or more in combined lines of credit and unused credit card balances; without careful fraud detection and alerting from card issuers, those same households might have to wait until their next statement to realize they've been victimized. Right now, the code to do all of the things described in the preceding list already exists in bits and pieces, so no new technology is needed to stitch them together and create a single program with all those characteristics.

Facing a threat of this nature, who cares if it's spyware or a Trojan? In fact, it's a blended threat and one with economic consequences of enormously grave proportions. Although I'm aware of nothing like this in the wild just yet, it's probably just a matter of time before something indeed comes along.

Why Install Anti-Spyware/Anti-Adware?

Financial Armageddon aside, less damaging forms of spyware and adware have their own downsides. From the standpoint of simple irritation (or user's rights), nobody likes to see an unwanted piece of software changing home page selections, resetting search engines, or installing unwanted toolbars, ad engines, or other things designed to enhance somebody else's opportunities to take advantage of your Internet access. Likewise, because some adware or spyware causes system performance to degrade, or makes systems unstable, it's simply got to go. In Chapter 4, you should have gotten the sense that manual removal of spyware or adware can be time-consuming, tedious, and

sometimes downright difficult. Because that's increasingly the case as new forms of adware and spyware are discovered, I believe installing anti-spyware/anti-adware software is both appropriate and effective.

Remember also that there are two ways in which anti-spyware/anti-adware software is designed to be used:

- **Scanning, detection, and removal** — This uses the software to systematically examine a system's memory, important data structures, and files to look for traces of spyware or adware. During the scanning process, all such identifications are logged and then reported to the PC's user. Users can decide on a wholesale or a per-item basis which items they might wish to keep or remove, after which the software handles cleanup and removal activities automatically for all selected items.
- **Real-time detection and blocking** — This requires that anti-spyware/anti-adware software be running all the time, and that it be allowed to inspect all incoming data on a PC — instant messages, file transfers, e-mail, Web pages (and active content), and so forth. If the anti-spyware/anti-adware software sees something it recognizes as malign, it can block it from entry and either alert the user or write a log entry to a file. If it sees something suspicious (or potentially risky, like a change to your Windows Startup Items), it can warn the user of a pending change or arrival and require the user to grant explicit permission before it will be allowed to proceed.

At this point, it's entirely reasonable to ask: "Where does anti-spyware/anti-adware software get the information it needs to recognize known items?" and "How does anti-spyware/anti-adware decide what represents suspicious behavior?" The answers both come from deep inspection and analysis of known instances of spyware and adware, as does the answer to another important question: "Given some known spyware or adware item, how does anti-spyware/anti-adware know how to clean up after it and remove all traces of its existence?"

In an important sense, all anti-spyware/anti-adware software consists of four important parts:

- Software that monitors system activity and is able to intercept certain types of activity or data transfer that might contain spyware or adware. This means inspecting incoming data and alerting users about specific types of behavior associated with adware or spyware (changing search or home page defaults, adding toolbars or Startup Items, and so forth). This maps to the blocking function that requires anti-spyware/anti-adware software always to be running in the background.
- A database of telltale file names, registry keys, and other information it can use to profile known spyware to compare against observed characteristics on some particular system, or in data seeking entry into a system. This kind of information is generally called a *definition* or a *signature* because it helps to identify specific items of adware, spyware, or other unwanted software. This database maps to the scanning and identification function whereby anti-spyware/anti-adware software inspects all files, memory, the Windows registry, and anywhere else such software might leave telltale traces behind.
- A database of cleanup activities associated with specific adware or spyware items, so that once they're recognized, cleanup and removal can be automated and users relieved of that responsibility and effort. Should a scan ever report signs of infection, this makes it relatively easy to initiate cleanup and removal operations.

- A reporting tool that can gather information about a system that shows symptoms of infestation, but where no known spyware or adware can be identified. (The software can also use the same facility to report bugs or other failures about itself as well.) Although users can refuse to share such data with software developers or vendors, this is a valuable means of data-gathering when new forms of adware or spyware are encountered in the wild, and provides important clues (and can often lead directly to the offending software) that will help in the creation of spyware or adware definitions and cleanup/removal tools to counter them.

Hopefully, it's obvious why any scan should be preceded by a download of the latest software updates and any new adware or spyware definitions: the latest and greatest software and databases will maximize chances of detecting and cleaning up after something new.

Tip

To get the best results from scanning a system for adware or spyware (or malware, too, for that matter), always make sure the scanning tool and its database of definitions are as current as possible before you start. It usually takes just a minute or two to check, and it's worth the extra time and effort involved—if only for increased peace of mind!

Scanning for Adware and Spyware

Assume you've installed anti-spyware/anti-adware software on your computer (if this assumption is incorrect, you might want to jump ahead to the "Top Anti-Spyware/Anti-Adware Picks" section, where you can read about candidates for and the processes involved in installing this kind of software on your PC). After such software is installed, you should use it immediately to scan for possible spyware or adware infestation. This guarantees a clean start for your system going forward (or will help you clean up and restore your system to a more or less pristine state).

This usually means digging into program menus and finding out how to use a program's scanning capabilities. Let's take a look at how you'd do this with Spybot-Search & Destroy (as I wrote this chapter Version 1.3 had just been released; the relevance of this description will vary as version numbers change, but it should still give you an idea about what's involved in this effort). Here are the opening steps involved in scanning and starting a repair (I'll describe the rest verbally, because system restarts make it nearly impossible to capture screenshots during that process):

1. Launch Spybot-Search & Destroy. I did so by clicking Start→All Programs→Spybot-Search & Destroy (menu heading)→Spybot-Search & Destroy (program name). You can also click Start→Run, type `%ProgramFiles%/Spybot - Search & Destroy/SpybotSD.exe` in the Open dialog box, and click OK. This produces the screen shown in Figure 7-1.

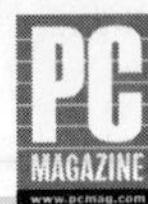

Note

%ProgramFiles% is a runtime variable that translates into the root directory where Windows XP puts programs by default. On an unaltered installation that's usually C:\Program Files.

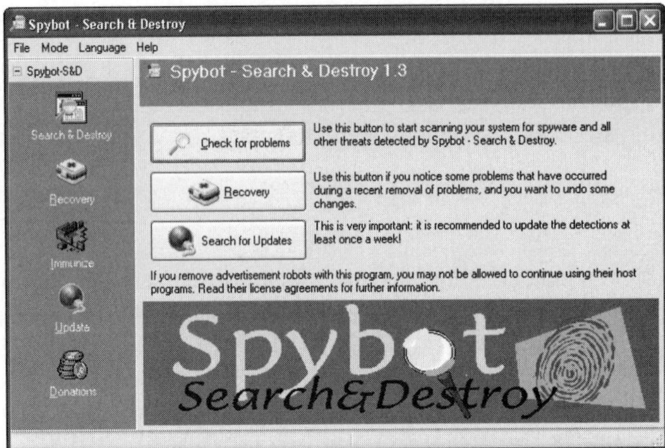

Figure 7-1: The startup screen for Spybot-Search & Destroy provides direct access to common program operations.

2. In keeping with best usage practices, click the Search for Updates button next. This will automatically look for, download, and install any software or definitions that have been added since the last time updates were checked.

3. To scan a system, click the Check for problems button. The program begins scanning the system on which it's running, showing a progress bar at the bottom of a window. When the scanning process completes, you'll see a screen like the one shown in Figure 7-2, which lists an issue with a DSO exploit as the only problem discovered.

Note

This vulnerability actually refers to potential vulnerabilities in Internet Explorer that relate to default Security Zone settings. Apparently, they're not fixed in the version of IE that ships with Windows XP SP2 because Spybot-Search & Destroy discovered them in a clean, unused installation. That said, the fix is minor, entirely automatic, and prevents a vulnerability that permits code to execute without requesting permission and without using Active Scripting or ActiveX. For more information on this common problem, see http://forums.net-integration.net/index.php?showtopic=9126&hl=dso+exploit.

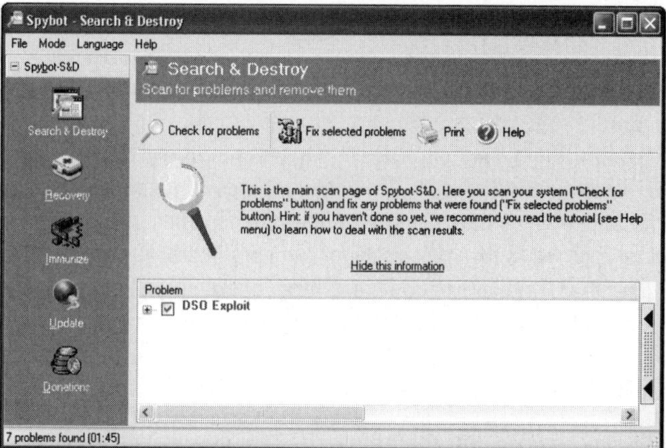

Figure 7-2: When Spybot-Search & Destroy finishes scanning, it displays anything it thinks needs fixing for your review.

4. At this point, you can clear any items you're not sure about (or you might even want to visit your favorite search engine and read up on problems by name to help you decide what to do). In most cases, however, it's entirely safe to leave everything selected and then click the Fix Selected Problems button to let the software do its thing. That's because Spybot-Search & Destroy saves backup copies of any items it removes, and you can always use the Recovery item in the left pane to restore something if your system gets flaky afterward. For the same reason, the software creates a System Restore point before it starts fixing any items, so you can always get back to where you started even if your system won't boot; this notification screen appears in Figure 7-3.

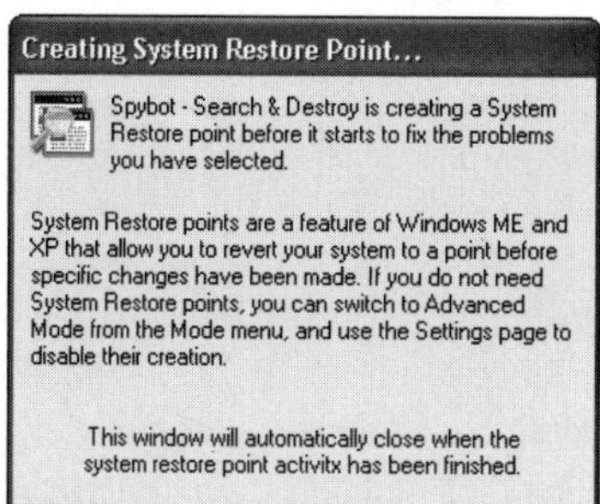

Figure 7-3: To make sure you can recover from changes, Spybot-Search & Destroy even creates a restore point to which you can return if problems occur, and all other recovery activities fail.

The Online Alternative

If you'd rather not install anti-spyware/anti-adware software on your system right away (or at all), you can still take advantage of numerous excellent scanning services online. I'll give you a list of URLs for such sites right after I explain why I don't consider this to be an entirely satisfactory alternative to installing this kind of software on your PC. It's because, for whatever reason, there don't seem to be any online scanning services that also offer cleanup and repair. Sure, they can find the stuff, but they don't seem to be inclined to fix it (probably for the very good reason that such software has incredible power to do harm as well as good, and most people aren't comfortable turning that level of system control over to a Web site). Keep this caveat in mind as you scan this short list of quality online spyware scanners (all of them download software to your system to do their jobs, by the way, but most of them remove all traces of same when they finish):

- PestPatrol's **PestScan** does an excellent job of ferreting out and reporting on spyware and adware `www.pestscan.com`).
- **Spy Audit** is the scanning part of Webroot's excellent Spy Sweeper product, or something very close to it (`www.webroot.com/services/spyaudit.htm`).
- XBlock's **X-Cleaner** is no longer available on its own site, but you can still access and use their tool through Spyware-Guide.com (`www.spywareguide.com/txt_onlinescan.html`).

For still more alternatives, visit your favorite search engine and use something like "free online spyware scan" as a search string. You'll be amazed at the number of offerings that pop up!

After this point, the software goes through cleanup and removal operations for each of the problems it attempts to fix. For DSO Exploit, this meant agreeing to permit the program (and the system) to shut down and restart. On that next startup (because Spybot-Search & Destroy inserted itself into the Run Once registry key), the program ran before normal program loads completed, so it could undertake cleanup operations on files that would otherwise be loaded into memory and therefore more difficult to remove. According to documentation I found on this problem (see the preceding Note), the program rewrites some registry entries that must be handled during startup. I experienced no problems from these changes and have observed outstanding results from everyday use of this software.

Notice that Spybot-Search & Destroy handles all the messy details that can make manual removal and cleanup so much work, right down to creating restore points and inserting itself into the Windows startup sequence. (This is why you had to boot in Safe Mode to conduct manual repairs, because handling keyboard input requires that bootup be completed.) I believe that automated repair is usually better than manual, because it takes all the precautions that human users in a hurry may sometimes be tempted to skip, and because it is presumably tested very thoroughly to make sure it's working (and safe for most systems) before it's released to the public.

Before I move to the next section and talk about blocking spyware and adware, I'd like to make one more valuable point about regular system scans. My point provides the answer to this question: "If you scan immediately after installing anti-spyware/anti-adware software, and keep that software updated, why are regular scans necessary?" Remember that there's always a time lag between discovery of spyware or adware in the wild and corresponding definitions and cleanup and removal routines. If you should get infested on Tuesday with something new, and download a new set of definitions and cleanup and removal routines on Friday, chances are pretty good that a Friday scan will also detect and repair that infestation. When it comes to spyware and adware, blocking is not always 100 percent effective, so regular scanning (and cleanup, when necessary) is absolutely essential!

Blocking Spyware and Adware

In the previous chapter, I explained that pop-up blockers work by inspecting incoming Hypertext Markup Language (HTML), Extensible Markup Language (XML), JavaScript, and other markup or code to look for evidence of pop-up advertisements. If such evidence appears, the browser is instructed not to open a new Window; if no such evidence is found, it's allowed to proceed. Blocking spyware and adware can be a bit trickier because there' s more, and more complex, code to read and decipher and because, in far too many cases, users deliberately (but usually neither consciously nor willingly) initiate the downloads without knowing that adware, spyware, or malware elements may lurk within their contents.

This is where recognition by element name (especially items like file names, DLL names, or registry keys and values) can usually permit identification to occur before requests to write such elements are allowed to go through. This works fine for known items of spyware and adware, because they have already been analyzed, profiled, and their telltale characteristics recorded and enshrined in various databases. But what about new spyware or adware that hasn't yet been dissected or cataloged?

That's why certain characteristic behaviors are often flagged for alerts by anti-spyware/anti-adware programs. Thus, when you install legitimate Windows programs that add to the Windows Startup Items, you'll be queried just to make sure those changes are on the up-and-up. They can't proceed until you give your permission, on the theory that you'll be expecting this interaction when you're installing wanted software, and warned about potential problems when unwanted software is trying to install itself. The same drill applies to default home page and search engine settings: If you jump into IE and change these settings for yourself after you've installed anti-spyware/anti-adware software, you'll have to approve those changes with the built-in monitor before they'll "take" for good.

Although this involves a little more activity and some possible minor inconvenience, I think it's worth it for the added sense of security this protection provides. In fact, you don't need to become at all concerned until such a dialog pops up without a good reason! At that point, some investigation — including updates to your software, and a scan for adware and spyware — is probably a good idea.

The next section presents some leading anti-spyware/anti-adware products. But with this market sector currently exploding, be aware that new products show up almost on a daily basis. Also check with your current anti-virus vendor to see what it might have to offer in this space. Nearly all of the major anti-virus players, such as Symantec, McAfee, Trend Micro, FRISK, and so forth, have recently begun to offer, or soon plan to offer, anti-spyware/anti-adware products, and to include such coverage in their current offerings or product suites.

Top Anti-Spyware/Anti-Adware Picks

Recent comparative reviews online and at *PC Magazine* award top spots to two products nearly unanimously. One is the commercial software product from Webroot known as Spy Sweeper, the other is a freeware (donation-ware, actually) product from Patrick M. Kolla called Spybot-Search & Destroy, who developed the package working with a host of volunteers and colleagues. In the paragraphs that follow, I describe both products (and a third, Lavasoft's Ad-Aware) and compare and contrast their features and functions in Table 7-1.

- **Spy Sweeper 3.0** is the version I tested for this book. It gets consistently high ratings for its ability to detect and remove more spyware and adware than any other product (and indeed, it found at least 40 items on every computer I tested, even though I'd been using Ad-Aware Plus on all of my systems for a year or more). Its scanning functions are reasonably fast (it took less than 15 minutes to scan 80,000-plus files on my biggest hard drives), accurate, and it did a great job of removing everything it found on my systems. The blocking functions are good, and will warn you as changes are attempted to default browser settings, as tracking cookies are placed on your system (requires changing a default program setting), and as sites attempt to download spyware onto your system or into your PC's memory. It doesn't catch all spyware in real time, but its scanner usually catches what its blocker cannot. As a result of researching this book, Spy Sweeper has become my anti-spyware/anti-adware product of choice. At $29.95 for a yearly update subscription, it's a reasonable price for a great piece of software (`www.webroot.com`).
- **Spybot-Search & Destroy 1.3** is the version I tested for this book. It, too, gets consistently high ratings for its ability to detect and remove lots of spyware and adware (and it, too, found numerous items on every computer I tested despite the prior use of Ad-Aware Plus on those computers). Its scanning functions are a bit slower than those for Spy Sweeper but still entirely acceptable, and its blocking functions are likewise more than adequate for the job. Unlike Spy Sweeper, Spybot-Search & Destroy does not include an auto-update function to automatically download new definitions (and software, if available) each time the program is run or scheduled to run. Because of the importance of currency, this is something that users must remember to do if they elect to use this program as their primary tool for blocking or scanning for adware and spyware. One thing that Spybot-Search & Destroy can do that Spy Sweeper can't is to automatically create a restore point for Windows XP just before it makes any repairs at the user's request. Although both programs offer rollback or recovery features to reverse such changes, only Spybot-Search & Destroy offers this failsafe mechanism (which I applaud as an excellent implementation of "belt and suspenders" protection) (`www.safer-networking.org/en/index.html`).
- **Lavasoft's Ad-Aware SE** is a freeware version of its well-known anti-spyware/adware program. It offers only scanning services and does a reasonably good job at the task. To add blocking functions, users must upgrade to one of two commercial versions of the software, either Ad-Aware SE Plus or Ad-Aware SE Professional; both include a separate program called Ad-Watch that watches for and blocks adware and spyware. The same is true for

numerous other features, as shown in Table 7-1. I originally included the previous edition of Ad-Aware here as a kind of "honorable mention," because so many users reported best results from scanning efforts with free anti-adware/spyware software when they combine Ad-Aware with Spybot-Search & Destroy. (Because only the latter has blocking features, there's no need to worry about "blocking conflicts.") But since then, *PC Magazine* has awarded the brand-new SE version of Ad-Aware — namely, Ad-Aware SE Plus and Ad-Aware SE Professional — its much-coveted "Editor's Choice" award, so it clearly belongs on this short list of choices from all perspectives (`www.lavasoftusa.com`).

Table 7-1 Comparing Spy Sweeper, Spybot-Search & Destroy, and Ad-Aware

Product Name	*Price*	*Defns*[1]	*Scanner*	*Blocker*	*Rollback*	*Restore*	*Scheduler*	*Cookies*	*AutoUpdate*
Spy Sweeper	$29.95/yr	27,191	Y	Y	Y	N	Y	Y	Y
Spybot-S&D	$0	15,016	Y	Y	Y	Y	Y[2]	Y	N[3]
Ad-Aware SE	$0	30,112	Y	N[4]	Y	Y	N[5]	N[6]	N[6]

Notes:

1 The number of definitions changes every time they're updated; these are as of July 20, 2004.

2 Spybot uses the built-in Windows Task Scheduler but does provide a built-in scheduling utility (requires running the program in Advanced Mode).

3 Although Spybot-Search & Destroy does not auto-update, it's easy to update manually just before starting a scan.

4 The free Ad-Aware includes no blocker but both for-a-fee versions (Plus and Professional) do include a separate blocking program, Ad-Watch.

5 Ad-Aware SE freeware and Plus versions omit this feature but include detailed instructions on how to use the Windows Task Scheduler or scripting tools to automate use of the tool.

6 The free Ad-Aware version omits these features, but they're included in both the Plus and Professional for-a-fee versions.

Note

Check the "Resources" section at the end of this chapter for citations of recent comparative reviews at TopTenReviews.com and *PC Magazine*. Therein, you'll find pointers to other anti-spyware/anti-adware software products. TopTenReviews covers a total of 17 products (3 of which use the same code base, although they offer different pricing and licensing terms). *PC Magazine* covers 13 products, including several that don't overlap with the TopTenReviews coverage. You'll find detailed feature/function comparisons at both sites, and lots of other information as well. If you don't like the top picks I present here, expect no trouble finding alternatives!

Installing and Using Anti-Spyware

All three of the top picks from the preceding section are pretty easy to install. Basically, just download the file and run the install utility to get the program set up and running. I'll step you through what's involved for Spy Sweeper as an example:

1. Go to `www.webroot.com/downloads/` and grab an evaluation copy of Spy Sweeper (or follow the links to purchase a registered copy instead). Both work identically (but the evaluation times out after 30 days), so download whichever version makes sense for you.

Tip

If you download it to your desktop, it'll be easy to find once there. Personally, I have a set of download directories set up on my PCs, wherein I sort items into categories named installed (for software I actually install and use), eval (for software I intend to evaluate to decide whether to keep it or pitch it), and ziphell (for software I'm not using, not evaluating, and don't have installed on my machine, but might want to install someday). Use a scheme that works for you!

2. Launch the executable installer file (my registered version's file name was `sspsetup 612_1749417422.exe`; yours may be different). You can type the file name into the Open dialog after clicking Start → Run, or open Windows Explorer and then find and double-click the file name. If it's on your desktop, you can double-click its icon from there. If you use a download directory scheme, open My Computer or Windows Explorer to get to that directory and double-click on it there to launch.

3. You'll step through some initial screens to indicate your acceptance of the license agreement (click "I agree" to continue) and proceed until you're asked to select your install type, as shown in Figure 7-4. You can simply click the Next button at the bottom of the Window, unless you know enough about Spy Sweeper to make use of the custom installation selections (not recommended for first-time users).

4. As soon as you click Next on the preceding screen, you'll see the Ready to Install screen shown in Figure 7-5. This simply enumerates the program's file system location, informs where it appears in the Start menu hierarchy, and lists other default configuration settings for the program. To change any of these settings, you'll need to click the Back button and select the Custom install type. For this example, simply click the Install button to begin the actual installation process.

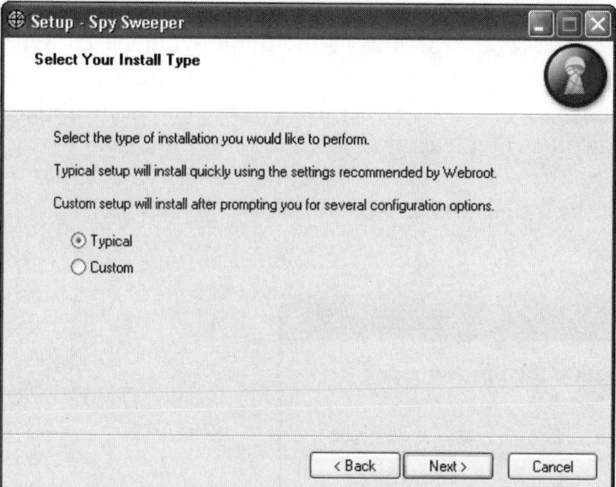

Figure 7-4: Until you learn more about how Spy Sweeper works, it's quickest (and easiest) to leave the Typical install option selected, as it is by default.

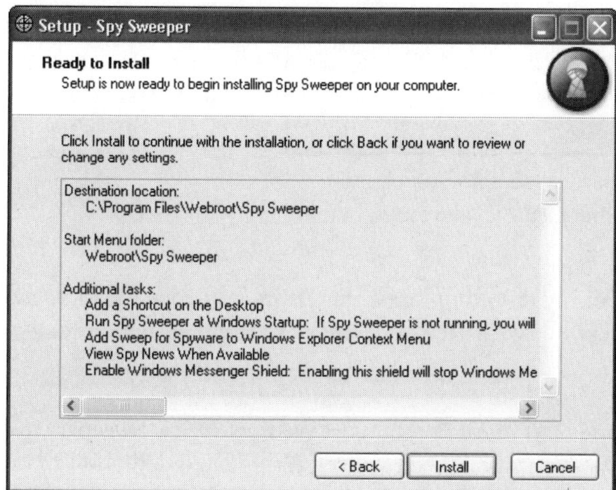

Figure 7-5: Unless you elect a custom installation, all the Ready to Install screen is good for is to tell you what the Install facility is going to do next, as soon as you click the Install button.

5. Next, you'll watch the program display a progress bar as it copies files, makes Registry changes, and goes through the rest of the motions involved in installing itself. When that process is complete, one more screen appears to signal that installation is nearly over; it's shown in Figure 7-6. It simply lets you decide whether or not you want the program to start immediately after installation completes, and whether or not you want to read the release notes (the former is selected by default, the latter not, as shown in Figure 7-6). Click the Finish button and the installation will be complete.

Figure 7-6: To complete the installation, select (or clear) whichever boxes you choose, and then click the Finish button.

That's all there is to it. On most of my test computers, this entire sequence took five minutes or less. You'll want to scan your PC next, to see what Spy Sweeper can find. You'll do that in the following step-by-step sequence:

1. Start Spy Sweeper by clicking Start → All Programs → Webroot → Spy Sweeper (folder) → Spy Sweeper (program). First, you'll be asked to check for updated definitions. Do so, and you'll see the screen shown in Figure 7-7 next. To start a scan, click the Sweep Now button at the upper left.

2. This brings up the Step 1: Sweep System screen shown in Figure 7-8. To start your system scan, simply click the Start button at the lower right in the upper-right pane.

Figure 7-7: The primary startup screen for Spy Sweeper includes numerous menu icons on the left; to scan your system, click the Sweep Now item.

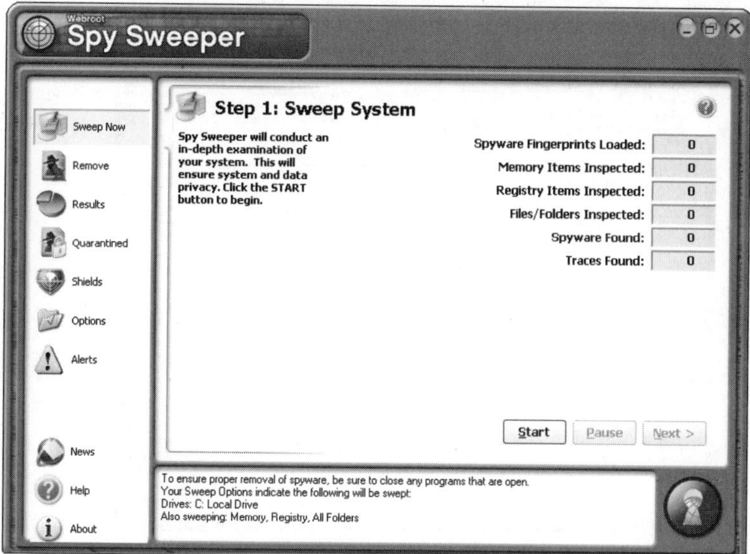

Figure 7-8: To start a system scan, all you need to do is click the Start button at the lower right.

3. When the scan is complete, the numbers for registry items, files/folders, spyware, and traces will be filled in, as shown in Figure 7-9. When anything that needs cleaning up appears — such as the single item for the Pointroll cookie described in the lower-right pane in Figure 7-9 — click the Next button to start that process. On more infected systems, it's not unusual to see 20 or more Spyware items reported, with 40 or more traces found. It's also not unusual for scans to take 30 minutes or more (for example, our technical editor's scan took 30 minutes, found 27 spyware items, with 63 traces — because some spyware or adware items have multiple traces, the count for items is usually slightly more than half the count for traces).

Note

By default, SpySweeper scans only drive C:. To change that, open the program, click the Options icon on the left, and then the Sweep Options icon on the top. Next, click the pull-down menu under "Select Drives to Sweep," click the check boxes on all hard disks you wish to scan (any where temporary Internet files go should be scanned), and then click the Apply button. Your next scan, automatic or manual, will use these new settings.

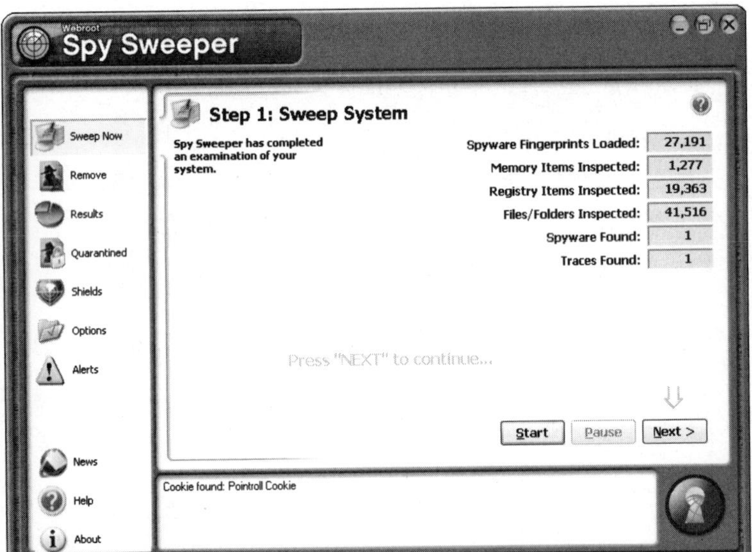

Figure 7-9: After the scan is complete, click the Next button to move onto Step 2: Removal.

4. The Step 2: Remove window appears next, with a complete list of all spyware/adware items found during the scan, as shown in Figure 7-10. Each item can be selected or cleared at the user's discretion — Spy Sweeper checks all items by default — based on their assessment as to whether they want to keep an item or remove it. By highlighting an item from

the list, and then clicking the "View more details online" hyperlink, users can read more information about that item from Webroot's database on its Web site. The information page for the Pointroll cookie appears in Figure 7-11 as an example (note that it's fairly innocuous, unlike other spyware or adware you're likely to encounter).

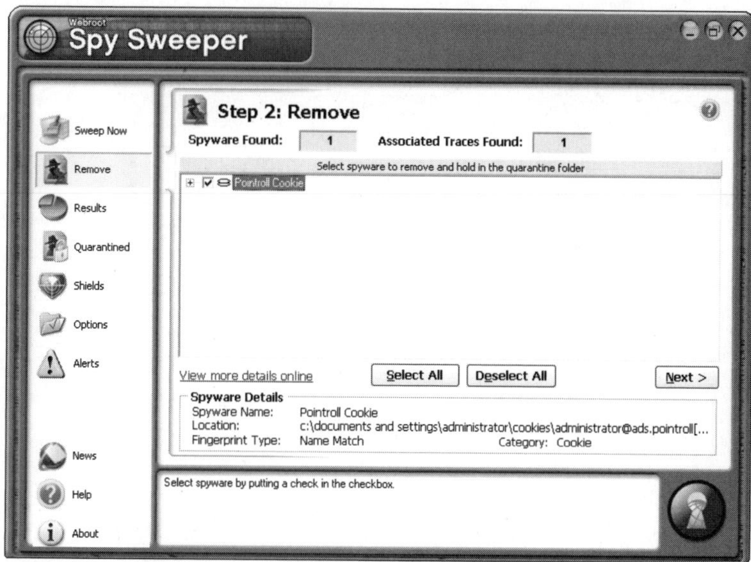

Figure 7-10: You can clear any items you wish to keep in the list of spyware uncovered by the scan. (All items are checked by default.)

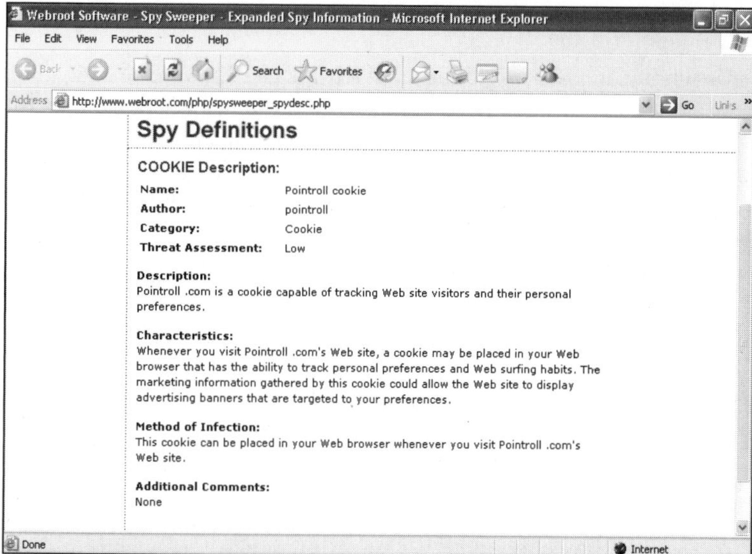

Figure 7-11: The Webroot database entry for the Pointroll cookie indicates it's a tracking item with spyware potential.

5. Click the Next button to begin the removal process, which also creates a backup item so that Spy Sweeper can reverse any changes later, if you choose. This produces the Step 3: Results screen shown in Figure 7-12, which shows you what the program has done as a result of your latest scan and clean-up operations. Simply click the Finish button, and you're done!

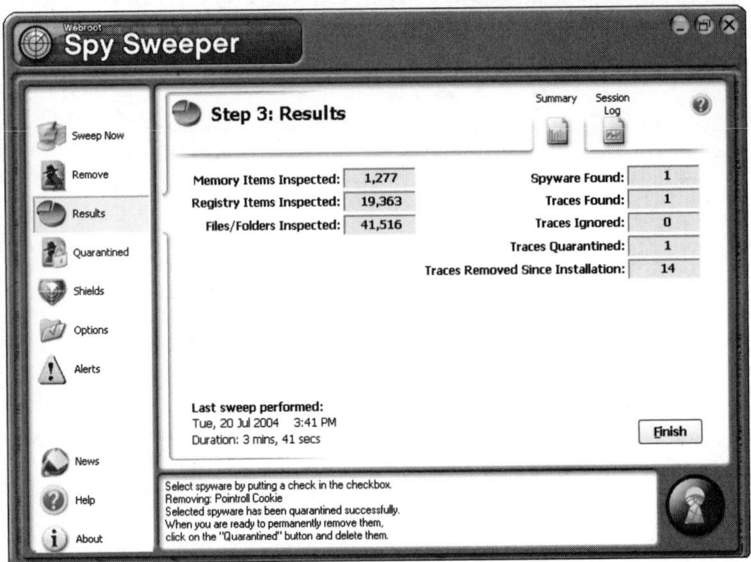

Figure 7-12: Click the Finish button to complete the post-scan removal process, and you're done!

To keep Spy Sweeper running in the background as an adware and spyware blocker, minimize the program after your scan is complete. If you click the shutdown button (the X in the upper-right corner), the program reminds you it can't protect you unless it's running and gives you the option to minimize it instead. I strongly recommend you keep some kind of blocker active on your system. So, unless you plan to use something different to block adware and spyware on your system, why not use Spy Sweeper to do that job?

Spy Sweeper's other icons provide information that documents the program's operations or configuration:

- **Quarantined** — This window lists all the items that Spy Sweeper has removed from your system since it was installed on your computer. You can also restore items from this view, but it's mostly a record of what's been cleaned up at your behest.
- **Shields** — This multi-tabbed window defaults to a summary of all the real-time protections that Spy Sweeper delivers. Figure 7-13 shows all the shields that Spy Sweeper installs by default with green check marks and those not installed by default with red Xs. Spy Sweeper blocks all changes to IE favorites, default home and search page changes, loading

of spyware into memory, installation of spyware or adware, introduction of new startup items, and more. By default, only shields against tracking cookies (which can't really do much harm) and common ad sites are not turned on.

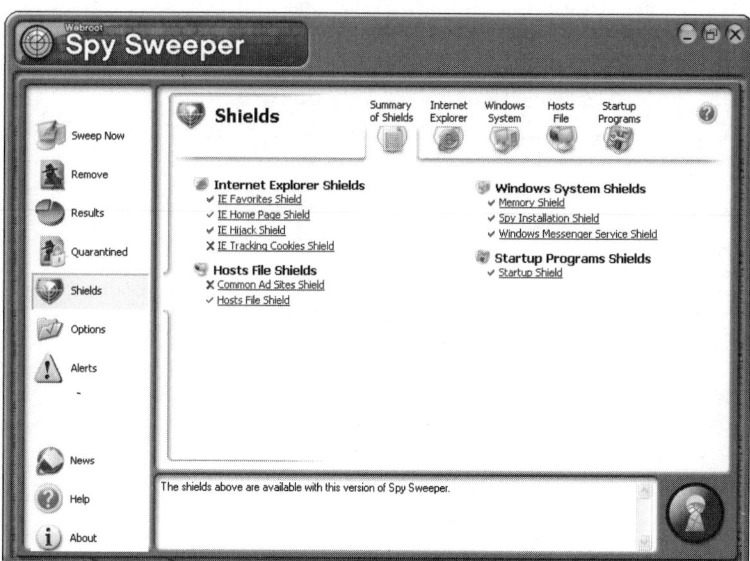

Figure 7-13: Spy Sweeper Shields provide real-time protection against various types of threats or changes.

- **Options** — This multi-tabbed window is where you find Spy Sweeper's program controls. It adds menu items to IE, enables automatic update checks, handles deletion of old items from Quarantined, and instructs Windows to load the program during startup, among lots of other options. Other tabs provide drive selections and exclusions for scanning (sweeps), permit automatic scheduling for scans, offer permanent inclusion and exclusion lists, and provide information about other Webroot products. Figure 7-14 shows the Program Options tab for the Options window, which provides controls that are easy to understand and use.
- **Alerts** — Provides an entry for each item it discovers that might need handling. You can elect to select or deselect all entries using a single button, and then to keep or remove selected items using buttons of the same name. Basically, you want to get rid of anything that shows up, except items related to valid new software installs (for example, the Microsoft GDI Detect tool [gdidet.exe] used to examine Windows systems to determine whether or not they're vulnerable to a graphics device interface vulnerability discovered in late summer 2004 showed up here, but because I recognized it as something desirable, I knew it was safe to keep).

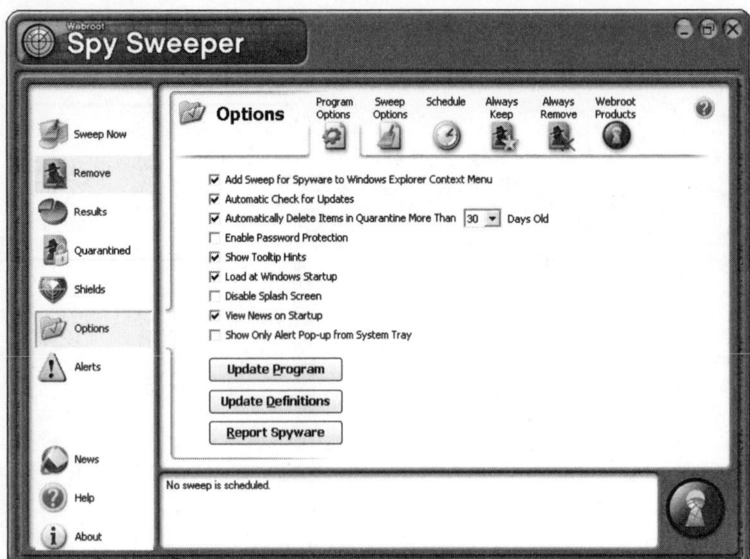

Figure 7-14: Spy Sweeper's Options window provides lots of controls (and tabs) to help you manage and schedule the program's behavior.

Tip

In general, if you're not sure whether to keep or remove something that Spy Sweeper puts into an alert, you can click a hyperlink next to it to see what information Webroot has about it (if nothing is available, it will tell you so). You can also jump to a Web browser window and search on the item name that Spy Sweeper supplies for you; in most cases, this can help you decide whether it's a keeper, or in need of removal. Also, whenever you install software; apply hot fixes, security updates, or service packs; create or invoke a restore point; and so forth, you'll often get alerts from Spy Sweeper that you can safely ignore. If you're still in doubt about what to do, remove it — it's always safer (though less convenient) to get rid of something safe than it is to let something suspect run on your machine!

You'll also see icons inside the main Spy Sweeper for News (visits the company Web site to see if you've got the latest news loaded; if not, it loads it for you), Help (provides access to the program's informative help facility, supplemented with more information on the Web site), and About (shows the version of the software you're running, which spyware definitions, your license key, and when your update subscription expires).

As you get to know your anti-spyware/anti-adware program, you'll begin to appreciate the kinds of things it can do for you. As long as you keep it current, keep it running to block adware and spyware, and perform regular scans, it should keep your system relatively safe and sound from the unwanted effects of adware and spyware.

Checking Your Work

After you install anti-spyware/anti-adware software, you'll want to scan your system to look for (and remove) any traces of such unwanted software or content on your PC. You can use a variety of Web-based (or accessible) tools to scan your PC as well. Because many experts recommend the use of multiple anti-spyware/anti-adware scanners (and this means scanners only, because you can easily avoid potential conflicts between multiple scanners by running only one at a time — see the next section for more information about potential related sources of trouble), visiting one or more of the sites listed in Table 7-2 regularly or occasionally may make a nice enhancement to your personal PC security regimen. If you use a product from one vendor, it's probably smart to try a scan from a different vendor to bring multiple sets of scanning tools (and signatures) to bear on your PC. It's also important to recognize that these tools (like many other forms of active content) work only inside Internet Explorer (likewise for Windows Update, which is why even those who use alternative browsers may have trouble doing away with IE completely).

Table 7-2 Online Spyware/Adware Scanners

Name	*Type*	*URL*
Spy Audit	.EXE	`www.webroot.com/services/spyaudit.htm`
PestScan	ActiveX control	`www.pestscan.com/`
X-Cleaner	ActiveX control	`www.spywareinfo.com/xscan.php`

Likewise, you can use more than one spyware/adware scanner to check your PC, as long as you run them in sequence. (It's not a good idea to run them in parallel.) To that end, even if you have a favorite tool, you might want to consider adding one or more of these freeware programs to your collection of PC security software as well. In particular, I've seen numerous reports from people who claim that the combination of Ad-Aware and Spybot-Search & Destroy beats anything else around when used in tandem. For pointers to some highly rated freeware programs that run on your PC and you can use to back up your primary tool, see Table 7-3.

Table 7-3 Freeware Spyware/Adware Scanners

Name	*URL*
Ad-Aware	`www.lavasoft.de/software/adaware/`
Bazooka Adware and Spyware Scanner	`www.kephyr.com/spywarescanner/index.html`
Spybot-Search & Destroy	`www.safer-networking.org/en/download/index.html`

Note

Seldom, if ever, is it necessary to remove adware or spyware manually because no tool exists to do the job. For example, though I tried aggressively and persistently to create problems or cause infestations on my test PC that spyware removers couldn't fix, I wasn't able to force a situation where manual cleanup was the only viable repair option. That said, some vendors or organizations may be quicker than others to release removal tools as new infestations are discovered and analyzed, and remedies and removal tools proffered. If your primary supplier for such software can't detect or remove something, it may be because it's new enough to not yet be covered. Don't let that stop you from seeking other remedies, or from checking back later for a fix if one isn't available immediately. In the unlikely event that manual cleanup is required for some reason or another, please check back into Chapter 4 for its observations and advice on such activities.

Using Multiple Spyware/Adware Blockers

This is a section that occurs in each chapter in Part III of this book; it addresses the question of running more than one program of the same type on a single PC. Because this is the anti-spyware/anti-adware chapter, I answer the question: "Should you run more than one anti-spyware/adware program at the same time on a single PC?"

This is an interesting question, whose answer is "That depends on what kind of anti-spyware/anti-adware software you're talking about." That's because this software provides two different kinds of functionality — for one it's okay to run multiple types of software; for the other it's not.

By now, you should be familiar with the distinction between a software/adware blocker and a software/adware scanner, as described earlier in this chapter. Here, it suffices to say that a blocker runs all the time looking for evidence that spyware, adware, or something else unwanted it knows how to recognize may be trying to gain a foothold on your system. Because blocker software runs in real time and essentially makes itself part of your PC's operating environment, it's bad idea to try to run more than one kind of blocker of the same type at the same time. Thus, if you're going to run Spy Sweeper, Spybot-Search & Destroy, or a similar program (whether mentioned in this chapter or not) all the time in the background, it should be the only anti-spyware/adware program that you use in that way. Typically, this means you'll configure this program to start up as Windows itself starts up, and leave it running all the time to keep an eye out for adware and spyware on your behalf.

But that doesn't mean you can't — and in fact, you probably should — at least occasionally scan your PC for spyware and adware using another software package that can do the same job. (Any of those mentioned in the previous section, whether run online or installed and run locally on your PC, will do.) That's because no single program can catch absolutely everything — you may be able to catch with one program what another program might miss. That said, if you do install something on your PC for this purpose, make sure not to add it to your list of Startup Items — otherwise, you're risking the very contention we're advising you to avoid!

Resources

The TopTenReviews piece cited in the "Top Anti-Spyware/Anti-Adware Picks" section of this chapter is called "Anti-Spyware Software Review." It's available online at `www.anti-spyware-review.toptenreviews.com/`. The introductory story on anti-spyware/anti-adware software at *PC Magazine* (which includes links to individual reviews of all 13 products covered, plus various comparison charts and related news and information) is entitled "Spy Stoppers," by Cade Metz, and appears in the March 2, 2004 issue. That story and all related links are available online at `www.pcmag.com/article2/0,1759,1524269,00.asp`. More information about Ad-Aware, including pointers to downloads or purchase instructions for commercial software, is available online at `www.lavasoftusa.com/`. You can also take a look at *PC Magazine*'s accolade of Editor's Choice for this program at `www.pcmag.com/article2/0,1759,1646811,00.asp`.

Summary

This chapter took a look at the various functions that anti-adware/spyware software can perform, with a special emphasis on two highly important activities: scanning a system to identify and target for removal any spyware or adware already resident and real-time blocking of any spyware or adware that may try to enter a system (normally, while the user is connected to the Internet). Along the way, I looked at how these kinds of protective programs are installed and used. I paid particular attention to two leading products—namely Webroot's Spy Sweeper and Patrick Kolla's Spybot-Search & Destroy (with honorable mention for Lavasoft's Ad-Aware and related commercial products). Given that plenty of free and commercial options are available, I strongly urge you to go out and pick one so you can start installing and using it immediately, if you don't have something to protect you from adware and spyware already in place. If you do have something in place, I encourage you to consider the costs and effort involved in switching to one of my top picks, assuming you're using something else.

The next chapter focuses on an even more important component in any well-constructed PC's security shield—namely, anti-virus software used to protect systems against infection from the many sorts of malware known to be lurking on the Internet. Here again, I'm hoping you're protected already, but I may be able to point you to some top options that offer better protection still!

Chapter 8

Anti-Virus Programs

It seems that not even a week goes by without some warning coming across about a new virus program that wreaks havoc on personal computers. If you've used e-mail for any length of time, you've no doubt received innumerable forwarded messages about the latest virus attacks, usually accompanied with some information about how you can protect yourself from them. Although many such e-mails can be hoaxes — which are fairly well documented by Web sites such as `www.vmyths.com` and `www.f-secure.com/virus-info/hoax/` — the fact remains that the number of viruses has skyrocketed in recent years, each finding stealthier ways to get into a system and cause damage. So, how many viruses are out there waiting to spring their malicious payloads on users? Early estimates in the 1990s reported roughly 500; that number has grown to an astonishing 60,000-plus, according to the list of known viruses from Symantec. Additionally, a report from Trend Micro, Inc., estimated that virus infections in 2003 cost companies an astonishing $55 billion in losses! Due to these costs, many Internet service providers (ISPs) are now offering free download and use of anti-virus software for subscribers (check with your ISP to see if this is an option for you).

This chapter's aim is not just to inform you about viruses, where they come from, and what they do, but also how to protect yourself from them. Here, you'll learn about some of the more sinister viruses roaming the wilds of the Internet. As in other chapters, I begin with a few definitions, explore the threats that viruses pose to computers and their contents, and discuss proper preventative measures, best practices, and avoidance. Finally, I examine some anti-virus software that can help clean your system and, hopefully, keep it that way.

Quick Virus Refresher

Although they may seem like a new threat to the computing world, viruses are actually the oldest form of malicious code around, born before the Internet experienced such widespread usage. Before the Internet was around to carry these nasty applications to your computer, they spread on physical storage media, such as floppy disks. So how do these viruses cause such mayhem? Unfortunately, there are as many ways to damage a system as there are viruses, but in a nutshell, once a virus is unleashed on a system — whether transmitted as an e-mail attachment, downloaded as a file, or ferried on a diskette or CD — it attaches itself to any acceptable operating system, user, and application files and carries out its own agenda — all too often, that means some form of detrimental deed or another. For example, an early type of macro virus would attach itself to an application, such as Microsoft Word or Excel, so that every time the application ran, the virus ran, too, enabling it to load

itself into memory and infect other applications and propagate further. Actions that a virus takes can range from the relatively harmless display of a message to the downright obliteration of a system.

Viruses come in many forms, namely, macro, boot sector and master boot record (MBR), and file infectors (please refer to Chapters 2 and 4 for a refresher on each type and what to do about them). Each virus takes its own devious course, but two factors are common to all of them: propagation and damage. There's a vast amount of information on the Internet and in various publications that document viruses and how they work. One such site is the CERT Coordination Center at `www.cert.org/other_sources/viruses.html`; it provides comprehensive materials ranging from lists of frequently asked questions and a virus database, to pointers to anti-virus organizations and publications. I'll leave you to your own explorations for now if you are the inquisitive type and focus instead on what you really need to know: how to stop the little buggers from getting into your system and causing harm.

Why Install Anti-Virus Software?

Anti-virus software is the penicillin of the PC world. These applications stand guard over your system, scan incoming files and applications, and, when necessary, quarantine and clean up viruses that aim to do ill on a system. However, it's important to note that even if you download and install an anti-virus application on your computer, your job isn't done yet! Because new viruses are discovered all the time, you must be vigilant and keep anti-virus software up to date, either manually or by enabling automatic download and installation of new virus definitions.

The fact is that if you don't have some form of anti-virus software installed on your system, you are vulnerable to innumerable attacks. If you don't mind losing all of your data, having to reinstall all your software, or permitting a random application to send e-mails to every contact in your address book, by all means, take your chances; but if you're reading this book, chances are you do indeed want to protect yourself, so read on to learn how anti-virus software works, how to install it on your system and keep it up-to-date, as well as deciding which software package is right for you.

If you're not sure which application to install, may I suggest as a starting point that you scan your system using one of a number of free online scanning utilities? Most anti-virus vendors provide this kind of service for free. To get a sense of how healthy your system is, or to watch what a virus scan looks like, check out one of these online scanners:

- **Trend Micro HouseCall** — `http://housecall.trendmicro.com/housecall/start_corp.asp`
- **Panda ActiveScan** — `www.pandasoftware.com/activescan/com/activescan_principal.htm`
- **BitDefender Scan** — `www.bitdefender.com/scan/index.html`
- **Symantec Security Check** — `http://security.symantec.com/sscv6/default.asp?productid=symhome&langid=ie&venid=sym`
- **McAfee FreeScan** — `http://us.mcafee.com/root/mfs/default.asp`

Given that so many online scanners are available for free, why bother with anti-virus software on your PC at all? If you've read the previous chapter, the answer will be a familiar refrain: Online scanners may be able to find things in need of fixing (adware or spyware in the last chapter, viruses and other malware in this chapter), but such scanners do not offer the kind of cleanup and repair capabilities that savvy (or worried) users want to have at their fingertips if suspicions are confirmed, and removal and cleanup are required.

Anti-Virus Software, Firewalls, SP2, and Windows Security Center

One of the nice new features about Windows XP SP2 is the Windows Security Center, a new Control Panel applet that watches the status of anti-virus software, firewall software, and automatic update status for the operating system itself (to make sure that current security updates are applied in a timely fashion). This new functionality does not, however, come without the need for some changes. For one thing, you will probably have to update your anti-virus and firewall software so that you can run a version that communicates with the Security Center and so that what it shows you about the status of your system corresponds to its actual status.

Launching the Windows Security Center is easy (and it will launch itself if it senses something it doesn't like). You can click Start → Control Panel → Security Center, or Start → Help and Support Center → Protecting Your PC: Security Basics → Use the Security Center to launch this tool. A "happy version" of the Windows Security Center appears in the sidebar figure; please note that all three of the indicators on the right-hand side for each item listed — namely Firewall, Automatic Updates, and Virus Protection — not only show a status of "On" but also appear in traffic signal green. When any of these items is questionable, it shows up as "Off" in bright red.

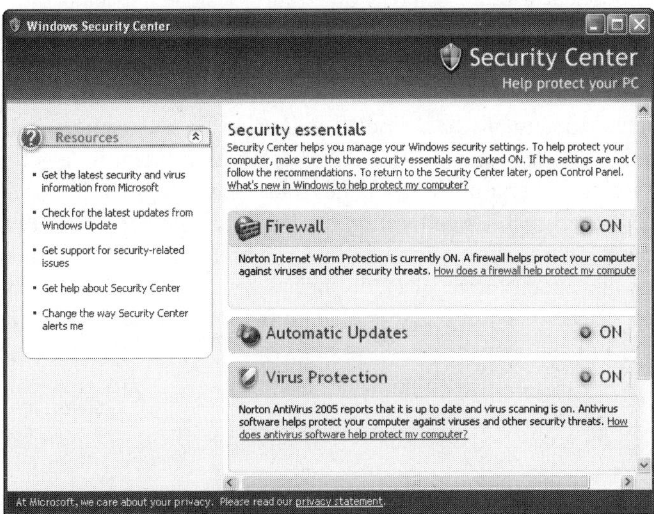

When Windows Security Center finds things to its liking, it shows status On in green; Off shows up in red.

Continued

Anti-Virus Software, Firewalls, SP2, and Windows Security Center *(Continued)*

Be prepared for some occasional eccentricities, too. For example, with BitDefender anti-virus installed (but the BitDefender firewall disabled in favor of Windows Firewall), Security Center kept telling me my anti-virus software wasn't installed (even though it was installed, up to date, and working just fine). But if I disabled the Windows Firewall and turned on the BitDefender firewall, then Security Center would tell me that everything on my system was fine, anti-virus and firewall both. The thing is, the Windows Firewall actually scores better on security scans than the BitDefender firewall does, so I learned to live with the false warnings from Security Center in exchange for the firewall and anti-virus coverage I wanted.

This does, however, illustrate why it's important to obtain the most current version of firewall and anti-virus software for use with Windows XP SP2. It certainly increases the chances that Security Center will report status correctly. During the transition from the beta version of SP2 to the final release, I saw how many anti-virus and firewall packages went from little or no integration with Security Center, to reasonably complete integration with Security Center. Even then, be prepared to investigate — and test — your installation, just to make sure what you think should be reasonably secure actually *is* reasonably secure.

How Anti-Virus Software Works

Dozens of anti-virus software packages are available today. These applications range in ability: some are designed to protect a single computer at a time, whereas others are designed specifically for servers, and others may take on entire enterprise-class networks. No matter what the scope of coverage involved might be, the underlying mechanisms for anti-virus software remain pretty much the same. Most anti-virus packages actively scan files as they are introduced to a system and rely on what's called *signature detection* to identify potentially hazardous files. Anti-virus applications maintain a database of known viruses and compare scanned files to that database to identify files that match the characteristics of known viruses. If a scanned file matches those characteristics, it is quarantined (which means moved to a new, presumably safe location on disk and renamed, so you can find it should you ever need it) so that it cannot affect other files on the system. Once a file is quarantined, the application can delete the file, attempt to repair it, or prompt you for a decision on what to do about the infected file. Signature detection is just one way of identifying viruses and is effective only if the virus database is up-to-date and contains the signature of a virus.

Note

Have I mentioned that it's important to keep your anti-virus definitions up-to-date yet?

In addition to signature detection, anti-virus programs also attempt to identify suspicious behavior from otherwise trustworthy applications. Examples of such behavior include an application attempting to write to an executable file, altering needed system files, making suspicious registry

entries, or adding to the list of items that execute automatically upon system startup. This approach helps protect against as yet unidentified or encrypted viruses and can alert you to suspicious behavior on your computer. Interestingly, this is an area where anti-spyware/anti-adware and anti-virus software often pick up on the same kinds of activities, because they're typical for adware and spyware as well as malware.

Top Anti-Virus Picks

With the array of anti-virus software available, how do you know which one will best suit your needs? As with most things, it's mostly a matter of price, but you should also consider the reputation of the software vendors and whether you want to maintain virus definitions manually or have updates performed automatically. As with other products discussed in this book, a number of qualified programs out there can handle the job, both for a fee and for free. There are so many, in fact, that I can't possibly cover all the available applications within the confines of this chapter.

On the Web

For additional reviews online, visit *PC Magazine*'s Web site at `www.pcmag.com` to see the latest reviews (search on "antivirus" or "anti-virus" for best results). TopTenReviews offers a comprehensive "Anti-Virus Review" that covers 11 products at `www.anti-virus-software-review.com/`. Well-known and respected security publication *The Virus Bulletin* provides test results for more than 20 anti-virus applications in the June 2004 issue at `www.virusbtn.com/vb100/archives/tests.xml`.

This section takes a look at the more popular anti-virus applications available and gives you an idea of which products are most effective at blocking malicious code from taking a toll on your computer. The top-rated anti-virus vendors include Symantec, McAfee, Trend Micro, BitDefender, and Panda Software. To begin, I want to examine the two biggest names in the fee-based anti-virus market: Symantec's Norton AntiVirus 2005 and McAfee VirusScan 8.0.

After I explore these fee-based applications, I will also take a look at some of the available freeware applications, including Grisoft's AVG Anti-Virus (free for home use) and ALWIL avast! 4 Home Edition.

Symantec Anti-Virus Products

Symantec is one of the most trusted purveyors of anti-virus software. Its line of Norton AntiVirus products has been around for quite a while. Its latest offering for the small and home office market, Norton AntiVirus 2005, protects systems from e-mail viruses as well as those introduced via instant messaging applications, including AOL Instant Messenger, MSN/Windows Messenger, and Yahoo! Messenger. This latest version from the anti-virus giant also includes detection of keystroke loggers, dialers, and spyware and scans compressed files. You can download a trial version of the software from `www.symantec.com`. The software costs $49.95 and includes a 12-month subscription to LiveUpdate (subsequent subscription renewals cost $19.95 per year; upgrades to new versions usually get at least a $20 discount), enabling your computer to update your anti-virus software and signatures automatically, according to whatever regular schedule you set.

Tip

As with many other vendors, Symantec offers a suite of products that it calls Norton Internet Security that combines anti-virus software, spam blocking software, a firewall, privacy controls, and numerous other items for less than double the price of most single software components, such as Norton AntiVirus. Thus, Norton Internet Security usually retails for $69.95, but also costs $19.95 a year for subscription services. For most people such suites offer convenience, easy installation, a single source for updates, and often cost far less in the aggregate than the individual pieces cost alone. Because I discuss the individual functions in separate chapters in this book, I tend to look at the pieces separately. But if you're interested in saving money and time, you should definitely think about bundles from strong reputable vendors like those mentioned in this book, and you should check out Appendix A, which devotes itself completely to security suites and what they have to offer. You'll also find the vexing issue of "Should I renew my subscription to an old version of software or buy the newest version?" covered in that appendix as well. (Hint: the answer depends on your willingness to save money in return for a slight increase in risk to your system's safety and security.)

McAfee Anti-Virus Products

For the home and home office user, McAfee's offering, VirusScan 8.0, provides protection equal to Norton's for an annual subscription fee of $39.99. VirusScan offers scanning of inbound and outbound e-mail and instant messaging applications; blocking of scripts and worms; detection of dialers, adware, and spyware; and provides direct integration with Microsoft Internet Explorer and Outlook. Visit `www.mcafee.com` for additional information on the anti-virus offerings from McAfee.

Tip

McAfee's bundle is called the Internet Security Suite, and retails for $69.99 (download only, add $10 if you want a box with a CD and printed documentation). It offers a wealth of items, including VirusScan, a personal firewall, a spam blocker, a privacy service, identity protection software, anti-spyware/anti-adware software, a pop-up blocker, Internet and newsgroup content filtering, and more.

Grisoft AVG Anti-Virus

Although it failed at some previous tests, recent comparisons by ICSA Labs and Virus Bulletin rate AVG Anti-Virus higher than in the past; it now passes their tests with flying colors. AVG provides e-mail scanning for Outlook, Outlook Express, Eudora, and Exchange clients, and also includes memory-resident scanners. The free version is available for download online at `http://free.grisoft.com/freeweb.php`. As I finalize this chapter, the company has just released new versions of its software that integrates with Windows XP SP2, including the freeware version.

ALWIL avast! 4 Home Edition

ALWIL offers its home edition free of charge to home and non-commercial users and specifies on its site that both criteria must be met for use of the free version. Like Grisoft AVG, avast! received Virus Bulletin's 100 percent rating, as well as certification from ICSA Labs. avast! provides automatic updates and resident protection from known viruses. The home version is available for free download at `www.asw.cz/eng/avast_4_home.html`, but as I finalize this chapter, this package does not yet integrate with Windows XP SP2 or the Security Center.

Installing and Using Anti-Virus Software

This section takes a detailed look at the installation and use of some of the free and fee-based anti-virus applications discussed in the previous section and compares ease of installation and use, available features, and other pertinent information.

Caution

It's always a good idea to perform a system backup and create a restore point in Windows XP before installing any new software on your system. In the vast majority of cases, you must perform the backup yourself, but Windows will create the Restore Point for you.

Norton AntiVirus 2005

The Norton AntiVirus (NAV) 2005 installation begins with a prompt to scan for viruses before installing Norton AntiVirus. In the interests of saving time and skipping descriptions for scan-related steps, I opted instead to proceed with regular setup before performing a system scan. This is not a good idea if your system has never had anti-virus software installed on it because this initial scan ensures that NAV gets installed onto a clean, virus-free system, in most cases (I felt I could get away with this in my case because I was installing onto a clean system image that had not yet accessed the Internet). The initial stages of installation included the standard warnings to exit Windows applications, accept the license agreement, and select the default installation folder. The component installation portion took about eight minutes.

During setup, NAV prompts you to select post-installation tasks you want it to perform, including:

- Running LiveUpdate
- Scanning for viruses
- Scheduling weekly scans of local hard drives
- Enabling auto-protection to scan the contents of compressed files

Automatic default settings include enabling auto-protect, scanning incoming and outgoing e-mail, script blocking, and automatic LiveUpdate. Once installed, registered, and activated, NAV presents the user with subscription information (the first service year runs for 366 days after the date of activation). Next, NAV does something curious: it presents a window labeled Security, as shown in Figure 8-1. On that screen, it recommends turning off Windows Firewall for optimal performance. Whether you accept the program's recommendations or not, it completes the configuration process and then launches LiveUpdate to grab the latest signatures and software updates.

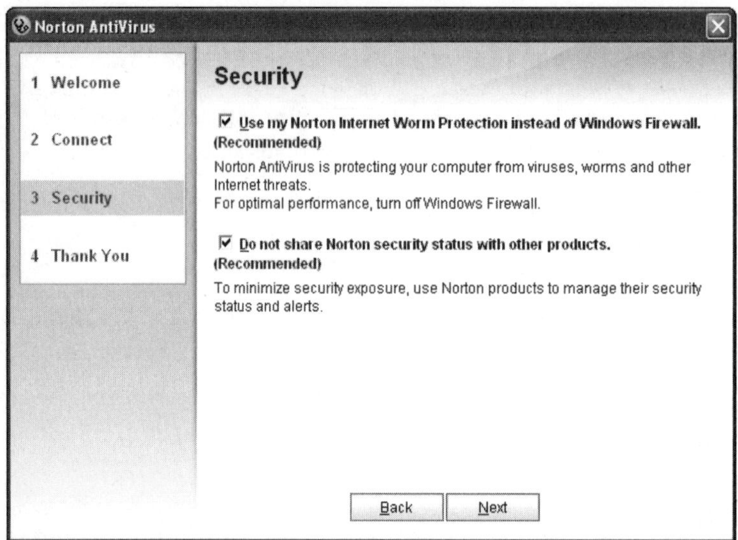

Figure 8-1: During post-installation configuration, NAV recommends using Worm Protection instead of Windows Firewall and against sharing information.

Later on, during the LiveUpdate process, the program remarks that it's changing the security settings on the firewall. It's often necessary to run LiveUpdate more than once immediately after installation to get the process fully completed (only one additional visit was needed to finish off NAV, but Norton Internet Security required three or more visits to finish the job). Even more interesting, Norton Internet Worm Protection shows up as a valid firewall in Security Center after the install, and NAV itself qualifies to make the anti-virus check happy as well.

I ran the resulting configuration through the Gibson Research ShieldsUP! (`http://grc.com`) and the Symantec SecurityResponse security scan. Not surprisingly, the Symantec check gives it a clean bill of health across the board. Gibson's results are less flattering: although his scan finds no ports open, he indicates that ports 1024 through 1030 (common Windows service ports), 1730 (NetMeeting), and 5000 (Universal Plug and Play, or UPnP) all show up as closed rather than fully stealthed. Because most security experts agree that complete stealthing is safest and the Windows Firewall tests as stealthed on all those ports, I'm not sure I agree with Symantec's recommendation that you disable it in favor of Norton Internet Worm Protection. That said, a closed port is not susceptible to attack per se, but it does show that your system is there and may invite repeated probes, scans, and related activity.

Careful inspection of a machine with NAV 2005 installed shows that Symantec is including a copy of Norton Internet Security 2004 with the newer anti-virus software, and that it's responsible for the "upgrade" to Norton Internet Worm Protection. Thus, another firewall does replace Windows Firewall. But because the versions of NIS 2004 I tested returned better results on the Gibson Research security scan, I'm still puzzled about the NAV 2005 results — especially because the default configuration for this firewall is to stealth blocked ports, and the only ports left open by default are those connected with Web access (80, 8080, and so forth).

Preliminary configuration completed, NAV launches into its System Status window, which details scanning features, shows that Internet Worm Protection (a.k.a. firewall) and e-mail scanning is in place, provides information about virus definitions, subscription renewal information, and shows that automatic updating is turned on (see Figure 8-2). As you can see in the figure, the system needs a full scan (and please remember to do this for yourself, should your system not have been scanned and pronounced healthy already).

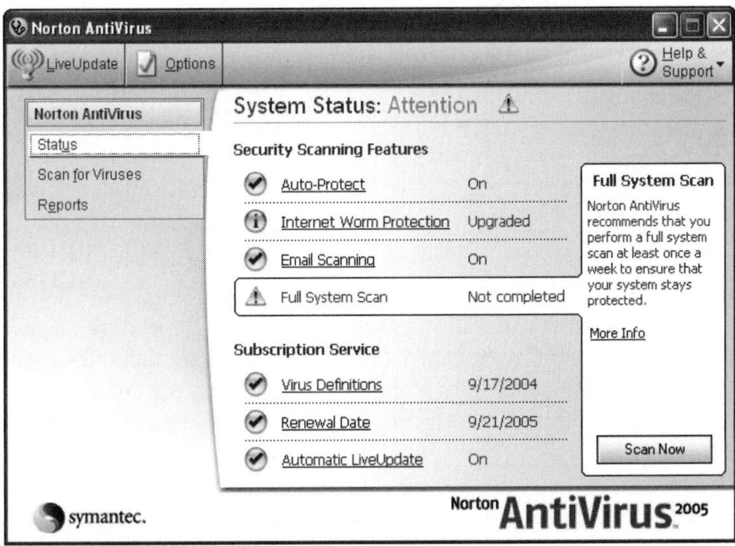

Figure 8-2: Norton AntiVirus 2005 displaying the System Status window.

Also, NAV notifies you when live updates are available by displaying a computer with two blinking red lights above it in the system taskbar (see Figure 8-3). The LiveUpdate process is very straightforward; simply click the icon in the taskbar and click Yes to run LiveUpdate. The Live Update configuration screen appears.

Figure 8-3: Norton AntiVirus 2005 notifies you of available updates with two blinking lights in the taskbar.

From the resulting LiveUpdate window, clicking the Next button prompts NAV to download and install available updates, if any are found. It's also possible to uncheck individual items, though all are checked by default for download (in Figure 8-4, I unchecked the URL download because it's over 24MB in size, and I don't use the Parental Controls that the package offers).

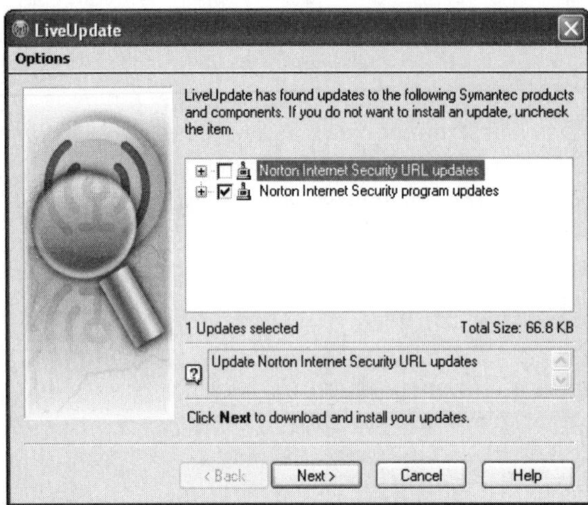

Figure 8-4: LiveUpdate identifies available downloads that you can elect to download or not, as you choose.

Clicking Next prompts NAV to download and install the available updates. Depending on the updates available, you may need to restart your computer. Once your LiveUpdate definitions are installed, you can move on to configure additional options within NAV by clicking the Options button on the main NAV screen (see Figure 8-5 to see the Options screen). Configurable options fall into numerous categories, as follows:

- **Auto-Protect** — Shown in Figure 8-5, this item controls NAV's background operation, and real-time scanning of all files accessed. It also offers various options for handling if malware is found (the default is automatic repair) and provides some controls over which types of files to scan. I strongly recommend checking the box next to "Scan within compressed files" to prevent malware, adware, and spyware from sneaking onto your system inside ZIP archives or other compressed files.
- **Script Blocking** — This screens incoming scripts (like those found on Web pages in JavaScript, Visual Basic Script, or other scripting languages) and stops those with malicious or suspect content from executing. If such content is identified, NAV asks you if you want to allow the script to run once, not at all, or provide blanket permission. In most cases, it's safest to deny permission altogether.
- **Manual Scan** — This terminology might suggest that NAV doesn't permit you to schedule scans but that's not the case. Manual or scheduled, this option panel lets you select which kinds of items you'd like to scan, and how to respond to malware discoveries.

Tip

To schedule scans with NAV 2005—if you didn't elect to set up a weekly scan during the initial program installation—you must use the Scan for Viruses panel. It shows all defined jobs. If you see a small green icon with an arrow pointing right, that indicates a schedule has been defined for this scan. Any time you create your own custom scans, you'll also have access to that icon so you can schedule it at your discretion. Best practice dictates that you scan your system at least once a week (and that's why NAV 2005 offers this as an installation default).

- **Bloodhound**—This is a name used to identify NAV's use of educated guesses about malware and other unwanted software (which goes by the name of heuristics) as it attempts to halt questionable software or activities in their tracks. By default, a medium level of protection is selected, but this can be tweaked higher or lower. I don't see any need to mess with this control.
- **Exclusions**—This lets you block files or directories from scanning (by default, the Quarantine area is blocked, so you don't need to worry about this). Use this only if you keep infected or infested files around for some reason, or if certain directories are prone to lots of false positives. I'd recommend moving this stuff to a separate drive whenever possible and maintaining tight access controls to keep the curious from harming themselves.
- **E-mail**—This scans all incoming e-mail (which checks all inbound messages and attachments, and should be left enabled) as well as outgoing stuff (which is a good idea to check; should a worm get loose on your system, this will stop it from infecting other systems). You can also specify malware-handling options here (the default attempts automatic repair), block worms, and receive alerts when e-mail attachments are scanned.
- **Internet Worm Protection**—These controls are grayed out, because the NIS 2004 firewall is taking over this job. You can manage that firewall through the NIS controls (available through a small globe icon in the system tray).
- **Instant Messenger**—This provides controls over MSN and Windows Messenger applications, AIM (version 4.7 or higher), and Yahoo! Messenger (version 5.0) or higher. Basically, it can monitor one or more of these IM services, and screen inbound attachments.
- **LiveUpdate**—This provides update controls, including automatic update downloads and signature applications, with notification of software updates (so you can decide when to apply them). It also launches a facility called QuickScan that immediately checks files most likely to cause trouble or contain malware, including files related to processes that are active during the scan, files with start-up instructions or .INI file entries, and files that appear in startup registry keys like `Run` and `Runonce`.
- **Threat Categories**—This tells NAV what to scan for above and beyond malware, which is included by default (and can't be turned off). But other items include some new elements in NAV: security risks (programs that may or may not be threats, but exhibit questionable behaviors), spyware, adware, dialers, joke programs, remote access software, and hack

tools (like keystroke loggers). If you decide to run a separate spyware/adware blocker like Spy Sweeper or Spybot-Search & Destroy, you'll probably want to turn these checks off.

- **Miscellaneous** — As the category name suggests, it lumps together otherwise unrelated program controls. These include how to handle attempted repairs to infected or infested files, the ability to enable or disable a plug-in for MS Office that scans for viruses, notification when anti-virus definitions get over two weeks old, and mechanisms to protect NAV itself from being tampered with (some malware, spyware, and adware tries to disable virus checks and other security software, if you'll recall).

All in all, there's a lot more functionality in NAV 2005 than there was in NAV 2004. By the same token, for about $30 more ($20 for those who qualify for upgrade pricing), you can get Norton Internet Security 2005 (which includes NAV 2005 plus the latest firewall, spam blocker, privacy tools, and more). To learn more about that security suite (the only one to include two top-rated elements — namely, the Norton Personal Firewall and Norton AntiSpam) check out Appendix A in this book.

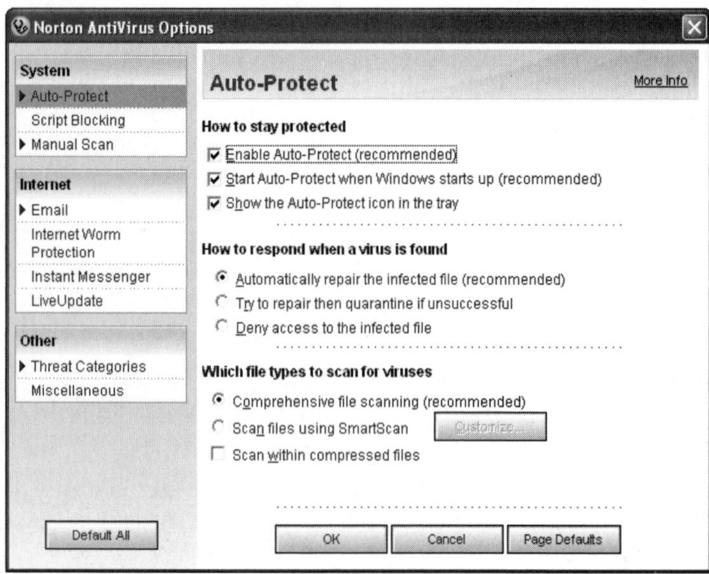

Figure 8-5: You can configure additional settings via the Options screen.

Once all updates have been downloaded and configuration options set, you can move on to scan your computer for viruses. This process usually takes some time, so you may want to schedule scanning for times when you aren't actively using your computer, such as late-night hours. If infected files are found during a scan, you can run the Repair Wizard to fix, quarantine, delete, or exclude the files, or view summary information.

After the system scan, you can view reports on quarantined items, visit the Online Virus Encyclopedia, and browse the Activity log (see Figure 8-6).

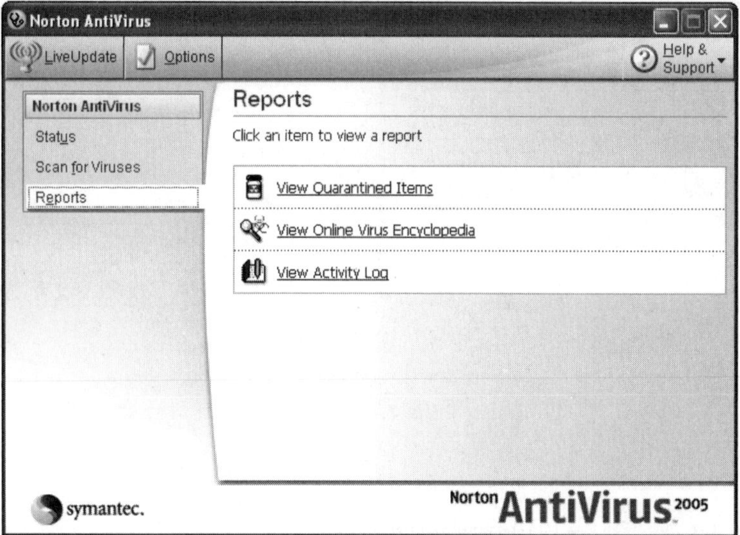

Figure 8-6: NAV provides three reports for your review.

Overall, NAV offers remarkably simple ease of use and is fully configurable for automatic updates and scanning, a key feature for those who prefer worry-free virus scanning. As you work with this product, or others like it, you'll notice lots of other small but informative behaviors (such as Norton's momentary addition of a small envelope icon in the System Tray as it scans incoming or outgoing e-mail, or its substitution of a text file for infected attachments to tell you they've been found and removed). This type of software offers lots of helpful conveniences to let you know what it's doing and when it finds things it doesn't like.

McAfee VirusScan 8.0

McAfee continually receives high marks for its anti-virus offerings. This review focuses on the latest release, VirusScan 8.0. The installation process was as straightforward as they come and took half the time to install that NAV required. The installation automatically included McAfee Security Center, which provides current virus advisories, detailed ratings of your system security, as well as a central location to control other McAfee security applications, including Personal Firewall, Privacy Service, and SpamKiller (see Figure 8-7).

The main window for virus scanning includes options to scan for viruses, configure options, manage quarantined files, view the World Virus Map, access the virus information database, and create a rescue disk for your system (see Figure 8-8).

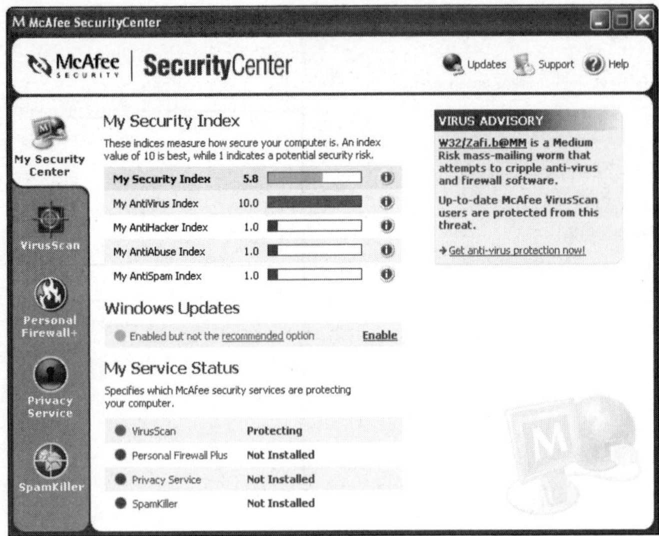

Figure 8-7: McAfee VirusScan includes installation of the McAfee Security Center.

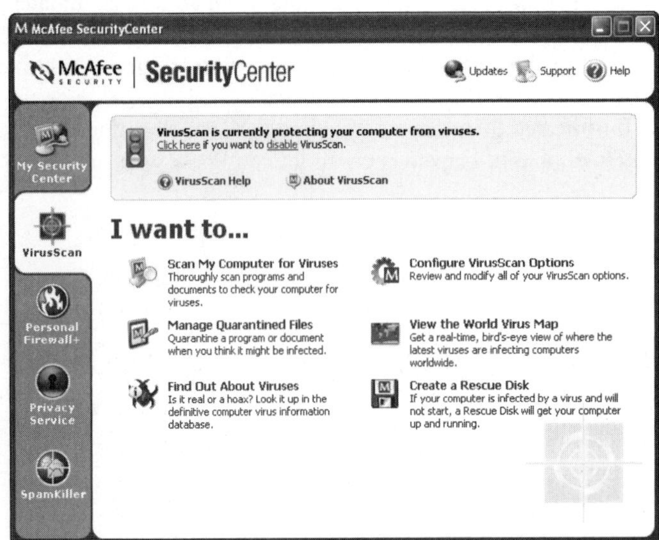

Figure 8-8: The McAfee VirusScan main management screen.

Configuration options for VirusScan fall in the same categories as those of other popular anti-virus applications, including specifying what sort of traffic to scan, options to participate in McAfee's Virus Map Reporting feature, and settings for automatic scheduling. A key feature to note for this application is that it automatically checks for updates and has options to install them automatically, download and notify you before installation, or notify before downloading, or you can disable the feature altogether. Also notable is an option to scan for spyware, adware, dialers, and other malware applications. Finally, VirusScan doesn't consume system resources like NAV does, so its impact on system performance is less noticeable.

Once you run a system scan, VirusScan provides a Scan Summary screen that reports any infected files it finds and then cleans them off your system automatically (see Figure 8-9). As far as ease of use goes, this package earns high ratings for staying up-to-date and performing its functions flawlessly, with minimal system impact.

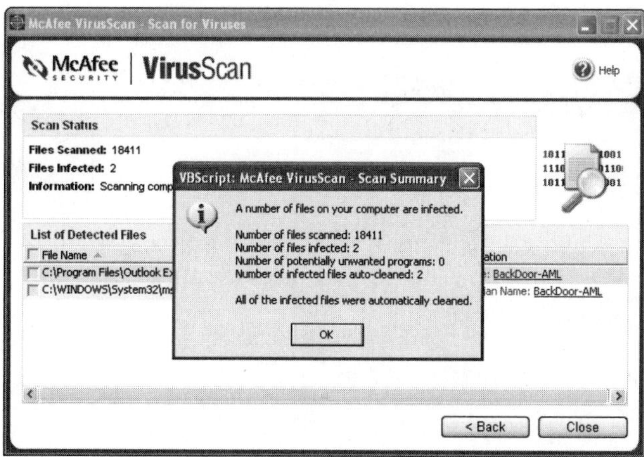

Figure 8-9: VirusScan automatically cleans infected files from your system.

Grisoft's AVG 6.0 Anti-Virus Free Edition

AVG is highly rated by both Virus Bulletin and ICSA Labs for its 100 percent detection rate of known viruses as of June 2004. The software provides standard anti-virus offerings, such as automatic virus definition updates, real-time e-mail and file scanning, and a virus vault for handling infected files. The free edition of this software is downloadable from `http://free.grisoft.com/freeweb.php`, where you must complete a registration form. Once downloaded (about 7MB), the installation routine provides the usual offerings of configuring the AVG Resident Shield, AVG E-mail Scanner, and the AVG Control Center. After installation, you must restart your computer before you can run the application. Upon rebooting, the Resident Shield immediately identified a virus present on the system I was testing (see Figure 8-10).

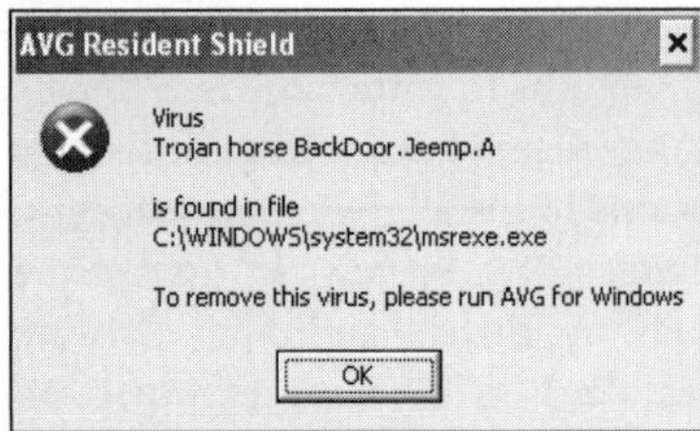

Figure 8-10: After installation and reboot, AVG automatically detected a virus.

When you launch AVG for the first time, the AVG First Run Wizard assists you in downloading the latest virus updates. Once downloaded, you can run a complete system test from the main program screen (see Figure 8-11).

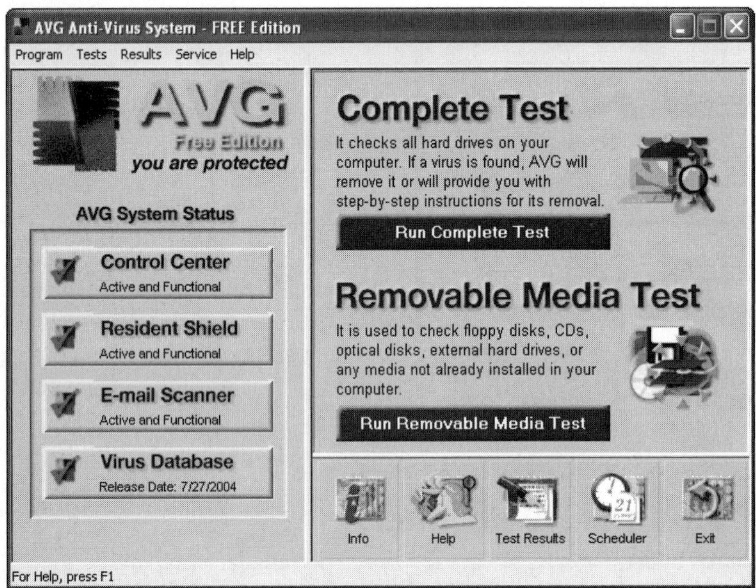

Figure 8-11: The AVG Free Edition main screen.

Overall, the AVG user interface is quite simple and easy to use and navigate. The Complete Test blazed through the system scan and the Test Finished screen (see Figure 8-12) provided information on the scan itself as well as infected files found and repaired on the system.

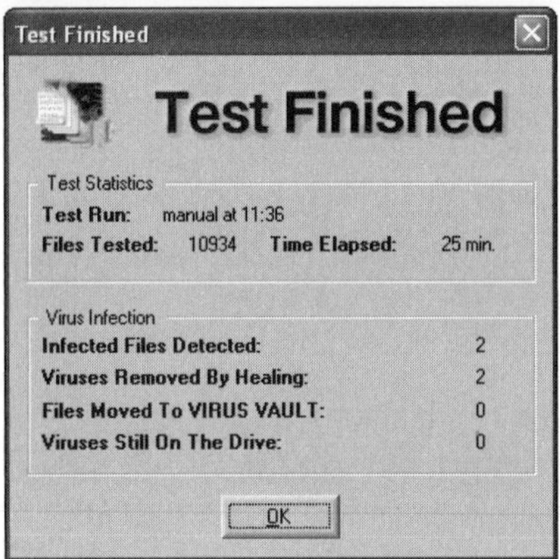

Figure 8-12: The AVG Test Finished screen.

The Test Results button launched a detailed list of which files it was not able to scan in addition to the file location, virus name, and status of each file. Overall, this product was extremely easy to use, efficient, and best of all, free! With free offerings such as this, those who need anti-virus protection but don't want to shell out for such coverage have no excuse!

ALWIL avast! 4 Home Edition

The final anti-virus application I'll cover here is Czech-based ALWIL Software's avast! 4.0 Home Edition. The Home Edition is free for home or non-commercial users after a brief registration process. The only shortcomings from this process is that you must wait up to 30 minutes to receive the activation key via e-mail; once you do get it and install the program, another key feature that's missing is script-blocking, which can leave your system more vulnerable than other applications we've reviewed here.

Once you've downloaded the software from the avast! Web page (about 7.5MB), the setup is as straightforward as the other applications discussed in this chapter, with the option to perform typical, minimal, and custom configurations. For this review, I installed the typical installation, which includes scanning for Internet and Outlook/Exchange e-mail, instant messaging, P2P shield, the standard shield, and application skins. During installation, you're given the option of performing a boot-time scan once you restart your computer; I opted to skip this step. Finally, note that you must register the product within 60 days to continue its use.

Once I rebooted the system, a virus was automatically detected (see Figure 8-13) and a notification screen popped up immediately, along with a blaring siren and an audible warning of its presence. You can move or rename, delete, or repair the file, or move the file to the chest. From there, you can also stop or continue the memory scan. Application configuration options are managed through the avast! Simple User Interface (see Figure 8-14), which you really have to explore yourself to find how to properly configure it, so it's not as simple as you might like.

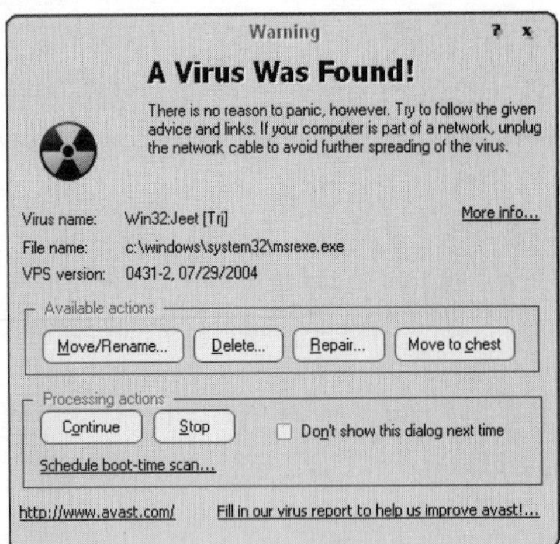

Figure 8-13: avast! detected a virus as soon as the system was rebooted via its resident memory scan.

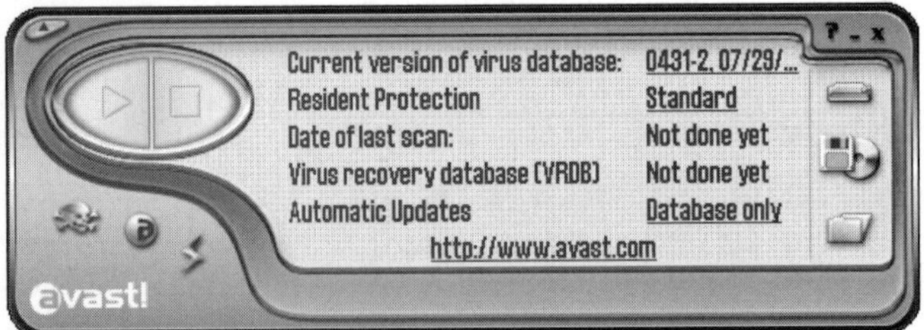

Figure 8-14: The avast! Simple User Interface provides controls to configure program settings (each button launches various parts of the interface).

You have to click the menu button at the top-left of this screen to get to the main menu (see Figure 8-15). Real program management comes from this menu. I promptly chose the Settings option to do away with the siren and audible warnings, but that's just my preference. This is where you configure program settings, automatic scans, and program updates. Note that the Enhanced User Interface isn't available with the Home Edition.

For the most part, avast! provides decent protection for your system, but frankly, I'd like to see more importance placed on protection mechanisms, such as script-blocking, rather than such an emphasis on a flashy interface.

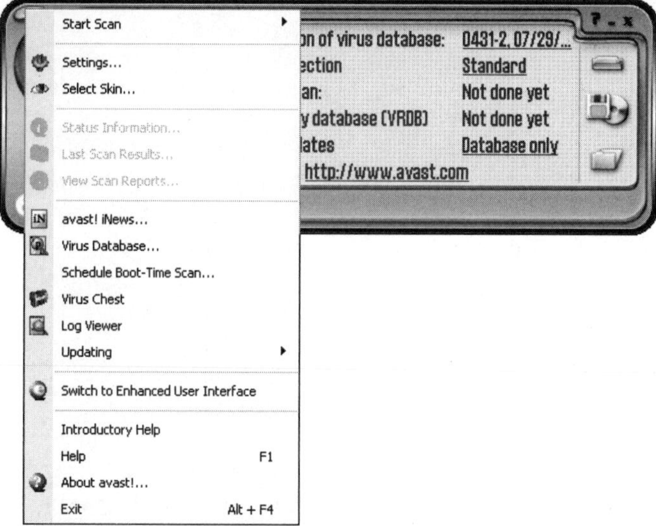

Figure 8-15: Program settings are accessed from the main menu of the avast! Simple User Interface.

Using Multiple Anti-Virus Packages

This is a section that occurs in each chapter in Part III of this book; it addresses the question of running more than one program of the same type on a single PC. Because this is the anti-virus chapter, I answer the question: "Should you run more than one anti-virus program at the same time on a single PC?" The answer to this question is a lot like the answer to the anti-spyware/anti-adware question in Chapter 7. That is, it's okay to use more than one scanner to search your file system, memory, and other system components for traces that may signal that some form of malware is present. But because real-time protection against viruses requires software to hook into input-output operations at a very low (or deep) level, you should keep only one anti-virus package running in the background to provide protection at runtime. In fact, I experienced my first truly nasty BSOD ("Blue Screen of Death," a cryptic error message screen that Windows produces when things fall apart in spectacular, unrecoverable fashion) back in the Windows NT 4.0 days when I decided to install a second anti-virus package on an otherwise well-configured and well-behaved machine because another vendor came out with a Melissa fix before my anti-virus vendor at the time did likewise. So remember: multiple scanners are okay, but install only one anti-virus package for background operation and runtime use.

Resources

Lots of folks out there dedicate their time and energy to investigating virus threats as they arise and work hard to keep the computing community in the know. Such resources can range from basic, introductory-level resources to full-blown virus encyclopedias. If you want to know more about viruses, consider exploring the vast amount of information available from the following resources:

- The International Computer Security Association, or ICSA (now part of TruSecure Corporation), runs some highly respected test labs that test all kinds of hardware and software to make sure they conform with the Labs' equally respected security criteria. Each year ICSA Labs lists all the anti-virus products that meet its certification criteria. To access its general anti-virus/virus info visit `www.icsalabs.com/html/communities/antivirus/index.shtml`. To see the list of ICSA certified anti-virus products, visit `www.icsalabs.com/html/communities/antivirus/certifiedproducts.shtml`. (Note: they're rated along a number of categories, so you'll have to follow more links to see any actual product names.) To read more about ICSA Labs certification criteria for anti-virus products, please see `www.icsalabs.com/html/communities/antivirus/certification.shtml`.
- Virus Bulletin (`www.virusbtn.com`) is an excellent source of virus news, information, and also has a great virus encyclopedia. It also publishes occasional ratings of anti-virus software, such as the ratings for 25 packages it tested on Windows XP Professional in June 2004. Check it out at `www.virusbtn.com/vb100/archives/tests.xml?200406`.
- The Anti-Virus Review Web site (`www.anti-virus-software-review.com/`) provides detailed reviews of anti-virus software.
- Douglas Schweitzer's *Securing the Network From Malicious Code* (Wiley 2002) covers more than viruses, discussing Trojans, worms, and other outright types of malware, and it does a good job of explaining their design and workings and exploring various tools and strategies to help block, foil, and repel attacks. Not as deep or detailed as the Skoudis and Seltzer book mentioned in Chapter 2, it's probably more useful to IT professionals or other interested computer users trying to figure out what to do about malware, rather than trying to understand malware at a deep and fundamental level.

This list should keep you occupied for many hours, and if you do perform additional investigations and take the information provided by these wonderful repositories, you'll be an anti-virus guru yourself in no time.

Summary

A major consideration when evaluating anti-virus software is why it's in such demand in the first place. Most of those in the know resoundingly agree: viruses have an easy target in Windows. But, you don't have to throw Windows out the window to keep your system safe. Any of the anti-virus applications mentioned here, if updated and run regularly, should keep your system safe from harm.

Other considerations for system security should include the use of a personal firewall and some good, old-fashioned common sense.

There's some strange predilection of humans to open anything that is sent to them — you must fight this urge with diligence if you want to keep your systems safe from these types of threats. Continuing the mantra throughout this book: If you're not sure, don't do it! If you don't know the sender of an e-mail or aren't expecting an attachment from a known contact, delete it, or at least check with those you know before you open unexpected attachments. These two simple exercises can keep your system safe — if you don't open a virus-infected file, it can't do anything to your system — and that's the goal in the first place!

Chapter 9

Spam Blockers

If there's one problem with unwanted material on the Internet that everybody can understand, it's spam. Given that *spam* refers to anything that shows up in an inbox unsolicited or unwanted, you've also identified the biggest component of all e-mail Internet traffic today. Mail handling company Brightmail (now a part of Symantec) reports that as of June 2004, more than 65 percent of all Internet e-mail qualifies as spam by somebody's estimation. Thus, the e-mail chaff now outnumbers the wheat to the point where nearly two messages out of every three are headed for oblivion at some point or another.

But bad enough as unwanted advertisements for bizarre or strange products or services might be, spam has a sinister edge as well. E-mail has become the distribution vector of choice for malware of all kinds, and is the special focus for worms, most of which are designed to use e-mail as one of a number of channels for propagation, if not the primary channel. Infected attachments are commonplace. For grins, I kept count of all infected attachments that showed up in my inboxes over the course of a week and was stunned to observe that they averaged more than 100 infected messages daily. That sounds like a lot, but when you stop to consider that the total average daily message count topped 1,000 (of which at most 70–100 were legitimate messages), at least this indicates that infected attachments don't represent a majority form of spam just yet.

In what should now be a familiar game of ongoing escalation — like the cops and robbers I've mentioned elsewhere in the book — as spam blocking technologies become more adept at identifying and stopping spam, spammers become more frenzied and inventive in their ways of slipping past such blocks. Fake or spoofed senders, fake domain names, enticing subject lines, assumed familiarity, or even impersonation of friends and family: all of these techniques are exploited daily to slip past the vigilance of software watching out for and seeking to eliminate spam as it travels from one mail server to the next, en route from its sender to its ultimate recipient. This chapter examines various techniques for identifying and blocking spam, and talks about what kinds of tools and services you can bring to bear to help get your spam problem under control.

Understanding E-mail Basics

Before I launch into the whys and wherefores of blocking, filtering, or otherwise getting rid of spam, it's important to understand some of the basic workings of Internet e-mail. The Simple Mail Transfer Protocol (SMTP) is a big part of what makes e-mail work. The other big part of Internet e-mail was originally specified in RFC 822, "Standard for the Format of ARPA Internet Text Messages," now

updated in RFC 2822 (this has also been extended by the Multipurpose Internet Mail Extensions [MIME] RFCs whose latest versions include 2045, 2046, and 2049).

Simply put, SMTP is what makes it possible for you to send e-mail to somebody else, and also defines various mechanisms for routing e-mail from one e-mail server to the next until it arrives at some e-mail server where your intended recipient can pick it up (or until some delivery or addressing problem prevents delivery). RFC (2)822 defines basic mail message formats, including a standard message header that acts like an electronic envelope for e-mail messages, and a message body, which is where the content that e-mail senders and receivers care about most reside. The MIME extensions are what makes it possible for you (and worms or spammers, alas) to attach all kinds of files—including infected binary attachments—to e-mail messages before sending them on their way.

From the standpoint of understanding how e-mail works:

- SMTP defines how e-mail is transmitted, stored, and forwarded until it reaches its intended recipient.
- RFC 2(822) defines what e-mail messages look like and how they are to be read and interpreted.
- The MIME extensions define what can (and can't) be transported along with e-mail messages, inside a single electronic envelope, as it were.

From the standpoint of spam, what makes e-mail so attractive a medium is that it consists at some fundamental level of nothing more than plain text. Anybody who takes the time to understand formatting and layout requirements for e-mail message headers (more on those in a minute) and contents can craft e-mail messages at will, using nothing more than a text editor (or software that emits the right kinds of plain text output). What's more, anybody who wants to take the time can craft e-mail headers for messages that attribute false identities to senders (or receivers) and all kinds of other identifying information as well. This not only prevents spammers from being identified, but it also helps malicious e-mail masquerade as coming from trusted sources and can thus provide potential points of entry (if not outright welcome, from the unwary) for worms, Trojans, or other malware payloads attached to e-mail messages.

Viewing RFC 822 Message Headers in Outlook and Outlook Express

To inspect the contents of the RFC 822 header in an e-mail message in Outlook, follow these steps:

1. Double-click a message item in one of your folders to select it. (Note: It might be necessary to do this twice, to force the message to open in its own window—this is essential, or the right menu option won't be available.)
2. Click the View item in the menu bar and then click Options. Notice the scrolling pane inside the Message Options window near the bottom. It's labeled Internet headers; this is where you'll find header information, as depicted in the accompanying sidebar figure.

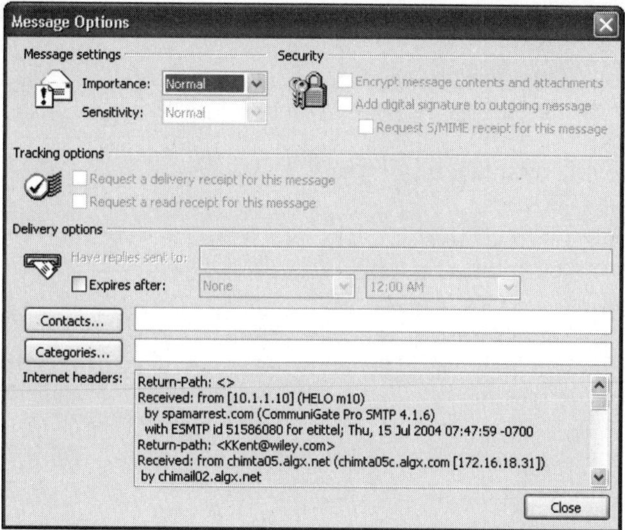

The RFC 822 header is accessible in the Message Options window in Outlook.

To do the same thing in Outlook Express, you must also open a message into its own window (double-clicking works here, too). Then click File → Properties, and select the Details tab in the resulting window that appears. The contents of the RFC 822 header show up in the text pane labeled "Internet headers for this message." If you click the Message Source button at the bottom of this window, you'll get a text window from which it's very easy to cut this header text for subsequent inspection and analysis.

I've learned it's easiest to view a message header by cutting the text from inside the Internet headers pane and then pasting it into a plain-text editor like Notepad. Because you can't resize the Message Options window, you can see only seven lines of message header text at a time. By cutting and pasting this information into a different program, you can see a screen full of header information in a single look — normally, in fact, this provides enough onscreen real estate to see the whole thing at once. It's a lot easier to read and understand when you can see more of the header, which hopefully explains why I recommend this approach!

Looking at an RFC 822 header can tell you all kinds of interesting information, so now I want to show the entire header for the message depicted in the preceding sidebar figure in a code listing. You can skip to the text that follows this listing, and I'll walk you through what's there to explain what's included therein, what it means, and what it can tell you about a message's journey from sender to receiver. For easy reference, I added line numbers for the text on the left-hand side; these do *not* appear in the original text that was cut and pasted from the Message Options window in Outlook.

```
 1 Return-Path: <>
 2 Received: from [10.1.1.10] (HELO m10)
 3   by spamarrest.com (CommuniGate Pro SMTP 4.1.6)
 4   with ESMTP id 51586080 for etittel; Thu, 15 Jul 2004 07:47:59 -0700
 5 Return-path: <KKent@wiley.com>
 6 Received: from chimta05.algx.net (chimta05c.algx.com [172.16.18.31])
 7  by chimail02.algx.net
 8  (iPlanet Messaging Server 5.2 HotFix 1.21 (built Sep  8 2003))
 9  with ESMTP id <0I0W00NTAEC14K@chimail02.algx.net> for etittel@jump.net; Thu,
10  15 Jul 2004 09:45:38 -0500 (CDT)
11 Received: from hmi2.northamerica.wileynet.net
12  (hmi2.hungryminds.com [168.215.86.70])
13  by chimmx05.algx.net (iPlanet Messaging Server 5.2 HotFix 1.16 (built May 14
14  2003)) with ESMTP id <0I0W00M51EBXD7@chimmx05.algx.net> for etittel@jump.net
15  (ORCPT etittel@jump.net); Thu, 15 Jul 2004 09:45:35 -0500 (CDT)
16 Date: Thu, 15 Jul 2004 09:45:26 -0500
17 From: KKent@wiley.com
18 Subject: Chapter 2, source material issue
19 To: etittel@jump.net
20 Cc: drader@austin.rr.com
21 Message-id:
22  <OFAF1274B9.5FCFE0F4-ON05256ED2.004EE9BA-
05256ED2.00511066@northamerica.wileynet.net>
23 MIME-version: 1.0
24 X-Mailer: Lotus Notes Release 6.5.1 January 21, 2004
25 Content-type: text/plain; charset=US-ASCII
26 X-MIMETrack: Serialize by Router on HMI2/Indianapolis/Wiley(651HF13 |
February
27  05, 2004) at 07/15/2004 09:45:24 AM
28  Original-recipient: rfc822;etittel@jump.net
```

Before I examine this information in some detail, two observations are essential:

- Indentation is meaningful. Thus, for example, because lines 3 and 4 are indented, this indicates they're part of the block of text that starts at line 2.
- Each line of text that starts on column 1 identifies what kind of information it is, by using a keyword (also known as a field name, or more simply, a field) followed by a colon. Thus, for example, you can see that in lines 2, 6, and 11, there are 3 `Received` items. Each of these indicates a transmission from one SMTP (e-mail) server to another, working from the original sender, `wileynet.net` (lines 11–15); through two e-mail servers at an Internet service provider (ISP; lines 6 through 10), `algx.net`; to the final server, `spamarrest.com` (lines 2 through 4, a spam screening service where I retrieve my e-mail).

Note

You can measure the transit time for messages from server to server by comparing receipt times in successive blocks of `Received` and other RFC 822 items. Time shows up in HH:MM:SS notation, followed by time zone. Time zone appears as a signed number, + or - HHMM, which may or may not have a label, as in line 10 where it's identified as CDT, or Central Daylight Time. Time zone is expressed as an offset from Universal Coordinated Time (UCT), a.k.a. Greenwich Mean Time (GMT), so that CDT is 5 hours behind, and Pacific Daylight Time, or PDT, 7 hours behind). Thus, you can see it took 2 seconds for the message to get out the door (to transit from the client through the local server) by comparing time stamps in lines 27 and 16. By comparing lines 16 and 15, you can see it took 9 seconds to get from the first server to the second. Likewise, by comparing lines 15 and 10, you see 3 seconds passed, and by comparing lines 10 and 4 you can see it took another 2 minutes and 11 seconds to transit two more time zones to the west.

The `Received` keyword shows the server transitions that this message made in moving from sender to receiver. Other keywords are equally important (but anything that occurs after line 11 on a legitimate server, or line 15 on a questionable one is also equally easy to falsify, or spoof, when generating e-mail messages for transmission). Here are other keywords of potential interest or note:

- `Return-Path` (line 5) — The e-mail address to use to reply to this message.
- `Date` (line 16) — This is the time stamp attached by an e-mail client when the initial send occurs (in Outlook, unless a rule prevents immediate transmission of a message when you click the Send/Receive button, outgoing messages will be sent following their order in the Outbox folder; as they leave the client, the time stamp is inserted just prior to transmission).
- `From` (Line 17) — This identifies the sender and may include a name (optional) but must include an e-mail address (required). This also appears in a standard Outlook message header (which does not include all RFC 822 fields).
- `Subject` (Line 18) — This identifies the message, to help the recipient understand what the message is about.
- `To` (Line 19) — The intended recipient or recipients for the message. More than one recipient may be listed, and multiples may be separated by commas or semicolons. Each recipient designation may include a name (optional) but must include an e-mail address (required). This appears in a standard Outlook message header.
- `Cc` (Line 20) — This stands for Carbon copy, and represents other designated recipients, usually as a courtesy or as a way of making sure they're kept informed about communications between sender and receiver. This field also appears by default in the standard Outlook message header. Another related field, `Bcc:` (which stands for Blind carbon copy, to indicate that blind copy recipients can't see who else gets a blind copy), does not appear by default in a standard Outlook header, but can be configured manually through the View menu item.

- MIME-version (Line 23) — Indicates which version of the MIME specification to which attachments must adhere.
- X-Mailer (Line 24) — Identifies the sending e-mail application from which the message originated.
- Content-type (Line 25) — Identifies the type of character encoding (text/plain) used for the message text, and the character set (charset) used to represent character data (US-ASCII, the common keyboard character set).

To learn more about other valid RFC 822 header fields and how to construe their contents, consult the text for the current RFC, 2822, or check the "Resources" section at the end of this chapter for pointers to some other online tutorials on this subject. Among many other locations online, you can read the RFC at www.faqs.org/rfcs/rfc2822.html. Although the contents and information in this header may seem kind of dry if not downright uninviting, knowing how to understand and interpret their contents can often help alert you to scams or spam. For example, "spoofed addresses" — mail that claims to originate from some sender with a specific e-mail address but actually comes from somewhere else — are easy to spot if you know how. That's why I dig into this information in more depth in Chapter 10, specifically when discussing spoofed addresses (a general spam technique) and "phishing" attacks (messages that purport to originate from banks, brokerages, or other places that might legitimately need your personal financial information, but that really come from third parties that want to steal and misuse this information for their benefit, not yours).

Why Block (or Otherwise Kill) Spam?

Plain and simple: spam is a hassle. Aside from the inconvenience involved in dealing with spam, there are lots of other issues to consider. For one thing, it takes bandwidth to transport messages that nobody wants, and consumes e-mail server and storage resources that could be used for other things. For another — ignoring the impact of spam that carries malware for the moment — there's a terrible cost in productivity. Brightmail conducted a survey of hundreds of companies and organizations and reports that most employers guess that it takes their workers at least 10 minutes every workday, sometimes longer, to deal with spam. In a business with 1,000 workers, that's 10,000 minutes, which translates into 166.67 hours, or 20.83 8-hour workdays, lost to handling spam every working day. Things get even worse on those days when spam volume goes up, and employees must spend even more time handling the extra influx.

Spam is also a vector — if not the major vector — that worms, and occasionally, other sorts of malware use to infect lots of systems. With the aggregate costs to the global economy of recent wildfire viruses estimated in the tens of millions to billions of dollars, productivity costs when something truly nasty takes root from an infected e-mail can really skyrocket.

In short, the primary reason to remove spam from inboxes everywhere is economic — namely, to avoid the losses in productivity that arise from time wasted dealing with spam, and the even greater amounts of time and effort that must be spent cleaning up in the wake of infections that spam can sometimes deliver. In the face of all the tools and technologies that have been brought to bear on the spam problem, it's a testament to the perverse ingenuity of mankind that spam remains a mounting problem, as the ever-increasing proportion of spam to legitimate e-mail (65 percent to 35 percent and climbing, according to figures cited earlier in this chapter) attests.

A Brief Taxonomy of Spam

In fact, not all forms of spam are alike, though all forms share the characteristic of arriving at inboxes uninvited (and usually also unwanted). Though the following list of types of spam is far from complete, it's reasonably representative of what most people dread finding in their inboxes on a more or less daily basis (in fact, I created it by saving and analyzing more than 5,000 spam items that showed up in my inboxes during the course of a single week):

- **Advertisements** — Ads for stocks, drugs, merchandise, auto warranties, insurance, degrees with no study, and all kinds of other stuff you probably don't need, and never asked to hear about.
- **Porn solicitation** — Opportunities to look at things you never heard of involving people you don't want to know. Some cause pictures to pop-up in e-mail viewers when HTML and graphics display are enabled. This can be a real problem, both at home and in the workplace.
- **Hustles or scams** — Family members of deceased Nigerian dictators want you to send them $20,000 so you can go to a bank and collect millions on their behalf. Yeah, right! E-mail fraud is, however, a growing problem and those who can least afford it (especially the elderly and unknowing) are the most likely to get victimized.
- **Identity theft attempts** — A genre of identity theft called "phishing" relies on credulous e-mail recipients believing that Citibank, PayPal, or American Express really would send an insecure e-mail and ask customers to provide personal, confidential information about themselves through this medium. Some even ask recipients to run software, which ends up installing spyware and Trojans on systems so that malefactors can steal all kinds of sensitive information from the unwitting or unwary. Others ask them to link to official-seeming Web pages and do likewise.

Caution

Any time a company with which you conduct business sends you e-mail and asks you to provide credit card numbers, Social Security data, account numbers, or anything else that could be misused in the wrong hands, don't provide any such information via e-mail. Instead, call the company and ask them about the e-mail. Chances are 99 out of 100 that they'll tell you it's not legitimate, because most such organizations do not trust e-mail to convey sensitive information any more than you should.

- **Sex aids/drugs/enhancements** — Pick the drug, device, or object of the moment, and chances are far too good that you'll get an e-mail offer to make it available to you discreetly, cheaply, and quickly. Explaining this kind of thing to the younger generation can be a real challenge!
- **Unwanted automated replies** — Far too many e-mail servers still generate automatic replies when they reject messages that they can't deliver (or won't deliver, because they're

infected with malware), even though it's been common knowledge since mid-2003 that numerous worms choose e-mail addresses from harvested address books and designate them as message senders. This has the unfortunate side effect of doubling malware-related e-mail, because each malicious message generates an automatic reply when blocked or detected (I have observed that between 20 and 30 percent of the spam I've received recently falls into this category).

- **Plays on curiosity** — By claiming to include racy photos of a well-known tennis star, hundreds of thousands of hapless recipients fell prey to a worm instead by attempting to view those snaps. Other common come-ons designed to get the unwitting or unwary to open unexpected (and far too often infected) attachments include subjects like "Here's the document I promised to send you" or "Please review this document," when they don't appeal to our baser instincts.
- **False familiarity** — This is a variation on the preceding item as senders attempt to capitalize on presumed friendship or intimacy, with subject lines like "Here are photos from the party" or "Check this out!" or even "Yo: Dude!!" By encouraging recipients to download messages and open attachments, predators seek voluntary surrender from their prey. Don't succumb to attempts to voluntarily breach your personal security.
- **Special offers/discounts/prizes** — Offers too good to be true usually are just that. How do you get a refund or a replacement from an e-mail address, when your stuff never arrives, or you get something different from what was promised in a once-in-a-lifetime deal. What else will these people use your credit card to pay for?
- **Strange character sets** — One strange side effect of the Internet's global scope occurs when messages you can't read show up in your inbox. This usually means you don't have Japanese, Korean, Chinese, or other non-Western alphabets loaded on your Windows machine. Lucky you! This makes it easier to tell that something you don't want or need to read is trying to get into your inbox.
- **Bizarre gibberish on the Subject line** — This means a program generated a subject line randomly, or somebody used code that expected substitutions that didn't work or weren't supplied. For example, a hop to one of my remote inboxes produced this subject line: `=?ISO-8859-1?b?U3RlbGxhciBTdG9jayBSZXBvcnQ=?=`. This sort of thing is a sure-fire sign of spam — moreover, spam from somebody using a spam generation program who really doesn't know what they're doing!

Of course, with a nearly infinite number of spam messages likely to show up in your inbox soon, I can't exhaust the many types of spam you'll encounter. But the foregoing list represents what I've been seeing in my inboxes recently, so I expect they're what you're seeing, too!

How (and When) to Block or Filter Spam

Every time an e-mail message gets forwarded from one SMTP server to the next, it's possible to subject it to inspection to see if it qualifies as spam or not. An increasing number of ISPs are doing just that, and enunciating e-mail policies that indicate they reserve the right to reject spam that shows up on their servers. The problem is that while some forms of spam are undeniable and relatively easy to detect (for example, an e-mail generated by a worm that contains an infected attachment recognizable to anti-virus software), other forms are more difficult to catch (such as highly personalized advertisements carefully crafted to look like real, solicited e-mail). Some legal scholars raise freedom of speech issues where spam is concerned and assert that despite its odious nature, spam is a form of protected speech that a carrier can't decide to accept or reject, only its intended recipient.

Legal controversy aside, spam is blocked or filtered at many stops along the path from sender to receiver. In fact, I think that savvy PC users should adopt a multi-step approach to dealing with spam where they can trade how much money they're willing to spend to avoid spam against how much time they're willing to spend dealing with it personally.

In its most extreme (and expensive) form, this involves a four-step approach:

1. **Hire an ISP to handle your e-mail that offers spam screening services and spam controls as part of its services.** Whether this means paying more than you would for unfiltered e-mail, or finding an ISP that routinely screens all incoming e-mail is up to you. It may cost somewhat more than unfiltered e-mail, but spam filtering seldom as much as doubles e-mail fees nowadays. These days, free e-mail account providers such as Yahoo!, Google, Hotmail, and so forth routinely screen spam from users' inboxes (even if they do include banner ads inside solicited mail). Many commercial ISPs also do likewise, including big-name outfits like AOL, EarthLink, AT&T Worldnet, and so forth.
2. **Consider signing up for a spam filtering or screening service** (I talk about specific companies that offer such services later in this section). For monthly fees that usually run from $3 to $5 a month, you can hire a company that specializes in handling e-mail and removing spam from your inbox. Some of the best-rated companies in this arena routinely score 98–99 percent spam removal rates, with few false positives (blocking mail you really do want) and false negatives (delivering mail you really don't want). Most such services allow you to view questionable messages through a Web page so you can decide what to download to your PC when the service can't identify it as either spam or desirable e-mail. This provides an opportunity to screen suspect e-mail in a very safe way—namely, while it's still sitting on a server somewhere, and can't possibly infect or affect your PC.
3. **Install special spam filtering or screening software on your PC.** This kind of software sits between your e-mail program and the Internet and inspects incoming e-mail to decide what gets into your inbox and what goes into the spam or suspect messages folder. Some of these programs can be taught to think like you do and can learn to separate spam from desirable mail over time. Other of these programs draw on their user communities to tell them what's spam and what's not. Either way, the best such programs also have great recognition and classification abilities. Some of these programs stand alone, whereas others work as plug-ins for e-mail packages like Outlook, Outlook Express, Eudora, and so forth. Either way, they inspect incoming e-mail first, perform their duties, and only then hand what's left over to your e-mail software.
4. **Use your e-mail software's built-in filters and recognition capabilities.** Most modern e-mail software includes its own built-in rules definition facilities and junk or adult sender recognition tools (including Outlook, Outlook Express, Eudora, and other browser-based e-mail packages like Netscape, Opera, and so forth). You can use these as your last line of

defense — they're usually too much work to set up and maintain as your only line of defense against spam — when it comes to guarding your e-mail inbox.

It's possible to argue that the foregoing strategy is overkill and that only one of items 2 or 3 is necessary to attain a reasonable level of spam filtering and control. I agree that this is probably a good place to start implementing an anti-spam strategy, but I also recommend item 2 over item 3 when it comes to picking which is best. I'd argue for this conclusion on two grounds:

- First, because a spam filtering service holds e-mail on the server and lets you inspect suspect messages remotely, it limits your exposure to malign influences.
- Second, because a service often includes automatic filtering and spam recognition updates as part of its offering, that means less effort for you in separating spam from good e-mail over time.

That said, you'll seldom spend more than $30 a year for spam-filtering or screening software that runs on your PC, and spam filtering services routinely cost more than that ($36 per year and up is typical). Ultimately, it comes down to the value you place on your time and which of these solutions involves the best combination of your time and money. I use both a spam-filtering service and local screening software because that's what produces the best productivity gains for me; you should feel free to evaluate your circumstances and come to different and appropriate conclusions that work for you.

The sections that follow describe the kinds of filters and blocks that are likely to operate at each of the four elements in the preceding strategy. Where appropriate — that is, for items 2 through 4 — I'll explore some of the many options available for each one, and do some hands-on, step-by-step activities to illustrate how things work.

Spam Handling at Your ISP

Not all ISPs offer spam handling as part of their basic e-mail services, but many of them do. Those that don't offer it for base-level accounts may sometimes offer it as an extra-cost option. But if you don't ask, you can't know what they can (or perhaps already) do to help you prevent spam from reaching your inbox. Some Internet experts go so far as to say that because customers usually have to pay for e-mail services, they should vote with their checkbooks for spam control assistance by taking their business only to ISPs that offer spam filtering and blocking as part and parcel of their e-mail services.

Indeed, it's the case that many ISPs do apply spam filters and controls to their e-mail servers, often purely in the interests of limiting the amount of storage space that unwanted messages can consume. If you recall the Brightmail statistic cited at the outset of this chapter — namely, that two of every three Internet e-mail messages are spam — and think about the impact this has on e-mail server storage requirements (which basically need three times as much storage to hold all incoming e-mail as they'd need to hold only desirable incoming e-mail), you can quickly understand why ISPs might seek to manage and block spam in their own best economic interests.

This is definitely a topic worth investigating, but if your ISP isn't willing to get involved in controlling spam, there's really not much you can do about it except to take your business elsewhere. I'm guessing that such uninterested parties will be in the minority, however, because spam is a problem that everyone involved with the Internet must face.

Spam Screening and Filtering Services

Numerous companies offer services whereby they pick up your e-mail, inspect it for spam, and clean it up on your behalf. This sort of service comes in two primary flavors, in fact:

- **Mailbox cleaning**—In this variation on the theme, the service company accesses your inbox on its home server and cleans out its contents for you. Most such services do this at least once an hour, so that as long as you don't read your e-mail too often, you'll not find too much spam waiting for you.
- **Alternate mailbox**—In this variation on the theme, you instruct your ISP to forward your mail to the spam filtering service, and you reset your e-mail client to download e-mail from the service rather than from your ISP. This lets the service check your inbox whenever new messages show up and perform spam screening, filtering, or classification as often as it polls the servers where its customers' e-mail accounts reside (at Spamarrest, for example, they do this once every 1 or 2 minutes depending on time of day and load factors).

When this kind of service is explained to them, some people voice objections on the basis of disruption that business failure could cause. If you go with a service that requires you to open a mailbox with them, even if such an outfit goes out of business, as soon as you can redirect your mail elsewhere you should be back in operation. This means disruptions of e-mail for less than a day in most cases, and usually for no more than a weekend in the worst case. Others worry that this kind of service can hold users up for higher fees at will and hold their e-mail hostage for same. Here again, you can always take your business elsewhere with the same disruption scenario. Still others worry about privacy and confidentiality by bringing yet another party into the e-mail delivery chain that leads to your inbox. Most such businesses make explicit promises in their terms of service to keep your e-mail confidential (except under legal compulsion, as from a subpoena or court order)—and that's pretty much the way things stand with any ISP you hire to handle your e-mail. Personally, I don't think any of these objections is sufficient to warrant skipping consideration of such services, but if you feel otherwise, feel free to keep them out of your personal spam-handling approach.

In any case, what you get from a spam screening or filtering service is an inspection of your inbox that results in classification of mail into multiple categories. The exact details vary, depending exactly how any particular service works, but classification schemes usually work according to one or more of the following filtering or recognition schemes:

- **Sender classification**—Users provide what's called a *white list* in e-mail terminology. This is a list of known senders from whose e-mail addresses you're inclined to accept any and all incoming e-mail. Service providers sometimes include what's called a *black list* in e-mail terminology, or require users to develop their own black lists over time. This is a list of e-mail addresses from which a user (and when items are supplied by the service provider, from which all users) will never accept incoming mail. In most cases, users can add entries to their own personal black lists as they discover senders from whom they wish to receive no further e-mail. Items that don't appear in either list must be reviewed by users for placement into one list or the other, or can simply be deleted.

Note

A controversial practice in e-mail circles is called *blacklisting*. This occurs when a domain is associated with the distribution of spam, either as a point of origination or forwarding of spam messages. Domains associated with known spammers are added to a black list, which basically defines a collection of domains from which no inbound e-mail will be accepted. Any number of services and individuals maintain black lists, but not all are viewed as completely fair or objective (for example, it's possible for spammers to use e-mail servers within domains outside their actual control for forwarding without obtaining the server operator's permission or even notifying the server operator that such activity is taking place). If you ever find you can't send e-mail to some specific recipient, it can sometimes be because your home domain has been added to somebody's black list somewhere. Work with your ISP to get this matter resolved, but be prepared to use an alternate e-mail address because it can take weeks or longer to get such listings changed sometimes.

- **Message inspection** — Content is a strong indicator as to whether a message is spam or desirable e-mail. Inspection can key in on certain kinds of sender addresses (like the gibberish ones I talked about earlier in this chapter); specific words, phrases, or entire subject lines; and specific words, phrases, or sentences in the message body to decide if a message is spam or not. Classification of e-mails as spam that meet various rules for inspection also explains why such services are sometimes said to use "rules-based classification."

Note

One of the biggest benefits from the best spam screening service providers depends on the aggregate intelligence of the entire community of users. That is, anybody who partakes of the service can identify specific messages as spam, but everybody who partakes of the service can benefit from such certification. Hence the message so familiar to users of Yahoo! e-mail, "Thanks! Every message you report helps SpamGuard perform better. The messages you selected were deleted and reported as spam." As new spam shows up, by reporting same, users make it easier for spam-handling software to make it go away. This applies to spam screening services that support user reporting as much as it does to e-mail services (like Yahoo!) that offer the same capabilities.

When you hire a spam screening service to clean up your e-mail, you'll have to interact with the service on some level. It may mean changing your client e-mail package to download your inbox from the screening service instead of your ISP (for those services that redirect e-mail), or it may mean installing and using a toolbar inside your e-mail package to add to the community's information about what is and isn't spam.

Let's take a look at what it's like to work with Spamarrest, a spam screening service that uses white list/black list classification techniques, to separate spam from desirable e-mail. This service depends on redirecting e-mail to its own server, where it can inspect and classify incoming mail on your behalf. At Spamarrest, all e-mail from senders on your white list — called "authorized senders" in Spamarrest lingo — goes into your inbox. Mail from senders on your black list — called "blocked senders" in Spamarrest lingo — is automatically deleted. Senders that appear nowhere in any of your white lists (which can also include authorized mailing lists and domains) nor anywhere in your black lists (which can also include blocked mailing lists and blocked domains) are called "unverified senders." These are dropped into an Unverified folder.

As shown in Figure 9-1, service users (called members) log in to the Spamarrest Web site to access their folders; unverified messages must be screened for placement into an appropriate category (authorized or blocked senders, and so forth) or deleted. Spamarrest recommends that obvious spam be deleted rather than blocked because sender addresses (and domains) are typically changed for each message that a spammer broadcasts (making their inclusion in the blocked senders list virtually meaningless, because it's unlikely a message from the same sender address will ever appear in your inbox again).

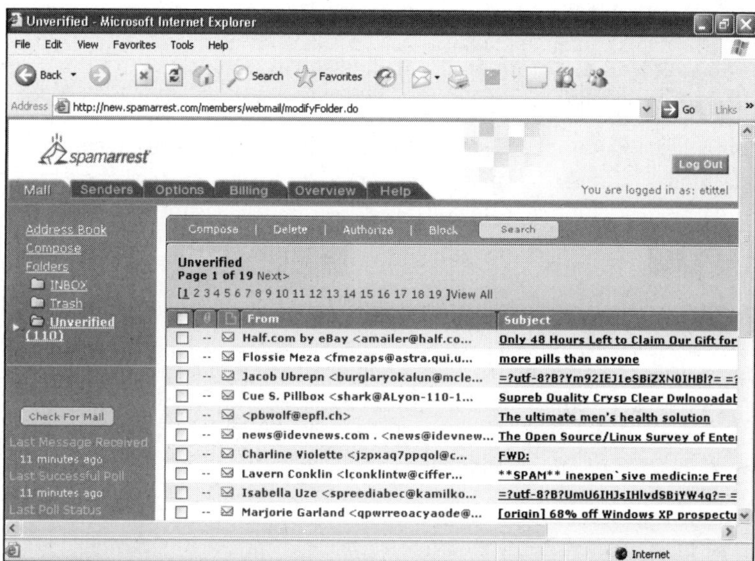

Figure 9-1: Unverified senders don't appear in any defined white or black lists and must be screened manually.

Verifying Senders

Some spam screening services send e-mail messages to addresses from senders not on white or black lists (as is the case with Spamarrest). These messages ask the recipient to read text from inside a graphic and key it into the body of a reply to that request. The notion is that the service is verifying that there's a human being on the other side of the connection, able to decipher a picture (which uses distorted numbers and letters that optical recognition software would presumably struggle to recognize), and verify that he or she has received the message, understood its contents, and sent a reply to verify his or her identity. All new senders who try to e-mail service users go through this process, unless the user manually adds the new sender's e-mail address to a white list in advance.

Managing senders in Spamarrest requires working with the Senders tab on the member site Web page. By default, this shows the member's list of authorized senders (his or her white list). But this interface also provides access to a number of other lists, as shown in the left-hand pane in Figure 9-2. Entries there include the following items (Authorized Senders doesn't appear here because it's already showing, so to speak):

- **Blocked Senders** — This is the black list for sender addresses. Any mail received from these senders is deleted automatically.
- **Mailing Lists** — Mailing lists often use consistent To: (recipient) addresses but dynamically generated From: (sender) addresses. This list lets you identify white mailing lists you've signed up for that use this approach, so you can approve their receipt when they arrive in your inbox.
- **Blocked Mailing Lists** — Works the same as the preceding item, except it identifies black mailing lists from which messages will be deleted upon receipt.
- **Authorized Domains** — Lets you accept e-mail from any sender within a specific domain (the right-hand side of a typical Internet e-mail address, so that adding wiley.com to this list would permit all messages with sender e-mail addresses of the form *name*@wiley.com to get through, no matter what *name* might actually be).
- **Blocked Domains** — Works the same as the preceding item, except it identifies black list domains from which all messages will be deleted upon receipt.
- **Import** — Lets you incorporate specially formatted text files containing e-mail addresses to help populate your authorized or blocked senders lists.
- **Export** — Lets you extract specially formatted text files containing e-mail addresses from your Spamarrest white and black lists.
- **Address Book** — Lets you create and manage an address book of your own inside Spamarrest (for those who read e-mail in another application like Outlook, this isn't terribly useful; for those who use Spamarrest as their primary e-mail interface, it's very helpful).

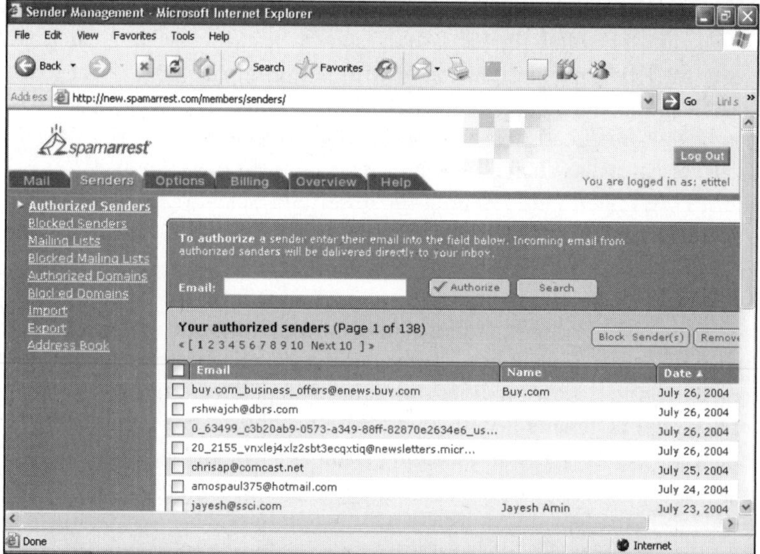

Figure 9-2: The Spamarrest Senders tab provides access to various types of white and black lists.

Spam screening services also report how much they're filtering and how much presumably desirable e-mail is getting through. I've been using Spamarrest for just over a year as I write this chapter, and it's handled over 160,000 e-mail messages, of which nearly 25,000 messages have been forwarded to my inbox. That's about 15 percent, which indicates that the Brightmail statistics notwithstanding, my personal spam-to-desirable-mail ratio is more like 6 or 7 to 1, rather than the 3 to 1 they report. Ouch!

Spam Screening and Filtering Software

As with spam screening services — which typically run remotely on a mail server somewhere — spam screening and filtering software — which typically runs on your PC (though some packages also have an external service component as well) — also come in two primary forms:

- **Standalone programs that insert themselves between the server where you pick up your incoming mail, and the client software you use to read that mail.** Thus, when you tell your client to download e-mail, hooks built into the other software tell your e-mail client to have it download e-mail instead, so it can screen and filter before depositing what's left over into your inbox.
- **E-mail client plug-ins that build themselves directly into whatever program you're already using to read e-mail.** Because Outlook and Outlook Express are by far the most popular e-mail clients in use on Windows PCs, you'll find that most such software works with both programs (but not always when those programs get their e-mail from an Exchange server, Microsoft's e-mail server platform, so be sure to check out your situation before settling on any product choices).

In most cases, interacting with the spam blocking software (be it standalone or plug-in) simply means identifying spam that does make it through the filter, so the software can learn what it can from your identifications and take over the job for you as it learns more about your notions of what's spam and what's not. Some spam blocking software also takes advantage of community intelligence in its workings as well, so that it can benefit from statistical analysis of what the entire user base thinks is (and isn't) spam, as well as whatever particular choices or selections you might make yourself.

Let's look at what working with high-rated Outlook plug-in Norton AntiSpam looks like, to get a sense of how this software works. Norton AntiSpam provides three kinds of spam controls:

- A security slider general control that offers three settings: Low, Medium, and High. By default, the software is set at Medium, which applies moderate filtering (including use of user-created and managed white and black lists), identifies most spam as such, and generates few false positives. By contrast, Low provides only a little predefined filtering, and doesn't identify spam as well, but generates virtually no false positives. The High setting aggressively blocks spam, identifies nearly all incoming spam as such, and generates the highest level of false positives. I was entirely comfortable with the default setting during my testing. The General tab in the Norton AntiSpam window proffers this slider control, as shown in Figure 9-3.

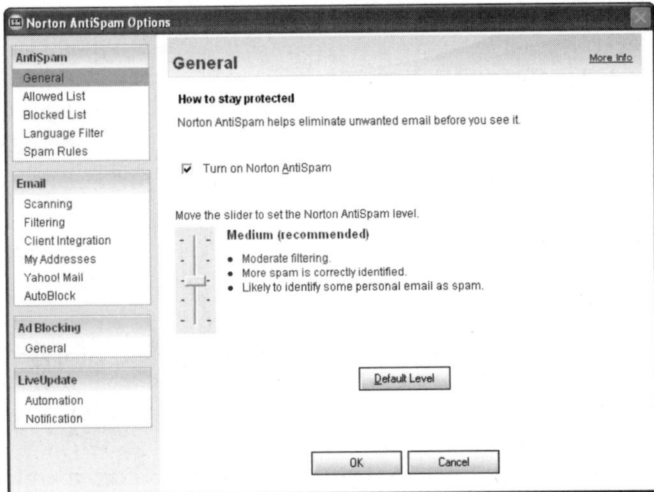

Figure 9-3: The General tab in Norton AntiSpam lets you manage spam-like security zones in Internet Explorer.

- Two additional entries in Norton AntiSpam are labeled Allowed List and Blocked List (you can see them at the top of the AntiSpam list on the upper left in Figure 9-3 as well). These provide white and black list capabilities for Internet e-mail addresses (though they must take complete address form as *name@domain.ext*). You can also import addresses from your Outlook or Outlook Express address book to seed your Allowed List in Norton AntiSpam, which is a handy feature.

- The Spam Rules pane is where you can design your own rule-based spam checks to screen incoming e-mail. This display is shown in Figure 9-4. Using this tool requires stepping through four stages when defining a new rule, but you can also use it to edit or delete existing rules, and to place rules in priority order (rules at the top are enforced first, those at the bottom last; important rules should be at or near the top of this list). Creating a new rule is covered in the step-by-step sequence that follows next. What results from such efforts, however, is a set of rules that you can use to classify incoming mail as spam. They're simple, powerful, and easier to understand and use than the rules facility built into Outlook itself.

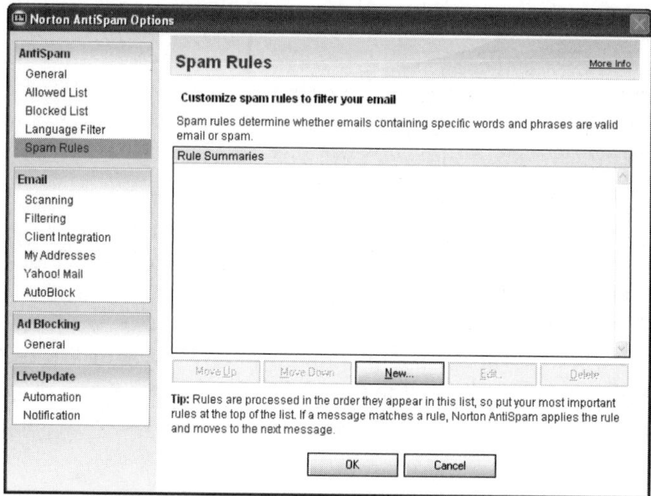

Figure 9-4: The Spam Rules pane is where you can create new or edit, delete, or prioritize existing spam rules.

1. Click the New button to start defining a new rule, and open a Custom Spam Rule window, as shown in Figure 9-5. This is where you can define key words or phrases that the rule can use to identify spam. I picked the name of a popular prescription drug often hawked on the Internet, as also shown in Figure 9-5. Note that spelling "smarts" in Norton AntiSpam means that by typing in a word or phrase, you also cover alternate spellings, uses of upper- and lowercase, insertion of punctuation marks, and other techniques spammers use to try to slip past pattern recognition routines. This one's pretty slick, as far as such things go.

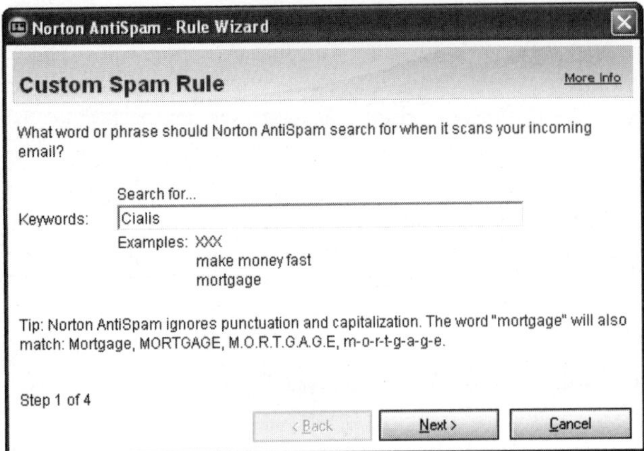

Figure 9-5: In Step 1, you enter one or more keywords or key phrases to tell the rule what to look for.

2. Click the Next button to proceed. This calls up Step 2, where you instruct the spam rule in what part of the message to seek the search string. Your options include the entire message (header and body), the sender (from) or receiver (recipient), the subject line, or the message body. It's a good idea to be as specific as possible here, because a more narrowly scoped search will also complete more quickly. In Figure 9-6 I selected the subject line by clicking the radio button to its left, because that's where drug names often show up in pharmaceutical spam.

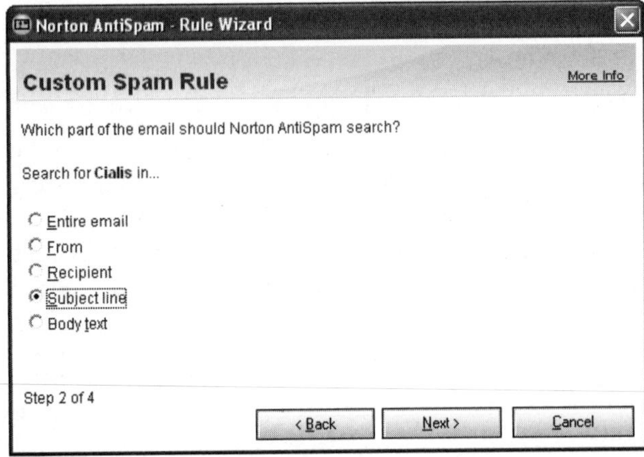

Figure 9-6: Step 2 tells the rule where in the message the search string should be sought.

3. Click the Next button to proceed to the screen shown in Figure 9-7. Step 3 is where you identify the rule as one that identifies spam (the default) or desirable e-mail (not spam). Click the right radio button — or in this case, nothing, because the default is just what we want.

Figure 9-7: Step 3 indicates if the rule identifies spam or desirable e-mail.

4. Click Next to proceed to Step 4. Here (see Figure 9-8) you see the rule restated in text form: "Search for **Cialis** in **subject line**. Classify matching messages as **spam**." where key terms are emphasized in blue on screen (bolded here). Click Finish and you've created a spam rule.

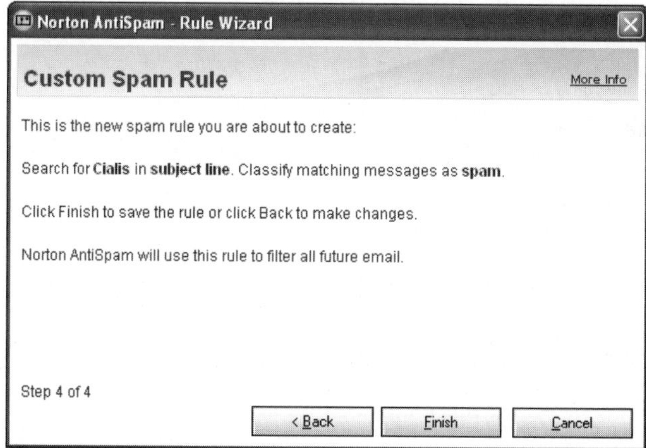

Figure 9-8: Step 4 restates the rule for final review in text form so it can be saved or edited as needed.

As you see and are able to identify more kinds of spam, you'll get pretty adept at creating rules to help you block it off. I find this capability especially useful for those messages where the sender identity changes with each instance, but all have identical subject lines. This can kill them all in a single blow!

Working with Rules in Outlook

Like Norton AntiSpam, Outlook has a Rules Wizard you can use to define rules for recognizing and handling spam. Unlike Norton AntiSpam, the rules in Outlook are more far-reaching and general in purpose, so that they can also be used for all kinds of other tasks besides handling spam. As I step through what's involved in defining rules in Outlook, you'll get a pretty good sense that this has its upside and its downside. As a last resort, it's certainly workable, but with other more efficient tools, you can build, test, and use rules much more quickly and easily. Here's a step-by-step hike into Outlook, where I define a rule that recognizes e-mail messages with a specific drug name in the subject line and then deletes that message:

1. To access the Rules Wizard shown in Figure 9-9, open Outlook, click the Tools menu entry, and select Rules and Alerts from the pop-up menu that results. If the E-mail Rules tab isn't selected, click it. Then click the New Rule entry at the far left to open the Rules Wizard.

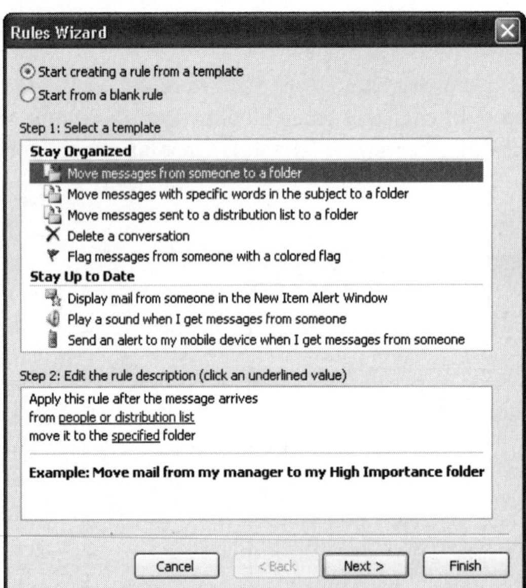

Figure 9-9: The Outlook Rules Wizard lets you start from a predefined template or create a new rule from scratch.

Note

The Rules Wizard gives you two radio buttons at the top of the window: one to create a rule from a predefined template (this is selected by default), the other to start from a blank rule (which means creating a new rule from scratch). Unfortunately, the predefined templates included with Outlook don't address spam issues, so you'll need to create spam rules starting from a blank rule.

2. Click the radio button to the left of the line that reads "Start from a blank rule" near the top of the Window (see Figure 9-10). Note that by default the Step 1 entry that reads "Check messages when they arrive" is highlighted. That's good, because that's what you want anyway when checking incoming messages. Click the Next button.

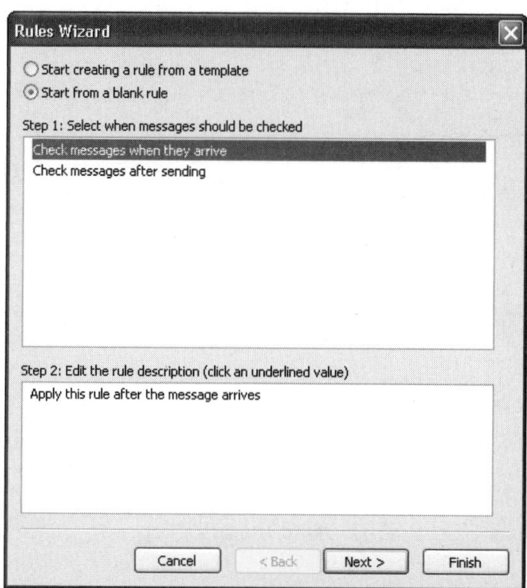

Figure 9-10: The template references disappear when you click the "Start from a blank rule" radio button.

3. Next, you must select the condition or conditions that trigger the rule. Click the check box to the left of the line that reads "with specific words in the subject" and then click the underlined text (specific words) in the lower pane and type the word ***levitra***. Click the Add button, and then click OK. This produces the information shown in Figure 9-11 and shows how you convert a general condition (shown in the upper pane) to a specific condition (shown in the lower pane). Click Next to proceed.

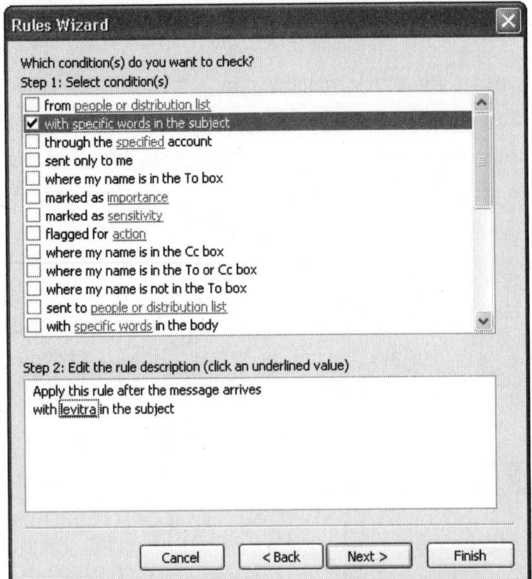

Figure 9-11: When you pick a specific word in the subject, the rule applies to any message whose subject line includes a match.

4. Having defined how to identify a message that meets a condition for being flagged as spam — though this is neither implicit nor explicit in the definition, as it was with Norton AntiSpam — you must do something with it. In this case, there are three different ways to delete a file. The most irreversible is to delete it permanently. Otherwise, moving it into the Deleted Items folder is the same thing as deleting the message. My selection requires that I also go down to the lower pane and select the Deleted Items folder from a pick list that appears there when I click the underlined word specified, and produces the rule shown in the lower pane in Figure 9-12. Click Next to move on to the next step.

Tip

Another less dangerous strategy might be to create a new folder named "Spam" or "Suspect Spam" and target that folder in your rule instead. That way, you'd always have the option of digging into the Spam or Suspect Spam folder later, without having to remember which items you deleted and which wound up in the Deleted Items folder because of a rule. Most anti-spam software packages take this more conservative approach, but also provide commands to empty the Spam folder with a couple of clicks (one to command, another to confirm the command).

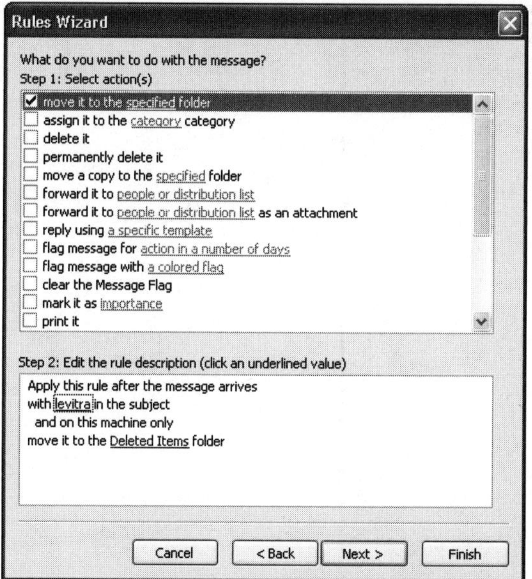

Figure 9-12: Given three ways to delete the identified spam, I do so by moving it into the Deleted Items folder.

5. As shown in Figure 9-13, you're presented with some rule controls that let you name the rule, manage options for its application and use, and give you one last chance to look things over before creating exceptions to its application. In this case, all the defaults work nicely (as depicted in Figure 9-13), so you can click the Finish button to complete the definition for this rule, before moving on to state any applicable exceptions.

6. There's one last step to traverse before the rule is completed, as shown in Figure 9-14. Here, you have the option of defining exceptions to your rule, based on a wide range of exceptions that include sender information, other message text, specific recipient information, and so forth. In this case, you don't need any exceptions — though you may want to scroll through the whole list to get a complete sense of the full range of options available (you may need them someday) — so you can click Finish again to complete the process.

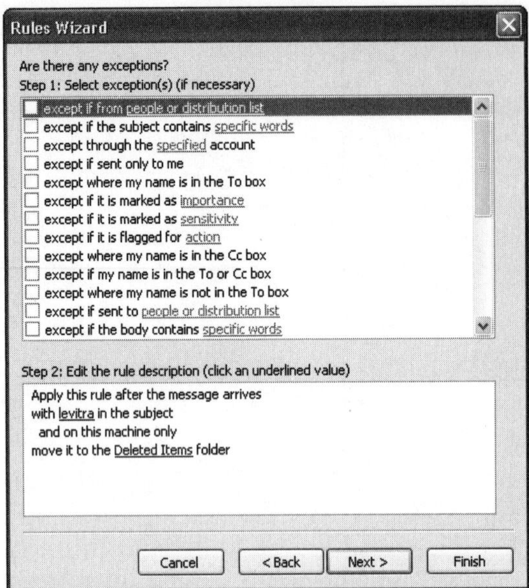

Figure 9-13: You have one last chance to review your rule before adding it to your rule set.

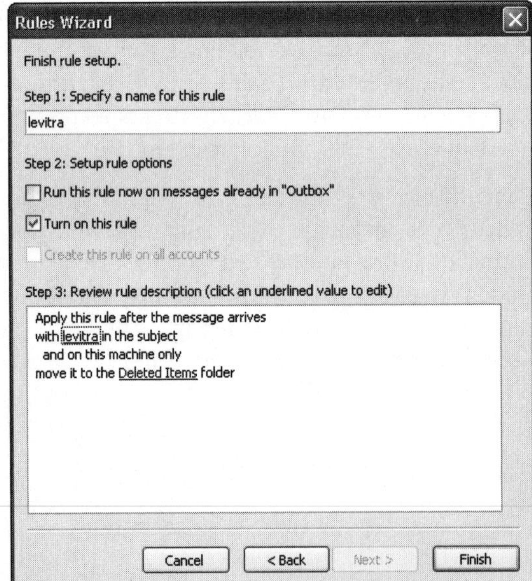

Figure 9-14: Once the rule is finalized, you're allowed to select from a large list of possible exceptions.

7. The finished rule appears in your list of defined rules (in fact, it's the only rule defined in Figure 9-15) as you return to the Rules and Alerts window. From here you can click OK to close out, create another new rule, edit or delete your sole existing rule, and so forth.

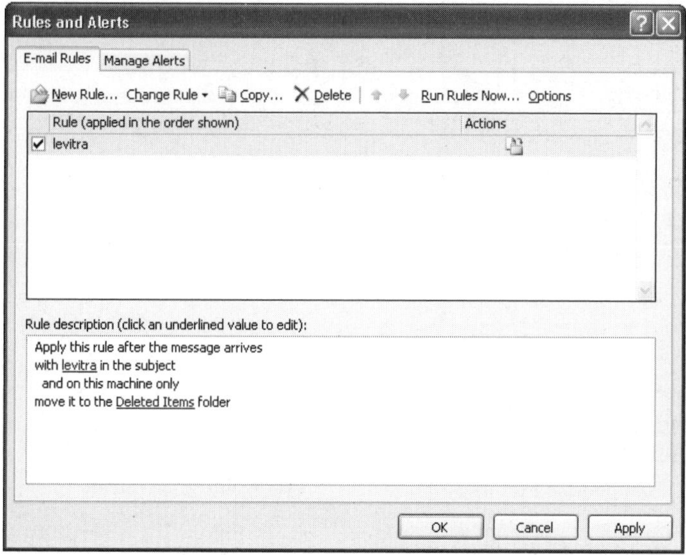

Figure 9-15: When the rule is truly finished it appears in the Rules list in the Rules and Alerts window.

Notice that what took four or five steps in Norton AntiSpam took seven in Outlook, not counting subsidiary text entry widgets you had to interact with along the way. Although the Outlook Rules Wizard can do the job, I think this walkthrough makes an excellent case for why a specialized tool is better for a specific job, even though a general tool that can do the job might be more capable and powerful (as indeed the Outlook Rules Wizard is).

What's New in Outlook 2003 SP1?

As I was writing this book, Microsoft released Service Pack 1 (SP1) for Outlook 2003. Though it didn't change the Rules Wizard any, it did add some significant functionality to help manage e-mail messages, including spam. This is best represented in the new look of the Junk E-mail tool once SP1 is installed. A quick peek at the tabs on the Junk E-mail Options window tells the story (access this window by clicking Actions→Junk E-mail→Junk E-mail Options), as shown in Figure 9-16.

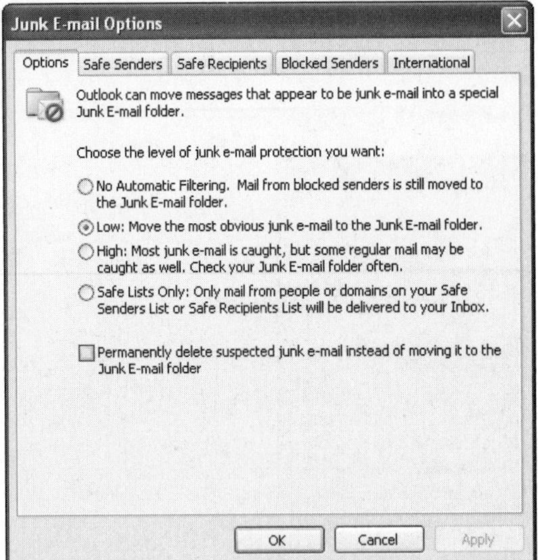

Figure 9-16: The Junk E-mail Options shows you can manage senders, recipients, and international traffic in various ways.

The Options tab showing in Figure 9-16 is where you set the level of junk e-mail protection for Outlook. By default, it tackles only obvious junk e-mail and moves it into a Junk E-mail folder. But you can elect to turn off automatic filtering — a major functionality addition to Outlook 2003 SP1 — for the lowest level of protection, if you so choose. Higher levels of protection turn up the filtering intensity, but require some occasional checking of the Junk E-mail folder to haul out false positives. The most extreme level of protection is to require you to define white lists for both senders and recipients, and to accept incoming e-mail only from the combined membership of both lists (in other words, you accept incoming e-mail only from those to whom you send e-mail, or from whom you're willing to receive e-mail).

The Safe Senders and Safe Recipients tabs control access to windows where you can add entries manually to your heart's content, import or export such data from or to files (handy if you also use an anti-spam service like Spamarrest), and indicate if people in your address book (the Contacts folder in Outlook terminology) are also trusted or not. Blocked Senders lets you establish and manage your own personal black list, and also includes file import/export capabilities. The International tab meets a need I've long felt for e-mail handling. First, it lets you block e-mail from top-level domains (which basically means the end of the sender's domain name and lets you stop traffic wholesale from certain countries if you like — such as `.ru` for the Russian Federation, `.ro` for Romania, and `.kr` for Korea). Second (and this is where my wish is answered), it lets you block incoming e-mails by the language encodings they use. Thus if you can't (or don't want to) read Korean, Chinese, Thai, or whatever other languages you might find yourself being asked to load character encodings for, you can block them right here very easily.

If you work with other anti-spam services, anti-spam software, or rules definition facilities in other e-mail packages, you'll quickly observe that while the details of their operation may differ, the basic principles of operation and use are pretty much the same. Thus, what I've shown for these various

categories of tools and facilities is pretty representative of each class, including the various additional members in the software and service categories I present in the next section of this chapter.

The Sum Is Greater Than the Individual Parts

In fact, the combination of multiple tools that work together often provides more (and easier) functionality than either tool can alone. For example, with Norton AntiSpam installed on a PC running Outlook, identifying spam is as easy as highlighting a message in your inbox and then clicking the This is Spam button in your NAS toolbar. As shown in Figure 9-17, this produces a confirmation window that asks you to verify that you do indeed want to add the sender to the blocked list. A simple yes or no suffices to do the deed. Likewise, you can open the Norton AntiSpam Folder, highlight any message therein, and then click the This is not Spam button to remove the sender from your blocked item list. This represents good integration between the two packages, even though you must still use the Rules and Alerts Rules Wizard to define spam rules for Outlook, or open NAS to use its Spam Rules separately.

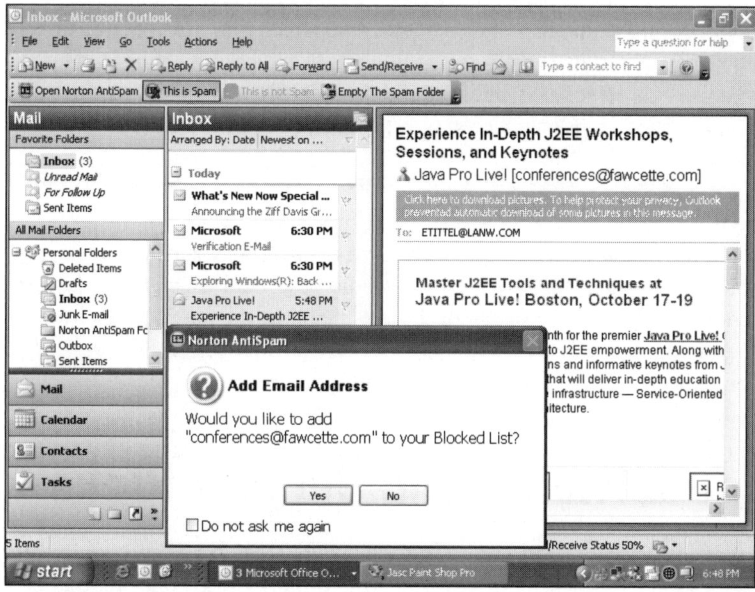

Figure 9-17: NAS highlights selected button actions in orange to show you what you're doing, then prompts you for decisions with pop-up windows.

If in a Lather, Switch, Don't Fight!

This book's technical editor, Mark Justice Hinton, observed that the complexity of working with anti-spam plug-ins and rules in Outlook drove him to distraction, and then to consider other alternatives. Just as you can find browsers to replace or supplement Internet Explorer, so also can you do for e-mail client software. The Mozilla Organization's Thunderbird e-mail client (`www.mozilla.org/products/thunderbird/`) gets uniformly high marks for its great built-in anti-spam capabilities, and for its ease of everyday customization and use.

If You Make The Rules, Can You Still Win the Game?

One thing that Outlook can do with rules that many anti-spam packages cannot is to import and export them. Originally designed to let users import rules developed in earlier versions of Outlook into newer versions following an upgrade, this capability also lets users import rules that others build on their behalf — including comprehensive collections of spam blocks and filters. At least two anti-spam products I know of use this approach to provide comprehensive, complex sets of rules, regularly updated, to help users stay ahead of spam: Flow Ruler (`www.flowruler.com`) is a shareware inbox organizer that includes spam blocker capabilities, and spamXpress (`www.spamxpress.com`) is an Outlook plug-in built around the mail rules engine accessed through the Rules and Alerts facility introduced earlier in this section.

This also raises the possibility of finding sources for predefined Outlook files (which end in an extension of `.rwz`) on the Web. These can be downloaded and imported into your Outlook, but should come only from reliable sources. Also, some testing of imported rules is necessary because Outlook uses nicknames that may or may not transfer successfully from the computer where they were defined and from which they were exported to the computer onto which they are imported to be used. Proceed with caution when importing Outlook rules (products like the two mentioned in the previous paragraph don't fall under this admonition, because they're designed and tested to work following the export-import cycle, or are programmatically re-created on your machine during the install process).

If you find yourself frustrated by following well-beaten tracks to controlling spam, you may want to try something different as well. Others also swear by alternative e-mail clients like Eudora (`www.eudora.com`) and Opera (`www.opera.com`), as well. In fact, many of the alternative browsers (FireFox, Mozilla, Netscape, and more) include e-mail clients as part of their offerings. These, too, can be worth checking out for those with a hankering for something different.

Top Anti-Spam Software and Service Picks

By scouring the Web and various publications I've put together a small collection of anti-spam software and anti-spam service offerings, along with a highly ranked and highly rated offering that can only be characterized as a hybrid, since it requires users to install an Outlook plug-in on their PCs, but also communicates over the Internet with the vendor's continuously updated spam database. All of these items are presented in Table 9-1, and include brief descriptions, along with name, type, and URL information.

Before you look at Table 9-1, perhaps some explanation of its terminology will be helpful. In that table, Type can take three values:

- SW — This indicates a software-based antispam package that operates on the user's desktop, either as a plug-in to his or her e-mail package, or as an intermediary program.

- **hybrid**—An offering that combines a client-side piece (in this case, an e-mail client plug-in) combined with Internet access to the vendor's continuously updated spam definitions, plus various white and black lists.
- **Svc**—A spam filtering and blocking service that operates remotely, either on the user's mailbox (denoted "(v)" in Table 9-1) or by redirecting mail to the service provider's server, where it is screened upon arrival (denoted "(r)" in Table 9-1).

In the Description field of Table 9-1, a rules-based approach means using word or phrase recognition techniques against e-mail messages in whole or in part. List-based means using various types of white and black lists to retain or remove e-mail from an inbox. The phrase *verifies users* means that the package or service automatically generates e-mail from unverified senders to attempt to verify their identities and prove they're not spammers. Note also that most anti-spam software and services include annual service or subscription fees, so that one-time purchase of anti-spam software does not mean no further outlays will be required (for most such products, annual fees or upgrades will be the norm, not the exception—this is sensible, because of vendor's ongoing costs to update rules databases and maintain white and black lists).

Table 9-1 Top-Rated Anti-Spam Software, Services, and Hybrid Offerings

Name	*Type*	*Cost*	*Description*	*URL*
Norton AntiSpam 2004	SW	$39.95*	Rules- and List-based	`www.symantec.com/antispam`
Spam Inspector 4.0@	SW	$29.95*^	Rules- and List-based	`www.giantcompany.com/`
Qurb 2.0	SW	$29.95	List-based, verifies users	`www.qurb.com`
Cloudmark SpamNet@	hybrid	$39.95+	Rules- and List-based	`www.cloudmark.com/`
Spamarrest@	Svc	$34.95#	List-based, verifies users (r)	`www.spamarrest.com`
SpamCop	Svc	$30.00	Rules- and List-based (r)	`http://mail.spamcop.net/individuals.php`
CleanMyMailbox	Svc	$30.00	Rules- and List-based (v)	`www.cleanmymailbox.com`

* Annual subscription fees also apply (first year of subscription services is free)

@ Works with POP3 e-mail clients: Outlook, Outlook Express, Netscape, IncrediMail, and so on

^ Occasional promotional discounts are available (price was $19.95 on a limited-time basis as I wrote this chapter)

+ Cloudmark SpamNet costs $3.99 a month, or $39.95 a year

$19.95 for 6 months, $54.95 for 2 years

(r) Users redirect mail from ISP to anti-spam service provider

(v) Anti-spam service provider visits and cleans user's mailbox

Note

Check the "Resources" section at the end of this chapter for citations of reviews where you can find these products mentioned. You'll find detailed feature/function comparisons at both sites, and lots of other information as well. If you don't like the top picks presented here, expect no trouble finding alternatives!

Once you've picked an anti-spam package or plug-in for your PC, you'll find that installation is entirely mundane, if not anticlimactic. Choosing Norton AntiSpam (NAS) as an example, you'll find that installation involves at most three or four steps and usually takes less than a minute — with one exception: NAS will import your Outlook address book to help you get your white list going. When I elected to do this, the more than 800 entries in my address book added about 15 minutes to the installation time overall, probably because I elected to review each entry and approve or deny it manually (if you elected to import without reviewing, it would add less than 3 minutes to the installation time). Of course, working with the program over time is what gives it most of its value, so installation represents a minuscule fraction of the time that you'll spend with such software if you want to make the most of its capabilities.

Checking Your Work

When it comes to checking spam blocking or filtering effectiveness, I couldn't find any online checks or services that rated the cleanliness of e-mail inboxes after filtering or blocking was applied. But since deciding what's spam (and what's not) is mostly in the eye of the e-mail recipient, it's really up to you to decide if your current spam-handling methods are working or not. If you're bound and determined to check things empirically, you could always harvest spam from your inbox, send it to a friend to help her check her setup, and then turn things around and have her help you check yours. But the real key here, as the rest of this discussion sets out, lies in answering the question "How much time do I (or must I) spend dealing with spam?" to your satisfaction.

The key is to track the time and effort you must spend in dealing with spam on a daily basis. If you are spending more than 10 minutes a day on such activities, it might be cost-justifiable to try other alternatives or options. Thus, checking your work in this case is a matter of gauging how satisfied you are with your current arrangements, and making changes if and when your frustration level, or your time expended, exceeds some threshold that only you can set.

Using Multiple Spam Blockers

This is a section that occurs in each chapter in Part III of this book; it addresses the question of running more than one program of the same type on a single PC. Since this is the anti-spam chapter, I answer the question: "Should you run more than one anti-spam program or service at the same time on a single PC?"

As the preceding text in this chapter indicates, it's definitely okay (but more expensive) to combine an anti-spam service with anti-spam software on your PC. Since the former runs on somebody else's server and manipulates your e-mail before you download it your client, there's really no opportunity for interference anyway.

But if you find yourself pondering the use of multiple services or multiple software packages, my advice is don't do it! While it's almost always possible to recover false positives from any service or software that misidentifies spam, this is a case where time and expense argues against using multiple instances of the same type of anti-spam technology. On the service side, you'd be doubling your costs (or close to it, anyway) without necessarily realizing substantial additional benefits. On the client side — that is, on your PC — you'd be lengthening delays involved in performing screening, and raising the old issue of primacy (which anti-spam package goes first, and which one second) when two programs or plug-ins are essentially trying to do the same job.

That said, it's still okay to use rules from your e-mail client software to filter e-mail that arrives in your inbox after all other filtering or blocking has been applied. I described this earlier as your last line of defense, and indeed, that's what it is! If you're lucky, it won't be necessary to use this capability very often, but if the occasional bit of spam shows up in your inbox and you can't figure out how to block it further up the line of safeguards you've put in place (whatever they may be) you can always define a rule to block it inside your e-mail package.

Resources

Brightmail (`www.brightmail.com`) maintains regular trends and statistics about the spam it handles on behalf of its large customer base (it routinely screens hundreds of billions of e-mail messages monthly). Its Web site is a valuable source of information. The only reason I don't mention its excellent products and services in this chapter is because its business focus in on enterprises and service providers; it doesn't cater to individual e-mail users.

If you want to learn more about reading and understanding RFC (2)822 e-mail headers, but don't necessarily want to dig deeply into the RFCs, you may find other resources easier to approach and appreciate. I've found these two online items to be particularly informative in explaining how to look for evidence of spam in an e-mail header: StopSpam's "Reading EMail Headers: All About Email Headers" (`www.stopspam.org/email/headers.html`) and a Charter Communications FAQ by Andy Olds entitled "Understanding E-mail message headers" (`http://swins.com/support/online/faqs/email_headers.html`).

Tom Pisello, writing for SearchSmallBizIT.com, did a very nice analysis of the costs of spam entitled "The ROI for anti-spam initiatives" (it actually looks at how much money anti-spam efforts can save, but in the process of doing so also explains how much spam costs as well). It's an interesting analysis and includes some different general industry stats from those reported by Brightmail and me (`http://searchsmallbizit.techtarget.com/columnItem/0,294698,sid44_gci991440,00.html?track=NL-118&ad=487443&Offer=smb728`).

Lots of organizations are focused on spam, including efforts to educate e-mail users on how to avoid or deal with spam, to promote legislation to help reduce spam, to report on spam costs and techniques, and much more. Of that multitude, I think two are worth a visit. First, there's the Coalitions Against Unsolicited Commercial E-mail, or CAUCE (`www.cauce.org`); of particular interest is its Resources page (`www.cauce.org/about/resources.shtml`). Second, there's EmailAbuse (`www.emailabuse.org`), which provides news and information about spam, and also provides pointers to all kinds of other great anti-spam resources.

Comparative product reviews on anti-spam products are widely available, but I turned to my "usual sources" for their insights and information in this chapter, as I've done in other chapters. My primary informants included TopTenReviews "Spam Filter Review" (www.spamfilterreview.com/), plus a nicely interlinked collection of items from *PC Magazine* constructed around Cade Metz's "Spam Blockers" story and numerous reviews of software packages of various types, with links to other Editor's Choice items from previous issues as well (February 17, 2004; www.pcmag.com/article2/0,1759,1615479,00.asp). See also Lance Ulanoff's article "Spam: A Reality Check" from the February 18, 2004, issue of *PC Magazine* for an interesting and thought-provoking discussion of anti-spam legislation and its ability to deal with the problem, or lack thereof (www.pcmag.com/article2/0,1759,1529243,00.asp).

More information about top-level domains or country codes like the ones mentioned in the discussion of the Outlook Junk E-mail Options controls is available through the Internet Assigned Numbers Authority (IANA). Check out its Root-Zone Whois Information (Index by TLD Code) Web page at www.iana.org/cctld/cctld-whois.htm.

Summary

This chapter looked at spam as a form of unwanted e-mail, and as a kind of general scourge of the Internet. In terms of unwanted content with significant impact, I described how spam occupies the undesirable spot at the top of this particular heap, both in terms of bandwidth consumed and human productivity wasted in carrying it and dealing with it, respectively. I also discussed four different opportunities that exist to screen, block, or filter spam: at any e-mail server where mail is forwarded from sender to receiver (but most importantly for you, at your ISP's e-mail server); through an Internet-based service that inspects and filters your incoming e-mail before you download it from your inbox; using local software on your PC to inspect and filter incoming e-mail on its way to your inbox; and rules to inspect and screen e-mail once it arrives in your inbox, courtesy of whatever e-mail client you're using to read that e-mail. I also toured the services and software (or rules facilities) that you can use, to show how they work and help to eliminate unwanted e-mail from your inbox, and presented a number of top picks in all these categories to help you make the most of every opportunity to reduce the spam that you must see and delete.

This also concludes Part III of this book, which looked at tools and techniques for dealing with all kinds of unwanted content and software on your PC. In the next part (and chapter) of this book, I change gears to discuss best practices when accessing or using the Internet. In fact, Chapter 10 maintains the focus of this chapter, but switches its viewpoint to talk about best practices for dealing with Internet e-mail — and spam of all kinds — as you go about your daily rounds and activities.

Part IV

Commonsense Rules for Safe Computing

IN THIS PART:

Part IV switches gears from tools and their application to rules and techniques, but with the same ultimate goal in mind: to help you avoid or bypass trouble, rather than falling into it. Here, you tackle two of the most common forms of online interaction or activity — namely, e-mail and Web surfing — and discover best practices to keep your PC safe and sound.

Chapter 10

Practicing E-mail Safety

Of all the potential sources of danger on the Internet, none is more obvious nor omnipresent than spam. Finding unwanted e-mail in one's inbox is an everyday occurrence, and something that anyone who uses the Internet should anticipate. This chapter stresses some important techniques for avoiding trouble. I also try my best to help you identify various tip-offs and other telltales that might help you separate e-mail you could and perhaps even should examine on your PC, from e-mail that you should (and perhaps must) delete as soon as it shows up in your inbox. Of course, if you're lucky, your anti-spam screening service or software or your e-mail software's spam screening tools will strip out the unwanted stuff before you even know it's there.

But even if anti-spam measures deliver the 98 to 99 percent spam diminution that many of them claim, that still leaves at least a handful or two of spam that slips through even the best nets designed to catch such stuff. Although I hope you don't have to apply what I cover here to too many test cases every day, I do seek to provide you with tips and techniques you can use to avoid trouble whenever possible, and to deal with spam safely and gingerly when it stares you in the face.

Never Open Unexpected Attachments

As I've said so many times already, if you can follow only one rule where e-mail is concerned, the title of this section of the chapter is the one to get behind 110 percent. That's because e-mail attachments are the most likely vehicles in which trouble will arrive on your desktop. Indeed, if you have a good anti-virus solution in place, it should detect and block any infected attachments that show up. Or at least, your anti-virus software will move infected and suspect attachments into a special storage area on your hard disk known as "quarantine"—I urge you not to venture into these precincts unless acting under instructions from an anti-virus provider to get something they want you to send them for further study.

Sender Spoofing

Be careful. A growing number of worms use a technique called "sender spoofing" whereby they harvest e-mail names from address books, Web pages, or other locations on an infected machine, then use those names in the From field in e-mails they send out in answer to their blind urge to propagate.

The next time you see an e-mail from your mother or your sister with the subject line "A great recipe for you to try" ask yourself these questions:

- Who really sent this message?
- Has sis ever sent me anything like this before?
- Does mom even know how to attach a document to an e-mail message?
- Am I expecting something like this?

Unless you talked to her on the phone yesterday and were promised an e-mail with recipe attached, you'd better proceed cautiously. In fact, other questions you should also answer include:

- Why send a recipe as an attachment (why not in the message body)?
- What type of file is that attachment? How big is it?

If it's an executable file or a ZIP, or it's more than 10K in length, tread even more carefully. You may just want to call and ask: "Did you e-mail me a recipe as an attachment recently?" Chances are depressingly high that the answer will come back "Why no, I didn't." Trash that attachment! You don't even want to know what's lurking inside!

Some people go so far as to turn off attachments in their e-mail packages to avoid any chance of something wicked piggybacking its way into their systems. Instead, they let friends and colleagues know that if they want to send a file, special arrangements will be necessary. This might mean using some kind of file transfer application instead or perhaps sharing a confidential (and preferably Web-based) second e-mail account specifically for accepting e-mail with attachments. If you've got friends or family who appear to have trouble resisting the urge to open any and all attachments that show up in their inboxes, you might want to share this admonition with them.

Benefits of Web-Based E-mail

As I informed you in Chapter 9, Web-based e-mail provides an opportunity to probe the insides of e-mail messages in a safe place — that is, through a Web browser that's looking at a file on a server someplace else. This lets you poke around inside e-mail messages safely, where you can examine them, check their headers, look at attachment file names and types, and do some sleuthing of your own before allowing unexpected attachments anywhere near your desktop. Based on my experiences with Spamarrest, I observed that it would screen out most infected messages from unknown senders for me, but would cheerfully forward spoofed e-mail with sender addresses on one of my white lists. That's why it's a good idea to check your inbox remotely when you can, as well as to check messages from unverified or unknown senders. Sure, the latter category is more likely to be a source of infection, but with the right worm around, the former category's not safe either.

Setting up a second e-mail account at MSN, Yahoo!, Google, Hotmail, or some other low-cost or free service gives you a way to make sure unexpected attachments never show up at your primary account, and it gives you a failsafe if your primary account ever goes offline for any reason. It also gives you the opportunity to use a Web client to screen your messages, to help you decide if you'd like to use a service to screen your primary account as well.

That said, because e-mail message bodies can contain active content they can pose some problems to those who read them without proper precautions in place (security zone set for some level of script blocking on Internet sites, pop-up blocker armed and ready, add-on or BHO monitor running, and so forth). In other words, even Web-based e-mail isn't completely safe, but it's definitely going to help you keep e-mail attachments at arm's length, so you can decide which ones merit downloading to your PC.

Blocking Attachments in Outlook

This requires some thinking on your part, to decide what kinds of files you don't want arriving in your inbox. Because there's no master switch in Outlook to permit you to disable all attachments in a single go, you'll want to check which extensions are turned off by default, then decide which ones you want to add. Here's how to check the default roster:

1. Launch Outlook, if the program isn't already open on your desktop. You can do this by choosing Start → All Programs → Microsoft Office and then Microsoft Outlook from the resulting pop-up menu. Or you can simply choose Start → Run, type `outlook.exe` in the Open dialog box, and then click the OK button.
2. Press F1, or click Help on the Menu bar, and then click Microsoft Office Outlook Help. The window shown in Figure 10-1 appears.

Figure 10-1: The Outlook Help facility holds the keys to documenting already blocked file types.

3. In the Search for dialog box in the Outlook Help pane in the upper-right portion of the display, type `block attachments`, and then click the green arrow to the right of the dialog box. When the search is complete, you'll see a display like that shown in Figure 10-2; click the item (third from the top) that reads "Attachment file types blocked by Outlook" (this is a list of all files blocked by default in Outlook 2003 SP1).

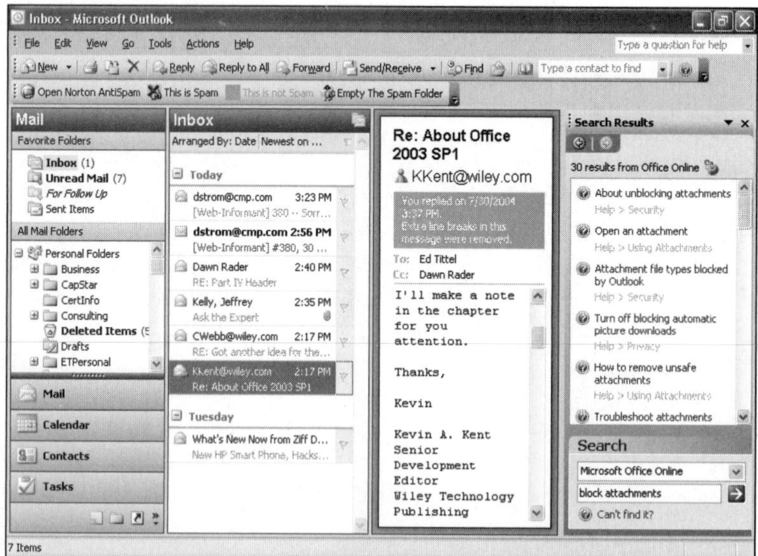

Figure 10-2: A whole list of topics appears in answer to the search string "block attachments."

4. A help window appears that lists all file types blocked by default in alphabetical order by file extension (see Figure 10-3). By no big surprise, this also matches the master list of executable and active content file types I mentioned in Chapter 2.

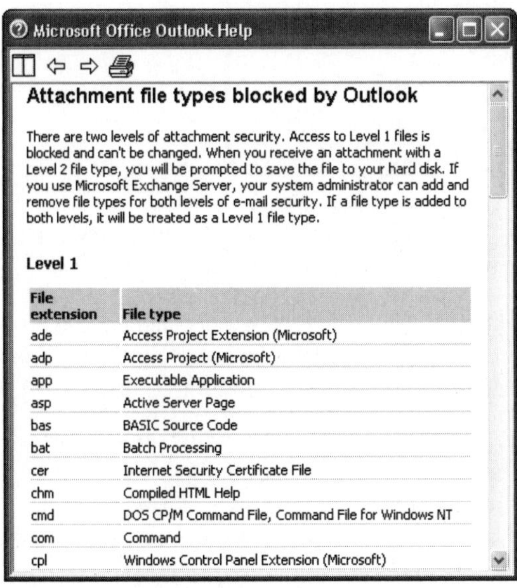

Microsoft Office Outlook Help

Attachment file types blocked by Outlook

There are two levels of attachment security. Access to Level 1 files is blocked and can't be changed. When you receive an attachment with a Level 2 file type, you will be prompted to save the file to your hard disk. If you use Microsoft Exchange Server, your system administrator can add and remove file types for both levels of e-mail security. If a file type is added to both levels, it will be treated as a Level 1 file type.

Level 1

File extension	File type
ade	Access Project Extension (Microsoft)
adp	Access Project (Microsoft)
app	Executable Application
asp	Active Server Page
bas	BASIC Source Code
bat	Batch Processing
cer	Internet Security Certificate File
chm	Compiled HTML Help
cmd	DOS CP/M Command File, Command File for Windows NT
com	Command
cpl	Windows Control Panel Extension (Microsoft)

Figure 10-3: A handy help file lists all file types that Outlook 2003 SP1 blocks by default.

After examining this list, you should have a pretty good idea of what's missing—namely, file types associated with common applications you probably use, or with common graphics formats. You can mark other file types in Outlook for special handling, but it requires editing the Windows registry. Here's a step-by-step set of instructions, subject as always to a warning to back up your registry before making changes (or at least creating a restore point so you can return to it later if something goes wrong; see the sidebar at the end of this section for instructions should you need them—for relevancy's sake I show you how to save the registry hive you'll be editing in the step-by-step that follows next):

1. Open the Registry Editor by choosing Start→Run, typing **`regedit.exe`** in the Open dialog box, and then clicking OK in the Run window.
2. Navigate to the following registry key (or use the Find command, F3, to jump straight to that entry) `HKCU\Software\Microsoft\Office\11.0\Outlook\Security` (`HKCU` is an abbreviation for `HKEY_CURRENT_USER`). This key is shown open, ready for editing in Figure 10-4.

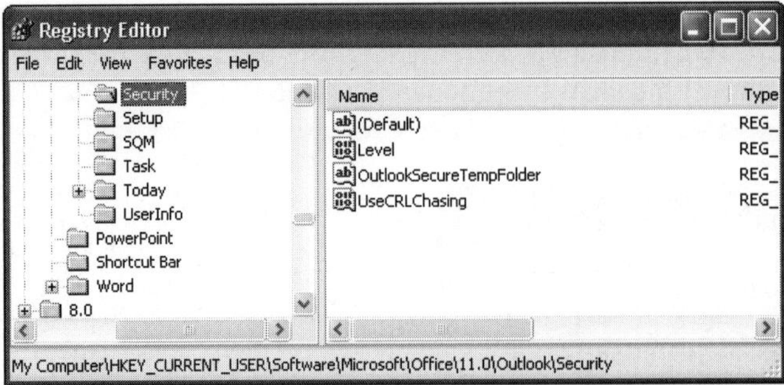

Figure 10-4: The . . .Outlook\Security key is where files can be blocked by type/extension, or marked for special handling.

3. Right-click the Security key in the left-hand pane, click New, and then choose String Value in the resulting pop-up menu. A string value labeled `New Value #1` appears in the bottom of the right-hand pane; type **`Level1Remove`** and press the Enter key.
4. Right-click the `Level1Remove` name, pick Modify from the resulting pop-up menu, and then type whatever file extensions you want to block, each beginning with a period, and separated by a semicolon, in the Value data textbox inside the Edit String Window. Figure 10-5 shows that I elected to handle a couple of bogus file types, `.kkk` and `.rpm` formats, purely as an example. You'd want to list whatever file types you want to force into special handling (for example, `doc;dot;rtf` would do a pretty good job of blocking most Word files) when using this for your own needs. Use of upper- or lowercase characters doesn't matter, but be sure to begin file extensions with periods and separate them using semicolons.

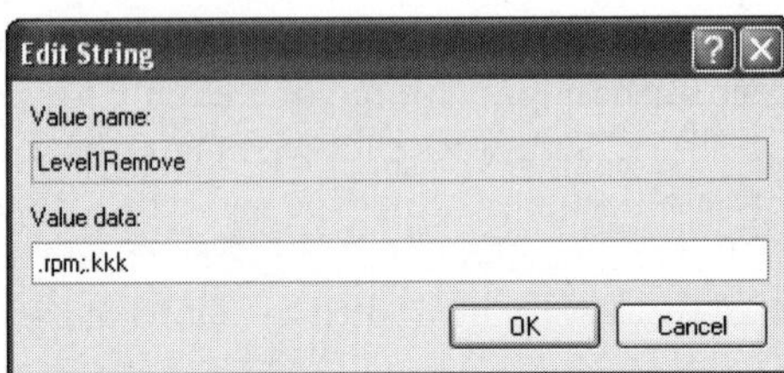

Figure 10-5: Create a string value named Level1Remove and then edit its contents to build a list of file extensions to mark for special handling, separated by semicolons.

If you check the list of file types in the Help file mentioned earlier in this section, you'll see that Microsoft has already handled most of the worrisome items for you. You can concentrate on those applications you use on your PC that may require special handling, or use it to add other extensions that aren't on the list likewise.

I hope you're asking the question by now "What does 'special handling' mean?" I'm glad you asked! If you try to open a file with an extension that's mentioned in the `Level1Remove` value list in Outlook, instead of opening the file immediately, you get a pop-up window with a security warning

that asks you to be sure that what you're opening is safe. In fact, it forces you to save it to disk, just to give anti-virus software another chance to check it over and stop it dead in its tracks.

Tip

If you don't like this approach to handling certain file types, you can follow the same recipe shown in the preceding step-by-step list using a string value named `Level1Add` instead of `Level1Remove`. This is a more draconian technique because it adds the values you supply to the list of attachment types that Outlook won't permit you to download to your machine. Thus, use this approach only if you're sure you won't ever need to receive such a file type by e-mail (or are willing to go back into the Registry Editor to remove that value from the `Level1Add` list, either temporarily or permanently).

Backing Up Registry Keys

In the preceding step-by-step instructions, you're asked to add a value to a key in the HKCU hive. To be as safe as possible when doing this sort of thing, you could back up that hive into a file before making the changes. Then should your changes cause problems, you could restore the contents of that file into the registry, thereby wiping out whatever caused those problems to occur. Here's how:

1. Open the Registry Editor (Start → Run, type `regedit` into the Open text field of the Run dialog box, and then click OK).
2. Right-click the hive key you want to back up (in this case that's HKEY_CURRENT_USER or HKCU).
3. Click the Export item in the resulting pop-up menu, as shown in the first sidebar figure.

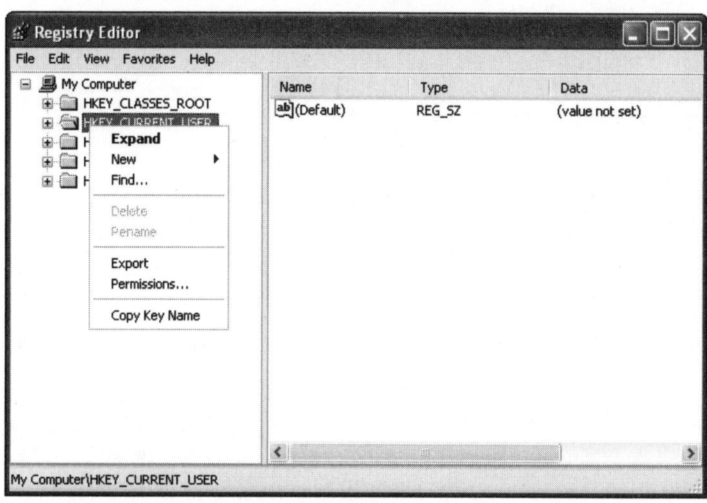

Exporting a hive key requires only that you right-click it in the left-hand pane and then pick Export from the pop-up menu.

Continued

Backing Up Registry Keys *(Continued)*

4. An Export Registry File window opens that prompts you to save the selected registry values (in this case an entire hive key, which this window identifies as a branch in the radio button selected on the lower left, as shown in the second sidebar figure). The save location defaults to My Documents, which is fine for demonstration purposes but may not be best for your needs. Notice the descriptive file name I used: `HKCU-bkup-040924` identifies the hive key, indicates it's a backup, and includes the date the snapshot occurred. You don't need to use this exactly, but it is a good idea to use names you can read and understand later.

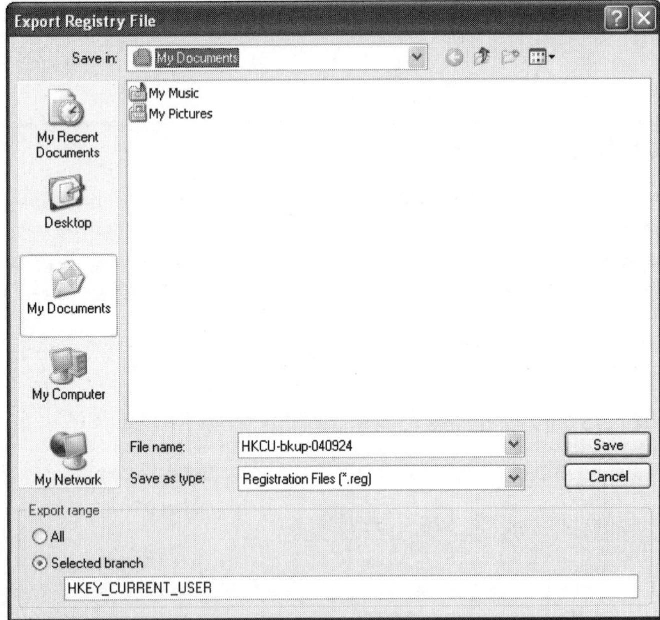

The Export Registry File window lets you specify a file name and a location for your saved registry contents.

That's what it takes to back up, or export in Registry Editor terminology, a registry hive key or branch. Here's what it takes to restore its contents to your registry, an operation that the Registry Editor identifies as an import:

1. Open the Registry Editor (Start→Run, type `regedit` into the Open text field of the Run dialog box, and then click OK).
2. Choose File→Import on the Registry Editor menu. This causes an Import Registry File window to open as shown in the following sidebar figure. By default, it opens to the My Documents folder for whoever's logged in, so there you see the exported file ready for import (that's why it makes a good demonstration). Select the `HKCU-bkup-040924.reg` file (or whatever you called yours) to target it for import.

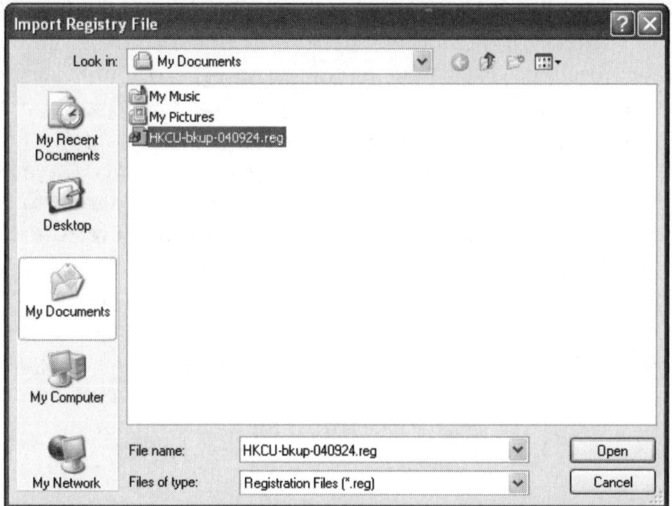

You must select the registry data file you want to import in the file selection area of the Import Registry File window.

3. Click the Open button at the lower right to perform the import operation. Watch closely! It's over in the blink of an eye.

Because you're replacing a part of the registry that's in use while you're running Windows, you may get an error message that states that not all keys could be replaced during the import operation. That's why it's essential to make sure Outlook is closed while you do this in this particular case (or whatever application or server closed, disabled, or shut down in the more general case) when you perform such operations. Otherwise, the changes you seek to undo may not take effect.

Other tools and techniques are available that you can use to back up and restore the registry. For that information check out Jerry Honeycutt's excellent book mentioned in the "Resources" section toward the end of this chapter or some of the other quality registry references available (these are cited in the "Resources" section of this and other chapters in this book).

Screen Your E-mail

When it comes to reducing total e-mail volume, nothing works like screening your e-mail. I don't care if you use a third-party service like Spamarrest or SpamCop, anti-spam software like Norton AntiSpam or Spam Inspector, or a hybrid solution like Cloudmark SpamNet—or something completely different of your own choosing. You can even rely on the updated spam blocking capabilities built into Outlook, if you like. The important thing is that you get some help and try to cut back on the volume of mail that you must inspect (and download) so you can concentrate on the messages you actually might want to read, and ignore those you don't want to see or read.

That said, I think it makes sense to try to block as much spam as possible before you ever download anything to your PC (and your e-mail inbox). To me, this argues eloquently in favor of hiring a

spam filtering service to do as much of this dirty work for you as possible. Though it is the case that local anti-spam software (or built-in e-mail client filters) can indeed block nearly all the spam you might receive, it's also true that this approach requires you to import that spam onto your PC before you toss it into the trash. I think it's a lot more efficient and effective to toss it out before you have to copy any messages from wherever you download your e-mail to your local machine.

With spam representing anywhere from 3 out of every 10 messages, to 13 out of every 20 messages, depending on whose statistics you believe, you're sure to save yourself some time and effort if you can avoid having to screen spam the old-fashioned way—namely, by looking it over yourself and manually separating the wheat from the chaff. According to my account information at Spamarrest, for example, I've received an average of more than 3,600 e-mail messages a day in the 391 days since I signed up for that service. On average, I've received only 59 or 60 desirable e-mails a day, and had to screen anywhere from 240 to as many as 600 unverified messages a day there (and some days, this seems like far too much)—but it's still less than 20 percent of what would have to be downloaded and screened manually, if a screening service weren't in the picture. Spam filtering is not a frill: it's an absolute necessity!

Recognizing Hoaxes and Spoofs

There is plenty of e-mail on the Web that doesn't contain any malicious content whatsoever, but that can lead to trouble anyway. Two big categories that fall under this heading are hoaxes and spoofs. Let's do some definitions, talk about some examples, and describe some workable identification and evasion strategies.

Hoaxes

Simply put, a *hoax* is an e-mail that attempts to convince you that something false and unreal is actually true and real, and often includes a "call to action" so you're unwittingly tricked into spreading the hoax to others. Thus, in some sense, a hoax is very much like a virus in that it includes a mechanism designed to assist in its propagation. Virus hoaxes are an obvious case in point (and I even know about a worm that was based on a virus hoax that actually spread the no-longer-completely-false hoax at the same time it spread itself to countless e-mail inboxes). But hoaxes are as varied and ingenious as the people who foment them.

One of my favorite antihoax Web sites, Hoax Busters (`www.hoaxbusters.org`), offers a list of five hoax giveaways that is worth paraphrasing here, because it so actually captures and represents this phenomenon:

- **A dire sense of urgency**—Hoaxes are fabulous consumers of exclamation points (the more, the better) and like to use lots of capitalization as well. Thus, common elements on hoax subject lines include terms like *`URGENT`*, *`VIRUS ALERT`*, or *`WARNING`*, often with three or more exclamation points.
- **Spread the word**—Hoaxes invariably include injunctions, admonitions, or outright pleas to be e-mailed to everybody in your address book in the public interest of getting the word out as quickly and broadly as possible.

- **Reality check/verification** — Hoaxes often include some kind of quote that will be attributed to a public official, a corporate officer, or somebody else with assumed credibility in whatever areas the hoax touches. In effect, this kind of statement implicitly (and sometimes even explicitly) asserts that this information is real, urgent, and important — not a hoax, in other words.
- **Terrible consequences for failing to participate** — The hoax will claim that horrible things can happen to those who may be victimized if you don't get the word out to everyone you know. A virus could wipe your hard drive, computer zombies could bring down the air traffic control network, or your pets could all get the mange!
- **Repeated forwarding** — The subject line may include lots of FWD:FWD:FWD: notations, to indicate the message has been forwarded a lot, or you might see various marks in the text (like lots of greater-than signs, >>>>), that indicate lots of forwarding as well.

Before you succumb to a hoax, ask yourself this: whose job is it to get the word out about whatever affliction you're supposed to help fight? Chances are pretty good it's really not yours, for sure. Virus bulletins are believable only when they emanate from software vendors (like Microsoft, Symantec, McAfee, and so forth) or security organizations (WildList, Virus Bulletin, CERT, and so on). Remember that a hoax just wants to appear in as many inboxes as possible, and let the forwarding stop at your inbox. If you feel really strongly about it, send a short e-mail to the person who sent it to you, tell them not to worry, it's just a hoax, and point them at one or more of the great antihoax sites on the Web (mentioned by name, with URLs, in the "Resources" section at the end of this chapter). Some of these sites will even backtrack through the senders lists embedded in the e-mail headers in such messages, and tell them it's a hoax and what to do about it on your behalf!

Spoofs

Where hoaxes can be irksome or disturbing, depending on your credulity, spoofs can be quite a bit scarier. A *spoof* is an e-mail message that pretends to originate from some (usually trusted) source, and usually includes both an attachment and some kind of call to action. Because the attachment may include Trojans, back doors, spyware, or outright malware, and the call to action is usually to execute the attachment, the results of falling prey to a spoof can be pretty dire indeed.

The most common form of spoof plays on people's fear about computer security, in fact. You might receive a message that claims to originate from Microsoft or a security product vendor that informs you a serious vulnerability has been discovered. Because you've registered for their security notification service, they've kindly attached a security update that fixes this serious vulnerability. Now, if you'll only take a few minutes to install it, you'll be safe and sound from here on out. Don't do it! Or rather, if you do it, expect to suffer somehow as a consequence.

The proper rule of Internet information delivery to recall in this case is that vendors never push security updates via e-mail to their customers (the term *push* refers to initiating the transfer of data on their end to the customer, in the form of an e-mail attachment). The problem, of course, is that e-mail is easy enough to spoof to make this a far too problematic a method for distributing any kind of security updates or information. You may get an e-mail that notifies you a security update is available from Microsoft and other vendors, but you'll never get an e-mail from them that includes any kind of security attachment, period, be it an update or something else.

Figure 10-6 shows a page on the Microsoft Web site that's entitled "How to Tell if a Microsoft Security-Related Message is Genuine." Although it looks just like a Microsoft Web page, it's the body of an e-mail message that was used to help spread the Swen worm starting in September 2003. Even for those very familiar with Microsoft security alerts, it's uncannily like the real thing. Thus, Microsoft points out ways you can tell it's not:

- **Microsoft Security Bulletins never contain attachments.** Instead they provide links to security bulletins on its Web site, where users can follow other links to digitally signed Web pages where verifiable copies of updates reside.
- **All Microsoft Security Bulletins are digitally signed.** Signatures can be verified by using Microsoft's public key, available through TechNet (see the "Resources" section for a pointer to a Web page where you can grab a copy of the key for comparison purposes).
- **All Microsoft Security Bulletins also appear on the MS Web site** (and e-mailed bulletins should include a link to same; monthly bulletin summaries include links to all covered security bulletins).

Careful examination of the Swen worm spoof shows, of course, that the spoof fails on all three counts.

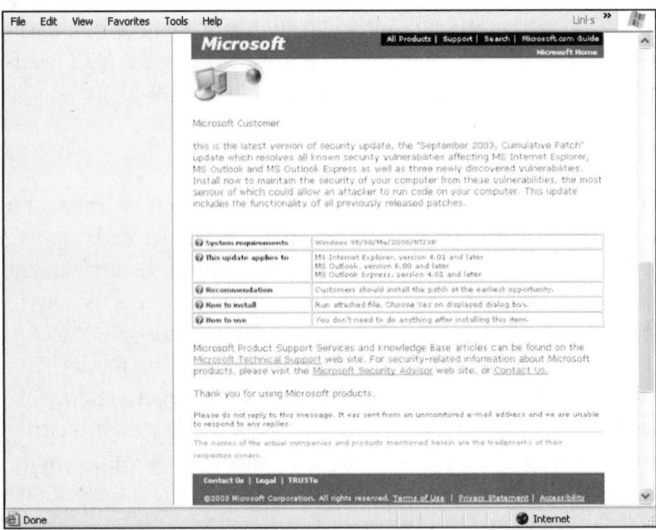

File Edit View Favorites Tools Help

Microsoft

All Products | Support | Search | Microsoft.com Guide

Microsoft Home

Microsoft Customer

this is the latest version of security update, the "September 2003, Cumulative Patch" update which resolves all known security vulnerabilities affecting MS Internet Explorer, MS Outlook and MS Outlook Express as well as three newly discovered vulnerabilities. Install now to maintain the security of your computer from these vulnerabilities, the most serious of which could allow an attacker to run code on your computer. This update includes the functionality of all previously released patches.

System requirements	Windows 95/98/Me/2000/NT/XP
This update applies to	MS Internet Explorer, version 4.01 and later MS Outlook, version 8.00 and later MS Outlook Express, version 4.01 and later
Recommendation	Customers should install the patch at the earliest opportunity.
How to install	Run attached file. Choose Yes on displayed dialog box.
How to use	You don't need to do anything after installing this item.

Microsoft Product Support Services and Knowledge Base articles can be found on the Microsoft Technical Support web site. For security-related information about Microsoft products, please visit the Microsoft Security Advisor web site, or Contact Us.

Thank you for using Microsoft products.

Please do not reply to this message. It was sent from an unmonitored e-mail address and we are unable to respond to any replies.

The names of the actual companies and products mentioned herein are the trademarks of their respective owners.

Contact Us | Legal | TRUSTe

©2003 Microsoft Corporation. All rights reserved. Terms of Use | Privacy Statement | Accessibility

Done Internet

Figure 10-6: Except for failing all key identity tests, the Swen worm spoof looks pretty convincing!

The secrets to avoiding spoofs are to learn and understand your vendor's policies regarding distribution of patches, fixes, and updates — especially anything that relates to repairing vulnerabilities or fending off known exploits. That said, I'm sure you'll find that as a rule vendors don't use e-mail as a vehicle for distributing such updates — only for distributing information about and pointers to

reliable sources for such updates. Thus, if an attachment that purports to be a security update shows up in your inbox, forward a copy to the vendor and then trash it!

Other more blatant attempts to steal from you can occur via e-mail as well, but even though they may use spoofing techniques to try to convince you they're legitimate, they're still considered a different type of spam. I'll cover e-mail fraud next, including outright scams designed to part people from their money, and phishing attacks, designed to steal people's confidential information (such as credit card numbers, account information, and other sensitive data with profound financial consequences should their theft lead further to stealing somebody's identity).

Generally, when organizations do communicate with their members or customers by e-mail, they not only use clear identification techniques (such as special logos, digital certificates, links to Web-based versions of the same information, and so forth), they also provide guidelines about what kind of business they won't conduct via e-mail. In fact, most such operations — including AOL, MSN, and EarthLink, for example — state that they will never ask for passwords or other personal, confidential information via e-mail as a matter of policy. Thus, any communication that purports to originate from them that does request such data *must* be a spoof.

Beware E-mail Fraud: Phishing, Scams, and More

Phishing (pronounced like fishing, in case you wondered) involves a metaphorical sort of fishing for information that requires a certain amount of credulity, or lack of caution, on the part of the fish. Let's say an e-mail shows up in your inbox that claims to originate from Citibank, US Bank, PayPal, Microsoft/MSN, or EarthLink. It asks you to visit a Web page, and provide some personal information to keep your account active, review a transaction, or some other plausible reason. Should you do this? Maybe, maybe not. Let's take a test to find out.

On the Web

Visit MailFrontier's Web site to take its Phishing IQ test (`http://survey.mailfrontier.com/survey/quiztest.html`): follow the links to 10 mocked-up e-mail messages, and try to separate the legitimate requests from those that could be phishing attempts. Compute your score marking each of those items as legitimate or otherwise, then click the "Get your score" button to see how you did. Anything over 80 percent is pretty good, but any answer where you mark something fraudulent as legitimate could have been a possible financial score against you. Ouch!

The key to recognizing phishing attacks requires a little persistence and a little patience, so I'll dig into an item from MailFrontier's Phishing IQ test as an example. It also requires a feel for cues and clues to fraud, both obvious and subtle. Take, for example, the text that shows up in your browser's status bar when you try to follow the PayPal link that shows up as `http://www.paypal.com/cgi-bin/webscr?cmd=_login-run` in one of the e-mail messages on the MailFrontier test: it's `http://194.65.136.141/.paypal/login.html`. Although that might look like a PayPal URL to

the untutored eye, the use of an IP address instead of a domain name should set off warning bells. Further check-ups show that 194.65.136.141 is in Portugal, that PayPal's primary IP address is 64.4.241.16, and its location is in the United States. Absolute confirmation comes when 194.65.136.141 comes up as a "non-existent domain" when performing a reverse DNS lookup (I'll explain this in a minute). This one's a stinker.

Of course, not all of these checkups require quite so much work (though most of them do). The URL in item 4 from the MailFrontier test is supposedly from US Bank; the text for the purported destination URL takes the form `https://www4.usbank.com/internetBanking/RequestRouter?requestCmdId=DisplayLoginPage` in the e-mail message, but appears in the browser tray area as `http://www.pmf.sc.gov.br/sadm/.UsBank/` when you mouse over the link. There are two things to note here that should set off immediate fraud alerts:

- First, a secure HTTP connection (indicated by the `https://` at the beginning of the original URL) should never turn into an insecure `http://` URL.
- Second, the real target domain is in Brazil (as denoted by a domain name ending in `.br`)— somewhat whacky for an institution named US Bank, don't you think?

Another stinker!

Here's a recipe you can follow if you want to take the time to determine if a link in an e-mail is legit or a sign of possible fraud. Following the recipe involves using the `nslookup` (name server lookup) utility that's built into Windows XP (and most other modern 32-bit versions of Windows). It's a command-line tool, so you'll start by opening a command prompt window:

1. Open a command prompt window by clicking Start → Run, typing **`cmd.exe`** into the Open dialog box, and clicking OK.
2. At the command line, type **`nslookup`** and press Enter. (I'm going to use the PayPal example discussed a couple of paragraphs earlier, using the IP address 194.65.136.141 and the domain name `www.paypal.com`.)
3. At the > prompt (which is what indicates you're inside the `nslookup` utility now) type **`www.paypal.com`** and press Enter. (Note that most of the IP addresses that appear in response start with 216.113.188, and a few others that start with 64—a sure-fire clue that 194.64.136 is not a related address.)
4. Next, you're going to do a "reverse DNS lookup" to try to produce a domain name for the mystery IP address. So you must first type **`set q=ptr`**, then press Enter, then type **`194.65.136.141`**, and then press Enter at the next > prompt. The complete results of this activity are depicted in Figure 10-7. Notice that the ultimate result of this lookup is `Non-existent domain`. Simply put, this means nobody has registered this domain, so it's bogus.

```
C:\>nslookup
Default Server:  aus-dns-cac-01-dmfe0.austin.rr.com
Address:  24.93.40.62

> www.paypal.com
Server:  aus-dns-cac-01-dmfe0.austin.rr.com
Address:  24.93.40.62

Non-authoritative answer:
Name:    www.paypal.com
Addresses:  216.113.188.64, 216.113.188.65, 216.113.188.66, 216.113.188.67
          64.4.241.16, 216.113.188.32, 216.113.188.33, 216.113.188.34, 216.113.1
88.35

> set q=ptr
> 194.65.136.141
Server:  aus-dns-cac-01-dmfe0.austin.rr.com
Address:  24.93.40.62

*** aus-dns-cac-01-dmfe0.austin.rr.com can't find 141.136.65.194.in-addr.arpa.:
Non-existent domain
>
```

Figure 10-7: This exercise clearly shows that the real PayPal and the address from the e-mail aren't related.

What we've just done here is first to check the real IP addresses associated with the PayPal Web server. When I checked at my PC, there were nine of them, eight of which started with 216.113.118 and the ninth with 64.4.241.16 (others who checked my work reported different results, indicating that results may vary by geographic location, or by the number of PayPal servers up and running at any given moment). The address from the e-mail is 194.65.136.141, so there's no numeric relationship between it and the others. The second part of the exercise tries to match a domain name with this 194.65.136.141 address and is unable to do so — a clear indication that it's not a PayPal Web site. This is all the evidence you need to know to avoid following that link.

On the other hand, why bother? If you want to conduct this kind of business with a service provider, a credit card company, a bank, or whatever other kind of institution might actually send you such an e-mail, they won't bat an eye if you call them on the phone instead and say: "Let's talk about that e-mail you sent me." Provided you can prove your identity to them, they'll be happy to take care of things by phone. And since you called them, you can be pretty sure you're talking to the right people. Just make sure you get the phone number you call from a reputable source, like their Web site or directory services — better still, from your last bill or statement from that company.

Scams and other attempts to defraud e-mail users come in many forms. The Nigerian scam is probably one of the best-known instances of this kind of thing and comes in a wide variety of forms nowadays. The scam hinges on a story that usually includes the following elements: Someone has lost a very wealthy relative, who's left millions of dollars in a bank account somewhere near you. This person needs a local representative to act on his or her behalf to go retrieve this money and offers to split the proceeds with the retriever. But first, a modest sum of money to help expedite the process is required; this amount is seldom less than a couple of thousand, sometimes as much as $20,000 or more. Those who get swindled part with the modest sum, but the retrieval (and split) of the promised millions never happens.

The Geography of IP Addresses

Earlier in this chapter, I told you that the 194.65.136.141 "PayPal" address was in Portugal. In the next section, I report that the originating address for a `W32.Bagle.A@mm` e-mail I received is in Singapore. This naturally leads to the question: "How do you look up IP address locations?" The answer is: "Get the right tool for the job."

You can try free Web sites to look up IP address locations. Here are two pretty good ones:

- **IP2Location** (`www.ip2location.com/free.asp`)
- **GeoBytes** (`www.geobytes.com/IpLocator.htm?GetLocation`)

The first site limits you to 20 free lookups a day, and the second can't always locate your target IP addresses. I use the IP Address to Country Mapping Tool included in NetScan Tools Pro 2004 (`www.netscantools.com`) and have also gotten good results from an evaluation copy of CallerIP (`www.visualware.com`). If you're just handling personal lookups, the free Web site links should be fine; if you're interested in more frequent or regular use, you might want to investigate the aforementioned commercial tools.

Other e-mail scams involve investments, phony health insurance, pyramid schemes, and much, much more. To get a sense of the breadth of offerings designed to part suckers from their funds, visit one or more of the Web sites that track such things:

- **ScamBusters.org (`www.scambusters.org`)** — Tracks all known e-mail and online scams, publishes monthly newsletter, and provides a search engine to look for scams on its site.
- **U.S. Securities and Exchange Commission (`www.sec.gov/investor/pubs/cyberfraud.htm`)** — "Internet Fraud: How to Avoid Internet Investment Scams" is a must-read for those interested in this topic.
- **Spamming Bureau's Email Fraud and Internet Fraud (`www.spammingbureau.com/email-fraud-and-internet-fraud.php`)** — Email Fraud and Internet Fraud (check fraud and other related listings under "General" heading in its Spam directory).

Although it may seem incredible, hundreds to thousands of people fall for e-mail scams every year; and some poor victims even lose their life savings. The moral of this story is, if somebody you don't know asks you for money by e-mail, don't even dignify such an e-mail with a reply. You don't want these swindlers to know that their spam has found a "live" e-mail address somewhere. Likewise, if somebody offers your anything on terms that are too good to be true, they probably are just that — and they're also designed to part you from your money, not to part them from theirs. Be careful!

In the next section, I distill rules and recommendations from e-mail and spam experts the world around into a series of short, sweet admonitions designed to help you play it safe with e-mail. Please read and heed them well, and ignore them at your peril.

Eleven Basic Rules for E-mail Safety

You can find lots of good advice on e-mail safety all over the Web. Here's a relatively short list of guidelines that distills the most common and practical elements from as much such advice as I could find, digest, and summarize for your benefit:

- **Filter your e-mail, and block as much spam as you can.** As I've said before it doesn't matter what combination of spam filtering services or tools you use, as long as you use something to turn down the volume of unwanted e-mail.
- **Never open unexpected attachments, or attachments from unknown senders.** Be careful with attachments from those you know and trust while you're at it, too!
- **Never reply to spam.** Sure, a lot of spam shows up with Remove links included, so you can tell them not to send you any more spam. But when you click that link, your e-mail address goes back with that reply, and you've just told the spammer that there's a person on the other end of that address. All this does is generate more spam, because spammers pay more for live e-mail addresses. Pitch it; don't answer it!
- **Don't post your real e-mail address.** If you alter your e-mail address before posting it somewhere, that makes it unusable to automated address harvesters. Something obvious will work for people, but probably not for machines, so that `johns@onda.com` could easily become `j0hns@REMOVETHISonda.c0m` or `johns@NOSPAMonda.com` and still work for human responders. The same goes when posting on Web sites, or other places that spiders and robots routinely troll for e-mail addresses. If your ISP permits e-mail address aliases, you can use them creatively to categorize incoming e-mail and catch a lot of spam.
- **Keep your primary e-mail address as private as possible**. Go ahead and sign up for one or more additional free e-mail addresses at Hotmail, MSN, Yahoo!, or wherever. Use that address when registering software, signing up for mailing lists, purchasing stuff online, or anything else where addresses might be resold. It's easy to create stringent white lists for screening mail on that address by including only those addresses of authorized senders from whom you expect (and want) e-mail. Distribute your primary e-mail address only to friends, family, and colleagues, people from whom you want e-mail.
- **Use privacy policies to your advantage.** Don't accept all the default options when you sign up for a newsletter, join a new members-oriented Web site, or anything else where you have to register and provide contact information (especially an e-mail address). Opt in to stuff you really want, opt out of everything else. Look for requests to have partners or third parties send you special offers or information — that's asking for permission to spam — and uncheck those options, or find other ways to decline such opportunities.
- **Keep a low or zero profile online.** Don't add your e-mail address to online directories (like those at Yahoo!, AnyWho, Bigfoot, or other similar sites). Don't post your profile on Web sites and if you do, alter your e-mail address so if harvested, it won't work (even spaces might do the job so that `johns@onda.com` could avoid some spam by entering `johns @ onda (dot) com` or by converting symbols to words as in `johns(at)onda(dot)com` instead — but I like altered characters better because it's harder for harvesters to get those conversions right).

- **Don't perpetuate hoaxes.** If you get a chain e-mail, or some kind of obvious hoax message, don't pass it on to anybody (except maybe to a hoax reporting site).
- **Don't encourage spammers by buying anything advertised in spam.** Microsoft performed an analysis recently that indicated how selling one item with an $11 profit margin would make it pay for spammers to send 100,000 e-mails for every purchase. If you buy, you're just paying for more spam, so if you must buy, buy it somewhere else or some other way — don't respond to an unsolicited e-mail pitch!
- **Never install software or updates delivered via e-mail.** Most reputable vendors do not distribute software or updates by e-mail, so that leaves only unreputable sources responsible when such things show up in your inbox. Don't install them: go to the vendor's Web site instead and download software and updates from there, or e-mail them a copy of the message and ask for their advice.
- **Don't respond to requests for money or sensitive information via e-mail.** If you must provide sensitive information, credit card numbers, or other data that might be used in identity theft, call the purported sender and offer to provide that information by phone (just be sure to use a reputable source, like a bill or statement, or directory services to get the number you call). If they need it, they'll make you prove your identity first and then accept it cheerfully by phone. As for money, don't give it away unless you can afford to do without it (chances are nearly 100 percent you'll never see that money again, or anything else in return).

If you can follow these 11 tips, you'll be able to avoid new spam, reduce your current spam load, and avoid potential sources of trouble and mischief that will show up in your mailbox.

When in Doubt, Play It Safe!

Sometimes, something will show up at your inbox that's absolutely baffling: It might look like it's from your boss or perhaps a family member. But by now, your sense of what's real and what's not should be pretty keen. If it somehow doesn't look or feel right, you're better off forwarding the message (but do remove any attachments it might have, especially infected ones) back to its putative sender with a subject line like "Did you really send this to me?"

Within hours of the discovery of sender spoofing worms in the wild — in this case the `W32.Beagle.A.worm@mm` (a.k.a. `W32/Bagle.A`) originally reported on January 18, 2004 — I received an e-mail supposedly from a colleague (with whom I'd worked on a security book, ironically enough). As I learned on January 19, this was simply a side effect of the worm choosing his address as the sender and one of my addresses as the recipient. But I wasn't hit by the virus for two reasons:

- First (and probably foremost), my anti-virus software blocked it, even though it was a brand-new, unreported virus at the time.
- Second (and equally important), because I wasn't expecting anything from him, I saw no reason to open an `.exe` attachment from him without checking with him first.

A quick exchange of e-mails confirmed he had nothing to do with the message in question. Some hasty e-mail header analysis after that confirmed that the originating IP address had no valid host name resolution, and certainly had nothing to do with his domain. In fact, the originating IP address is in Singapore, whereas the colleague's root domain is in the Miami, Florida, metropolitan area.

Because I was sensitive to something seeming out of whack, even though the supposed sender was (and still is) on my white lists, I was able to avoid trouble. Some experts describe this as developing a sense of healthy paranoia. Although you need not look for black helicopters around every corner, it's smart to question whatever shows up in your inbox, and to be suspicious of the unknown, the unexpected, and the nonsensical. If something seems funny, it probably is — trash it, and play safe!

Resources

A pretty comprehensive list of free e-mail services is available online at EmailAddresses.com — enough to fill five Web pages in fact. You'll find all the old familiars here — Yahoo!, Google, Hotmail, MSN — plus lots of unfamiliars, too (`www.emailaddresses.com/email_web.htm`).

Microsoft Knowledge Base Article 837388, entitled "How to configure Outlook to block additional attachment file name extensions," not only covers the details involved for Outlook 2003, but it also goes three additional Outlook versions back as well (`http://support.microsoft.com/default.aspx?scid=kb;en-us;837388`).

Microsoft has oodles of resources on spam, many well worth spending some time with. Microsoft Research has a report entitled "99,999 Innocent Bystanders Spammed" that explains the remarkable economics and paybacks for spam (`http://research.microsoft.com/displayArticle.aspx?id=672`). Bill Gates also wrote an "Executive E-mail" on Spam in June 2004, wherein he lays out the company's views on spam and anti-spam technology directions. It's definitely worth a quick read (`www.microsoft.com/mscorp/execmail/2004/06-28antispam.asp`). The company's spam page is updated regularly and includes pointers to lots of useful news and information. See also Microsoft's "Fight Spam" pages and documents in its "security at home" offerings (`www.microsoft.com/athome/security/spam/default.mspx`).

Anti-spam capabilities in Outlook 2003 got a significant boost from the release of the Microsoft Office 2003 Service Pack 1 (SP1) in July 2004. For a good overview of new and enhanced capabilities, start with the product information brief entitled "Outlook 2003 Junk E-mail Filter" (`www.microsoft.com/office/outlook/prodinfo/filter.mspx`). Then check the Outlook Help files for an item named "About the Junk E-mail Filter" (if you've installed Outlook 2003 SP1, it marks all the new and enhanced features with a colored asterisk). If you're using Outlook Express, you will want to read about security enhancements in Windows XP SP2 in an article entitled "Use the New Security Enhancements in Outlook Express" (`www.microsoft.com/windowsxp/using/web/sp2_oe.mspx`); these include expanded and improved program settings, virus protection settings, and improved spam handling capabilities.

If you're interested in learning more about the registry in general, or more specifically, about registry backups and restores (or exports and imports, if you prefer) you could do worse than grabbing a copy of Jerry Honeycutt's *Microsoft Windows XP Registry Guide* (Microsoft Press, 2003), and if you're not in a hurry Jerry's busy at work on a second edition that should be available in early 2005. Knowledge Base article 322756 "How to back up, edit, and restore the Registry in Windows XP and

Windows Server 2003" is also worth a read (http://support.microsoft.com/default.aspx?kbid=322756).

Lots of e-mail hoax, fraud, and abuse sites are on the Internet, so if you don't like the ones I recommend, fire up your favorite search engine and you'll have no trouble finding lots more to choose from. My favorites include Hoax Busters (www.hoaxbusters.org), TruthOrFiction.com (www.truthorfiction.org), The U.S. Department of Energy's Computer Incident Advisory Center (CIAC) Hoaxbusters page (http://hoaxbusters.ciac.org/), Jeff Richards' Virus Hoaxes and Netlore (http://hoaxinfo.com), and HoaxKill (www.hoaxkill.com)—the outfit I mentioned earlier in the chapter that will do hoax backtracking and e-mailing on your behalf, if you request them to.

The Microsoft article "How to Tell if a Microsoft Security-Related Message is Genuine" is situated inside the company's security Web pages. You can find it at: www.microsoft.com/security/incident/authenticate_mail.mspx; poke around at www.microsoft.com/security/ for all kinds of other security-related stuff.

Lots of good articles on phishing are available these days. Some of the best coverage I found while researching this book was at *PC Magazine*: Neil J. Rubenking's "Can you sniff out fraud?" (July 28, 2004; www.pcmag.com/article2/0,1759,1628424,00.asp) introduced me to the MailFrontier phishing test, and Lance Ulanoff's "Opting into Identity Theft" (July 21, 2004; www.pcmag.com/article2/0,1759,1625608,00.asp) does as good a job of explaining the risks and methods of this phenomenon as anything I've found. Microsoft's article "What you need to know about phishing" (www.microsoft.com/athome/security/spam/phishing.mspx) also does a great job of explaining phishing and how to stay safe from phishing attempts.

If you're going to check the veracity of e-mail headers, IP addresses, URLs, and other suspect invitations to venture online, you'll want to learn more about the nslookup command mentioned briefly in this chapter and built into Windows XP. A good overview is included in the Windows XP Professional Product Documentation. Entitled "Nslookup," it provides syntax details and mentions the many associated subcommands briefly, but if you follow the link to Nslookup subcommands at the end of this document, you'll find lots of useful details there (www.microsoft.com/resources/documentation/windows/xp/all/proddocs/en-us/nslookup.mspx). If you really get interested in this stuff, a newer utility called DNS Dig does the job in a more user-friendly way than nslookup, as does the Name Server Lookup tool in NetScan Tools Pro 2004. If you want to try out this tool, you can use a free, Web-based version of DNS Dig at the AnalogX Web site (www.analogx.com/contents/dnsdig.htm). Numerous other freeware implementations you can run on your own PC are also available.

Finally, well-known information security company GFI (makers of the LANGuard intrusion detection and monitoring products, plus numerous e-mail security offerings) provides access to a peachy "Email Security Testing Zone" (www.gfi.com/emailsecuritytest/) on its Web site. You can pick from a pretty comprehensive battery of nearly 19 e-mail security tests, and by providing your e-mail address, subject your e-mail environment to a good checkup of its capabilities and pinpoint potential weaknesses or causes for concern.

Summary

This chapter offered numerous tips and techniques for practicing e-mail safety. In particular I've explored the dangers that e-mail attachments can pose, reviewed the benefits of screening incoming e-mail to remove as much spam as possible, and talked about ways to recognize and avoid e-mail spoofs, phishing attempts, swindles, scams, and other attempts to defraud the unwary. In fact, I believe that if you can follow the 11 rules for e-mail safety enumerated near the end of this chapter, you'll be well-protected against most of the common, garden-variety threats to your inbox, your PC, your identity, and your net worth.

The next chapter changes focus to Web safety. I explore various aspects of Web browser security and hardening techniques, explain ways to spend money safely online, and talk about the importance of keeping up with security updates, as well as maintaining current lists of virus, spyware, adware, and other signatures calculated to keep unwanted software and content from entering your PC from the Web.

Chapter 11

Practicing Web Safety

If you've gotten this far, you know all about the various threats that you're up against in regard to Internet security. You know that there are folks out there who want to break into your system, seemingly useful applications can actually wreak havoc on your system, and others want to get as much information about you as possible (with or without your consent). Fortunately, you can take a number of steps to lock down your system to protect yourself from online woes.

For many years, the majority of users out there have had positive, beneficial online experiences. So why now are there so many dangers to consider and guard against? The simple answer is that hackers have not only gotten more advanced, there are also a lot more of them. In other words, as the numbers of benign users have grown, so too have the legions working the darker side. But, by tweaking some settings and using some good, old-fashioned common sense, you can lock down your browser and your PC to ensure safe surfing—on the Web, that is (I can't do much to improve your odds of hanging 10 on a real wave. . .).

Understanding Browser Security

Web browsers rely on a number of protocols and technologies to perform various actions on the Web. The most basic of these is the Hypertext Transfer Protocol (HTTP), which is the underlying communication mechanism for the Web that controls how Web pages are transmitted across the Internet. The other major standard that regulates Web communication is the Hypertext Markup Language (HTML). There are more books and resources on these two topics than you can shake a stick at, so I'm not going to explore the nitty-gritty details of these standards here. However, if you have interest in exploring these topics further, please see the resources listed at the end of this chapter. Finally, a number of other technologies impact how Web pages are transmitted and displayed, including the following:

- **ActiveX Controls**—An extension to other Microsoft technologies, namely object linking and embedding (OLE) and the Component Object Model (COM), that allows full system access to a process initiated on a Web page. Obviously, this is a dangerous capability in the wrong hands, so Microsoft has begun registering ActiveX controls for authentication before they can be run on a system. For additional information on ActiveX controls, visit the Microsoft Web site at `www.microsoft.com/com/tech/activex.asp`.

- **Java** — Developed by Sun Microsystems, Java is an object-oriented programming language similar to C++. Java applets are ideally suited to the Web due to their small size and universal availability across platforms and browsers. For all things Java, visit the Sun Web site at `http://java.sun.com/`.
- **JavaScript** — A scripting language developed by Netscape for the creation of interactive, dynamic Web sites. For more information, go to the definitive guide to JavaScript at `www.javascript.com/`.

Again, the details on these technologies are beyond the scope of this book, but resources for further study are listed at the end of this chapter. For now, suffice it to say that, although these technologies drive the development of advanced Web sites and technologies, they also pose a threat to any system's security. A seemingly innocuous Web page that includes the wrong ActiveX control, for example, can lead unwary or unwitting visitors into any of the dire situations discussed throughout this book, be it the introduction of a virus, a Trojan horse, spyware, adware, other malware, and so forth.

Keep in mind that a large number of attacks that play out across the Web have a specific target: Internet Explorer (IE). Many industry experts therefore recommend using an alternative browser for common Web browsing, and using IE only when visiting those sites that require it (such as Windows Update, for example). A later section explores the specifics of how to lock down IE, so I won't go into that just yet. For now, take a look at some of the other more popular browser offerings available.

Cross-Reference

If you want to revisit the discussion of TCP/IP and protocols, you'll find that material covered earlier in this book, in Chapter 5. For a refresher on active Web content and the kinds of dangers it can pose to an unprotected PC, please consult Chapter 3.

Firefox from Mozilla

Major features include pop-up blocking, tabbed browsing, built-in search capabilities (via Google), privacy tools for blocking ActiveX controls and spyware, and streamlined download capabilities. Firefox can import settings from Mozilla 1.*x*, Netscape Navigator, IE, and Opera, including Favorites, history, cookies, and passwords.

The Firefox interface, as with most browsers, uses buttons and menus that will be familiar to anyone who's ever used a browser (see Figure 11-1). This download is available at no cost from the Mozilla Project Web site (click the Windows hyperlink under the Firefox heading, and it will initiate a download to your PC).

Once downloaded, Firefox easily imports settings from IE, to help users make the switch easily. Those who troll message forums, blogging sites, and other places where people with strong opinions share them with others online will discover that Firefox has an enthusiastic following, one whose relatively small size (compared to IE) is more than compensated for by its members' strong loyalties and fierce devotion. Like the version of Internet Explorer included with Windows XP SP2, Firefox includes a built-in advertising pop-up blocker, and its capabilities are rated about the same as well.

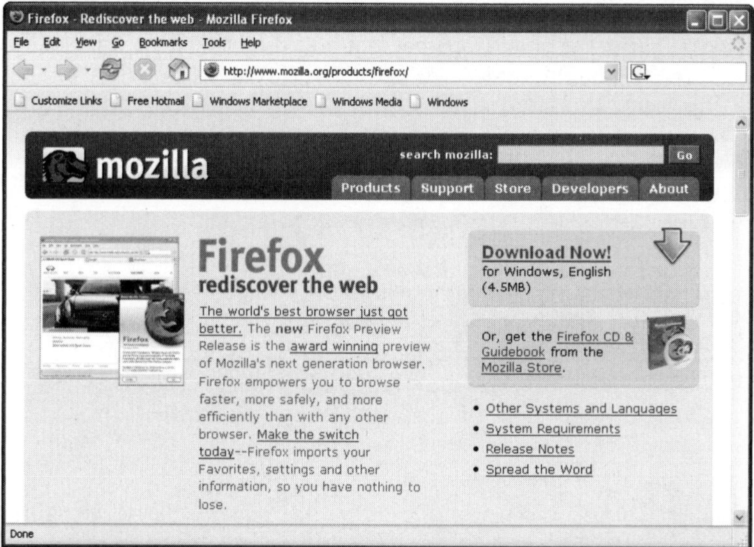

Figure 11-1: Those not paying close attention might be inclined to confuse Firefox and IE, especially because Firefox can import all IE settings and defaults.

Opera from Opera Software

Opera Software is the brainchild of Håkon Lie, one of the creators of the Cascading Style Sheets (CSS) specifications for Web pages at the World Wide Web Consortium (W3C) and a well-known figure in the Web community, along with a star-studded cast of software developers. Based in Norway, since 1994, Opera Software creates high-quality Web browsers for numerous platforms and operating systems, including Windows, Linux, Macintosh OS, Solaris, FreeBSD, QNX (a real-time version of Unix), and various types of smart phones and PDAs (personal digital assistants). It even makes a version for OS/2 for diehard adherents of that now-outmoded operating system.

The Opera Web browser comes in two forms:

- A freeware version that's supported by ad revenues (which means that blocking in-line/in-page ads in that version is not an option).
- A commercial option (at a cost of $39 U.S. per copy to license) that eschews the ads and provides one of the best built-in ad blockers available anywhere (note further that this version includes a very nice built-in e-mail client as well).

You can visit the company's Web site at `www.opera.com` and easily locate either version: Simply click the Download button on the home page to grab the freeware version, or the Buy button to pay for a download of the commercial version.

The current version of Opera is 7.54, and it generally comes in two forms: one that includes the Java Virtual Machine (JVM) and a version that omits the JVM. You need the JVM version only if Java isn't already installed on your machine (and it makes up about 12MB of that download, so it's probably a good idea to check if you're not sure). Figure 11-2 shows what the unregistered/freeware

version of Opera looks like, and Figure 11-3 shows the registered version; the only real visible difference is the lack of the Google ad bar in the latter (for some, the added e-mail client will make a difference; for others, it may not signify much).

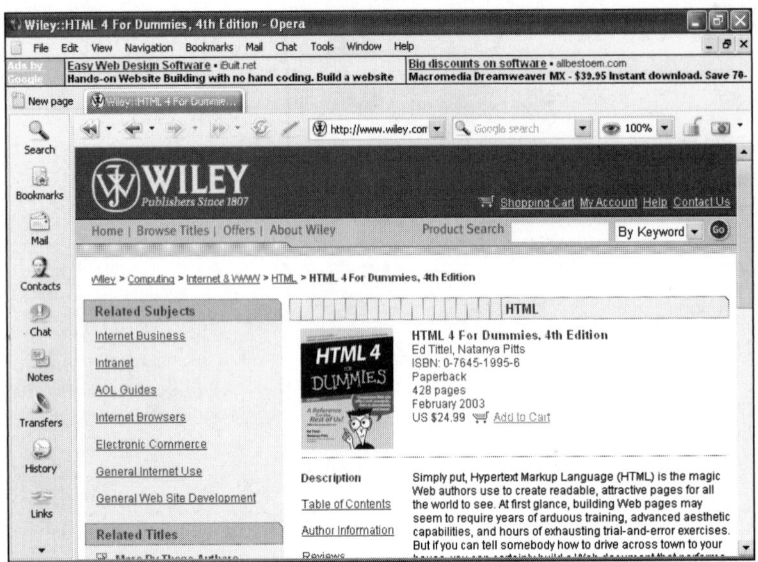

Figure 11-2: The freeware version of Opera includes built-in advertisement areas and pop-ups.

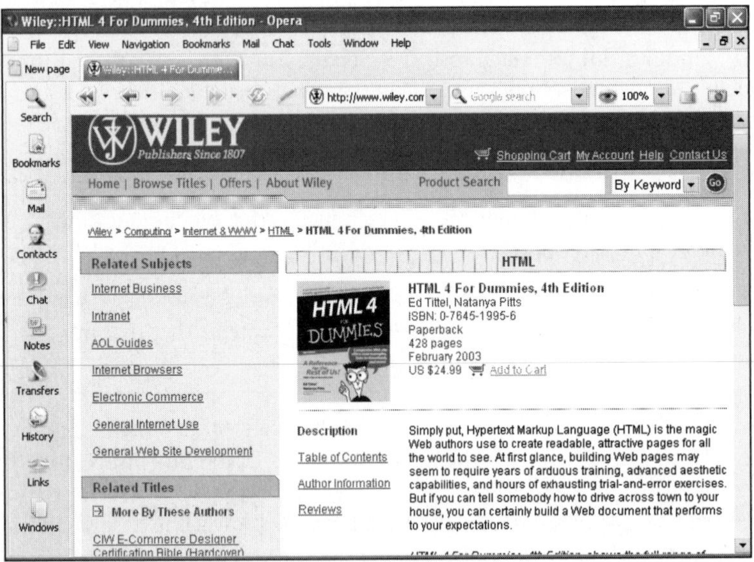

Figure 11-3: Registering Opera does away with ads by Google and annoying pop-ups.

How to Tell if You've Got the JVM Installed

On new installations of Windows XP, it's highly likely that Java will not be installed on your machine, but there's an easy way to tell for sure. Here's how:

1. Open a command window (Start → Run, type cmd in the Open text field of the Run dialog box, and then click OK).
2. At the command line, type `java -version` and press the Enter key.
3. Check the output. If it looks something like what's shown in the first figure in this sidebar, you've got the Sun Java Virtual Machine installed (or a reasonable facsimile thereof); if it looks like the second sidebar figure, it's not installed.

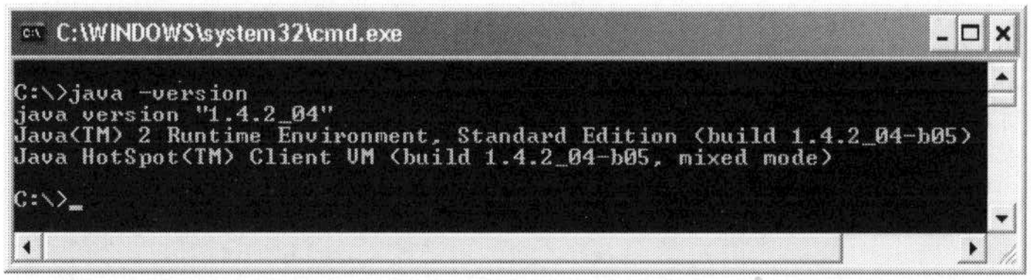

```
C:\WINDOWS\system32\cmd.exe

C:\>java -version
java version "1.4.2_04"
Java(TM) 2 Runtime Environment, Standard Edition (build 1.4.2_04-b05)
Java HotSpot(TM) Client VM (build 1.4.2_04-b05, mixed mode)

C:\>_
```

If a JVM is installed, Windows responds to java at the command line.

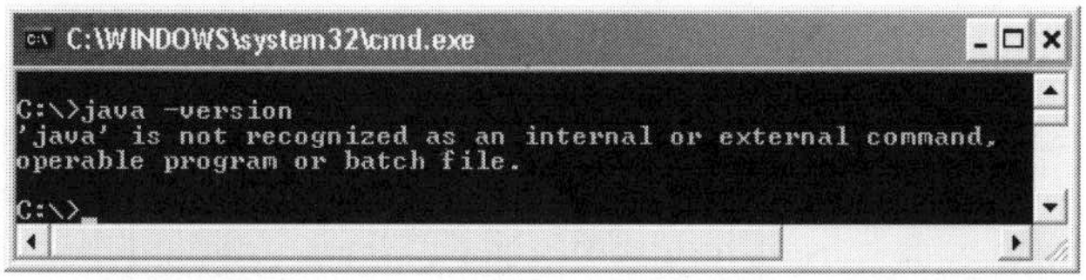

```
C:\WINDOWS\system32\cmd.exe

C:\>java -version
'java' is not recognized as an internal or external command,
operable program or batch file.

C:\>_
```

If a JVM isn't installed, java is not recognized at the command line.

As an alternative, you can search the hard drive where Windows resides (`%systemdrive%`) for Java using Windows Explorer (you'll usually see a set of related directories in `%systemroot%\Program Files` that include `java` and the version number in their names).

If the two alternative browsers mentioned here don't engage your interest, there are plenty of others to choose from. Visit your favorite search engine and use "IE alternatives" as a search string, and you should see what I mean. Among many other good articles and Web pages on this topic, Robert Varnosi's article for CNET Reviews is helpful in identifying leading candidates for the role of "other browser" or "replacement browser" (see the "Resources" section for a pointer to this and other sites and stories on the subject of IE alternatives).

Exploring Common IE Security Settings

Internet Explorer has been organized around the idea of security zones since the days of Internet Explorer 4.0. Basically, this mechanism groups common security settings around various different external kinds of sites and networks, as well as around My Computer (those settings are not accessible

through IE, however), to help organize how security is applied to each such group. Figure 11-4 shows the zones that are accessible through Internet Explorer on Windows XP SP2:

- **Internet** — By default all Web sites fall into this category, meant to represent otherwise uncategorized sites you'd encounter on the Internet, "in the wild" as it were.
- **Local intranet** — This is meant to include sites on an organizational intranet and can include sites that bypass a local proxy server and sites accessible using Universal Naming Convention (UNC) names — which means they're on a network where NetBIOS traffic is permitted and thus presumably inside the local firewall as well. Organizational Web sites and other Web-accessible servers are typically the only entries that appear in this category.
- **Trusted sites** — This is meant to include Web sites you trust not to pose a threat to your PC or the data it contains. Typically, only trusted vendor, partner, or customer Web sites and other Web-accessible servers would be placed into this category.
- **Restricted sites** — These are sites known to be potentially hazardous to your PC and the data it contains. Normally, it's safer to block these sites at a firewall, but you can also tag them for special handling and very limited access and capabilities by placing them into this security zone as well.

The idea that motivates security zones is that each zone has an associated collection of specific security settings — Internet Explorer 6.0 recognizes nearly 40 distinct kinds of such settings — that are set by default en masse when a site is assigned to some other zone (or left in the default Internet zone).

To access the Security tab shown in Figure 11-4 in IE, simply click the Tools menu entry and then select Internet Options in the resulting pop-up menu (or you can simply double-click the zone icon in the browser's status bar). Clicking the Security tab at the top of the Internet Options window produces the list of zones depicted in Figure 11-4. For a little more detail, I want to step through a big-picture description of the defaults associated with each zone. For any given zone, you can do this by clicking the icon for the desired Web content zone and then clicking the Default Level button near the bottom of the Internet Options window. As I discuss each one in the sections that follow, I'll also provide screen shots for each one.

Internet Content Zone

Microsoft uses a slider control to manage security zones as a whole, so you'll see a similar display to the one shown here in the three sections that follow as well. By default, the Internet zone is set up to allow normal Web surfing to proceed safely but with all precautions necessary to prevent potentially risky sites from posing a problem for you and your PC. Thus, it's set up to prompt you before downloading anything questionable — which Microsoft defines as potentially unsafe content, as well as unsigned ActiveX controls. Remember, all Web sites you visit will belong to this zone unless you move them into another zone (or a Group Policy Object for Internet Explorer that makes such assignments is applied to your PC; this won't typically occur on home PCs, but may and often does occur in the workplace). Figure 11-5 shows the Default Level for the Internet zone.

In the Default Level view, the position of the Internet slider tells the story for how each zone compares to the other. The Internet zone is set at a Medium level, with prompting for questionable or risky stuff, but otherwise a pretty wide-open security screen (more details on this in Table 11-1 and the discussion that follows its appearance later in this chapter).

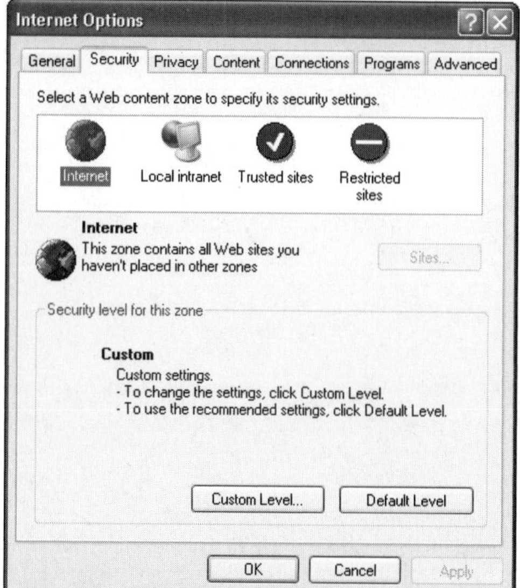

Figure 11-4: Internet Explorer 6 permits Web sites to be placed into four named security zones.

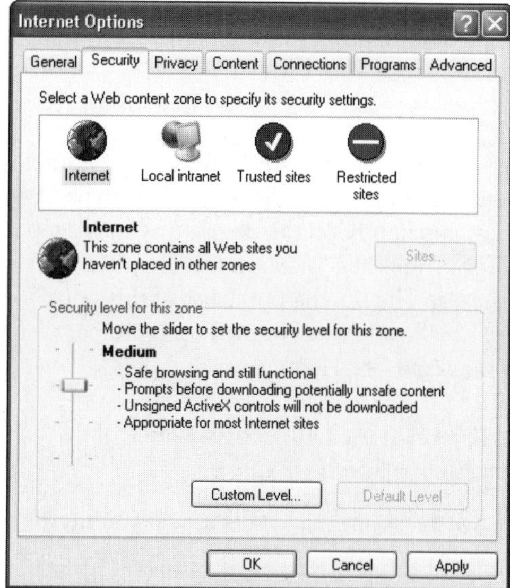

Figure 11-5: The slider sits at Medium for the Internet content zone.

Local Intranet Content Zone

As a more trusted source of data, software, and information than the Internet, the Local intranet zone adopts a more relaxed security posture. Instead of prompting for permission when potentially risky

or questionable stuff is encountered, much of it is allowed to proceed unhindered on the theory that only relatively safe sites should be moved into this zone at all. Figure 11-6 shows the Default Level description for this zone.

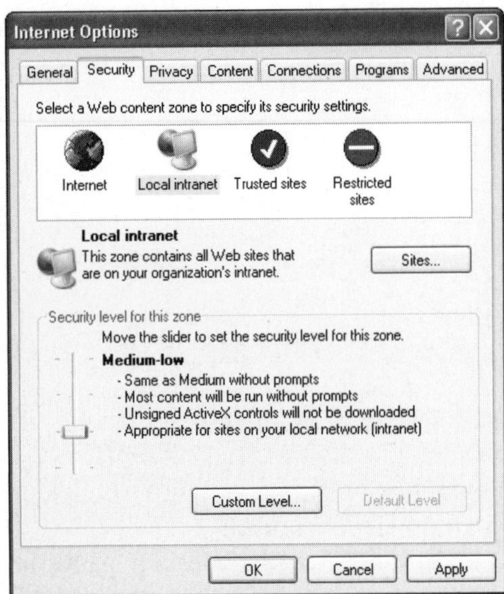

Figure 11-6: As the level of trust increases, the slider moves down.

Note that at the Medium-low slider setting, unsigned and potentially unsafe ActiveX controls aren't downloaded, but otherwise most prompts to warn about questionable or risky stuff are bypassed. Interestingly, the pop-up blocker is disabled for such sites, apparently on the theory that only "good pop-ups" will appear on such sites. The gory details appear in Table 11-1 later in this chapter.

I work with a number of companies that have Web sites, so I'll pick the publisher of this book—namely John Wiley & Sons—as an example to show you how to add a site to the Local intranet content zone and then explain what that does to your browser's controls. Here's how it's done:

1. Open Internet Explorer (I usually just click the IE icon in the Quick Launch area of the taskbar, but you can also choose Start→All Programs→Internet Explorer).
2. In IE, choose Tools→Options, and select the Security tab on the resulting pop-up Internet Options window.
3. Click the Local intranet content zone in the upper pane on the Internet Options window, as shown in Figure 11-7.
4. Click the Sites button to open the Local intranet window and then click the Advanced tab therein to open the Local Intranet window shown in Figure 11-8, where I added the Wiley URL (or you can add other sites you trust to a fair degree yourself as you choose). Type the URL into the upper text box and then click Add so it shows up in the Web sites text box as shown in the figure.

Figure 11-7: Selecting the Local intranet content zone.

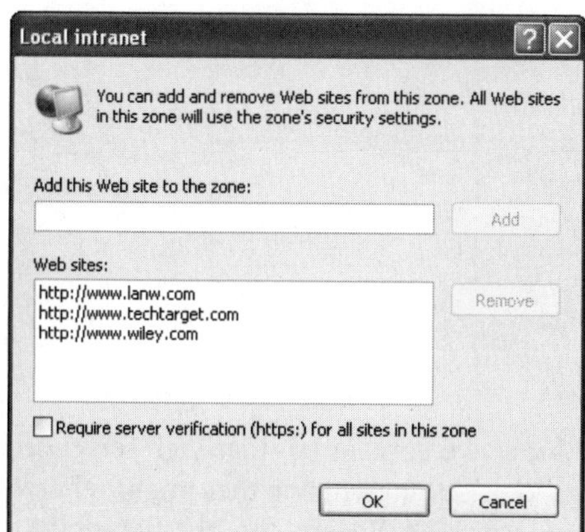

Figure 11-8: Adding a URL in the Local intranet window.

Click the OK button three times to close all open Windows, and you're done!

The implications of this change are worth pondering carefully before you go elevating Web site privileges in this way (and even more so to the Trusted content zone covered in the next section). That's because most active content from such sites will run on your PC without warnings or prompts, although unsigned ActiveX controls will still not be downloaded or executed.

Trusted Sites Content Zone

This zone is even more trusted than the Local intranet zone, so it should include only sites that you're willing to vouch for unquestioningly. As Figure 11-9 indicates, it sets very few limits on what such sites can send (and do) to your PC, which means that you must be extremely picky about the sites you move into this category. To do that in any category display (other than in the Internet zone, where that button's grayed-out because all sites arrive there by default anyway), click the Sites button, then paste or type the URL for the site into the "Add this Web site to the zone" textbox.

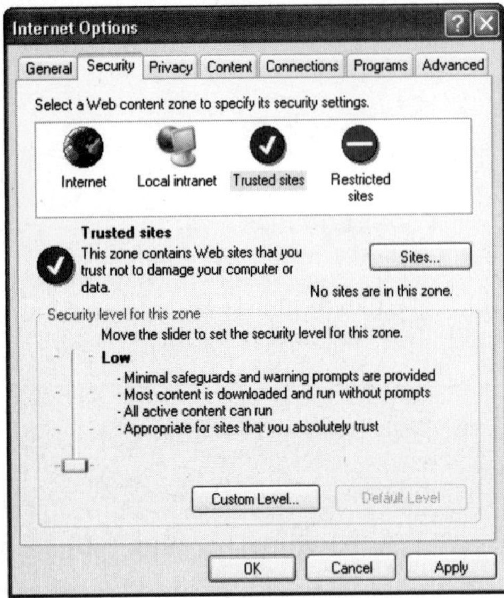

Figure 11-9: The Low setting on the security slider is as lax as IE gets—and that's pretty lax indeed!

On sites in the Trusted zone, everything goes for active content (so that Web server security on trusted sites had better be strong enough to avoid outside interference that might otherwise place spyware, adware, or malware there and put you in harm's way). Here, too, the pop-up blocker will be disabled by default. Interestingly, though, Web sites that belong to less secure zones are blocked from navigating into this zone, so you won't be able to follow links into these sites in some cases, nor can they otherwise steer you into these sites. You must visit them directly.

Note

As a point of potential reference, the only Web site that's in my Trusted sites list is my own `www.lanw.com`. Occasionally when I'm working on somebody else's Web site, I'll add their site to this list temporarily, but only as long as I'm actively engaged in working on that site (and usually also have some degree of control over its behavior).

Restricted Sites Content Zone

This one is the "bad boy" of security zones. Nearly everything that IE can block is blocked or prompted for, and anything potentially questionable or risky is disabled. Scripting and active content are not allowed, Java is disabled, any data exchange that's not encrypted requires the user to grant explicit permission for it to proceed, and all access that requires authentication forces the user to supply a valid account name and password. Figure 11-10 shows a pretty good summary of what it's like to lock IE up tight.

Figure 11-10: Sites in the Restricted zone have only limited capability and access to your PC.

Anything in the Restricted sites zone can't really do much for you, because it won't be allowed to do much to your PC. This kind of treatment makes some sites less attractive and causes others to be unable to offer normal services. *PC Magazine*'s Web site, for example, routinely runs JavaScript routines to produce product summaries, comparison ratings, and other tabular data; if that site were placed into the Restricted sites zone, you'd be unable to execute the scripts and thus unable to see any of that data. For sites that are heavily dependent on ActiveX and other IE-focused or -specific technologies, they won't work properly if put into this zone (and sometimes, that's what it's like to view these sites using an alternative browser that doesn't support things that IE does, or whose own security settings prevent them from working).

Summing up Security Settings

Table 11-1 shows all of the security settings associated with Internet Explorer 6 and how they're set for each of the four security zones described in the previous sections. Note the correlation of slider settings to how tight or relaxed such settings can be, but that some behaviors are restricted everywhere but in

the Trusted zone. As such things go, Microsoft's defaults are fairly realistic, though I have a few recommendations or suggestions after Table 11-1 to explain where some additional tightening up may be warranted.

Table 11-1 Windows Internet Explorer 6.0 Security Settings

Category	*Security Zones*			
.NET Framework-reliant components	Internet	Local	Trusted	Restricted
Run components not signed with Authenticode	Enable	Enable	Enable	Disable
Run components signed with Authenticode	Enable	Enable	Enable	Disable
ActiveX controls and plug-ins				
Automatic prompting for ActiveX controls	Disable	Enable	Enable	Disable
Binary and script behaviors	Enable	Enable	Enable	Disable
Download signed ActiveX controls	N/A	Prompt	Enable	Disable
Download unsigned ActiveX controls	N/A	Disable	Prompt	Disable
Initialize and script ActiveX controls not marked as safe	Disable	Disable	Prompt	Disable
Run ActiveX controls and plug-ins	Enable	Enable	Enable	Disable
Script ActiveX controls marked safe for scripting	Enable	Enable	Enable	Disable
Downloads				
Automatic prompting for file downloads	Disable	Enable	Enable	Disable
File download	Enable	Enable	Enable	Disable
Font download	N/A	Enable	Enable	Prompt
Java VM				
Java permissions	Hisafe	Medsafe	Losafe	DisJava
Miscellaneous				
Access data sources across domains	Disable	Prompt	Enable	Disable
Allow META REFRESH	Enable	Enable	Enable	Disable
Allow scripting of IE Web browser control	Disable	Enable	Enable	Disable
Allow script-initiated windows without size or position controls	Disable	Enable	Enable	Disable
Allow Web pages to use restricted protocols for active content	Prompt	Prompt	Prompt	Disable
Display mixed content	Prompt	Prompt	Prompt	Prompt
Don't prompt for client certificate selection when no certificate or only one certificate exists	Disable	Enable	Enable	Disable

Category	***Security Zones***			
Drag and drop or copy and paste files	Enable	Enable	Enable	Prompt
Installation of desktop items	Prompt	Prompt	Enable	Disable
Launching programs and files in an IFRAME	Prompt	Prompt	Enable	Disable
Navigate sub-frames across different domains	Enable	Enable	Enable	Disable
Open files based on content, not on file extension	Enable	Enable	Enable	Disable
Software channel permissions	Medsafe	Medsafe	Medsafe	Hisafe
Submit nonecrypted form data	Prompt	Enable	Enable	Prompt
Use Pop-up Blocker	Enable	Disable	Disable	Enable
Userdata persistence	Enable	Enable	Enable	Disable
Web sites in less privileged Web content zone can navigate into this zone	Enable	Enable	Prompt	Disable
Scripting				
Active scripting	Enable	Enable	Enable	Disable
Allow paste operations via script	Enable	Enable	Enable	Disable
Scripting of Java applets	Enable	Enable	Enable	Disable
User Authentication				
Logon	Auto only	Auto only	Auto logon	Prompt4

Actual Entry	**As shown**
Administrator approved	adminapp
Disable	Disable
Enable	Enable
Prompt	Prompt
Does not appear	N/A
Custom	Custom
Disable Java	DisJava
High safety	Hisafe
Low safety	Losafe
Medium safety	Medsafe
Anonymous logon	Anon log
Automatic logon only in Intranet zone	Auto only
Automatic logon with current username and password	Auto logon
Prompt for user name and password	Prompt4

Customizing Your Security Settings

When it comes to dealing with security settings in Internet Explorer, the preceding table might cause you to feel a little overwhelmed, but please don't be. You'll notice that it lists only a small number of settings for each of the many items in that table. In fact, the three most common settings are as follows (as shown in Figure 11-11):

- **Enable** — Turn this setting on so that whatever action it governs occurs (for example, Binary and Script behaviors for ActiveX controls and plug-ins are enabled by default for the Internet content zone, as indicated in Figure 11-11).
- **Disable** — Turn this setting off so that whatever action it governs does not occur (for example, Automatic prompting for ActiveX controls is disabled by default for the Internet content zone, as indicated in Figure 11-11).
- **Prompt** — Before executing or performing whatever action a setting governs, present the user with a pop-up dialog box and specifically ask for permission (for example, IE prompts the user for permission by default before it downloads any signed ActiveX controls in the Internet zone, as shown in Figure 11-11).

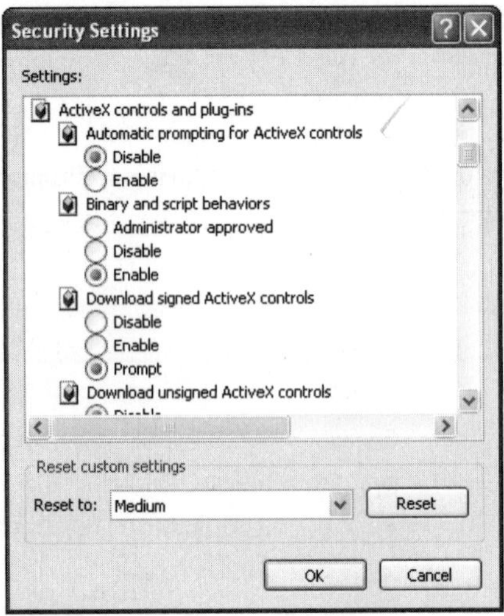

Figure 11-11: The Security Settings window lets you manage IE security settings by clicking specific radio buttons associated with each one.

Another setting you'll sometimes see in the lists, but won't see selected unless you're working in an environment that runs under Active Directory, or that has had a detailed security policy defined and applied, is Administrator approved. This means a network administrator has reviewed and approved a list of specific choices as a matter of policy, and that policy has been defined (and will be enforced through) a Group Policy Object (for example, the Binary and script behaviors setting for ActiveX controls and plug-ins shown in Figure 11-11 includes this option, but it won't be set unless a corresponding policy has been defined for your PC).

The sections that follow have been organized to correspond to the way Table 11-1 is structured. You might have to do a little scrolling around in the Security Settings window in IE to find these items, but rest assured — they're all there! To access these settings for any given content zone, from inside IE, choose Tools → Internet Options, then select a Web content zone (I used the Internet zone as the basis for the preceding examples, since it's the zone assigned to Web sites by default, and therefore the most likely one you'll need to dig into), and click the Custom Level button. That's what opens the Security Settings window for whatever content zone you choose and provides access to the settings documented in Table 11-1.

.NET FRAMEWORK-RELIANT COMPONENTS

This section of settings basically distinguishes between .NET Framework items that use Microsoft's Authenticode technology and those that don't. To be as brief as possible, Authenticode uses valid and up-to-date digital certificates to "sign" code components to prove that they originate from a known and presumably trusted source. Signed components are assumed to be safer than unsigned ones, but interestingly the default settings for all security zones except Restricted sites is to allow both unsigned and signed components to run. The unsigned components setting may be worth disabling for the Internet zone, if you're concerned about possible system exposures.

Note

In case you're not familiar with the term (or the concepts behind it), Microsoft's .NET is a comprehensive development environment that's intended to make it easy for developers to build networked applications, so that PCs can access information on servers on their local networks, or across the Internet, with aplomb and ease. Microsoft looks at this technology as a great enabler, and promises it will make all kinds of applications and services possible that otherwise would be very difficult to build. More skeptical (or paranoid) outsiders look at .NET as a way for Microsoft to lock developers and users to the Windows platform, thereby ensuring the company's continued market dominance. To be perfectly fair, both points of view have some validity, but .NET is sweeping Windows desktops (and thus, the world) for good or for ill. For more information on this fascinating technology visit `www.microsoft.com/net/` for the Microsoft view, but check independent technology news media (*PC Magazine*, for example) for more objective external viewpoints.

ACTIVEX CONTROLS AND PLUG-INS

ActiveX is a key Microsoft technology used for providing active Web content of all kinds, so IE has lots of settings related to this technology. All ActiveX capabilities are disabled by default in the Restricted sites zone, and either enabled or prompted for in the Trusted zone. Again, if you're concerned about possible system exposure in the Internet zone, it may be worth changing those values set to Enable to Prompt users for permission instead. Some experimentation will show what makes sense for your browsing habits.

DOWNLOADS

Download settings apply to three kinds of access:

- First, they establish whether or not downloads are prompted for automatically. By default, this occurs only in the Trusted and Intranet zones (and perhaps should also be enabled for the Internet zone); the other two are disabled.
- Second, they determine whether downloads are allowed or disabled. The default setting is Enabled for all zones except Restricted sites (and is fine to leave as-is).
- The third setting establishes whether or not fonts may be downloaded. This is enabled only for the Local intranet and Trusted site zones; it's not an option for the Internet zone and is disabled for Restricted sites. It also applies only to the version of IE that's included with Windows XP SP2, so if you're using a different version you won't see this option at all.

JAVA VM

The Java Virtual Machine settings have declined dramatically since Microsoft abandoned Java in favor of .NET technologies. Where there used to be 20-plus settings for Java in IE 5, there's only one in IE 6. This has to do with levels of permission and access granted to scripting of Java applets in the browser — which means how invocations of small Java programs from inside Web pages are to be handled. Here's how this lone Java control in IE is set by default: it's entirely disabled for the Restricted sites zone and is set to low, medium, and high safety for the Trusted, Local intranet, and Internet zones, respectively — just as you'd expect, because that way safety controls and these applications' ability to access and manipulate your PC declines as the level of trust goes down. Unless these settings cause difficulties with Java code elements on sites you visit regularly, leave them as-is.

MISCELLANEOUS

Because it's something of a grab bag of items, this category includes the largest number of settings — as many as 17 items in all. Of these, some few bear particular watching (but the defaults for the various security zones are generally workable):

- **Script-initiated windows without size or position controls** — Small, practically invisible browser windows are a stock in trade for adware and some rogue spyware active content and controls. Thus, they're rightfully disabled for the Internet and Restricted sites zones. Depending on how you stock the Local intranet and Trusted zones with sites (and their programming practices), it may be wise to change the default Enabled values to Prompt instead.
- **Drag and drop or copy and paste files** — Given recent reports of vulnerabilities based on this capability, it may be wise to change this value to Prompt for the Internet zone, but other defaults should be okay.
- **Navigate sub-frames across different domains** — This is enabled for all zones except Restricted sites (where it's disabled) by default. Given the potential for those different domains to be questionable on the Internet, it may make sense to change the setting for that zone to Prompt instead.

- **Use pop-up blocker** — Disabled by default for Local intranet and Trusted site zones, you may want to enable it on one or both depending on your experience with pop-ups in sites you place there.

Other items of potential interest include how actions in special browser window areas called IFRAMEs (which act like independent windows, even though they occupy just a portion of the browser window on your screen) and how nonencrypted form data are handled. In the first case, tricky programming could allow rogue code in an IFRAME to take advantage of whatever zone the primary window is in to try to get away with something. In the second case, this setting would let the user know if he or she was being asked to send potentially sensitive data (like credit card numbers or other financial data) in clear text to a server (which makes it easy for any eavesdroppers to grab and possibly use such information). That explains why these items are set to prompt users by default for the Internet content zone for both cases!

Outside these items, other defaults should work acceptably. But don't be afraid to dig further into them if vulnerability or exploit reports suggest potential areas of concern. And because all kinds of interested parties are banging hard on IE all the time — including "good guys" looking for ways to improve on or add tools to baseline IE functions, and "bad guys" seeking to exploit possible weaknesses or vulnerabilities — you can rest assured it's just a matter of time before some (or all) of these items require more attention and understanding.

SCRIPTING

Scripting controls are wide open for all zones except the Restricted sites zone. It may make sense to tighten up (at least with Prompt settings instead) in the Internet zone, at a minimum. After making such a change you'll be able to decide whether to keep it that way or roll back to the default, based on the number of prompts you must handle.

USER AUTHENTICATION

This single setting describes how logon controls work for users in each zone. Possible values include the following:

- **Anonymous logon** — All requests for access to a resource will be granted without checking user credentials. This is workable only for sites and items designed for unrestricted public access; by default this value is assigned to none of the security zones.
- **Automatic logon only in the Intranet zone** — This means users logon with their standard account names and passwords in the Intranet zone, but are prompted for that information in all other zones. It's a workable setup because of the trust (and usually local nature) of the Intranet zone by design. By default, this value applies to both the Internet and Local intranet zones.
- **Automatic logon with current username and password** — Automatically presents user credentials in effect for automatic logon. Because this involves the highest possible level of trust for credentials, it applies only in the Trusted sites zone.

- **Prompt for username and password** — Requires users to present credentials when seeking access to controlled resources. Applies by default to all sites in the Restricted sites zone, and by implication to all sites in the Internet zone as well (because its default is to grant automatic logon only within the Local intranet zone, this means credentials are requested in the Internet zone).

For most situations, these settings should be okay. For more details and information on these security settings, check out the Roger Grimes white paper on Authenticode technology in the "Resources" section. The portion entitled "Configuring Custom Settings" is particularly informative, though the default settings documented there differ somewhat from the defaults associated with the version of IE 6 included with Windows XP SP2 and later versions. Be sure to cross-reference this information with the data in Table 11-1 to figure out what applies and what doesn't.

PRIME CANDIDATES FOR "TIGHTENING UP"

If you must rein security in from the defaults to some extent, the following items can be changed from "Enable" to "Prompt" settings:

- In the .NET Framework component category, at least the "Components not signed with Authenticode."
- In the ActiveX controls and plug-ins category, the "Binary and script behaviors" and "Run ActiveX controls and plug-ins."
- In the Miscellaneous items section, the "Drag and drop or copy and paste files," "Navigate sub-frames across different domains," and "Web sites in less privileged web content zone can navigate into this zone."
- In the Scripting category, you might want to experiment likewise with Prompts for all three entries — namely "Active scripting," "Allow paste operations via script," and "Scripting of Java applets," but be prepared to back off if this causes too much interruption or browser interaction (which I found it did for me when I used those settings for a few days).

As long as you don't try to change too many things at once, you can experiment with these settings and see what works best for you. If in doubt, making things more secure may limit your browser's capabilities, but it will also lessen your exposure to potential dangers.

Managing Cookies

Internet Explorer manages Web *cookies* — those blobs of information that Web sites collect about users for their own purposes. Sometimes benign and sometimes mysterious or downright nefarious, cookies also have characteristics that permit them to be tagged and characterized and managed to support functionality you want or need and to deny information transfers you don't want to allow.

Cross-Reference

Chapter 1 defines cookies in more detail and discusses the sort of threats they pose. Turn there for more information.

Controlling Cookies with Privacy Settings for Web Content Zones

The same kind of slider control applies to cookies that applies to Web content zones, but you need to manage cookies only for the Internet zone (Restricted sites are just that where cookies are concerned, and cookies are permitted to work unhindered in both the Local intranet and Trusted sites zones). You can pick a privacy setting for the Internet zone, but you can also manage sites as to whether cookies are allowed or blocked through the Sites button.

To access Internet Explorer 6 cookie controls, choose Tools → Internet Options and then click the Privacy tab. This produces the display shown in Figure 11-12; this always applies to the Internet zone and shows default settings.

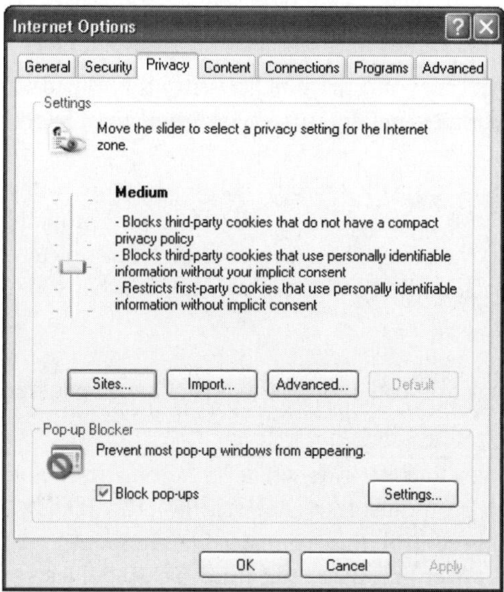

Figure 11-12: By default, IE 6 blocks suspect or potentially dangerous cookies, but lets others work unhindered.

The Privacy slider can occupy one of six positions; by default it takes a middle-of-the-road stance at the Medium privacy setting. This setting blocks only cookies that do not conform to standard privacy policy specifications (this is called a "compact privacy policy" in the language of the specification; see

the "Resources" section for more information on what this means, where to find the specification, and what it's intended to accomplish) or that seek to harvest and use personal information without obtaining implicit consent (this usually means they don't explain what information they intend to gather, nor how they will use it, thereby depriving you of your opportunity to deny such access). As defaults go, it's a pretty reasonable position to establish. The other five slider positions may be named and described as follows (taken in order from least secure to most secure; the Medium default setting occurs between the Low and Medium High settings in this list):

- **Accept all cookies** — All cookies will be saved, and Web sites that created cookies can also read them.
- **Low** — Restricts third-party cookies (cookies associated with sites affiliated or linked with the site you're visiting at any given moment) that lack a compact privacy policy, and also restricts third-party cookies that seek to use personal information without obtaining implicit consent.
- **Medium High** — Blocks third-party cookies that lack a compact privacy policy, or that seek to use personal information without obtaining your explicit consent. Also blocks first-party cookies (those created and managed by the site you're visiting) that seek to use personal information without obtaining your implicit consent.
- **High** — Blocks cookies that lack a compact security policy and cookies that seek to use personal information without obtaining explicit consent.
- **Block all cookies** — Blocks cookies from all Web sites and permits no Web sites to read any existing cookies on your PC. Thus, this setting essentially turns cookies off completely.

Individuals concerned about cookie security may feel (and will certainly be) more secure at the Medium High or High security settings. Because many Web sites require cookies to behave properly and to deliver the best user experience, you'll seldom enjoy surfing if you turn cookies off completely.

You have two other mechanisms for managing cookies in the Privacy tab, no matter what slider setting you choose for the Internet zone:

- One is accessible through the Sites button, where you can either explicitly allow all cookies or block all cookies on a per-site basis.
- The other is through the Advanced tab, where you can override whatever automatic cookie handling that the slider setting establishes. Here, you must first check the box that reads "Override automatic cookie handling" to put this control in place instead of automatic handling, after which you can establish controls over first-party and third-party cookies separately. Either class can be accepted, blocked, or set to prompt for your permission to proceed. Also, session cookies (information that keeps track of your activities while accessing — and often, logged into — a Web site) can be allowed through a separate check box. If you decide to take this approach, I recommend setting first- and third-party cookies to Prompt to begin with, and checking the "Always allow session cookies" box. You'll quickly be able to decide if this is workable for you or not (I tried this and similar controls from third-party software for a couple of days and was overwhelmed by the vast number of prompts I had to field as a result).

And indeed, if managing cookies is something of interest to you, you'll find plenty of ways to do this outside the privacy controls built into IE 6. If you use an alternative browser, you'll find similar cookie management capabilities built into the vast majority of available options as well. If you also use spyware/adware-blocking software, you'll find that many such packages also include cookie management facilities, as do some anti-virus packages. These days, the majority of security suites (see Appendix A later in this book for more information on these all-in-one collections of tools) include cookie management among their multifarious capabilities, too.

Viewing Privacy Policy and Cookie Information in IE

If you want to see what's lurking on any page you visit, you can use the Privacy Report feature built into Internet Explorer to show the URLs for all objects referenced on that page. This can be tedious, because it will often involve looking at lengthy lists of items (and sometimes, they're all from the same site as on the Web page at `www.lanw.com`, which doesn't even use cookies) — but it will tell you exactly what's inside the source markup for whatever page you're viewing. Here's how:

1. Inside Internet Explorer, visit any Web page you like. Once you have a page loaded, choose View → Privacy Report. A Privacy Report window opens, as shown in Figure 11-13.

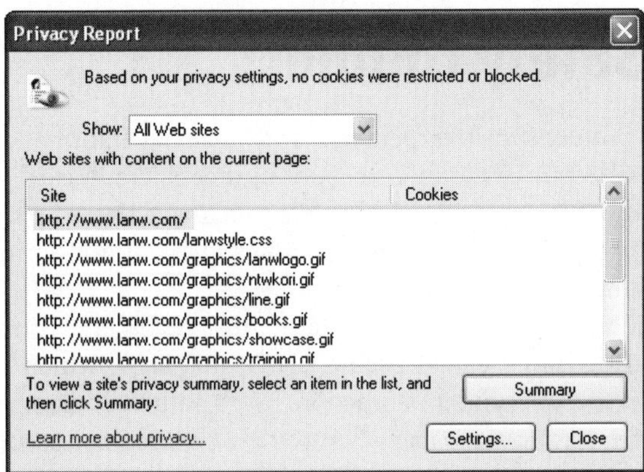

Figure 11-13: The Privacy Report window shows URLs for all objects referenced within the current, open Web page.

2. Scan the interestingly titled list box to see all the objects referenced inside the page (the title is "Web sites with content on the current page" but it shows URLs for all objects called or used inside the page). Any links to an advertising or other tracking site will stand out in such a list.

3. You can see a summary of the site's privacy policy by clicking the Summary button at the bottom of the page (note that my site, `www.lanw.com`, has no privacy policy because it collects no information from visitors except what the visiting browser routinely supplies). Cookie handling in IE actually works by comparing compact policy details to your own settings, then acting accordingly.

Privacy settings are also available here through the button (these are the same as those discussed in the preceding section) at the bottom of the Privacy Report window. You can use the objects listed on this window to see if the page makes references to unsavory sites, and get information about the privacy policy for any item that shows up in the list. This may help you to decide when to block all cookies from specific sites, not just because of their own practices, but because of the sites they link to.

Whatever options for managing cookies you choose, you'll have to make two tradeoffs as you establish the level of control that works for you. On the one hand, your interaction with cookie management facilities or tools will increase as you choose to be prompted or informed about questionable cookie activities. Such cookie activities might be defined as cookie warnings occurring when you don't expect them, or occurring from sites where you'd rather not be tracked (or there's no real reason, like return or repeat business, that justifies recording your activities). On the other hand, functionality on some Web sites where you restrict cookies may be likewise inhibited because cookies are no longer allowed to behave as the site expects. This is especially true on sites like Amazon.com, where that company invests a lot in creating custom user profiles and tailoring its offerings to what's been observed about your past interests and activities. Both of these phenomena are valid and inevitable, but only you can decide whether or not (and at what level) they're acceptable.

Spending Money Safely Online

By understanding that it's your job to protect sensitive personal and financial information when you're active online — such as your Social Security number, account numbers, credit card information, passwords and access codes, and so forth — you should be able to manage the security of that information, and keep it safe from prying eyes. The secrets are to know what you can do to protect yourself, and how to make sure such data is sent as securely as possible.

Make sure your browser is doing its job. Ensure your browser supports 128-bit encryption. Most secure transactions use another version of HTTP called Secure HTTP (HTTPS), which uses the Secure Sockets Layer (SSL) to conduct secure, encrypted transactions. Web addresses using this protocol begin with `https://`. Additionally, most browsers flag when you are engaged in a secure transaction by showing a padlock icon in the status bar. Figure 11-14, for example, shows a fictitious checkout window from Wiley's online bookstore. Note that the URL starts `https://customer.wiley.com/ . . .`, indicating that secure HTTP is in use; note further the locked padlock in the status bar at the lower right in the window. If you right-click the padlock, in fact, it will tell you what type of encryption is in use (in this case it's SSL 128-bit, which indicates a special communications protocol called the Secure Sockets Layer, or SSL, is using 128-bit keys to scramble data sent between my PC and the Web server, so as to render all communications unintelligible to third parties).

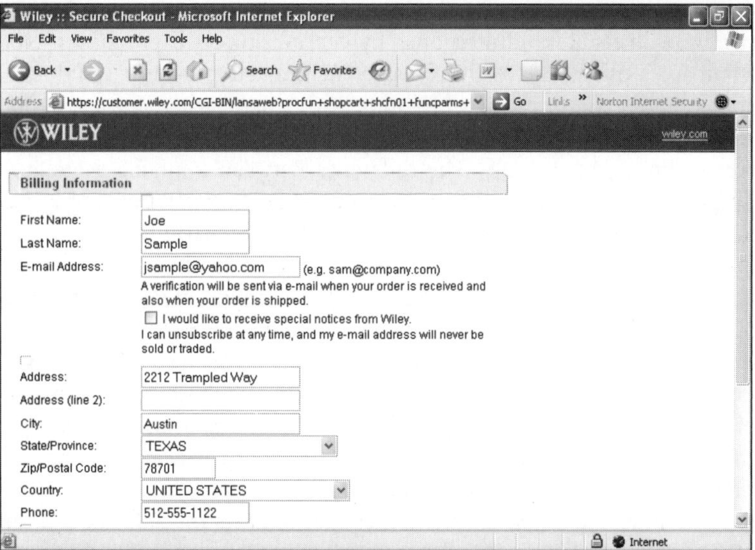

Figure 11-14: When you conduct a secure transaction online, you'll see `https://` in the URL and a locked padlock icon in the browser's status bar.

How Server Security Is Established and Managed

How can you be sure that a server really is what it claims to be? Likewise, how can you be sure that you're really doing business with the party you think you're accessing? The secret's in a system of highly secured digital certificates. Certificates are issued by (and can be checked with) trusted third parties — in business, this means companies like VeriSign, Thawte, or GE Financial, that provide companies with long, complex, special bit patterns that are practically impossible to forge.

When you begin a transaction with a secured server, an initial step that occurs is a request for the server's digital certificate, followed by a check with a third party that verifies its authenticity and also its currency (since certificates can be revoked, and because all come with time stamps after which they expire). Thus, when you see the `https://www.wiley.com/ . . .` URL, you can be sure that Wiley's certificate is valid and current, and conduct business with them with reasonable assurance that they'll get the money for the book you want to buy, and that they'll ship you the book as soon as the credit card transaction clears!

Get a credit card (not a debit card) that is reserved only for online purchases. This simplifies the process of tracking real expenditures versus fraudulent ones by centralizing such purchases. Not only do many credit card companies offer cards with 100 percent protection against fraudulent charges, but others hold you accountable for only $50 of fraudulent purchases when notified about such transactions. Also, make sure that card has the ability to be monitored online and check regularly for unauthorized charges to limit your liability. The difference between notifying a creditor immediately after a charge is made, versus 60 days later, can mean the difference between a $50 or a $500 liability for you. If you ever find something you can't account for on a charge statement, call the credit company immediately to block additional charges from being made to that vendor account. If you ever find yourself in this situation, follow up any call with written correspondence that describes the details of the charge(s) reported, any changes or adjustments made, and the account representative's name, plus the date and time of the call.

Know how the information a vendor gathers about you will be used. Not only should you investigate how information a vendor collects about you will be used (and this means wading through lengthy and sometimes obtuse privacy policy documents), you should not dispense any information that's irrelevant to a transaction. For example, there's no need for a legitimate vendor to require your Social Security number, annual income, or birth date. If a vendor requires this information for a purchase, don't provide it! This is how many people fall prey to identity theft.

Don't engage in online transactions with obscure merchants. Investigate any merchant to whom you must hand over your credit information beforehand: check the Web for postings about that company to ensure that you're dealing with a bona fide retailer, not someone who's going to take your money and run. At a minimum, browse the Web site for a physical mailing address for the company and search an online business directory for that address. Also, check the Better Business Bureau (BBB) to seek positive or negative interactions with a business at `www.bbb.org`. Likewise, check for entries at the Federal Trade Commission (FTC) Web site for consumers at `www.ftc.gov/ftc/consumer.htm` for listings on companies, as well as for a great source of up-to-date information regarding e-commerce transactions.

Investigate your options for returns or upon failure to deliver. Start by researching whether a vendor's delivery policy is guaranteed. If a vendor doesn't deliver a purchase within 30 days or the time allotted, you must be notified and allowed to cancel your order if you so choose. If you use a little common sense about how you can make sure you get what you're paying for, you can avoid lots of potential problems down the road.

If a vendor is concerned about security, it's bound to have a posting regarding its security policy for online transactions. Seek out such documentation and read it carefully to ensure you're making a wise decision in trusting that entity to handle your credit information with due diligence and care.

Educate those close to you about providing information online. Most notable in this group are children and the elderly. Make sure that others in or near your computing environment understand how online interactions can lead to danger and potential theft or loss. If you think about the way that the phishing scams described in Chapter 10 work, and how the imposters can be detected, that provides an excellent demonstration or teaching tool to show others how to avoid falling prey to such wiles.

Tip

Want to check your browser's encryption capabilities when using SSL? It's easy: just point it at `www.fortify.net/sslcheck.html` and see what that page reports to you. Most IE users should see that they're using the RC4 cipher, 128-bit key. Here's what the site says about this encryption technology: "You have connected to this web server using the RC4-MD5 encryption cipher with a secret key length of 128 bits. This is a high-grade encryption connection, regarded by most experts as being suitable for sending or receiving even the most sensitive or valuable information across a network." There! Don't you feel better already?

The Importance of Security Updates

Although news reports may heighten your sense of concern for security issues with Internet Explorer, it's important to keep any Web browser you use patched and up to date. Because browsers are used more than any other software — except perhaps e-mail — to access the Internet, this means keeping up with security bulletins and alerts, and installing patches, security updates, and so forth fairly quickly once they're released. The only possible exception to this rule applies when a facility or capability you don't have installed on your PC is covered: in that case, because you don't run that code, you won't be affected by the presence or absence of a related patch or update.

Caution

It's the presence or absence of code on your machine, not whether you actually use it, that makes the difference between needing to install updates and being able to skip them. Outlook Express (OE) is an example to which most Windows users can relate: Because it's installed by default along with Internet Explorer, and therefore present on nearly every Windows machine, vulnerabilities in OE should be patched whenever applicable updates come along. Alas, just because you don't use it doesn't mean it can't hurt you. Generally, the Windows Update scan does a great job of identifying what is installed on your PC and won't recommend updates for things you don't have installed on your machine.

Although it may seem subject to more security flaws than other alternatives, Internet Explorer is also the most targeted browser for attack and exploit. That's because of its widespread use — somewhere between 6 percent and 70 percent of Web surfers use IE 6, and another 6–7 percent still use other IE versions as I write this chapter — making IE the obvious target of opportunity. If another browser eclipses or approaches IE's market share, you can be sure it too will become more of a focus for attacks and exploits as well.

But no matter which browser (or browsers) you use, it's important to track updates and apply all that are related to security or that update or enhance functionality you use, whether security-related or otherwise.

When in Doubt, Be Safe!

Remember that although attacks are always possible, most adware, spyware, and plenty of other malware finds its way onto PCs because users invite, approve, or encourage its presence. Just as you should never open unexpected e-mail attachments, no matter what the source, so also should you refuse downloads and active content from Web sites you don't already know and trust.

By managing your security and privacy settings you can configure your browser to tell you when suspicious or potentially damaging actions occur, and when transfers of sensitive information are attempted. If you refuse to permit these things to proceed you can play it safe on a case-by-case basis; if you block these things from occurring, you'll be as safe as can be. Only you can decide if dealing with lots of prompts and alerts is worth the extra functionality you'll be able to exercise by request (and with your permission), or if you simply want to skip risk-taking activity and information transfers altogether.

Resources

Information about Web standards of all kinds is at home in three primary locations. One is the IETF, also home to TCP/IP and other Internet protocol and service standards; you can visit this site and standards documents through `www.ietf.org`. The second is the World Wide Web Consortium, or W3C, which is responsible for Web markup languages such as HTML, XHTML, XML, and so forth, plus basic Web services and information description and delivery applications; you can visit this site at `www.w3.org`. The third is OASIS, the Organization for the Advancement of Structured Information Standards. It's a consortium of business, research, academic, and other interests that develops and promotes information standards and services that are industry- or market-focused and aim to help consolidate and unify how they define, transport, and exchange information. Visit this site at `www.oasis-open.org`.

When it comes to dealing with the various languages most commonly used to create active Web content, it's important to note that the first two references I supply — namely, for ActiveX and Java — are company pages for their proprietary products. It's harder to provide a definitive resource for JavaScript, though the item supplied earlier in this chapter comes close. If you're interested in other authoritative references, you may want to check out `http://devedge.netscape.com/central/javascript/`. For a standards-based alternative (albeit one that's designed for European use), you can check out a redefinition of JavaScript in standards-based form called ECMAScript at `www.ecma-international.org/publications/standards/Ecma-262.htm` (ECMA is the European Computer Manufacturer's Association and acts as a default clearinghouse for all kinds of standards in the European community).

Robert Varnosi's article at CNET Reviews is entitled "Alternatives to Internet Explorer," and appeared on July 6, 2004; it mentions only the "usual suspects" — that is, the most popular options (`http://reviews.cnet.com/4520-3513_7-5142616.html`). Likewise, Matthew D. Sarrel's "Time to Find an IE Alternative" (*PC Magazine*, July 9, 2004; `www.pcmag.com/article2/0,1759,1622109,00.asp`) covers only two options — namely, Opera and Mozilla — but does so pretty nicely. If you're in search of all the options, an exhaustive list of same appears at "Replacements for

Explorer" on the Microsoft Boycott Campaign's Web site (www.msboycott.com/thealt/alts/internetexplorer.shtml)—its slant should be clear from the site's name!

When it comes to understanding and using Internet Explorer 6, one of the best all-around resources is the *Microsoft Internet Explorer 6 Resource Kit* (Microsoft Press, 2001). Although it's available in hard copy for about $60 U.S. list price, you can access it online for free (though that won't give you access to the extra tools, help files, and other goodies on the book's CD) at www.microsoft.com/resources/documentation/ie/6/all/reskit/en-us/default.mspx). Also, you should find the new online appendix entitled "A Description of the Changes to the Security Settings of the Web Content Zones in Internet Explorer 6" of great interest because of its focus on Windows XP SP2 (http://support.microsoft.com/default.aspx?scid=kb;en-us;300443).

For more information about Microsoft's Authenticode technology check out the Roger Grimes white paper on this topic. It defines Authenticode, explains how it works, includes a brief and informative digital certificate tutorial, and explains how IE uses this technology to decide whether or not it should permit potentially dangerous content to run on your PC (www.microsoft.com/technet/security/topics/secapps/authcode.mspx).

Numerous Microsoft Knowledge Base articles deal with Internet Explorer and Web security issues. In particular, the following articles should be of interest:

- **The Default Privacy Settings for Internet Explorer 6**—http://support.microsoft.com/default.aspx?scid=kb;EN-US;293222
- **Description of Cookies**—http://support.microsoft.com/default.aspx?scid=kb;EN-US;260971
- **Description of Persistent and Per-Session Cookies in Internet Explorer**—http://support.microsoft.com/default.aspx?scid=kb;EN-US;223799
- **How to Manage Cookies in Internet Explorer 6**—http://support.microsoft.com/default.aspx?scid=kb;EN-US;283185
- **How to Delete Cookie Files**—http://support.microsoft.com/default.aspx?scid=kb;EN-US;278835

If you want to learn even more about cookies, persistent user data on the Web, and so forth, a bit of browsing and exploration inside Microsoft Technet is also strongly recommended (www.microsoft.com/technet). Also, www.cookiecentral.com has to be one of the best places to learn more about these weird and sometimes dangerous "information bins" designed to help servers recognize and know more about you.

Starting in 2004, W3 Schools has updated its browser statistics page monthly (data for every other month is available for 2002 and 2003). It's a good source for tracking trends in browser usage (www.w3schools.com/browsers/browsers_stats.asp). Lots of other sources are available online (and differ to some extent depending on populations monitored and length of monitoring period); try your favorite search engine with "browser statistics" or "browser usages statistics" to see what's available.

If you want to learn more about digital certificates, you can also find lots of good information in TechNet. In particular, Knowledge Base article 297142, "Overview of Digital Certificates," is a good

place to start digging more deeply into this topic. For a more server-centric set of documents, see the "Certificates" page for the Windows 2000 Internet Information Server (a.k.a. IIS; `www.microsoft.com/windows2000/en/server/iis/default.asp?url=/windows2000/en/server/iis/htm/core/iicerts.htm`). By digging into this stuff, you'll learn how Web servers get and use certificates, and how Web clients check them when conducting secured transactions.

Summary

This chapter discussed all kinds of topics related to safe surfing. In particular, I examined Internet Explorer's security settings, Web content zones, privacy controls, and other aspects of its behavior designed to help you navigate the sometimes risky waters of the Internet with relative safety (if not always relative ease). I also looked at what's involved in spending money safely online, and some tricks to keep your online financial activities separate from the rest of your fiscal life. Along the way, you should have learned various ways to restrict, limit, or lock down IE's sometimes wild and wacky ways.

In the next chapter the focus turns to your PC's primary program: the operating system itself. There, you'll review much of what you've learned about establishing and maintaining a secure Windows PC, along with lots of tips and tricks to help you get secure, and keep things that way.

Chapter 12

Practicing System Safety

To a large extent, practicing system safety is based on knowledge. That is, you have to know what's normal and regular on your system before you can recognize what's abnormal or irregular. In addition, there are plenty of commonsense rules of safe computing that are easy to practice given the installation, use, and proper maintenance of the right tools to help you stay safe, online and off. Throw in a few good working habits, and exercise a little due diligence before downloading software, and you're most of the way safe.

But as the old saying goes: "eternal vigilance is the price of liberty" (Wendell Phillips, 1852). Practicing safe computing means keeping up with current threats and vulnerabilities, so as to be better prepared to encounter and foil them. It also means keeping a constant eye on your system and its behavior to look for the odd, the unwanted, the unexpected, or other signs that malign forces may be at work somewhere. This chapter explains how to recognize a clean and safe PC, and how to keep your PC secure and pristine!

Baselining Your System

Once you've done the scanning necessary — for viruses, spyware, adware, and so forth — to make reasonably sure your PC isn't operating under a cloud of sorts, you can take a look around your system to see what's normal. Computer geeks sometimes call this kind of activity "baselining" a system, because it's intended to provide you with a snapshot of what's normal for your PC.

You'll find several components of interest when establishing a baseline for your PC. One of the most important components involves taking a look at what processes are running and active on your system right after startup, before you fire off any applications. That way, they'll include only those processes that Windows itself launches at startup to do its job, and those associated with other programs that normally launch during startup (many items in this latter category will be related to the firewalls, anti-virus, anti-spyware, and other security or safety components I recommend elsewhere in this book, in fact). In the sections that follow, I describe some methods for taking snapshots of a normal baseline, including process and file inventories.

Creating a Process Inventory

It's easy to take a process inventory at any time on a Windows XP machine. Simply right-click the task bar (usually at the bottom of your display area unless you've moved it) and select Task Manager from the resulting pop-up menu. To see the list of processes running on your PC, click the Processes tab at the top of the window, as shown in Figure 12-1.

Tip

By clicking the heading button in any column on the Task Manager Processes tab, you can cause the processes to be sorted on that field value. Thus, for example, click CPU Time to sort processes according to the amount of CPU time they've consumed since the last reboot (hint: System Idle Process always wins, so look in line 2 and lower for potential causes for concern). Click again on the same heading to reverse the sort order (by default, the highest values show up first, so clicking again causes the lowest values to show up first). Same thing goes for Mem Usage (memory usage), which can also be pretty revealing when it comes to understanding where your system resources are going.

Applications | Processes | Performance | Networking

Image Name	PID	User Name	CPU	Mem Usage
alg.exe	124	LOCAL SERVICE	00	2,584 K
CCAPP.EXE	1296	Administrator	00	23,892 K
CCEVTMGR.EXE	1632	SYSTEM	00	3,716 K
CCPROXY.EXE	1912	SYSTEM	00	6,140 K
CCSETMGR.EXE	1608	SYSTEM	00	4,304 K
csrss.exe	928	SYSTEM	00	2,516 K
explorer.exe	1520	Administrator	00	19,528 K
lsass.exe	1020	SYSTEM	00	856 K
mgabg.exe	1960	SYSTEM	00	1,840 K
msmsgs.exe	748	Administrator	00	2,952 K
NAVAPSVC.EXE	1992	SYSTEM	00	8,224 K
NOPDB.EXE	500	SYSTEM	00	10,096 K
NPROTECT.EXE	236	SYSTEM	00	5,288 K
psp.exe	1440	Administrator	00	992 K
SAVSCAN.EXE	300	SYSTEM	00	216 K
services.exe	1008	SYSTEM	00	3,508 K
smss.exe	404	SYSTEM	00	408 K
SNDSrvc.exe	464	SYSTEM	00	3,360 K
spoolsv.exe	1788	SYSTEM	00	5,052 K
SpySweeper.exe	1284	Administrator	00	10,408 K
svchost.exe	624	SYSTEM	00	3,272 K
svchost.exe	1180	SYSTEM	00	4,768 K
svchost.exe	1228	NETWORK SERVICE	00	3,696 K
svchost.exe	1308	SYSTEM	00	27,172 K
svchost.exe	1356	NETWORK SERVICE	00	2,472 K
svchost.exe	1408	LOCAL SERVICE	00	3,484 K
symlcsvc.exe	532	SYSTEM	00	520 K

☑ Show processes from all users End Process

Processes: 31 CPU Usage: 0% Commit Charge: 240M / 3434M

Figure 12-1: The Processes tab in Task Manager shows you all the processes active on your PC.

Of course, unless you want to copy all this information by hand, it might be more sensible to record it to a file. That way, you've got something to compare things with later when you go back to check this list. Because you're trying to compare current conditions to what passes for normal on your PC, I recommend you do this right after startup, before launching any additional applications. Fortunately, the built-in Windows `tasklist` command makes this job easy; here's how you can ensconce this data safely in a file named tasklist-*yymmdd*.txt (substitute two-digit codes for the year, month, and day so you can tell when the snapshot was taken):

1. Open a Command Prompt window by choosing Start → Run, typing **`cmd`** (or **`cmd.exe`**, if you prefer) in the Open text field of the Run dialog box, and then clicking OK to execute those instructions.
2. To see a list of active tasks on your system, type **`tasklist`** at the command prompt. This produces a display like that shown in Figure 12-2. For more information on the `tasklist` command, type **`tasklist /?`** to display online command help. Also, you can sort the process names alphabetically by typing **`tasklist /nh | sort`** (this drops the column headings from the output and then sends the resulting process names and info to a sort utility to sort them in descending alphabetical order by process name).

```
Microsoft Windows XP [Version 5.1.2600]
(C) Copyright 1985-2001 Microsoft Corp.

C:\Documents and Settings\Administrator>tasklist

Image Name                   PID Session Name     Session#    Mem Usage
========================= ====== ================ ======== ============
System Idle Process            0 Console                 0         16 K
System                         4 Console                 0        224 K
smss.exe                     404 Console                 0        408 K
csrss.exe                    928 Console                 0      2,772 K
winlogon.exe                 964 Console                 0      1,400 K
services.exe                1008 Console                 0      3,508 K
lsass.exe                   1020 Console                 0      1,364 K
svchost.exe                 1180 Console                 0      4,780 K
svchost.exe                 1228 Console                 0      3,696 K
svchost.exe                 1308 Console                 0     27,172 K
svchost.exe                 1356 Console                 0      2,472 K
svchost.exe                 1408 Console                 0      3,476 K
CCSETMGR.EXE                1608 Console                 0      4,356 K
CCEVTMGR.EXE                1632 Console                 0      3,724 K
spoolsv.exe                 1788 Console                 0      5,052 K
CCPROXY.EXE                 1912 Console                 0      6,140 K
mgabg.exe                   1960 Console                 0      1,840 K
NAVAPSVC.EXE                1992 Console                 0      8,224 K
NPROTECT.EXE                 236 Console                 0      5,288 K
SAVSCAN.EXE                  300 Console                 0        216 K
SNDSrvc.exe                  464 Console                 0      3,360 K
NOPDB.EXE                    500 Console                 0     10,096 K
symlcsvc.exe                 532 Console                 0        520 K
alg.exe                      124 Console                 0      2,584 K
explorer.exe                1520 Console                 0     19,544 K
CCAPP.EXE                   1296 Console                 0     22,276 K
msmsgs.exe                   748 Console                 0      2,956 K
SpySweeper.exe              1284 Console                 0     10,408 K
svchost.exe                  624 Console                 0      3,272 K
psp.exe                     1440 Console                 0      1,200 K
cmd.exe                     2696 Console                 0      1,688 K
tasklist.exe                2264 Console                 0      3,592 K
wmiprvse.exe                2272 Console                 0      4,568 K

C:\Documents and Settings\Administrator>_
```

Figure 12-2: The tasklist command provides a list of all processes active on Windows XP.

3. At the command prompt, type **`tasklist > C:\tasklist-yymmdd.txt`**, where you substitute two-digit values for year for *yy*, month for *mm*, and day for *dd*.

Note

Indeed you could cut and paste the text directly from the command window that's shown in Figure 12-2, but I go on to Step 3 and have you repeat the command, piping the output directly into a file. I think it's an easier and more straightforward way to grab this information and put it some place you can find it again. The syntax I show for the command writes the output to the root of the C:\ drive. If you follow those instructions verbatim, you may want to move that file somewhere else so you can find it more easily at another time.

4. Type `exit` at the command line or click the x-shaped close control in the upper right-hand corner of the command window to close this window.

Understanding What You See

For each entry under the Image Name heading (appears in both the Task Manager Processes display and in `tasklist` command output), you determine what it represents and whether it's benign (as it should be) or malign (which means it needs rooting out). Let's look at a reformatted version of the tasklist output in Table 12-1 (entries were alphabetized and some column data removed), which ties into the 16-item numbered list shown after Table 12-1.

Table 12-1 Tasklist Command Output

Image Name	*PID*	*Mem Usage*	*Explanation*
`alg.exe`	124	2,584K	Application Layer Gateway (1)
`CCAPP.EXE`	1296	23,892K	Common Client application (NAV; 2)
`CCEVTMGR.EXE`	1632	3,732K	Symantec Common Client Event Mgr Svc (NAV; 3)
`CCPROXY.EXE`	1912	6,076K	Symantec Common Client Proxy Server (4)
`CCSETMGR.EXE`	1608	4,312K	Background task associated with NIS (5)
`cmd.exe`	2884	872K	Windows command shell (Command prompt window)
`csrss.exe`	928	816K	Windows client server runtime subsystem (6)
`explorer.exe`	1520	19,180K	Windows Program Manager a.k.a. Windows Explorer
`explorer.exe`	2784	2,696K	Child process of Windows Program Manager
`hh.exe`	2556	16,748K	Windows help program
`iexplore.exe`	2776	22,480K	Microsoft Internet Explorer (7)
`lsass.exe`	1020	1,348K	Windows Local Security Authority Service (8)
`mgabg.exe`	1960	1,840K	Matrox BIOS Guard (works with graphics card)
`msmsgs.exe`	748	2,944K	MSN Messenger Traybar service (9)

Image Name	*PID*	*Mem Usage*	*Explanation*
NAVAPSVC.EXE	1992	8,220K	Norton AntiVirus auto-protect service (10)
NOPDB.EXE	500	10,096K	Norton Speed Disk process (11)
NPROTECT.EXE	236	5,284K	Norton process protects recycle bin (12)
pdesk.exe	552	3,620K	System tray app for Matrox graphics card
realsched.exe	2896	176K	Scheduler program: prompts for RealOne updates
SAVSCAN.EXE	300	616K	Symantec's anti-virus scanning software
services.exe	1008	3,504K	Used to start, stop, and manage system services
smss.exe	404	408K	Session Manager Subsystem (13)
SNDSrvc.exe	464	3,360K	Symantec Network Driver Svc (part of NIS2003/4)
spoolsv.exe	1788	5,036K	Windows print spooler service (14)
SpySweeper.exe	1284	10,196K	SpySweeper anti-spyware/anti-adware background task
svchost.exe	624	3,272K	Windows system process to service dynamic link libraries (DLLs) (15)
svchost.exe	1180	4,772K	Windows system process to service DLLs (15)
svchost.exe	1228	3,688K	Windows system process to service DLLs (15)
svchost.exe	1308	27,376K	Windows system process to service DLLs (15)
svchost.exe	1356	2,440K	Windows system process to service DLLs (15)
svchost.exe	1408	3,484K	Windows system process to service DLLs (15)
symlcsvc.exe	532	520K	Symantec Core Library Code (common code items)
System	4	224K	The Windows System process
System Idle Process	0	16K	Runs whenever CPU is idle
ups.exe	572	1,788K	PowerChute uninterruptible power supply (UPS) monitoring tool
winlogon.exe	964	7,964K	Windows process to manage user logon and logoff
wmiprvse.exe	3924	4,560K	Windows Management Interface (WMI) provider service (16)

1. The Application Layer Gateway is a Microsoft executable that provides functionality for the Windows Firewall and for Internet Connection Sharing for Windows XP. I find no evidence to indicate this process may be impersonated or subverted by spyware, adware, or malware, but many attacks that attempt to shut down local security will attempt to shut down this process as part of that effort.

Note

All of the executables that start with CC are part of the Symantec Common Client runtime environment, used for Norton Internet Security (which includes Norton Personal Firewall, Norton AntiVirus, Norton AntiSpam, and various other components in the test installation). This includes entries 2, 3, 4, and 5 on this list. There are no known attacks that impersonate these Norton components, as best I can discover.

2. `CCAPP.EXE` is part of the Norton AntiVirus system. No documented attacks or impersonations on many of these components, though some malware may attempt to shut down one or more of these components to bring down Norton security shields.
3. `CCEVTMGR.EXE` provides a general event management registration and reporting service for all Norton Internet Security components.
4. `CCPROXY.EXE` provides a mechanism for proxying Web access requests within Windows environments where the Norton Personal Firewall is active; it's designed to let the software screen outgoing Web requests according to security and suitability criteria (the latter in connection with Norton Internet Security's Parental Controls).
5. `CCSETMGR.EXE` provides a mechanism for launching various Norton Internet Security or Norton AntiVirus components at startup, and for scheduling LiveUpdate automated downloads.
6. `cmd.exe` is the Windows executable for the command-line environment (this appears only if you have a command prompt window open when the snapshot is taken). No known impersonation or attacks are documented, though some malware may open this process to handle scripts if system security is sufficiently compromised.
7. `csrss.exe` is the Windows client server runtime subsystem. Its job is to provide common windows, thread management, and graphics capabilities to all subsystems running in the Windows environment.

Caution

At least one known virus impersonates `csrss.exe`, so be very suspicious if you see more than one instance with this name (there should be only one).

8. `lsass.exe` is the Windows local security authority subsystem service that handles the logon process, user authentication, and generates session-specific security tokens that are compared with user and group permissions to determine whether resource access requests are granted or denied. The Sasser worm specifically attacks this system component, as do some varieties of Nimos and Lovgate.

9. msmsgs.exe is what the MSN messenger service users to advertise its presence, and to include a traybar icon on the Windows XP desktop (installed by default in Windows XP and subsequent service packs). Although no attacks on this component are documented, some attacks use file transfers inside the application to try to deliver infected payloads to users.

Caution

Several documented viruses use msmsgs.exe as their process names. You should never see more than one instance of this process name (or even one if you disable the Windows Messenger application). If you don't use Windows Messenger, in fact, it's perfectly safe to terminate this process. If you don't use Messenger at all, or if you don't mind starting it up manually yourself (use the Run command, type msmsgs.exe in the Open: text box, then click OK), you can stop it from running on startup as follows: Start→All Programs→ Windows Messenger→Tools→Preferences and then uncheck the check box that reads "Run Windows Messenger when Windows starts."

10. NAVAPSVC.EXE is Norton AntiVirus's auto-protect service; its job is to screen inbound and outbound file transfers, e-mail attachments, and so forth to block viruses from entering or leaving your PC. No known attacks are documented, but this is clearly something many types of malware will try to turn off if possible.
11. NOPDB.EXE is associated with the Norton Speed Disk utility in Norton SystemWorks; its job is to permit Speed Disk to launch during startup when the user requests this service. No known attacks are documented, nor any attempts to turn off or defeat this service. You won't see this on your machine unless it's also running Norton SystemWorks.
12. NPROTECT.EXE is associated with the Norton Protected Recycle Bin set up as part of Norton SystemWorks; its job is to prevent the Recycle Bin from being emptied without obtaining user confirmation. No known attacks are documented, nor any attempts to turn off or defeat this service.
13. smss.exe is a Microsoft process involved with creating, managing, and deleting user sessions.

Caution

Numerous viruses run using the smss.exe image name, so be sure to preserve only that version that resides inside the C:\Windows\System32 folder (all others are illegitimate). Search on smss.exe to look for multiple instances, and delete any that show up!

14. spoolsv.exe is the Microsoft print spooler service, which stores pending print jobs on your PC until they can be sent to the designated printer for output.

Caution

Numerous viruses run using the `spoolsv.exe` image name, so preserve only that version that resides inside the `C:\Windows\System32` folder (you can even end this process, too — you just won't be able to print unless you manually restart the Printer Spooler service or reboot your machine).

15. `svchost.exe` runs as a process that supports common Windows dynamic link libraries (DLLs) for lots of services. In fact, you'll see one instance of this executable in the processes display for each such group of services that shares a common set of DLLs in the Windows runtime environment. Figure 12-3 shows tasklist output that's been crafted to document what services are involved in each of the six `svchost.exe` instances present in `svchost` that appear therein — notice the wide variety and large number of services involved. No known attacks or attempts to turn off this process are documented, but it too should be found only resident in the `C:\Windows\System32` folder (though you will find copies in service pack or CD image folders as well).

```
C:\Documents and Settings\Administrator>tasklist /svc /fi "imagename eq svchost.
exe"

Image Name                   PID Services
========================= ====== =============================================
svchost.exe                 1180 DcomLaunch, TermService
svchost.exe                 1228 RpcSs
svchost.exe                 1308 AudioSrv, Browser, CryptSvc, Dhcp, dmserver,
                                 ERSvc, EventSystem, helpsvc, lanmanserver,
                                 lanmanworkstation, Netman, Nla, RasMan,
                                 Schedule, seclogon, SENS, SharedAccess,
                                 ShellHWDetection, srservice, TapiSrv,
                                 Themes, TrkWks, W32Time, winmgmt, wscsvc,
                                 wuauserv, WZCSVC
svchost.exe                 1356 Dnscache
svchost.exe                 1408 LmHosts, RemoteRegistry, WebClient
svchost.exe                  624 stisvc

C:\Documents and Settings\Administrator>_
```

Figure 12-3: The tasklist command can tell you which services are using svchost.exe instances.

Note

The precise command syntax in Figure 12-3 is `tasklist /svc /fi "imagename eq svchost.exe"`. Restated in something closer to English, this means show me all the DLLs for the services that every instance of the `svchost.exe` file uses. What you see in that display are various instances of `svchost`, where the first relates to distributed communications and terminal services, the second to remote procedure call services, the third to a whole bunch of services that call common presentation dlls, the fourth to DNS caching behavior, the fifth to various kinds of remote access, and the sixth to a still digital imaging service that runs in Windows XP.

16. `wmiprvse.exe` is a manifestation of Microsoft's system management application program interfaces (APIs) at the runtime level; it's a rearchitected version of the Windows Management Interface (WMI) introduced in Windows XP (and also supported in Windows Server 2003) to support all WMI services through a single provider service. That's why you'll find it running on your system someday because you've recently installed an application that draws on WMI support, or a Microsoft update that does likewise. As with `svchost.exe`, you will occasionally encounter multiple instances of this software running at the same time—this is normal.

Caution

Some viruses that impersonate this service have been reported—most notably Sonebot.B, Gletta.A.Trojan, and various flavors of Sasser. The only valid instance of this code resides within the `C:\Windows\System32\wbem` directory.

By getting a sense of what's normal for your system, you can use Task Manager or the `tasklist` command at any time you've got reason to be concerned about your system to check one snapshot against the other. If you do your homework on the initial snapshot, you'll need to check up only on new items to figure out where they're coming from, and what kinds of trouble they might portend, if any.

This probably leads to a perfectly valid question: "How do I find out about process names on my PC?" Indeed, my own listings here are examples that will contain some (but not all) of the items that will show up on your machine. To document your unique collection of processes, open Task Manager and check the Processes tab, or create your own `tasklist` output file as described earlier. Then, you can use the various entries in the Image Name column on Google, Yahoo!, or the search engine of your choice to learn more about these processes—especially, whether they should be causes for concern or otherwise. I got my information from a whole variety of sources online, along with an excellent tool from Liutilities called WinTasks 5 Professional (see the "Resources" section toward the end of the chapter for more details on this offering).

Note

To get a definite sense of what "Safe mode" really means for Windows XP, try booting your machine into that mode (hold the F8 key down just as Windows starts booting and then select Boot in Safe mode from the resulting character mode menu that appears on your screen). Whereas my normal Windows XP boot shows 30-plus processes, in Safe mode I get only 12 (not counting `taskmgr.exe`, which runs only to show me the other process names), and those include only basic system elements necessary for operation: `csrss.exe`, `explorer.exe`, `lsass.exe`, `services.exe`, `smss.exe`, `System`, `System Idle Process`, and `winlogon.exe`, plus "only" three instances of `svchost.exe`! This really shows how few elements are needed to run a minimal, stripped-down version of Windows.

Rough and Ready Performance Metrics

Although Windows XP does include a marvelous utility called Performance (it's in the Administrative Tools folder in the Control Panel) that you can use to measure system performance very accurately, you don't really need that tool to get a sense of what's normal on your PC. Instead, you can use a watch with a second hand because pinpoint accuracy isn't really overwhelmingly important (hence the title for this section).

Instead, create a text file or take notes with results from timing typical activities on your machine. They should include some or all of the following items:

- **Normal startup time (cold boot)** — Start timing as soon as you turn on the power to your PC and stop when the Windows login prompt appears (if applicable), or when the booting process has completed (if not).
- **Normal restart time (warm boot)** — Restart Windows XP (Start → Turn Off Computer and then click the Restart button) and start timing simultaneously; stop timing when the Windows login prompt appears (if applicable), or when the booting process has completed (if not).
- **Start time for commonly used applications** — These might include Office components, Internet Explorer (or whatever Web browser you use), and other applications that take at least a short time to launch (to give you enough time to have something to measure). Launch them from the Start → All Programs menu sequence and start timing as you click the application name on its pop-up menu. Stop timing when the application is ready for your input.

By comparing your baseline timings with those taken at another time, you'll be able to tell if your machine is running more slowly than usual or not.

Other Snapshots Worth Gathering

Most professionals who go looking for signs of unwanted or malicious activity also depend on comparing before and after snapshots of key directories in the Windows file system and in the Windows registry. I touched on some of the techniques and tools involved in Chapter 4 of this book. If you decide you might want to use them on your own system, you'll need to get familiar with some new tools and techniques yourself.

The Windows directories where untoward things often happen include the `%windir%` directory (this environment variable usually points to `C:\Windows` on most Windows XP computers, but to `C:\WINNT` on Windows NT and 2000) and the `%windir%\System32` subdirectory (a.k.a. `C:\Windows\System32`). By monitoring the contents of these directories, you can sometimes discover signs of unwanted software at work. By following the same steps to create a baseline snapshot now, and a comparison snapshot later, you can create a basis for investigation and see what's changed. Here's how:

1. Open a Command prompt window (Start → Run, type **`cmd.exe`** in the Open text field of the Run dialog box, and then click OK).

2. Type the following at the command line: **`dir %windir% /o:-d > winfiles-yymmdd.txt`**, where *yy* is the two-digit year, *mm* the two-digit month, and *dd* the two-digit day. Note that this captures only the files in this directory (you'd use the `/s -d` attribute instead of `/a: -d` to capture subdirectory data as well).

3. Type the following at the command line: **`dir %windir%\System32 /s /o:-d > win32files-yymmdd.txt`**, where *yy* is the two-digit year, *mm* the two-digit month, and *dd* the two-digit day. Note that this captures all the files in the `. . .\System 32` directory and all of its subdirectories, so this can be a big file.

If you use this same process for your baseline and then when you're conducting an investigation, compare the various files for the different dates involved, and you may be able to spot some differences. Files will be listed newest first, so hopefully, you won't have to look too deeply into any list to see new or unexpected items in the "after" snapshots that are missing from the "before" snapshots.

Tip

Finding differences isn't necessarily a bad thing—especially if you've installed a security update or a service pack since the last snapshot (in that case, you should expect to see things change so much that you'll really want to create a new baseline after performing such actions). The same thing applies whenever you install new or update existing software as well: make a new baseline! In general, it's only when you find instances of familiar file names in directories where they're not supposed to be (or in new directories for which you have no idea where they came from.) that you really have cause for concern.

You can also apply the same technique to your Windows registry, but it takes a bit more effort. The idea is to snapshot and export the contents of major registry keys (`HKEY_CLASSES_ROOT` or `HKCR`, `HKEY_CURRENT_USER` or `HKCU`, `HKEY_LOCAL_MACHINE` or `HKLM`, and so forth) or subkeys subject to change—for example, the `HKLM\SOFTWARE` key is the item to grab for before and after snapshots when installing software on your PC—to provide a basis for comparison.

If you don't want to spring for one of the tools I recommend in Chapter 4 (such as Registry Watch or Active Registry Monitor, which can perform such comparisons for you more or less automatically), you'll have to do a certain amount of setup and legwork to implement my suggestions (see also the next section, which specifically addresses issues involved in comparing snapshots to one another). Here's how to snapshot your major registry keys:

1. Launch the Windows Registry Editor: Start→Run, type **`regedit.exe`** in the Open dialog box, and then click OK.

2. Highlight the first major key in the registry, `HKEY_CLASSES_ROOT`, as shown in Figure 12-4.

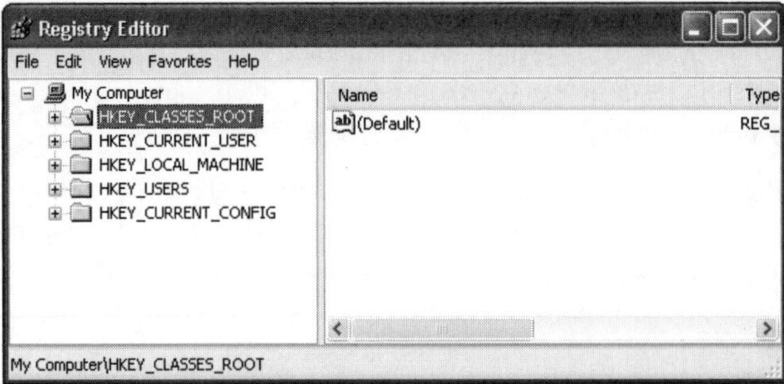

Figure 12-4: To write registry data to a file, select a key (or subkey) in the left-hand pane before using File → Export.

3. Click File and then Export in the resulting pull-down menu. The Export Registry File window appears, as depicted in Figure 12-5. Notice the file naming convention I used: `RegSnap-HKCR-`*`yymmdd`*`.reg`. This helps you to identify and reimport that data should you ever need to and provides the basis for automated comparisons explained in the next section.

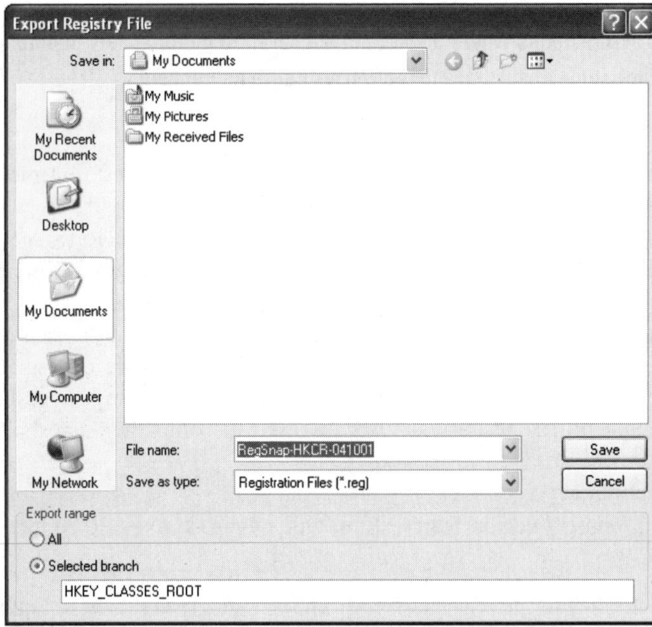

Figure 12-5: Save your files someplace where you can find them later, using recognizable names.

Note

The Registry Editor saves exported files by default in `.reg` format. That's good, because if you want to read data exported from your registry, or want the ability to restore only specific, individual keys and values, stick with the default registry file type (`.reg` extension). You will find other sources that recommend that you save such snapshots in hive file format (which usually take the `.hiv` extension) but if you do so, please follow other instructions carefully, realizing that you won't be able to read the contents of those files (even using WinDiff they're pretty incomprehensible for the most part) and that you can import only entire hive files in one go. In addition to being human readable, you can also pick and choose the keys and/or values you want to import from `.reg` files into your registry, which makes them preferable for most uses, in my opinion.

4. By default, the file is saved in your My Documents folder, but you can navigate inside the My Computer or My Network controls to store its contents elsewhere. Click the Save button, and you're done.
5. Repeat for the other major registry keys (`HKCU`, `HKLM`, and `HKU`—you don't need to capture `HKCC` because it's dynamically rebuilt each time Windows starts up).
6. Close the Registry Editor (click the x in the upper right-hand corner, or use Registry→Exit menu commands).

Here again, you'll need to repeat this exercise later, so you'll have "after" snapshots to compare to your original baselines.

Tip

If you want to be sure you're comparing "after" snapshots to current known good working "before" snapshots, it's essential to rebuild your baseline snapshots every time you change something about your PC. This means after installing new applications or utilities, service packs or security updates; adding new (or removing old) hardware; and so on. All of these things change the Windows registry, file system, and the list of processes active on your PC. Without keeping up with changes, you may end up chasing phantoms instead of real problems. Thus, it might be a good idea to get in the habit of building new baselines each time you make a system change, and at least once a month (perhaps on the same day of each month, driven by an Outlook reminder?) to be doubly darn sure you're working from the latest and greatest known good working baseline of your PC.

Comparing Differences

If you've a mind to avoid lots of reading and manual labor when comparing differences between one snapshot file and another, you're not alone. In fact, Microsoft includes a special tool called `Windiff.exe` that's designed to compare two versions of the same file (or two similar files, as will be the case here) to one another.

INSTALLING WINDIFF

WinDiff isn't installed as part of Windows XP (or other Windows versions) by default. You have to load your Windows XP CD or your latest Service Pack CD and install it from there. Here's how:

1. Insert the CD into your CD drive; the autorun program on the CD should launch the Windows XP install utility, as show in Figure 12-6.

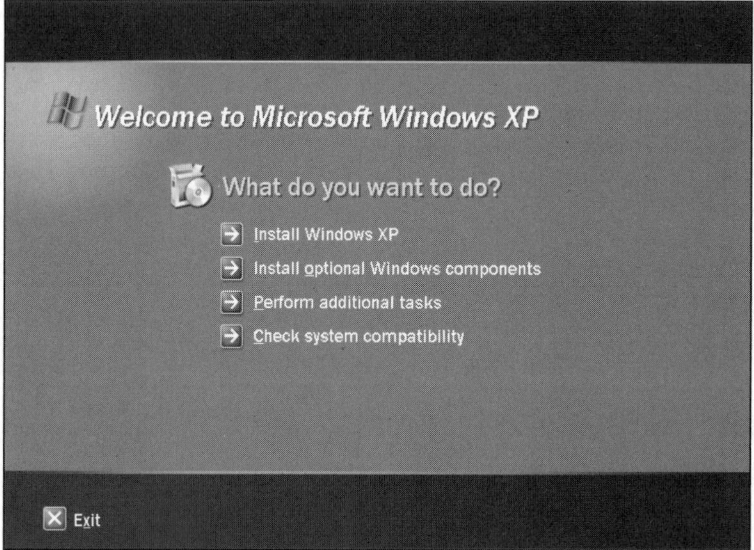

Figure 12-6: When the XP welcome screen appears, it offers various activities you can use it to perform.

2. Click the "Perform additional tasks" link that appears in Figure 12-6 and then click the Browse this CD button (this produces the display shown in Figure 12-7).

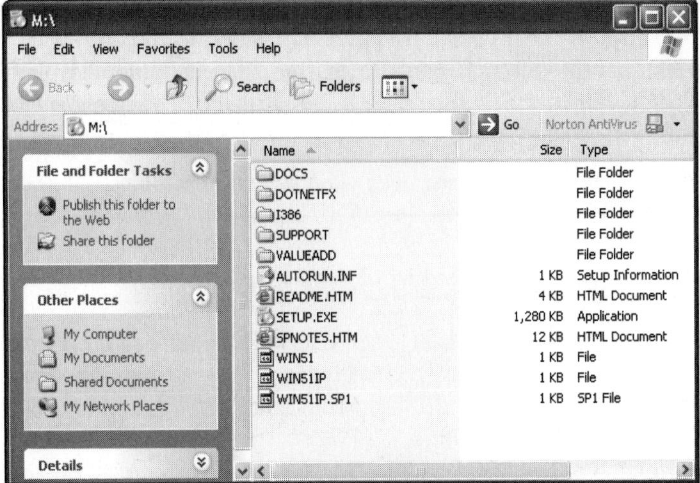

Figure 12-7: When you browse the XP CD, you open Windows Explorer to view its contents.

3. Open the SUPPORT folder to access the setup utility for the Windows Support Tools, as shown in Figure 12-8.

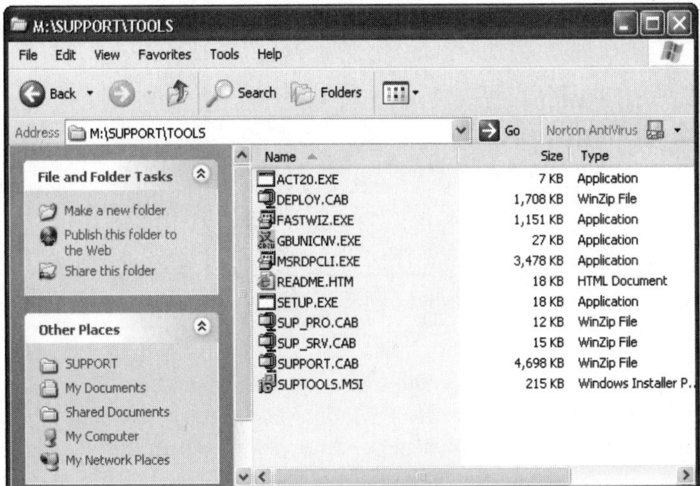

Figure 12-8: The SUPPORT\TOOLS directory is where the necessary setup utility resides.

4. Double-click SETUP.EXE to launch the Windows Support Tools installation wizard. It will lead you through the rest of the installation process. If you decide you don't want to install the complete collection of Windows Support Tools, you can elect to install Typical Tools (rather than the complete set, which also includes Optional Tools) because WinDiff is included in the former subset.

5. When the installation is finished, close all open windows and you'll be able to start using WinDiff.

USING WINDIFF

Once you've installed WinDiff, it shows up by default in a directory named `%ProgramFiles%/Support Tools` (for most readers, this means `C:\Program Files\Support Tools`). Using it requires a little preparation and understanding, but it's really not that bad. Here's how:

1. To launch the program, double-click the entry named WinDiff (or WinDiff.exe) in the Support Tools directory. Alternatively, you can click the WinLogo key and R and then type **`"%programfiles%\Support Tools\WinDiff"`** into the Open text field of the Run dialog box (note: the quotes around the string are necessary because the file specification has blanks in it). Either way, you should see a display like the one shown in Figure 12-9.

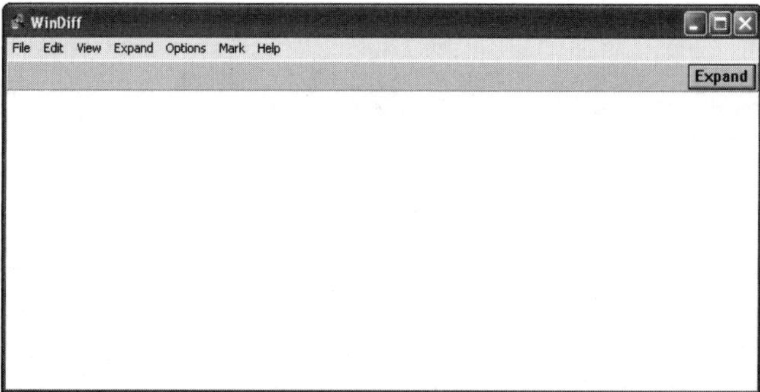

Figure 12-9: When WinDiff opens, it looks like a whole lotta nothing.

2. Next, click the File command in the WinDiff toolbar menu. There, the first two commands are Compare files and Compare directories. This admittedly contrived example hinges on comparing two directory lists I made of some product keys I keep around, one before I went in and added a file and changed some values in another file, the other after making such changes. These two files appear side-by-side to show the raw data in the following code lines:

```
Volume in drive D is Data and Storage                             Volume in
drive D is Data and Storage
 Volume Serial Number is 2803-B30D                                Volume Serial
Number is 2803-B30D

 Directory of d:\Test040928                                       Directory of
d:\Test040928

08/05/2004  05:07 PM          39 bitdefender-key.txt             08/05/2004
05:07 PM        39 bitdefender-key.txt
09/19/2004  06:33 PM          60 NAV2005upg-install-key.txt      09/19/2004
06:33 PM        60 NAV2005upg-install-key.txt
08/05/2004  04:40 PM          76 NIS2004-install-key.txt         08/05/2004
04:40 PM        76 NIS2004-install-key.txt
09/17/2004  09:50 PM         368 NIS2005-install-key.txt         09/17/2004
09:50 PM       368 NIS2005-install-key.txt
07/11/2004  04:41 PM          30 NortonInetSecurityKey.txt       09/28/2004
04:45 PM       400 NIS2006-install-key.txt
08/23/2004  06:25 PM          58 opera-7-regcode.txt             07/11/2004
04:41 PM        30 NortonInetSecurityKey.txt
06/15/2004  03:23 PM          28 spysweeperkey.txt               08/23/2004
06:25 PM        58 opera-7-regcode.txt
                                                                 09/28/2004
04:46 PM        54 spysweeperkey.txt
               7 File(s)   659 bytes
8 File(s)          1,085 bytes
               0 Dir(s)  100,493,692,928 bytes free
0 Dir(s)  100,493,692,928 bytes free
```

Note: I did take some liberties with these listings, including deleting unnecessary white space to fit it onto the page, and adding a blank line to the right-hand file listing to make the file count and free space lines match for both files.

3. If you click the Compare Files menu in WinDiff, the first window that pops open in response lets you pick the first file for comparison. Once you specify that file, a second window that lets you pick the second file pops up next. In my case, I compared a couple of directory listings named `keyfilev1.txt` and `keyfilev2.txt` that I deposited into the My Documents folder. After making these selections, a display like the one shown in Figure 12-10 appears (an analysis of this display, which is the meat of this whole section appears after the final step in this step-by-step sequence that follows the figure).

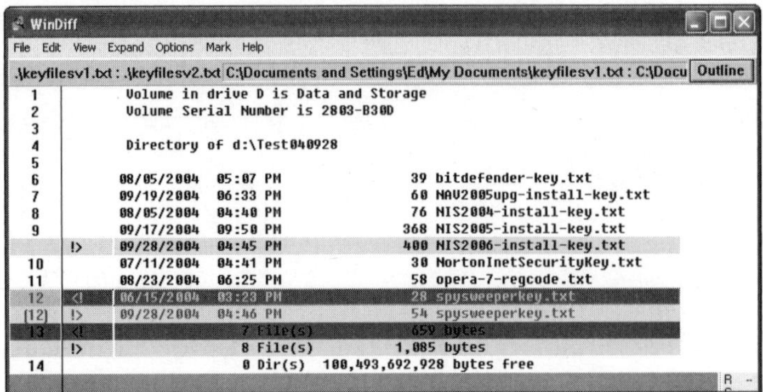

Figure 12-10: Color highlights help display file differences in WinDiff, but they don't jump out in a black and white rendering as much.

4. Once you're finished with WinDiff, click the red x in the upper right-hand corner, or select File → Exit to close the application.

The top line of the WinDiff display area shows the two files being compared. In the actual listing, lines with differences between the two files show up in yellow for the file 2 information, red for the file 1 information. This means that a line that's present in file 2 but not in file 1 (an added line) shows up only in yellow. This is the case for the unnumbered line between line numbers 9 and 10, where the listing for file `NIS2006-install-key.txt` shows up. A line that was present in file 1 but absent in file 2 would show up in red only (this does not occur in this example). A line that differs between the two files shows up in red first for the file 1 version and yellow second for the file 2 version. This is the case for lines 12 and [12] and for lines 13 and the unnumbered line that follows immediately afterward. These pairs of lines show that the file size for `spysweeperkey.txt` changed from 28 in file 1 to 56 in file 2, and that the total byte count for file 1 is 659, but 1,085 for file 2. This is just the kind of information you need to compare directory contents, registry files, and other items that may have changed. The appearance of a new file (for a product as yet unannounced, and by no means available) is a sure sign of monkey business, as are the changes in file size for the Spy Sweeper key and for the directory itself.

Working with WinDiff takes a little time and practice, but basically it takes two file names or directory specifications as input parameters (so it can have two things to compare to one another). By way of output, it creates a list of all the differences between the two files it finds, using color and other flags to show differences. This is merely handy when comparing process lists, which seldom exceed 40 or 50 items; it's absolutely essential when comparing Windows files or registry values, because they can easily number in the thousands!

That said, how can you tell when a change is significant? As I mentioned in earlier chapters in this book, anything that changes Internet Explorer defaults unexpectedly or unwontedly, adds entries to programs that are run automatically at startup (either in keys that end in `\Run`, `\RunOnce`, or buried in class definitions elsewhere in the registry), or removes other entries from those keys (so as to disable firewalls, anti-virus, or anti-spyware software, for example) is suspect. If a little practice doesn't build up your confidence, visit anti-virus and anti-spyware sites and look at the files, registry data, and other items they mention in documenting adware, spyware, and malware, and the items deleted or modified when removing such things manually. These all represent the kinds of things you're looking for and should help you zoom in on your local targets quickly and effectively.

Monitoring System Security

One of the biggest and best improvements in Windows XP SP2 is the introduction of the Security Center. This is a centralized utility that reports on what Windows knows about your system's current level of security, and that provides access to information to address any problems it reports (or at least, advice on what to check to make sure such problems don't exist). On a test PC running Norton Internet Security, for example, although Windows can tell that a firewall and anti-virus software are installed, it apparently can't report on their update status, as shown in Figure 12-11.

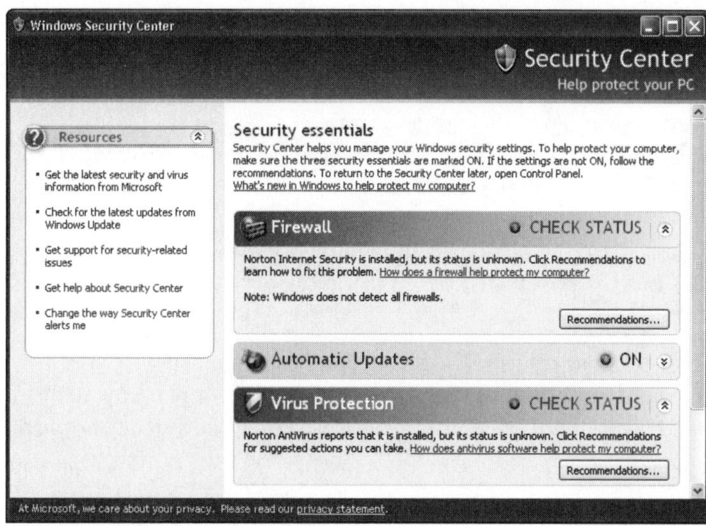

Figure 12-11: My test PC is running Norton Internet Security 2004, fully updated, but Security Center can't tell.

You can check in on this utility from time to time to see how Windows thinks you're doing in the security department. On the other hand, each time Windows starts up if there's a need to check status in any of the areas that the Security Center monitors, it'll pop up a warning message that tells you there's something going on that needs looking into. It's a vast step forward over anything else Microsoft has ever done before by way of security monitoring. That said, because it doesn't yet detect all anti-virus programs equally (I tried Norton AntiVirus 2004, BitDefender, and other packages mentioned in Chapter 9, but it could not access status information for all of those it could recognize) nor could it do the same for all third-party firewalls. I imagine this situation will improve as Windows XP SP2 becomes the norm, and more vendors add the necessary hooks into their products to communicate with the Security Center. For example, if I didn't use both the firewall and the anti-virus software built into BitDefender Professional v7.2, the program would report to Security Center

that anti-virus software was not enabled, even though it was running and working properly. On the other hand, Norton Internet Security 2005 integrated with Security Center perfectly and would accurately report all status changes in the firewall and anti-virus capabilities separately and correctly. Again, I think this situation should improve with time, as these kinks are worked out where necessary.

Of course, I still think automatic update is the right approach for all security-related software, whether or not Security Center can track its currency and update status. With automatic update turned on and a current subscription, you're guaranteed to be able to keep up with what's likely to show up in your inbox or security perimeter next! My only regret is that Microsoft didn't choose to include anti-spam and anti-spyware/anti-adware monitoring features in the Security Center as well. Maybe in Windows XP SP 3?

Proper Password Handling

I'm going to make some recommendations about password structure and also about how to keep your passwords safe and sound. In an age where many Web sites have passwords, where you probably use a password to log into your Windows computer, and where even some programs and utilities may have passwords, there certainly are enough of them to go around.

So I want to start by shaking the foundations of your universe and say that your password is probably insecure if one or more of the following conditions are true:

- If your password appears in any kind of dictionary, it might be reproduced the same way (or at least from a word list that matches the entries in that dictionary, if not the definitions and other stuff).
- If you use familiar data in or for your password — like the names of your spouse, your children, or your pets, or perhaps your phone number, street number, or part of your Social Security number — crackers often customize their dictionaries with such data when attacking you.
- Same goes for birthdays, anniversaries, and other numbers that relate to you and your loved ones.

Since I just described most passwords that people use, what's a person to do? The answer lies in a good working understanding of password complexity. A sufficiently complex password is much more difficult to guess, and makes whatever that password protects much less likely to succumb to a dictionary-based attack. But what are the ingredients of a complex password? Glad you asked! According to Microsoft, and lots of other experts who provide password guidelines, a complex password contains:

- At least 8 characters, preferably as many as 14
- A mix of upper- and lowercase letters, numbers, punctuation marks, and other symbols

It also:

- sufficiently strange and random to be difficult to guess, and unlikely to be in anybody's dictionary
- Follows some logic you understand, or some structure you can re-create, but that's unlikely for somebody else to be able to do likewise (unless you tell them, in which case you've violated a major password security rule)

Most dictionary attacks are smart enough to try obvious substitutions for vowels (@ for a, 3 for e, 1 for i, 0 for o, and so forth) so please don't fall prey to the idea that simple replacements for dictionary words gets you off the hook, either. An old friend and colleague of mine likes to explain what this means by using the example password Ie4PoTw/3I:Ps&O as an acronym for "I eat four pizzas on Thursdays, with three ingredients: pepperoni, sausage, and onions." Note that every other alphabetic character is upper- or lowercase, and there are a couple of numbers and three punctuation marks for good measure (and good complexity) thrown in. Use this approach as an example, but don't use this password, please: because it's in print, it just might show up in somebody's dictionary for that reason!

Next, here are five simple rules for passwords that you should violate only at your peril:

- Never write down passwords, unless they're stored in a very secure location (preferably a safe, but hidden in a locked drawer or lockbox is okay).
- Don't share your passwords with anybody. You never know when they'll violate any of the password rules. Administrators, bosses, and security staff are the only possible exceptions.
- Never e-mail your password to anybody (besides, doing so violates the previous rule, right?).
- Change your passwords regularly — at least every 6 months or so (frequency usually varies by how sensitive the materials and information you work with might be: in government top-secret workplaces, they routinely change passwords monthly, and sometimes, even more often than that).
- Don't use the same password for multiple sites, logins, or other password-protected assets. Otherwise, compromising one can lead to compromising them all (or as many as share the same password, anyway).

"Holy cow!" I hear you saying, "I need about 20 passwords! How am I going to remember all that stuff?" Good question! Fortunately, oodles and scads of password manager programs are available nowadays, so the only password you really need to remember is the one that unlocks that program (but that means it better be a really good password, *comprende*?). Numerous commercial password managers are available, but I mention a handful of my favorite freeware tools here believing that buying some or all of a firewall, anti-virus, anti-spyware/anti-adware, and possibly even anti-spam software or services has probably depleted your budget somewhat by now. See Table 12-2 for some recommendations (use your favorite search engine with "free password manager" as a search string if you decide you don't like any of these).

Table 12-2 A Handful of Free Password Manager Programs

Name	*Description*	*URL*
RoboForm	Password generation, storage, and autotext app	www.roboform.com/
HyperSafe	Provides local or Web-based access to passwords	www.passwordsafe.com/
KeyWallet	Provides local password storage and access	www.keywallet.com/
Password Safe	Bruce Schneier's open source password safe	www.schneier.com/passsafe.html
Secure Data Manager	Open source password manager with annotations	http://sdm.sourceforge.net/

Grab one and use it with your newly invigorated and incredibly innovative collection of passwords. For my own part, I'm entranced with Schneier's Password Safe (he's a real star in the computer security world, and his stuff is great) as well as the Secure Data Manager (also known as SDM). Other possible do-it-yourself approaches might include creating password-protected files in Word or Excel, or perhaps using a password manager built into a third-party browser (Internet Explorer will happily manage passwords for you, too, but its protection schemes have been cracked enough in the past for me to be nervous about recommending that approach without this warning).

Stay Away from Risky Downloads

It's a truism I've mentioned throughout this book that most unwanted content and software arrive by invitation on most PCs, rather than by insidious or nefarious means. At this point, I assume you're convinced that threats are everywhere and that vulnerabilities can be exploited given the right opportunity. If you've installed a firewall, anti-virus software, anti-spyware/anti-adware software and have done what you can to protect your system from these threats, that doesn't mean you can do anything you want on the Internet.

It's important to recall that signatures and other means of positive identification inform most of what protective software can do for your PC. Indeed, the presence of anti-virus and anti-spyware/anti-adware software on your machine should protect you from known threats — but what about new or unknown ones? I look at software downloads much the same way as I do at e-mail attachments: okay if they come from a known and trusted source, but questionable if not downright dangerous otherwise.

To make my point as directly as possible, don't download software from unknown or untrusted sources. If you can't find a glowing review of some shareware or freeware program in a reputable publication or on a well-known Web site, you're tempting fate (and risking infection or infestation) if you copy a download to your PC, and then install the software it contains. Stick to well-known sources of

shareware and freeware and resist the temptation to grab a cool-sounding or -looking tool or utility. Just because you can download anything you want, doesn't necessarily mean that you should.

When in Doubt, Play It Safe!

When you're working with your PC, cruising the Internet, reading e-mail, or diverting yourself in some hopefully enjoyable way, don't take unnecessary chances with unknown and potentially unsafe materials. Even though there is often some subterfuge or covert activity involved when unwanted software makes itself at home on a PC, it usually enters that machine through the front door, buried inside some supposed prize or possible treasure that users download. Although the protective software you install on your PC should protect you from routine threats, it's just not smart to open the door to potential infestation or infection.

The key to playing it safe is to do some homework before downloading anything. The best way into a download is through a link provided in a reputable publication (such as *PC Magazine* and other well-known publications that cover computing topics, tools, and technologies) or from a Web site that you know and trust (elsewhere in this book, I've cited sites such as The Ultimate Collection of Windows Software a.k.a. `tucows.com`, CNET's `Shareware.com`, ZDNet at `www.zdnet.com/downloads`, and so forth). Even if you find pointers to a program somewhere else on the Web, if the program's got sufficient capability and has generated real interest in the user community, you can probably find a copy of somewhere safer—if you take the time to look. Save yourself some possible grief, and do just that!

Resources

Legions of great resources are available that explain what processes run on a Windows machines, which ones are benign and necessary, which ones are benign and possibly unnecessary (and how to do away with them if you decide you don't need them), and which ones are potentially dangerous or outright malign. I found three stellar resources while researching this chapter, but given the time I know I could find more.

- There's very good built-in process info at the "I am Not a Geek" (sez you!) Web site at `www.iamnotageek.com/`, but a search engine like Google seems to be the best way to dig into its contents because I couldn't find many of the articles Google turned up for me by trying to navigate my way into that site top-down. If you simply search on process names, you'll find this site popping up repeatedly, so why not just take the most obvious approach?
- The Los Angeles Free Net has a great collection of Web pages called "Startup Programs and Executables Listing" that includes links to information for a sizable and reasonably comprehensive collection of process image names (`www.lafn.org/webconnect/mentor/startup/PENINDEX.HTM`).
- Paul Collins maintains a decidedly comprehensive startup programs list that includes most process executables plus a raft of other items; you can access a search engine against that list at `www.sysinfo.org` or jump straight to the list at `www.sysinfo.org/startuplist.php`.

If you're going to dig into the many command-line utilities that Windows supports, please avail yourself of Windows XP's built-in "Command Line Reference" for syntax information and examples to help you get things right. To access this reference, choose Start→Help and Support, and then type **`command line reference`** into the Search box in the upper left-hand corner of the resulting screen.

You can learn more about the WinTasks program at `www.liutilities.com`. I also found ready access to some, but not all, of the process information from my Task Manager list on its site by typing URLs constructed as follows: `http://www.liutilities.com/products/wintaskspro/processlibrary/`*<img>*`/`, where you substitute the image name without the `.exe` extension for *<img>* (so that looking up the Application Layer Gateway service, or `alg.exe`, would use */alg/* at the end of the aforementioned URL).

Although I already mentioned Jerry Honeycutt's outstanding book *Microsoft Windows XP Registry Guide* (Microsoft Press, 2002) in Chapter 4, because he explains how to compare registry versions using WinDiff therein, I think it's worth another mention here. He also wrote a peachy article for Microsoft entitled "Safekeeping the Windows XP Registry." Published on March 17, 2003, you can access it at `www.microsoft.com/windowsxp/using/setup/expert/honeycutt_03march17.mspx`.

Microsoft's WinDiff utility is an amazing tool, if you're willing to take the time to learn how to use it. To that end, you'll find Microsoft Knowledge Base Article 159214 "How to Use the Windiff.exe Utility" extraordinarily informative (`http://support.microsoft.com/default.aspx?scid=kb;en-us;159214`). If you're not really interested in lots of cryptic character display Chris Maunder has created WinDiff UI, a graphical interface for the program that's much easier to use and understand than WinDiff itself. You can read more about this tool and download an executable at `www.codeproject.com/tools/runwindiff.asp`.

The Windows XP product documentation includes a short but detailed technical description entitled "Password must meet complexity requirements" (`www.microsoft.com/resources/documentation/windows/xp/all/proddocs/en-us/504.mspx`). To see the company's official take on what makes a password sufficiently complex, please consult that Web page.

Summary

This chapter offered numerous tips and techniques for practicing system safety. In particular, I explored the process of creating a system baseline to use as a comparison if things ever start to get weird on your computer, as well as some thoughts regarding monitoring system security, managing passwords, and some commonsense rules for downloading anything off the Internet.

The next chapter moves on to the final part of this book, and changes focus to reviewing the kinds of regular security routines that you should practice. I explore a regular security regimen in Chapter 13 to help you keep up with the current state of security (whatever it may be), and also describe in Chapter 14 the kind of automated scans and checks you should be performing on your PC on a regular basis. The idea is to maintain a level of security awareness and checks that will minimize the chances of an unpleasant surprise appearing from out of the blue!

Part V

The Habit of Security

IN THIS PART:

Part V brings the book to a close with an emphasis on what it takes to keep systems safe and secure, covering what's involved in establishing routine security and talking about the kinds of things you must watch (and watch out for) to make sure your protection remains both current and adequate.

Chapter 13 deals with the routines and schedules that you must establish to maintain system security in advance of new threats, vulnerabilities, and exploits. Chapter 14 explains what kinds of news and information you should follow and how you can anticipate or react to events in time to head off trouble before it takes up residence on your computer. Given the right routines, the right state of watchfulness, and the right tools, all it takes is a bit of time and effort to remain safe and secure.

Chapter 13

Safety Is a Matter of Routine

By now, you already know what kinds of tools and software you should be using to establish a reasonably safe and secure computing environment for yourself. But once this exalted state has been attained, you can't just pull up the drawbridge and blithely ignore the rest of the world — at least, not if you want to keep using the Internet, sending and receiving e-mail, and visiting "the wild" (however briefly and cautiously you venture outside the confines of your own system or network).

In the face of daily discoveries of new malware, spyware, adware, and so forth, and with a limitless supply of scams and swindles to contend with, safety and security are states that require regular ongoing attention and maintenance. That's why these things have to become a matter of routine, at least in part. A regular schedule of activities — automated whenever and however possible, to be sure — related to checking on, updating, and occasionally even testing things just to make doubly darn sure they're okay is your ticket to remaining safe and secure over time.

Where to Focus Your Routines

Chapter 5 introduced a collection of Microsoft Web pages that operate under the general title of "Protect Your PC." This is where Microsoft dispenses the points of advice it believes are absolutely essential to protect PCs against the threats they face in our modern world. The three primary points of its advice are stated briefly (in these very terms) as:

- Use an Internet firewall
- Get computer updates
- Use up-to-date anti-virus software

Notice that even in this extremely abbreviated prescription for safe, secure computing, keeping current is emphasized as much as is using the right (and right kinds) of ingredients. Thus, obtaining updates is vital because they help systems stay safe from new threats and vulnerabilities, and anti-virus software must not only be used, but kept up-to-date as well.

On the Web

The "Protect Your PC" pages reside online at www.microsoft.com/athome/security/protect/. Windows XP SP2 is gaining increasing coverage there as I write this chapter.

Lots of experts agree with Microsoft's advice, both inside and outside the information security field. About the only thing I'd add to its prescription are the following elements:

- **Use a pop-up blocker**—Windows XP SP2 builds one into Internet Explorer 6.0, but plenty of other options are available (I explored these topics in Chapter 6).
- **Use anti-spyware/anti-adware software**—At least one such program should run as a background process on your PC, and you may want to keep other such programs around for occasional extra scans (I explored this topic in Chapter 7).
- **Take steps to eliminate spam**—Chapters 9 and 10 make a strong case for multiple layers of screening and filtering.
- **Perform regular scans to identify and clean up unwanted software and content on your PC**—This is discussed throughout the entire book, with particular emphasis in Chapter 4.

By now, you may be saying something like "Okay, I buy it—but where's the routine part?" Great question! The answer is that some part of your security and safety routine should be devoted to all of the software, services, and system components you use on your PC. That's what I talk about in this chapter. Another part of your routine should be to look at what's happening in the wild, and in the outside world, that might potentially pose a threat to your system's safety and security. That's what I talk about in the next chapter.

Cover All the Bases

To begin with, you'll probably want to make an inventory of the various items on your system you depend on to help keep your system safe and secure. Just for grins, I took such an inventory of one of my test machines to present as an example, which you'll see laid out in Table 13-1. Notice that by extending a simple list of names with some additional information that's easy to gather from these items, you get a pretty good sense of what kind of security routine will be necessary to follow to keep things safe and secure from here on out.

Table 13-1 Security Software Inventory and Other Info

Name	*Type*	*Update*	*Subscription*	*Notes*
BitDefender v7.2	Antivirus	Auto	Yes: 8/5/2005	Can prompt prior to update install
BHO Demon 2.0	BHO monitor	Manual	None	Prompts for updates each time you reboot

Name	***Type***	***Update***	***Subscription***	***Notes***
IE 6 Pop-up Blocker	Pop-up blocker	Auto	None	Handles with Windows Auto Update
Security scans	Security scan	Manual	None	Autoreminder on first of the month for regular sites
Spam filter	BitDefender item	Auto	Yes: 8/5/2005	Updated when BitDefender updates
Spam filter	Outlook 2003	Manual	None	Check for updates every other Friday
Spam service	Spamarrest	Auto (svc)	Yes: 7/5/2005	Third-party service, no handling needed
Spy Sweeper 3.0	Anti-ad/spyware	Auto	Yes: 7/25/2005	Runs every Friday at midnight
SpyBot-Search & Destroy	Anti-ad/spyware	Manual	None	Run once a month for backup check, update then
Windows Firewall	Firewall	Auto	None	Handled with Windows Auto Update
Windows XP SP2	OS	Auto	None	Automatically downloads updates, prompts for install

If you compare the items listed in Table 13-1 against the items recommended in the preceding section of this chapter, it shouldn't be terribly surprising that all those bases are covered. Practicing what I preach isn't just for appearance's sake, either — I've learned the hard way that all this stuff really is necessary to get (and stay) out of trouble. Although the items that populate the entries for all of the various types — and sometimes, their number (I, for example, occasionally run a backup adware/spyware check on my systems to look for things the other tool might miss; I use multiple layers of spam filtering as well) — may vary, you should make sure you've got something of each type installed on your system, too.

Notice that some entries in the Update column in Table 13-1 read *manual*, whereas others read *auto*. The manual entry means that you must remember to perform updates and checks on a regular schedule, or see the level of system security diminished. The automatic entry means that the component to which it applies automatically downloads (and sometimes applies) updates. Where Windows itself is concerned, it downloads updates and then reminds you that they're available so that you can install them at your earliest convenience. Following a little research to see if known problems attach to security updates, I tend to install 8 out of 10 such items within 12 hours of their arrival on my machines.

I've developed a technique for dealing with manual updates. Implementation details on your system may differ (especially if you don't use the software that drives this example), but the idea that drives the technique should work, even if you have to jump through some extra hoops to make it happen. Because I use Outlook for e-mail, I've come to rely on its calendaring and scheduling capabilities. For the regular, manual activities in my security routine, this means I've set up recurring reminders to urge me to perform and complete these tasks.

I'll use the "Security scans" item as an example. I've set up an automatic reminder for the first of each month that not only tells me to run the scans, but also provides their URLs for easiest possible access (even in my own behavior, I've learned the more you can do to make the effort mindless and easy, the more likely it is to happen). Here's how:

1. Open Outlook. (Click once on the Outlook icon in the Quick Launch area of the task bar or choose Start → All Programs → Microsoft Office 2003 → Microsoft Outlook 2003 instead.)
2. Click the Calendar entry in the left-hand column. The resulting display appears in Figure 13-1.

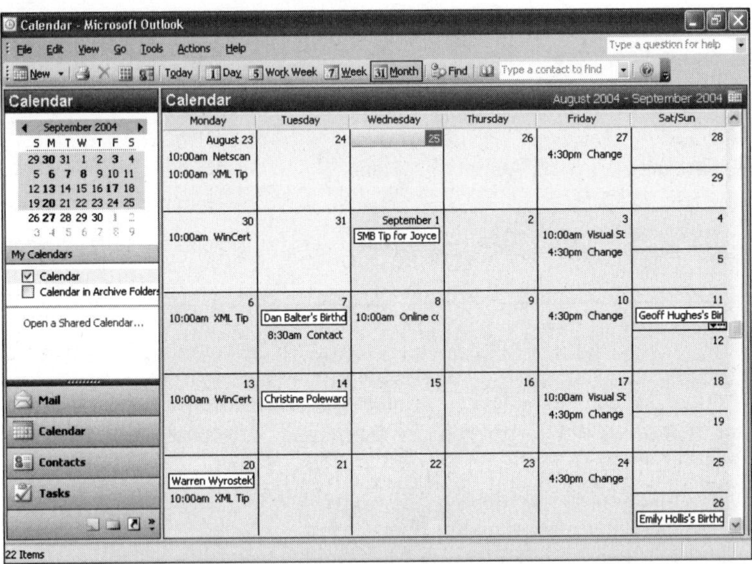

Figure 13-1: From the Calendar view in Outlook, it's easy to create recurring reminders.

2. As an example, and since it's August as I write this, if you want to get a reminder on the first of each month, double-click the September 1 area inside that date box. An Untitled Event window opens, which you'll fill out next. In the Subject field, type **Monthly security scan**. In the Location box, type the PC's name: for me, it's PC Winxppro-152. Set the start time at 5:00 p.m. on September 1 (the next first of the month from the current perspective) and the end time at 5:30 p.m., and then send the reminder 9 hours in advance so that Outlook reminds you about this all day long. Also type in the URLs for the scan sites you want to visit in the Notes text box, just to help you remember where to go. The results of this data entry appear in Figure 13-2.

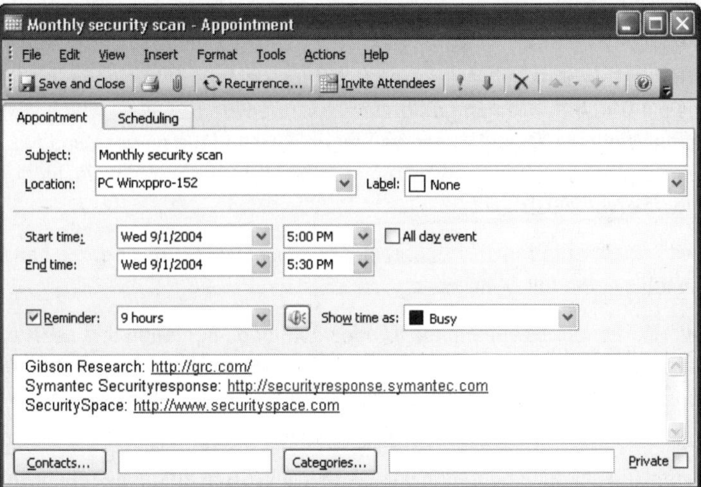

Figure 13-2: The event reminder for my monthly security scan goes into Outlook's Appointment calendar.

4. To turn this into a regularly scheduled thing, double-click the Recurrence button at the top of this window. The Appointment Recurrence window pops up on top. In the Recurrence pattern pane, click the radio button labeled Monthly and then click the Day button to the right. This creates an ongoing reminder every first day of the month that you can depend on to help you remember your security scan, as shown in Figure 13-3.

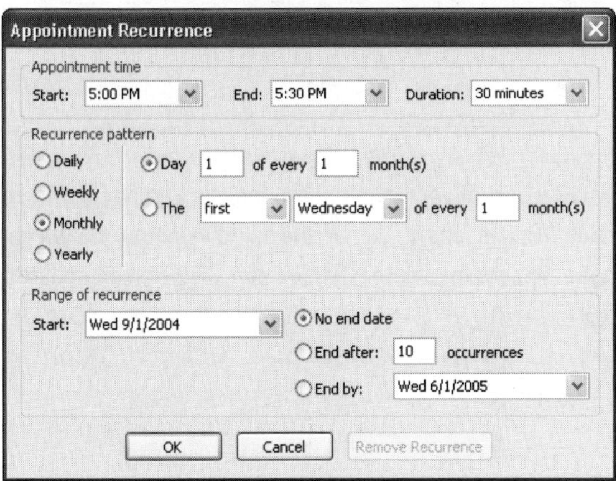

Figure 13-3: The security scan reminder is set to repeat forever on the first day of every month.

5. Click OK to set the recurrence pattern and then click OK to make this a regular appointment. If you want to quit Outlook, you can click the X in the upper right-hand corner of its window, or choose File→Exit instead.

Scripting: The Other Automation Alternative

It's a little beyond the scope of this book, but Windows itself supports at least two scripting languages — namely, the old DOS batch language (forever enshrined in `.bat` files, which Windows still runs cheerfully even on Windows XP and Windows Server 2003) and the newer Windows Scripting Host (whose files end in `.wsh` and likewise run on most Windows versions including Windows XP and Windows Server 2003).

You can use the Windows scheduler to run scripts at regular times of your choosing. You can learn more about these built-in tools at the following sites:

- "Using Batch Files" is Microsoft's entry in the Windows XP documentation that deals with this topic. You can learn how to build such files, invoke parameters, employ filters, redirect command output, and about all the commands that work in such files at `www.microsoft.com/resources/documentation/windows/xp/all/proddocs/en-us/batch.mspx`.
- Although you can find tons of documentation on how to use WSH to automate repetitive tasks on TechNet (`www.technet.com`), the "Windows Script Host overview" is a great place to start learning about this tool. Read more at `www.microsoft.com/resources/documentation/windows/xp/all/proddocs/en-us/wsh_overview.mspx`.

If you really want to automate manual tasks, you can try these tools, or you can look into third-party products that can even capture keyboard entry and mouse clicks to completely take you out of the loop (which is often what you really want). Good products in this category include Wilson Window Ware WinBatch (`www.winbatch.com`) and OpalisRobot (`www.opalis.com`, check under the products heading). Once you set up scripts in these environments, you can schedule just about anything to run automatically that you can do with a mouse and a keyboard!

Tip

Any time you've got a manual task that should be part of your security routine, it's a good idea to set up a recurring reminder to help you stay on schedule. This means if you had the same inventory shown earlier in the chapter, you would also set up recurring reminders to look for Outlook and BHO demon updates every other Friday, as per the schedule in Table 13-1.

Keep Your Software Current

Whether you rely on built-in update scheduling, script updates to occur automatically, or schedule yourself to do the dirty work, the key to maintaining security and safety lies in keeping your software current. This includes your operating system, all the security items already mentioned in this chapter, and all the applications that you use regularly. It's a taxing, time-consuming job that's best driven with a checklist and regular checkups — that's one reason why I schedule regular security check-ups to make sure I'm keeping up with what I must.

Microsoft actually provides a tool that will also help you check currency on the Microsoft components in your system (but probably won't help much with other stuff, which is why you still need a schedule, regular reminders, and a checklist to stay on top). This tool is known as the Microsoft Security Baseline Analyzer (MBSA), and it will cheerfully inspect your entire system configuration and tell you where security updates, service packs, or other patches and fixes are needed.

MBSA is a free tool available on the Microsoft Web site for download that you can install and run on your system as needed (it might be a good item to add to your monthly scanning tools list, for example, or you might even decide to use the Task Scheduler to tell it to run on the first or second day of each month). If you visit `www.microsoft.com` and search on "MBSA" the most current version of that program should show up near or at the top of the resulting listing (at the time of writing, that's version 1.2.1, designed to work with Windows XP SP2).

On the Web

Predicting what happens to Microsoft URLs in the future is sometimes risky, because they have ways of changing over time. That said, the current version MBSA URL appears to be built to last for a while, so you might want to try this instead of the search technique outlined in the preceding paragraph: `www.microsoft.com/technet/security/tools/mbsahome.mspx` (in fact, `www.microsoft.com/mbsa/` works, too). But whereas these URLs may someday break, the search technique should tell you something as long as MBSA remains available.

After downloading the software, you need only double-click on the single file you'll receive to install MBSA (it took less than 2 minutes on each of my several test machines to complete this process). Once installed, you should see an icon that looks like a padlock with a check mark on (and alongside) it on a desktop shortcut named Microsoft Baseline Sec. . . (see Figure 13-4) or something similar.

Figure 13-4: By default, the MBSA installer places a shortcut to the program on your desktop.

Here's a step-by-step description of how to scan your computer using MBSA, with some limited discussion of how to scan and read the most significant results:

1. To launch MBSA, double-click the shortcut shown, or choose Start → All Programs → Microsoft Baseline Security Analyzer. A display like the one in Figure 13-5 appears.

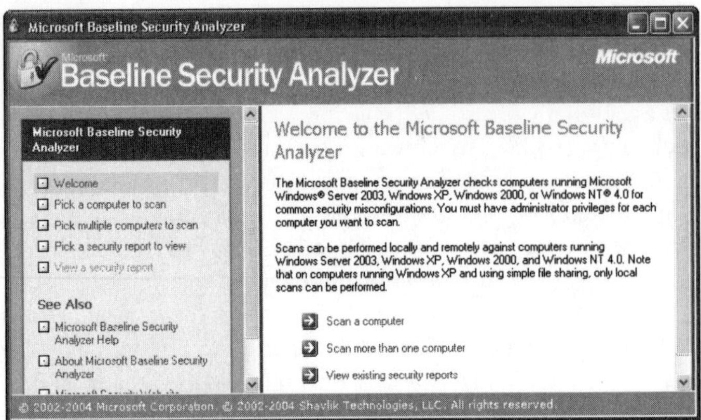

Figure 13-5: The MBSA welcome screen provides options for scanning, and for viewing scan results.

2. To scan your computer, click the green arrow to the left of "Scan a computer" in the right-hand pane, as depicted in Figure 13-5. Because MBSA always scans the computer where it's running by default, this is easy to do, but first, you'll have to click through another setup screen like the one shown in Figure 13-6.

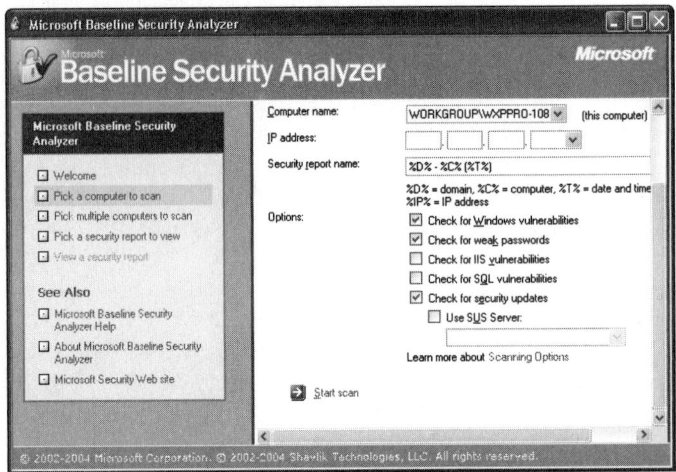

Figure 13-6: By default, MBSA is set up to scan the machine where it's running.

3. Click the green arrow to the left of the Start scan instruction at the bottom of the right-hand pane to put MBSA to work. While it's chunking away at its job, you'll see status information on resulting screens, including one that tells when its downloading the latest

set of update information (to give MBSA something current to check your system against) and when it's scanning your system, seeing what it can see. On most computers, this will take anywhere from 1 to 5 minutes to complete. When its scan is complete, you'll see a display like the one shown in Figure 13-7.

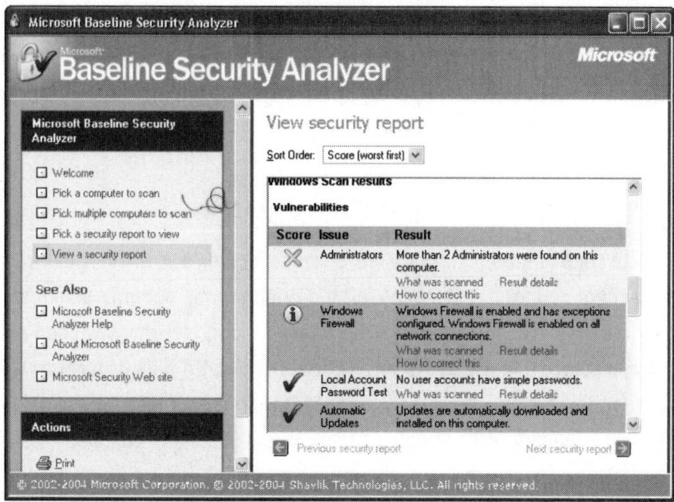

Figure 13-7: To view the Windows Scan Results shown in the right-hand pane, you must scroll down a bit.

4. After looking over the MBSA report to your heart's content, you can close the application by clicking the red X in the upper right-hand corner of its window. Note that each item has two or more hyperlinks that lead to additional information:

   - **What was scanned** tells you what MBSA looks at under this heading.
   - **Result details** tell you what it found.
   - **How to correct this** appears when MBSA has advice for you on how to mitigate or remediate the cause or causes of its findings. It's pretty simple to use, easy to dig through, and provides plenty of detail to help you figure out what to do (or when to yell for outside help).

Because the test machine is a relatively clean installation just upgraded to Windows XP Professional Service Pack 2, MBSA finds very little to remark about. Anything with a green check mark is okay, but a blue I means MBSA has information for you to read, and a yellow X indicates MBSA finds some cause for concern (though I had none in my report, a red X indicates a need for immediate action). Through the yellow X shown, MBSA calls attention to the existence of three accounts with administrative privilege on this machine and warns to make sure all such accounts are truly necessary. Through the blue I, MBSA also reports that the Windows Firewall has exceptions

defined (and of course, any exception in a firewall creates a potential point of ingress or egress). But in both cases, further investigation shows no cause for concern: The three administrative accounts include a system-level account that users can't access, plus the default Administrator account, and a personal account. The exceptions in the Firewall settings are to permit file and print services to work only on the local network (essential for file sharing and printer access). The latter information condition results from the Windows XP SP2 default setup, in fact, so mark this report up to MBSA's sensitivity and thoroughness.

Final result: the report card from MBSA on this system consisted entirely of green check marks, with the only other items discussed in the previous paragraph. I give myself an A for this report card, and hope your MBSA results are as quick and easy to investigate and dispel.

Note

If MBSA doesn't give you a complete slate of green check marks, do some looking and thinking before you let this bother you. This book's tech editor reported that because he'd changed his security settings for the Internet Web content zone for Internet Explorer, that caused a red X (even though he only switched a couple of disabled settings to prompt him instead). Clearly, while any information MBSA may present to you that indicates a problem may exist is worth looking into, it's not necessarily true that looking into things will require you to fix or change anything, especially if it's flagging some change you made yourself, consciously and of your own choosing.

If It's Important or Valuable, Back It Up!

Everybody keeps all kinds of important and valuable data on their computers, though they far too often don't realize that until some mistake or failure renders it inaccessible or unusable. Although most people have no trouble recognizing the value of certain files — important documents, financial spreadsheets, or precious photos or movies, for example — many forget that other kinds of information is worth time and effort or may also contain important information. One excellent case in point is the personal store (`.pst`) files in which Outlook stores current and archived e-mail messages (by default, in files named `Outlook.pst` and `archive.pst`). Although it may not occur to you to make backup copies of these files, you may keenly notice their lack or loss should those files get corrupted or damaged beyond repair. For some people, their "e-mail trail" is the only record of their activities they've really got!

In short, anything you might need to access again someday is something worth protecting and, hence, also worth backing up. Windows XP includes a built-in backup utility you can use to copy the contents of your My Documents folder and your personalized system settings (or the same information for all users on the machine, if there's more than one user account), or all the information on your computer. It's smart to opt for the latter, though the resulting data sets can be huge (current backup images from the test machines run from 11 to 26GB in size).

Tip

You can simplify backing up your files and data if you check the Preferences in the tools and applications you use and set things up to write your files to a subfolder you set up in your personal My Documents folder. That way, to save what is purely and truly yours, you need back up only the contents of the My Documents folder. In most cases, this will all fit quite nicely onto a USB Flash drive or CD (especially now that 512MB and bigger Flash drives have become so much more affordable).

When it comes to establishing a backup frequency, do it at least once a month, if not more often than that (I do it once a week, and copy important files to a network drive every night). You can back up to floppy disks, to a tape drive (if you've got one on your PC), to a USB- or FireWire-based external hard disk, or a networked drive — the bigger the better, if you opt to back up your entire system; small is okay if you copy only your personal documents and settings.

This is an important activity and deserves to be part of your system maintenance routine. Sometimes cleaning up from spyware, adware, or malware requires backing up damaged files or even restoring a damaged system. If you don't have a backup (or at least, reasonably current copies) of those files somewhere, you won't be able to come out of cleanup unscathed.

Unfortunately, walking through the details of backing up Windows XP systems and restoring them as needed goes a bit beyond the scope of this book. If you're interested in learning more about how to do this, take a look at some great documents from the Microsoft Web site to help you in your quest for further knowledge:

- Ed Bott's article "Windows XP Backup Made Easy" (July 14, 2003) is a real peach of a reference. For XP Home users, it explains how to install this utility (installed by default with Windows XP Professional); for all XP users it explains how, when, and why to use this tool. It also talks a bit about third-party options (`www.microsoft.com/windowsxp/using/setup/learnmore/bott_03july14.mspx`).
- "Backup Overview" is a good introductory element from Microsoft's Windows XP product documentation; you can visit this document at `www.microsoft.com/resources/documentation/windows/xp/all/proddocs/en-us/what_is_ntbackup.mspx`.
- "Backup Types" explains in detail the types of backups that the built-in Windows Backup utility can create, along with why and when to use them. You can visit this document at `www.microsoft.com/resources/documentation/Windows/XP/all/reskit/en-us/prdg_dsm_mxqs.asp`. You might also want to check out Chapter 14 of the Windows XP Resource Kit online, which is entirely devoted to backup and restore activities and tools (`www.microsoft.com/resources/documentation/Windows/XP/all/reskit/en-us/prdg_dsm_htwo.asp?frame=true`).

You can — and should — schedule backup tasks to run at off hours. They can take some time to complete, and consume lots of system resources while running. Best to get them out of the way while you're not using your computer. As with other routine tasks in your system and security regimens, automating them makes sure they're taken care of without factoring human frailty into the situation!

Making the Rounds

Once you've established your security routine, set up your reminders, and automated whatever you can, the important thing is to stick to it. Once you start to let things slide, you're creating unwanted potential for bad things to happen to your computer. Sure, you can dismiss those reminders when they pop up without actually doing the work involved to take care of them, but think about who suffers when things go wrong — yes, I'm talking about you.

If you want to keep your system safe and secure, it's not enough just to set things up and go through the motions once or twice. It's something you have to approach with sincerity, if not enthusiasm, and with commitment, if not with curiosity and a real desire to learn and grow. This may seem like a horrible chore sometimes, especially when you're busy with other parts of your life. But if you slog through the routine come heck or high water, you'll be rewarded with a system that keeps on chugging and with greatly diminished chances of having to clean up from major downtime resulting from infection or infestation.

If the idea that prevention is better than cure doesn't sway you to my way of thinking, look at it this way: It's better to suffer a little bit at a time, on a regular, predictable schedule than it is to suffer hugely and occasionally on an irregular, unpredictable schedule that can turn your whole life upside-down. But hey, it's entirely up to you what you do with your routine. If you're serious about wanting to be safe and secure, it will become just a part of what you do (like buying insurance and paying taxes) to protect yourself from being overrun by the whims of fate, or by vandals and other barbarians.

Resources

When it comes to establishing the pieces and parts that go into putting a working and properly protected PC together, opinions and advice are as varied as the individuals who dispense it. Nevertheless, Jeremy Cohn put a nice article together for LockerGnome called "To Do List - When your Buy a New Computer/Install a New OS." It deals with all the items that Cohn finds invaluable and all the tweaks and configuration tasks he finds necessary before he considers a computer safe, secure, and ready to use. It provides some great advice and not coincidentally agrees with the kinds of security elements I find worthwhile these days, too. Read it at `http://channels.lockergnome.com/windows/archives/20040823_to_do_list_when_you_buy_a_new_computerinstall_a_new_os.phtml`.

If you want to make sure your security inventory is complete, take another once-over on the Processes tab in Windows Task Manager. Look up everything, and inevitably you'll find all of the security elements that stay resident in the background on your PC along the way. This may not cover items you use only for occasional scanning, but it should include everything security related that runs regularly on your PC.

Some people find Windows scripting icky; others think it's the greatest thing around to automate anything and everything they do. If your tendencies are more to the former skip to the next paragraph, if to the latter, check out the following books:

Hill, Timothy. *Windows NT Shell Scripting*. Pearson Education, 1998, and *Windows Script Host*. Que, 1999. Although somewhat dated by now, these concise, well-focused books offer good explanations, great examples, and also work well as desktop references for script writers.

Knittel, Brian. *Windows XP Under the Hood: Hardcore Windows Scripting and Command Line Power*. Que, 2002. The title, in this case, really says it all.

Microsoft Corporation. *Windows 2000 Scripting Guide*. Microsoft Press, 2002. Although it aims mostly at system administrators, this book also provides great information on designing, building, testing, and using Windows scripting capabilities to the max.

If you don't like these options, visit your favorite online bookstore and search on "Windows scripting"; you'll find at least a dozen other titles on this topic from which you can choose.

If you are willing to spend the time to really dig in and learn what MBSA can do, it's a pretty amazing tool, especially when you consider Microsoft gives it away for free (it can do a lot of things with Windows services more likely to be found on a server than on a Windows XP desktop, so you may never get the chance to appreciate its entire arsenal of wonders). But if you want to learn more about this tool read "How to Use Microsoft Security Baseline Analyzer." It will tell you lots of useful stuff, and probably covers more than you wanted to know. Find this document online at `www.microsoft.com/technet/security/guidance/secmod112.mspx`.

Summary

This chapter showed you what kinds of things relate to system safety and security need regular attention and talked through various ways to automate reminders to take care of these chores, if not to let the computer do the dirty work (which you should do whenever possible). It also talked about the importance of keeping software and security data up-to-date, and how to establish a routine to make this a matter of course. Along the way you learned how to create reminders, what kinds of things might warrant such treatment, and about the snazzy Microsoft Baseline Security Analyzer tool. If you want to maintain the safety and security that using the right tools and best practices can deliver, create and stick to a security routine that helps you stay on top of your situation.

The next chapter in this book is also its final element. This chapter talked about the round of activities that goes into performing regular security upkeep and maintenance. You might say therefore that it looked at the schedule-driven and predictable side of this game. The concluding chapter looks at security from an event-driven perspective instead and explains how you find out (and if necessary, pre-empt or deal with) the possibility of ominous or perhaps even dire security threats and exploits that might head your way if you don't take evasive action. Actually, things will seldom be that scary, but I will talk about how you can keep up with what's going on in the continual back and forth between threats and exploits and relevant countermeasures and mitigation or avoidance strategies. It's more a matter of becoming and staying vigilant than of reacting to continual crises.

Chapter 14

Safety Requires Constant Vigilance

Alas, not everything about dealing with unwanted software or content is purely a matter of routine. Although the routine is undoubtedly important and a key ingredient when it comes to maintaining safe and secure computing, sometimes you must take steps to anticipate or head off oncoming trouble before it shows up in your immediate neighborhood. Thus another necessary part of the security routine that isn't really a form of maintenance is a matter of listening or watching carefully for potential signs of danger or vulnerability "in the wild."

Occasionally, particularly virulent forms of malware or other unwanted software will come along. Sometimes, it's something new against which signature-based defenses can't work — at least, not until the software is identified, analyzed, and a signature created. Sometimes it's something for which a security update may be available — but only just recently — and systems will become infected or infested because those updates may not yet have been applied.

But unless you know that something wicked may be heading in your direction (or more probably, simply out there on the Internet) that shows unusually broad distribution, strong virulence, or high damage potential, you might be caught not only unaware but also unprotected. Ignorance may not be much of an excuse in this case, but it's the lack of protection that will cause the most problems for you and your PC.

So what's a person to do, faced with this kind of possibility? First and foremost because this situation occurs only infrequently — for example, the Symantec Virus Encyclopedia shows that only nine Category 4 types of malware (which lumps multiple malware in the same family, such as the numerous variants of the Klez, Nimda, Mydoom, or Netsky mass-mailing worms, at least one each of which attained Category 4 status, sometimes more) have been identified since 1999. Roughly speaking, that appears to indicate that something like this has happened about twice a year: If you believe that recent history is a good predictor of the future (and it often is, but not always), then that's about the kind of frequency you're looking at going forward.

Cross-Reference

If you're a little hazy on the ratings categories for malware, please reread the discussion of that topic in Chapter 2.

Category 4 Characteristics

Recall the definition of a Category 4 malware item (which is typically a mass-mailing worm nowadays, but may be any kind of malware). To meet the criteria for this classification, which poses what Symantec labels as a Severe threat, malware must have a high Wild metric, and be ranked High for either Damage or Distribution.

- The **Wild** metric includes numbers of sites and computers infected, geographical distribution of infection, ability of current technologies to combat a threat, and the complexity of the malware item so labeled.
- The **Damage** metric measures how much damage or harm a malware item can inflict based on how many events are spawned, server congestions or shutdowns, deleted or altered files, access to and release of confidential or sensitive data, performance problems caused, difficulty of repair, and so forth.
- The **Distribution** metric measures how quickly malware can propagate and identifies the scale of e-mail and instant messaging or executable attacks (worms and viruses, respectively), speed of download or copy propagations (Trojan horse), network drive infection capabilities, and difficulty of removal or repair.

Thus, by virtue of its classification criteria, Category 4 malware usually causes serious problems, inflicts outright damage or productivity losses, and affects large numbers of systems and networks before it fades into relative obscurity (most Category 4 items are still around two or more years after discovery, but most have been demoted to Category 2 by that time).

Table 14-1 lists the nine Category 4 items mentioned in the previous section (see the "On the Web" item that follows the table to learn how to generate URLs to read more about them, if you're interested). It also lists each item's discovery date and its current Category rating as well (and note also that only one of the former Category 4 items, BugBear.B, remains a Category 4 to this day).

Table 14-1 Category 4 Items/Types Back to 1999

Formal Name	*Discovery Date*	*Current Rating*
W32.Badtrans.B@mm	11/24/2001	2
W32.Bugbear.B@mm	6/4/2003	4
W32.Funlove.4099	9/11/1999	2
W32.Klez.gen@mm	11/9/2001	2*
W32.Mydoom.M@mm	7/26/2004	3
W32.Netsky.D@mm	3/1/2004	3
W32.Nimda.A@mm	9/18/2001	2
W32.Sircam.worm@mm	7/17/2001	2
Wscript.Kakworm	12/30/1999	2

*Upgraded from Category 3 to Category 4 some time after discovery

On the Web

To find the Virus Encyclopedia entry that corresponds to each item in Table 14-1, stick the following URL string before the item's name recast in lowercase characters: `www.symantec.com/avcenter/venc/data/`, then add `.html` to the end. Thus, the W32.Funlove.4099 entry resides at `www.symantec.com/avcenter/venc/data/w32.funlove.4099.html`.

Now that you've seen the summary of these malware items, all of which caused at least consternation among Internet connected individuals and organizations (and for hundreds of thousands of systems, also led to infection as well), I want to talk about why and how they were able to spread so far and fast, and why they were able to set up residence on so many systems:

- Updates or patches to offset the vulnerabilities that these items could exploit were already available, in most cases (in only two cases did these malware items find and exploit previously unknown or unrecognized vulnerabilities). Thus, the primary piece of advice to avoid infection remains something you've heard repeatedly in this book: Keep your operating system and applications updated, and apply security updates as soon after their release as is possible. One especially nasty vulnerability permitted incoming worms in e-mail to execute automatically, without the user opening the attachment explicitly. Ordinarily, not overtly opening an attachment is enough to prevent infection, but in this case unless the patch was applied, recipients got much more than they bargained for from such messages.

Tip

Whenever you install a security update, Windows automatically creates a restore point for you. Thus, you can always roll back to the prior state by restoring that checkpoint later. Choose Start → Help and Support Center and then click "Undo changes to your computer with System Restore" in the Pick a Task section. This launches the System Restore utility with the restore option selected by default (note: you can easily switch to the create a restore point option if that's your intent, if Windows XP doesn't create an automatic restore point for you, as it does whenever Automatic Update applies changes to your system). Thus, you can install all updates as they're released and, if you encounter problems later on, roll back to the prior state (as long as too much time hasn't elapsed, because you'll lose all system changes in the interim) as you keep on working on whatever it is you use your PC to do. Reactive though this strategy may be, it's pretty workable for home office or hobbyist users.

- The malware made creative use of techniques for propagation, including broadcasts to entire address books, use of network file shares, or other techniques that permitted quick and easy spreading. Here again, if you follow the other prescriptions discussed thus far in this book — including installing and using a firewall and spam blocking software or services — you should be protected from most such threats already.

- Some of the mass-mailing worms used creative techniques to disguise their intent, such as harvesting e-mail addresses from address books and using them to spoof sender addresses, as well as to identify target recipients. In cases where recipients knew the spoofed sender, this could cause them to lower their guards and open attachments they otherwise would never touch. If you can remember to avoid opening any and all attachments you're not actually expecting—but do feel free to e-mail the putative sender to find out if the attachment is for real—you should remain immune to this kind of ploy. As long as you also patch vulnerabilities like the one mentioned for automatic execution of attachments earlier in this list, you should be able to avoid most such hazards altogether.
- In about half the cases, the malware item belonged to a family of similar items that shared at least some identifying characteristics with older, known malware that updated anti-virus software could easily catch. Thus, most people with up-to-date anti-virus software were often protected from newer, more virulent variants. Hopefully, this phenomenon adds credence to Microsoft's "Protect Your PC" mantra that includes "Use up-to-date anti-virus software."

By now, you may be feeling a bit less paranoid about a constant need to see around corners, or to know what's going to happen to your PC tomorrow. It's really not that bad—as the list of truly bad malware now indicates, even most of these items could have been foiled had users followed best security practices, applied updates on a timely basis, and used up-to-date anti-virus software. Only a couple of items qualify as genuine surprises, and those are what I'd like to explain how to look out for next!

Eyeing Security Events

Although it's possible that you yourself might someday be the first (or an early) recipient of some new form of spyware, adware, or malware, the odds are against it. Look at things this way: Hundreds of millions of users are on the Internet at any given moment. Indeed somebody's got to be first, but even if the odds of filling that slot aren't completely random (and I don't see how they could be) they're at least millions to one in favor of the proposition that somebody else will be the first victim of new attacks or unwanted software. In fact, the odds are still pretty high that a significant number of individuals will be exposed to malefic influences before they ever head in your direction.

Thus, in most cases if you keep an eye on sources of news about unwanted software and content, you'll often be warned at least hours and usually days in advance of exposure to actual danger. Most anti-virus vendors do a fantastic job of posting signatures (and when needed, anti-virus software updates) within 24 hours of the discovery of new malware, and anti-spyware/anti-adware vendors usually meet this admittedly high standard. When operating system or application patches or updates are required, things can sometimes take longer (and in some cases—as with the Abstract Syntax Notation or ASN.1 flaw discovered in the summer of 2003 but not patched until late spring 2004—it will take a LOT longer). But in such cases, the vendors or organizations involved will often post warnings and, where possible, describe temporary workarounds to allow businesses and organizations to keep working and stay relatively safe and secure in the face of such threats.

What does this mean in terms of keeping abreast of new developments or discoveries where malware, spyware, adware, and so forth are concerned? It means watching technology news in general (which often report highly mobile or infectious unwanted software within a day of its discovery), but it also means watching two specific sources for news about unwanted software or content that are highly relevant to your situation:

- General sources of security news and information, especially those with a stated and definite interest in unwanted software. This primarily includes news and industry organizations, trade groups, and interested individuals, along with consulting or technical services companies that focus on malware, adware, spyware, and so forth but that don't sell products in that space.
- Vendors of products that handle malware, adware, spyware, and so forth want to take care of their customers (and in some cases, may be contractually required to do so) and attract more buyers. Thus, they're also very quick to publicize and respond to new threats, including unwanted software and content.

All of these sources of information bear watching, so I'll describe a hypothetical Windows XP configuration by completing an inventory like the one I suggested in the previous chapter (in Table 13-1) and use that information to recommend general and specific sources of information worth watching. Of course, I'll abbreviate that inventory here in Table 14-2 because information about its update methods, subscription status, and most notes aren't really relevant to the situation where you're trying to figure out where to turn for vendor-specific sources of relevant news and information.

Table 14-2 A Hypothetical Windows XP Machine's Security Components

Name	*Type*	*Notes*
Norton AntiVirus 2005	Anti-virus	Symantec Security Response and newsletters are great sources of news and information.
Norton AntiSpam	Spam blocker	See Norton AntiVirus entry.
BHO Demon 2.0	BHO monitor	Check `www.castlecops.biz` for updates and information. (Look in the Top 20 lists, for "most downloaded files.")
Google toolbar	Pop-up blocker	Includes automatic updates, not much other info available.
Security scans	Security Scan	Visit `grc.com`; `securityresponse.symantec.com`; `www.securityspace.com`.
Outlook 2003	Spam filter	Check `officeupdate.microsoft.com`, but not much breaking news.
SpySweeper 3.0	Anti-ad/spyware	Built-in news updates occur with update checks.
SpyBot-Search & Destroy	Anti-ad/spyware	Run once a month for backup check, update and check for news then.
Windows Firewall	Firewall	Check MS Security home and bulletins pages.
Windows XP SP2	OS	Ditto above entry.

When it comes to following up on this kind of inventory, remember you must check both presumably neutral, objective third-party sites that cover security news and information as well as sites specific to whatever collection of components you may happen to have installed on your PC. I'll tackle neutral third parties first, and vendors or developers second in the sections that follow. The good news here is that you can sign up for e-mail–based newsletters, alerts, and bulletins from many of these sources, so you may find the very information you need in your inbox, instead of being forced to search for it yourself.

Third-Party Threat Information

Chapter 2 talked about numerous third-party sites that provide information about vulnerabilities and about malware that may exploit them. During that discussion, I mentioned sites such as the Common Vulnerabilities and Exposures (`www.cve.mitre.org`) and the Computer Emergency Readiness Team (`www.cert.org`), along with many other sites. In this context, it's important to observe that vulnerabilities and exposures listings tend to concentrate on known bugs, flaws, or problems with software that makes threats possible, whereas the kind of information you're after in this context will mention or document specific threats that probably seeks to exploit such things. They're not one and the same, so that while your research may sometimes lead you to CVE or CERT, you won't usually start there.

The kinds of general resources you're most likely to find useful in this context include the usual roster of weekly or monthly computer trade publications, especially those that offer security-related newsletters that tend to address new malware, spyware, adware, and other discoveries of unwanted software early and often. There are tons of options in this category, so if you have a favorite publication or ask around for recommendation you'll be able to supplement or supplant my favorites with very little effort. These are as follows:

- eWeek.com operates a strong online presence, including a topic center on security matters that's updated daily. It invariably carries news and information about all breaking malware, adware, and spyware, and is thus worth checking whenever news or rumors about such things surface through any channel. Check in on `www.eweek.com/category2/0,1738,1237860,00.asp` regularly, or as needed (an RSS feed is available, if you have an RSS newsreader and the interest to use it for such information).
- The SANS Institute is a highly regarded source of security news, information, updates, and training. It publishes two newsletters of likely interest to readers: *@Risk: The Consensus Vulnerability Alert* and *SANS Newsbites*. Visit `www.sans.org/newsletters/` to see what newsletters are available, and to sign up.
- TechTarget.com operates numerous Web sites that offer security content and information, including regular newsletters. Visit any or all of the following: `www.SearchSecurity.com`, `www.SearchWindowsSecurity.com`, and `www.SearchWin2000.com`. You'll be asked to register and set up an account to access site content; when you do, you can sign up for a variety of newsletters, many of them security oriented. Their breaking news coverage is especially helpful and informative, as is their Security Perspectives newsletter, an offshoot of *Information Security* (another TechTarget property; `www.infosecmag.com`)—one of the best information security publications around.

Of course, hundreds of other similar newsletters and publications exist that you could tune into, but even this relatively short list — which I candidly confess reflects my history, if not my biases — provides more input than most people can read on a regular basis. The important thing is to establish some reliable, regular sources of information and to use them when news stories, alerts, or other signals of impending trouble may impel you to dig deeper than usual.

All this said, I didn't have as much luck finding reliable, objective third-party information resources on spyware and adware that offer anywhere near the same depth of coverage, the kinds of newsletters and mailing lists, and so forth as you'll find for malware and general Windows security topics. I did, however, find some Web sites that offer regularly updated news and information in this area, including the following:

- Topix.net, which advertises itself as "The Internet's largest news site," runs a thread on spyware that aggregates spyware-related stories from newsfeeds of all kinds. It's updated daily and pretty comprehensive, but doesn't separate out alerts or bulletins from other kinds of coverage. You can sign up for daily or weekly e-mail alerts as new content appears in this thread, but it doesn't distinguish ordinary spyware related news and information from genuine spyware alerts or bulletins (`www.topix.net/tech/spyware`).
- Surfer Beware offers coverage of all kinds of Web-related security topics, including spyware, viruses, cookies, pop-ups, spam, Web safety, and firewalls. As with Topix, however, it's more of a news aggregator than an alert or bulletin provider, though it does offer lots of interesting articles and how-tos on the site as well (`http://spyware.surferbeware.com/spyware-news.htm`).
- Spyware Info (`www.spywareinfo.com`) doesn't appear to provide alerts or bulletins, per se, but it does run a set of well-used and moderated newsgroups (`http://forums.spywareinfo.com`) and offers a newsletter called the "Spyware Weekly" (subscription information is available in the Web site, forums, and newsletter message thread).
- Spyware Warrior (`www.spywarewarrior.com`) operates a pretty nice general spyware site, which includes a message forum entitled "Spyware news and warnings" that's pretty informative but the content, while moderated, is pretty much unfiltered so you'll find rants and raves as well as real news and information there.

Other general sites such as Spyware Guide (`www.spywareguide.com`) don't appear to offer general alerts or bulletin services at this time, either.

Outside the publication or training worlds, numerous third-party companies or organizations specialize in finding and reporting on security vulnerabilities. Some regard this activity as a demonstration of capabilities, some as a form of harassment. But whatever the real take on this activity might be, these firms are well known for their hard-hitting, informative coverage of vulnerabilities and exposures that might otherwise go unreported. These can be very valuable sites indeed, and include:

- Secunia (`http://secunia.com`) — This is one of the most consistent breakers of early news and information on threats and vulnerabilities, especially for Windows platforms; its security advisories are always worth checking out, and often worth further digging into. You can sign up for mailing lists on advisories and virus alerts as well.

- eEye Digital Security (www.eeye.com)—This company shows up frequently in news reports when it breaks advisories or alerts on security threats and vulnerabilities. Check out its Research section for information on security alerts, advisories (see upcoming advisories for a list of stuff Microsoft has yet to handle), and more; it also offers a security alert newsletter.
- SecurityFocus (www.securityfocus.com)—Not only runs a vulnerabilities database, reports on security news, and operates various interesting newsletters and mailing lists, it's also home to Russ Cooper's BugTraq, which aggregates bug, threat, exploit, and vulnerability reports from all over the world. Definitely worth checking out!

Here again, careful digging will turn up many other reputable and valuable sources of such information. The key is to find sources you can trust that tend to come up with important news and information sooner rather than later, because of the time sensitivity for this kind of information.

Vendor Threat Information

For each security product or service you use, you'll want to investigate what its parent organization has to offer. Our earlier inventory includes big players like Microsoft and Symantec, along with numerous smaller players and individuals, such as WebRoot Software (Spy Sweeper), Larry Leonard (BHO Demon), and Patrick M. Kolla (Spybot-Search & Destroy). In each case, the secret is to investigate what each party has to offer (or which other third parties they recommend) and to make the most of what's available. Because I've already covered much of this material in other chapters in this book, here's a short, swift recap of the most important and relevant points to this discussion:

- Visit the vendor's Web site and look for information. At Microsoft, for example, you must log into the company's subscription center at http://go.microsoft.com/?linkid=317769 with a Passport ID (see the following sidebar discussing Passport for more details). Symantec offers a security response document called "Symantec alerting offerings" that explains the many types of alerts and information it offers via e-mail or you can sign up for its Security Alert at http://nct.symantecstore.com/virusalert/). Results and information available vary from vendor to vendor. This is a case where a little digging goes a long way. If possible you want to sign up for security alerts and bulletins related to malware, spyware, adware, and other topics of potential concern (as many as possible, or at least, as many as you can handle).

A Passport To . . . All Kinds of Things

If you visit the aforementioned Microsoft URL, instead of jumping straight to a subscription sign-up page, you'll see the page depicted in the following figure instead. That's because Microsoft requires users to identify themselves to sign up for newsletters and to access all kinds of other resources to which they'd either like to control access (like for-a-fee developer or partner sites, for example—to access those, you must pay an annual fee, or the material is not available) or because they want to know who's interested in them. The Microsoft Passport was formally called the Microsoft .NET Passport because it's based on the company's .NET development framework for distributed services and applications (of which the Passport service is a sort of flagship example, as it happens).

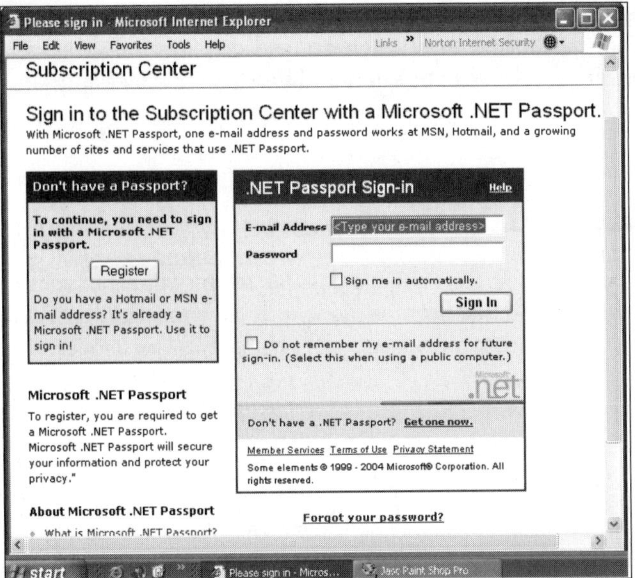

Signing up for a Microsoft Passport is ridiculously easy: All you have to do is provide an e-mail address, create a password, and agree to the terms of use and the privacy policy for the service. What it buys you (theoretically, anyway) is access to all kinds of resources from Microsoft, and from the numerous third parties who also use the Microsoft Passport to identify users. What it costs you in money is nothing, but it does provide a way for people who use the Passport service to reach you through an e-mail address (or at least, to know that there's a real person lurking behind that e-mail address). According to Microsoft's privacy policy, it won't use that information except to notify you about services of potential interest — and I've had a Passport for more than three years now and haven't even noticed it adding to my spam load one bit — but third parties who use the service can request (and use) additional information from you as they see fit. So proceed with some caution, limit what you disclose, and everything should be okay.

- Look for news and information on the vendor's home page (or security pages, at Microsoft and Symantec) and for newsletter sign-ups. At Webroot, for example, you can find regularly maintained lists of Top Threats and Spyware news updates (Spy Sweeper users will see the most current news entry in the New window of their software; Web site visitors can scroll back through previous new items as well). For its news offerings, visit `www.webroot.com/spywareinformation/spywarenews/`; for its general Spyware Information center, cut the last bit off of the preceding URL.
- Make sure to check for automatic or scheduled updates to vendor software, signature files or databases, and other regularly updated elements that help keep your coverage up-to-date. Whenever possible try to apply such updates automatically (though for Microsoft updates, you'll be informed they've been downloaded to your PC and asked to install them at your earliest opportunity — keeping potential conflicts and use of restore points in mind, please do this as soon as you can).

In general, you want to explore the vendor or developer's Web site, learn more about what's there, sign up for any alerts, bulletins, or related newsletters you can find, and do everything you can to keep up with breaking news that could affect your system's safety and security and make sure you've got the latest and greatest software and information needed to keep things safe and secure.

Avoiding Potential Trouble

Okay, let's assume you've heard some late-breaking news about a possible security threat to your PC. In most cases, the safest strategy is summed up in that horrible old joke about a man and his doctor, where the man says, "Doc, it hurts when I do this (demonstrates)," and the doctor replies "Well, don't do that any more!"

When you become aware of threats you may be able to avoid incurring excessive risk without suspending your use of a service completely, however. For example, if you learned about a new threat that could force e-mail attachments to show up and execute on your desktop without human intervention, you'd be smart to stop downloading e-mail to your PC until a fix became available. But does that mean you'd have to stop reading e-mail completely? Not necessarily—if you sign up for a backup e-mail account at one of the free services like Yahoo!, Google, or Hotmail, for example, it's still safe to read e-mail through a Web interface (because it doesn't download attachments to your desktop until you tell it to, and attachments sitting on a Web server can't be downloaded from and executed on your PC without your express involvement and approval). Thus, if a serious threat like the one described emerged, you could temporarily forward all e-mail from your primary account to the backup account and still keep up with e-mail, sort of at a safe distance, without incurring risks directly. That said, because nothing in this world is completely safe, if somebody invents a clever Web-based active content exploit that finds its way into HTML-based e-mail, even a Web-based e-mail client can't be judged 100 percent safe. So far, however, this has not posed a serious threat to e-mail readers.

Likewise, if you hear about a new malware threat that anti-virus software can't yet detect, it might be wise to suspend downloads long enough for that situation to be remedied and for new signatures and possibly software updates to become available before resuming such activity. The same thing is true for particular applications that may experience certain threats as well; although it may be painful or difficult to "do without" for a while, it will be safer and smarter to endure a (hopefully short) period of privation rather than to risk infestation or infection.

The key here, of course, is foreknowledge—information that may not be in advance of the actual threat, but that you should try to act upon (or stop other risky acts as a consequence of learning about them) as quickly as possible. That's why I recommend so strongly that you stay in touch with relevant news, alerts, and bulletins. They'll tell you when you should proceed with caution (if you proceed at all) and they'll also let you know when it's safe to resume your normal working routine.

If worst comes to worst and you do catch something, the responsible reaction is to disconnect from the Internet and wait for a fix to become available. Hopefully, this means a repair tool of some kind or an update to the software whose job it is to deal with whatever you've got (anti-virus for malware infections, anti-spyware/anti-adware for such infestations, and so forth). If you must reconnect to the Internet to grab such tools or solutions, stay connected only as long as is necessary to download them, then disconnect again and stay disconnected until you've got the situation cleaned up. This is a situation in which access to another known good (and clean) computer is invaluable because it allows you to keep your machine disconnected while still gathering the resources necessary to conduct cleanup and repair (for more information on this process, please consult Chapter 4 of this book).

The Personal PC Security Audit

In addition to the matters of security routine described in Chapter 13, you may want to consider adapting a well-established practice in the corporate world for use on your own PC (or PCs if you've got more than one). It's derived from the practice (which is tantamount to a legal requirement in publicly traded companies) of conducting an annual accounting audit, where the guiding idea is to subject internal record-keeping and financial reporting to an outside review in the hopes of verifying completeness and accuracy, and with the intent of catching and correcting errors, omissions, oversights, and so forth. When applied to matters of security, it means looking things over carefully and closely, questioning current approaches, tools, and even the very security routine you've established, with the idea of improving overall security and coverage as a result.

You probably won't be able to afford a real, objective third-party review, but you can take these principles and put them to work by planning and conducting a once-a-year review to summarize and analyze your current security posture and practices. That's when you can weigh how satisfied you are with current choices and methods, and research potential changes. It's also when you can look around to see if anything new has eluded your notice in the interim since your last audit, and decide if you need to add to your coverage, upgrade tools or software, and so forth.

This is a time when you might even want to think about spending a little money. Thus, instead of opting for the free security scanners recommended as part of your monthly routine in the previous chapter, you might want to visit `www.securityspace.com` and sign up for its $10 desktop audit or even its $49 single-shot standard audit (if you don't run any services on your machine and nobody needs to connect to you for that purpose, the former is fine; otherwise, consider spending the money for the latter). Also, if you haven't yet tried the free services at AuditMyPC (`www.auditmypc.com`) this is a good time to give them a try as well. The main thing is to use different tools from your customary ones, so as to get a different take on your system's security.

This is also when you may need to tackle some thorny issues related to renewing subscriptions to older software versus upgrading to newer software. Such considerations apply to everything in your environment, to be sure, but are usually most painful when dealing with commercial software or pondering a version upgrade for Windows. In both cases, the costs of upgrades usually exceed those of renewal, as does the work involved in making the switch from one version to another. In this situation, it's wise to consider what new functionality you're getting as a result of your expenditures. In most cases renewing a subscription to older software (take anti-virus as an example) may prevent you from exercising new capabilities available in current versions of the same package, but seldom grandfathered into older versions.

If you have to choose between diminished protection against current threats and less expense, versus up-to-date and complete coverage of current threats and more expense, the price difference (which normally falls somewhere between $20 and $40 and is almost always less than $100) is still probably less than the value of your time should you have to clean up after something to which your parsimony makes you subject. Only you can make this tradeoff, of course, but it's one that should be

made carefully and should include some additional "insurance value" against future threats that newer software will have, but older software may not.

Sometimes, this may lead you in unexpected directions. Here's an example: In the release from Norton AntiVirus (NAV) 2002 to 2003, the company started checking for Windows platform types in the software. The workstation version of NAV 2002 also worked on Windows 2000 Server, but the same version of NAV 2003 did not, and the server version of the same software cost more than $300 with no upgrade provision from the workstation version. Thus, instead of ponying up the $240 plus for the price differential, I switched the anti-virus software on that machine to BitDefender Professional instead (which runs equally well on both Windows workstation and server operating systems; for a free evaluation download visit `www.bitdefender.com/index.php?tab=0` and then click the Try button on that page).

Occasionally, cost alone may be enough to lead to such changes. But you can also take advantage of a forthcoming annual audit to look at recent software reviews and comparisons, not just to check ratings and information about current choices, but also to look for new products or offerings, or updates to other products or offerings, that might offer better value for the money, more functionality, improved convenience, or other inducements to make a switch. If you find yourself going down that road, don't forget to ask about pricing for competitive upgrades. In many cases, when you switch from one vendor's product to another, you can still get upgrade pricing (although it usually won't be as good a deal as moving from one version to the next of the same product, it will be cheaper than full retail for a brand-new, first-time purchase).

This exercise may also have to occur at odd intervals sometimes—the recent introduction of Windows XP SP2 as I write this book is a compelling case in point. Whereas prior to Windows XP SP2 you had no choice but to turn to third parties for pop-up blockers and browser add-on (BHO) management tools, that new software made Microsoft's built-in offerings not just an option among many, but a highly competitive option among market leaders in both categories. Likewise, the upgrade from Internet Connection Firewall (ICF) to Windows Firewall suddenly took a substandard facility that few took seriously and replaced it with a firewall that tests in the same league as leading third-party products (at least, for incoming traffic — unlike most other third-party firewalls, however, Windows Firewall doesn't screen or manage outgoing traffic). When these things happen, it's easiest to make such a switch if the new option you adopt is also a no-cost option (as is the case with the items just mentioned). But when compelling new capabilities, improved security, or better convenience are involved, you can weigh the costs of making a switch before the annual subscription runs out against the value that the new choice will return in exchange. Here again is another trade-off that only you can make for yourself, but one that's often well worth pondering (and even adopting, from time to time).

Finally, you may decide that new feature or functions in a new release aren't to your liking, have too much negative effect on system performance, or interfere with normal working procedures sufficiently to make a change potentially worthwhile. For example, between one version of a major anti-virus software release and the next, the vendor started not only requiring anti-virus checks every time an MS Office application performed an autosave (which I have configured to occur every 5 minutes) but also pushed a Windows icon onto the application tray with a wait message that made the application unusable for anywhere from 30 to 60 seconds. Because this caused a 10 to 20 percent loss of productivity, I had to consider (and ended up) selecting a different, less intrusive product as a consequence.

Staying Subscribed

No matter which products you use, or how many times you switch, you can't afford to let subscriptions lapse for anti-virus, anti-spyware/anti-adware, and your firewall. Because these are all essential tools in your ongoing battle to protect yourself from loss and harm, you can't just decide to do without and save the $20 to $30 a year that's typical for such services.

Tip

Although most such software will remind you when subscriptions are about to elapse, most companies don't credit you for renewing early — so that unless you wait until the day of expiration to renew, you'll lose whatever number of paid-up days still hold on last year's subscription — making a reminder of your own both important and essential.

During your annual security audit, please check to make sure you've set up reminders for the various expiration days you face, to make sure you get to use the full subscription period you paid for. The same observation holds when upgrading from one version to another, so you might also want to think about timing your software upgrades to coincide with subscription expirations as well. On my systems, such considerations apply to anti-virus software and to some of my firewalls and anti-spyware /anti-adware software, so I've got Outlook reminders set up for all of them, with early reminders a month in advance in case travel or vacation plans overlap with renewal dates.

Please note further than when your subscription related to some product runs out, be it for a security suite, anti-virus software, anti-spyware/anti-adware, or whatever, it doesn't stop working. You normally just can't access updates automatically any more (in many cases, you can still obtain updates by downloading them yourself, but this "product life extension" capability seldom lasts more than a year or two longer), though in some cases you may not be able to access updates at all. This situation offers you three choices:

- **Do without updates** — Given the importance of keeping this kind of software current, this practice exposes you to increasing levels of risk and vulnerability as your software continues to age. Not recommended!
- **Re-up your existing subscription** — This is a medium-cost option, where you keep using the same old software, but sign up for another year's worth of updates and subscriptions. Eventually, however, this will result in reduced functionality or capability (although new features and functions are added to current or pending software releases, they seldom if ever make it into last year's model) over time. This is okay for a year or so; beyond that, it too starts exposing you to risk and potential vulnerability.
- **Upgrade to the newest version** — This is the highest-cost option, but the one that offers the best protection and minimizes risk and exposure to vulnerability. If you've got the necessary funds, this is the recommended strategy.

If this sounds like a fiendish plot to extract as much of your money as possible, you can't be blamed for feeling this way. But you do have to weigh the costs, benefits, and risks of the various possible approaches just outlined, and do what's best for you. If it's any consolation, you'll usually get a year's subscription along with upgraded software whenever you take that path. On many occasions, budget constraints have caused me to upgrade only every other year, and renew subscriptions in between. As far as I can tell, that's a workable compromise for those seeking to keep covered yet also keep expenses to a practical minimum.

Where (or When) Will It End?

As I bring this book to a close, the question in this heading seems a good one to address. Certainly, trends and statistics related to spyware, adware, malware, and other PC pests indicate only that over time there are more of them to contend with, and each current generation seems to be more clever, dangerous, and malefic than the last. While I've been writing this book for example, an exploit based on embedding malware in the kinds of images that routinely appear in Web pages (namely, graphics files that take extensions like `.jpg` or `.gif`, among others) has appeared. It's even led to a pretty major security update, because the vulnerability exploited is part of the Windows Graphical Device Interface (GDI) that's used to draw Windows, icons, and other graphical objects on your display, as well as for many other graphical purposes. (If you're running Windows XP SP2, Windows itself isn't vulnerable to this exploit, but other Microsoft software on your machine — including various versions of Office, Visio, and many other programs — may very well be.)

To me, this illustrates the frailty and fallibility of human nature at the same time that it celebrates its ingenuity and cunning. As long as human beings keep creating software, flaws and vulnerabilities will be discovered. Once discovered, such flaws and vulnerabilities will inevitably be exploited. This cycle is what keeps the flow of adware, spyware, and malware ongoing, and what makes keeping yourself up-to-date and as protected as possible so very necessary.

So it looks like this situation is ongoing, with no end in sight. But what does appear to be in the works is a heightened sensitivity to such matters, and an increasing sense that getting and staying protected is simply part of building, using, and maintaining a PC. Although the threats will change, and the kinds of exploits fomented will vary over time, the need for vigilance and a safe computing mindset must therefore be never-ending as well.

Resources

To a large extent, this chapter itself is nothing more than a collection of resources designed to supplement and cement content presented elsewhere in this book. Nevertheless, I'd like to throw a few more carefully chosen security resources here as a final set of suggested additional reading and information if you're interested in digging deeper or learning more about the subject of Windows security and related software and tools used to provide the best safety and protection possible.

Microsoft offers an amazing collection of security-related news, information, white papers, training, and more on its Web site. This is all available through two primary security portals: general security stuff through `www.microsoft.com/security/` and more technical security information through `www.microsoft.com/technet/security` (this page will be redirected, but it's shorter than typing default.aspx at the end of the URL, which is otherwise required). Be sure to look for additional resources on these pages, including Microsoft's Security Guidance Center, references to books, pointers to security checklists of all kinds, plus security how-tos, and lots more. Investigate the offerings here, and visit these pages regularly because this content is changed and expanded all the time. At present, I am finding updates to all major guides and documentation to incorporate complete coverage of Windows XP SP2.

Symantec also offers lots of security news and information, including a FAQ, numerous white papers, and its own newsletter through its Security Response pages (http://securityresponse.symantec.com)—check the Reference Area at the bottom of that page. Be sure to check out its Windows XP Service Pack 2 information center as well, and to look at the FAQ and support documents tabs at www.symantec.com/techsupp/sp2/faq.html. The many documents referenced through the Security Response FAQ itself are also worth consulting, at http://securityresponse.symantec.com/avcenter/faq.html.

For more information on some of the specific items mentioned in this chapter, visit the following Web sites:

- Spy Sweeper—Its SpyWare Information Center (www.webroot.com/wb/spywareinformation/) provides access to all kinds of useful data. Above and beyond the news and top threats mentioned in this chapter, you'll also find instructions and tutorials on spyware terms, concepts, software, and removal operations.
- Larry Leonard's Web site at www.definitivesolutions.com is subject to periods of unavailability owing to access limits set by his Internet service provider (ISP) and the demand for BHO Demon. It's still worth a look.
- Patrick Kolla operates the Spybot-Search & Destroy pages through www.spybot.info. You can find some news and articles there, plus lots of other interesting resources, but nothing like alerts or bulletins. He also led me to Andrew Clover's excellent, but eclectic site at www.doxdesk.com, which includes great spyware/adware information and pointers under the general heading of parasites, but again no bulletins or alerts.

The most current information on the JPEG processing technology vulnerability also known as the GDI+ exploit is documented on the Microsoft site extensively. You can find general coverage on this topic at www.microsoft.com/security/bulletins/200409_jpeg.mspx. Knowledge Base article 833987, "Buffer Overrun in JPEG Processing (GDI+) Could Allow Code Execution" has all the technical details (www.microsoft.com/technet/security/bulletin/MS04-028.mspx).

Summary

This concluding chapter of the book talked about how to find out if and when serious potential security threats occur. This included a detailed discussion of the kinds of resources involved, places to obtain alerts and bulletins with indications of severity, possible workarounds or fixes, and other relevant information. I also described what kinds of reactions to such news might be typical, which I can sum up as "find an alternative or do without until the fix is in!" After that, I talked about the need for and benefits of performing annual (or more frequent) security audits using different tools

from those that are part of the customary routine and reviewed the pros and cons of upgrading older software for newer versions and the reasons for, and tradeoffs sometimes involved in, switching from one product to another.

Though this concludes the main body of the book, you'll still find a few bits of ancillary material on the pages that follow. This includes Appendix A, which discusses the pros, cons, and costs of using security suites to simplify software updates and maintenance; Appendix B, which provides a complete bibliography for all books and articles cited in this book; and a Glossary, which includes definitions for all technical terms introduced and used in this book. Of course, you'll also find the Index at the very end, which you can use to locate coverage of specific terms and topics.

Appendix A

The Security Suite Life

Throughout this book, I've discussed a number of items or elements that I think are important, if not downright essential, to securing a PC and making it safe for regular, everyday Internet use. If you enumerate the types of various items I've talked about most, you'll see that there are at least six of them — namely:

- Anti-spyware/anti-adware software
- Anti-virus software
- Browser Helper Object (add-ons) manager
- Firewall
- Pop-up blocker
- Spam blocking software and/or service

If you're okay with Windows XP SP2 and happy with the way Internet Explorer 6 works, you don't need to worry about the pop-up blocker (there's one built into the browser itself, accessible through the Tools→Pop-up blocker menu entry). You may not need to worry about BHO management software, either — Microsoft's Add-ons manager will warn you whenever one seeks to be installed and also lets you manage those that are already installed on Internet Explorer (it's accessible through the Tools→Manage add-ons menu entry). Finally, there's Windows Firewall, which also does a pretty reasonable job of protecting your system from unwanted and unauthorized external access attempts.

Assuming you're okay with these built-in components, that still leaves at least three additional elements to add onto your Windows XP system: anti-spyware/anti-adware software, anti-virus software, and some kind of spam blocking software (with or without the third-party spam filtering service recommended in Chapters 9 and 10 of this book). For some people, finding, installing and managing three or more software packages is all in a day's work and strikes them as no big deal; for others, it may seem like too much trouble to deal with.

The purpose of this appendix is to inform and remind you that you do have another option besides going out and bagging best-of-breed software packages one at a time for the various elements you choose to acquire from somebody other than Microsoft (though you might not have to mess with several items in the preceding paragraph, that doesn't mean you might not choose to do so anyway). Of course if you're not using Windows XP SP2, those other items won't be built into Windows, and you will indeed want and need to get them elsewhere.

That's where the other option mentioned (and the topic of this appendix)—namely, security suites—comes into play. Many vendors offer varying collections of security and protection software to their customers under the general heading of security suite software. Today, most of these offerings cover everything except for anti-adware/spyware software (though there is ample evidence that this will change soon, and that most major vendors will bundle this functionality in their suites as well) and browser add-on or BHO management software (on this subject, it's a little harder to tell if it will become a standard component or not).

For those who prefer a one-stop solution, security suites make good sense. For those willing to spend some money, but for whom budgets may be tight, the fact that most security suites cost less than the combined cost of commercial options for most (or all) of the software they include may be an added incentive to look in this direction for a security solution for their PCs. And finally, the observation that security suites nearly universally offer automatic update services to their owners (thereby relieving you of most of the responsibility involved in keeping your security software current and up-to-date) may be just the kicker that some folks need to move them further in that direction.

But it's up to you to decide whether you want to use products from multiple vendors and try to find the best in each category or whether the convenience, cost savings, and easy updates that security suites offer is right for you. I confess to an unwavering curiosity about the best in each category, so I waffle and use some components from a security suite along with other third-party "best of breed" items in my search for a real nonpareil solution. But that does take extra time and effort, and costs more too, so I'll let you look over some representative security suites here and decide which way you'd like to go yourself.

Security Suite Offerings

Although this appendix can't claim to offer an exhaustive survey of security suite software, you won't suffer from a lack of options if you decide to dig more deeply into this product niche for yourself. Here I'll list some leading offerings, then lay out their components in a single table so you can see who's got what on a single page, along with how much you might be asked to pay for these products.

I begin with a list of seven leading security suite products, each with an associated abbreviation I'll use in Table A-1 and a URL where you can learn more, along with a few remarks on topics of potential interest:

- **BitDefender Professional Edition 8** (abbreviation: BDP; `www.bitdefender.com/bd/site/products.php?p_id=25`)—Another outgrowth from a well-known anti-virus company, BitDefender adds a firewall, spam blocker, content and privacy controls to its anti-virus technologies. It also markets a standard version that omits the firewall and anti-spam features for those seeking a top-notch anti-virus package.
- **Computer Associates eTrust EZ Armor Security Suite** (abbreviation: EZT; `www.my-etrust.com/microsoft/index.cfm?`)—Although this offering has the fewest capabilities or additional bells and whistles, it's available for free for the first year of updates, and its purchase and subscription costs are lower than those for other suites mentioned here. CA has recently acquired PestPatrol (a leading anti-spyware/anti-adware company), so it seems likely it'll be adding this functionality to its suite in the relatively near future.

- **F-Secure Internet Security 2004** (abbreviation: FSI; `www.f-secure.com/products/anti-virus/fsis2004/details.shtml`)—F-secure is based in Finland, and widely used in Europe. It's a bit on the pricey side, especially considering that it doesn't cover anything but firewall and anti-virus capabilities.
- **McAfee Internet Security Suite 6.0** (abbreviation: MIS; `http://us.mcafee.com/root/package.asp?pkgid=144&cid=10353`)—Long a leading name in anti-virus technology, McAfee offers pretty comprehensive coverage of most elements listed in Table A-1, but comes in second to Norton Internet Security in many reviews.
- **Norton Internet Security 2005** (abbreviation: NIS; `www.symantec.com/sabu/nis/nis_pe/index.html`)—Not only does NIS cover most of the bases in my list, but it also leads the market in the firewall and spam blocking categories and comes in for honorable mention in anti-virus coverage.
- **Panda Platinum Internet Security** (abbreviation: PPI; `www.pandasoftware.com/products/platinum_is/`)—Another European outfit, Panda's products are also well-known and widely used outside the United States. It's the most expensive product suite here, but also offers very good functionality for the price.
- **ZoneAlarm Security Suite** (abbreviation: ZAS; `www.zonelabs.com/store/content/catalog/products/zass/zass_details.jsp`)—A market leader in personal firewalls, ZoneAlarm offers the most comprehensive coverage of all security elements I mention at a market average price.

Use the abbreviations introduced in the list items above to identify the specific suites covered. In the headings, FW stands for firewall, AV for anti-virus software, AS/A for anti-spyware/anti-adware software, PB for pop-up blocker, SB for spam blocker, and BHO for Browser Helper Object manager. Unfortunately, most of the offerings in the table are so new that nobody (including me) has really had time to test claimed anti-spyware/anti-adware capabilities seriously. While I (and other reviewers) can stand behind other entries in the table with a fair degree of confidence, it's really not yet clear how these suites stack up against leading anti-spyware/anti-adware products like Webroot Spy Sweeper, SpyBot-Search & Destroy, or Ad-Aware. Fortunately, it's easy to supplement this functionality with free tools like SpyBot-Search & Destroy or Ad-Aware if you buy a suite and find this part of its capabilities aren't completely up to snuff. Please note also that except for the McAfee Internet Security suite, all the products mentioned feature free trial or evaluation versions you can download from their Web sites, so in most cases you can try before you buy to see if you like it or not.

Table A-1 Comparing Security Suite Offerings

Abbrev	*FW*	*AV*	*AS/A*	*PB*	*SB*	*BHO*	*Cost/Upgrade*	*Notes*
BDP	Y	Y	N	N	Y	N	\$39.95/\$22.48	More capability than EZT for less cost
EZT	Y	Y	N	N	N	N	Free or \$50[1]/\$20	Few bells and whistles, good basic protection

Continued

Table A-1 Comparing Security Suite Offerings *(continued)*

Abbrev	*FW*	*AV*	*AS/A*	*PB*	*SB*	*BHO*	*Cost/Upgrade*	*Notes*
FSI	Y	Y	N	N[2]	N	N	$78/$49	Offers great simplicity, ease-of-use
MIS	Y	Y	Y	Y	Y	N	$70[3]/$40	Privacy, parental controls, and more
NIS	Y	Y	Y	Y	Y	N	$70/$30	Privacy, parental controls, and more
PPI	Y	Y	Y	N	Y	N	$90/$NA[4]	Content filtering and privacy controls
ZAS	Y	Y	Y[5]	Y	Y	N	$70/$70	Privacy, cookie controls, ID lock, and more

1 Visit the Microsoft Protect Your PC page to get access to one free year of this product, which costs $50 otherwise, $19.95 per year thereafter.

2 I couldn't determine with complete certainty whether or not a pop-up blocker was included with this product, so I erred on the side of caution.

3 Price is $10 higher for those who want to receive a CD and printed documentation.

4 I was unable to confirm U.S. upgrade pricing, though several newsgroup posts suggest it's in the neighborhood of $50.

5 From reading over the ZoneAlarm documentation, it appears that spyware/adware coverage in the current version is less than complete.

On the Web

Microsoft maintains a reasonably comprehensive list of anti-virus software vendors — many of whom also offer security suites — in Knowledge Base Article 49500 (`http://support.microsoft.com/kb/q49500/`). If you want to look for more offerings, visiting the Web sites mentioned here is a pretty good place to start looking. You can also use your favorite search engine with a string like "security suite" or "internet security suite" and get some pretty good results as well.

Shopping Advice

If you decide you're interested in one of these security suites, or in buying any of the commercial software packages mentioned throughout this book, you might be able to save a little money with some simple shopping advice. Some Web sites make it easy to comparison shop on price or other criteria as long as you know the name of the product you're shopping for. I recommend that you visit sites like `www.shopper.com` to try to find the best deals on software whenever possible. Interestingly

enough, you may sometimes be able to save more by going to a store and buying a shrink-wrapped software package than by downloading the same thing from the Internet. But if you go looking for good prices online, whether you buy online or not, you should be able to determine if discounts are available, and if so, to find them fairly easily.

You may occasionally get what look like incredible deals from aftermarket retailers who sell software that's one or two revisions back from the current version. Thus, for example, you may see advertisements for Norton Internet Security 2003 at less than half the list price in Table A-1 for Norton Internet Security 2005. But before you succumb to such temptations, think about what it means to upgrade (possibly through two versions; if you're lucky, only to the most current version) to maintain a subscription and keep your software up-to-date (fortunately, all the software that requires a subscription to grab updates, automatically or otherwise, also makes it easy for you to find out when your subscription expires). What looks very cheap may not be such a great deal if you have to turn around and pay full retail (or look for another low-ball purveyor) in the next few months to a year. It's generally a good idea to add the upgrade price (in this case it's $29.95 or $39.95, depending on which version you've got) to the purchase price of the original product before making the call. If the result is still less than the price of the new product, it's probably worth it as long as you can meet proof of purchase requirements to upgrade; otherwise, skip it!

Also, as you shop around, be on the lookout for rebates (money back from your purchase price, although you must usually jump through some documentation or proof of purchase hoops to qualify) or for so-called "competitive upgrade pricing" (a discount on your current purchase so long as you can prove you've owned a competitive product in the past; be sure to check documentation and proof of purchase requirements here, too). You can occasionally save some serious money on your purchase by looking for such offerings and taking the best advantage of them that you can. Another purchase strategy is to look for discounts at outlets like Costco, Buy.com, or other mass marketers; sometimes, you can find some remarkable deals that way. Students and teachers may qualify for educational discounts, too. Where there's a will to save money on this stuff, remember, too, that there's almost always a way!

Appendix B

References

You can find many of the links mentioned in this appendix by pointing your browser at `www.wiley.com/go/pcmag`. Once there, you can find the links to the book's references by selecting the companion site for this book, or you can explore some of the other great *PC Magazine* titles available.

Microsoft Knowledge Base

Microsoft Knowledge Base articles are available online at `support.microsoft.com/`.

A Description of the Changes to the Security Settings of the Web Content Zones in Internet Explorer 6 (Article 300443)

How To Configure Outlook To Block Additional Attachment File Name Extensions (Article 837388)

How To Disable Active Content in Internet Explorer (Article 154036)

How To Restore the Operating System to a Previous State in Windows XP (Article 306084)

How To Use Security Zones in Internet Explorer (Article 174360)

How To Use the Windiff.exe Utility (Article 159214)

You can stick the KB article number into this stub URL to locate any of these items: `http://support.microsoft.com/kb/q`*<number>*`/`

Books and Articles

Comer, Douglas E. *Internetworking with TCP/IP: Principles, Protocols, and Architecture, Volume 1*, 4th edition. Pearson Education, 2000.

Hafner, Katie and John Markoff. *Cyberpunk: Outlaws and Hackers on the Computer Frontier*. New York, NY: Simon & Schuster, 1991.

Honeycutt, Jerry. *The Windows XP Registry Guide*. Redmond, WA: Microsoft Press, 2002.

Rubenking, Neil J. "11 Signs of Spyware." *PC Magazine,* March 2, 2004.

Schweitzer, Douglas. *Securing the Network from Malicious Code.* Indianapolis, IN: Wiley Publishing, Inc., 2002.

Scrimger, Rod, et al. *TCP/IP Bible.* New York, NY: John Wiley & Sons, 2001.

Skoudis, Ed and Lenny Zeltser. *Malware: Fighting Malicious Code.* Indianapolis, IN: Prentice Hall PTR, 2003.

Safe Download Sites

CNET (Outstanding source for all kinds of software) — `www.downloads.com`

Free Downloads Center (Popular freeware source) — `www.freedownloadscenter.com`

The Free Site (Popular freeware source) — `www.thefreesite.com`

Shareware.com (Offers both shareware and freeware) — `www.shareware.com`

Tucows (The ultimate compilation of Windows software) — `www.tucows.com`

Online Security Scanners

For malware, spyware, and adware

Ad-Aware — `www.lavasoft.de/software/adaware/`

Bazooka Adware and Spyware Scanner — `www.kephyr.com/spywarescanner/index.html`

BitDefender (Online virus scan. Follow prompts) — `www.bitdefender.com/scan/license.php`

Housecall (Click Scan Now, follow prompts) — `housecall.trendmicro.com/`

Pest Scan (For spyware and adware. Follow prompts.) — `www.pestscan.com/`

Spy Audit .EXE (Scans for spy- and adware.) — `www.webroot.com/services/spyaudit.htm`

Spybot-Search & Destroy — `www.safer-networking.org/en/download/index.html`

Symantec (Virus detection. Click Check for Security Risks, follow prompts.) — `securityresponse.symantec.com`

X-Cleaner ActiveX control (Scans for spy- and adware.) — `www.spywareinfo.com/xscan.php`

Spam

Coalition Against Unsolicited Commercial Email (CAUCE) — www.cauce.org

EmailAbuse — www.emailabuse.org

Gates, Bill. "Executive E-mail: Preserving and Enhancing the Benefits of Email — A Progress Report." — www.microsoft.com/mscorp/execmail/2004/06-28antispam.asp

Microsoft. "99,999 Innocent Bystanders Spammed." — research.microsoft.com/displayArticle.aspx?id=672

Microsoft. "Outlook 2003 Junk E-mail Filter." — www.microsoft.com/office/outlook/prodinfo/filter.mspx

Microsoft. "Windows Script Host overview." — www.microsoft.com/windowsxp/home/using/productdoc/en/wsh_overview.asp

Other online security scanners

HackerWhacker (Free Tools: click Run Test. HackerWhacker offers a one-week membership, with complete access to all scans, for $9.99.) — omega.hackerwhacker.com/freetools.php

Security Space (Click Security Audit, select Single Test. Security Space offers a year's worth of end-user scans for a paltry $9.95; a great deal!) — www.securityspace.com

Steve Gibson Research, ShieldsUP! (Gibson is very generous with his remediation advice to help you fix anything amiss that might pop up. Definitely worth a visit.) — grc.com

Symantec Security Check (Offers AV and security check. Also worth a visit.) — securityresponse.symantec.com

Blocking Software

Pop-up Killer Review (Sergei Kaul's Web site full of information, discussion, and additional information on pop-ups, including a comprehensive list of 116 pop-up blockers.) — www.popup-killer-review.com

PopUpCheck.com (Jim Maurer's Web site offers descriptions of 19 tests you can perform to check your browser's ability to block pop-ups. His standard pop-up test covers 9 of those items, his miscellaneous pop-up tests cover another 4, and his advanced pop-up tests cover the rest.) — www.popupcheck.com

Password Management

AI RoboForm (Password generation, storage, and autotext application) — www.roboform.com/

HyperSafe (Provides local or Web-based access to passwords) — www.passwordsafe.com/

KeyWallet (Provides local password storage and access) — www.keywallet.com/

Password Safe (Bruce Schneier's open source Password Safe) — www.schneier.com/passsafe.html

Secure Data Manager (Open source password manager with annotations) — sdm.sourceforge.net/

Security Issues and Information

Active Registry Monitor — www.protect-me.com/arm/

Anti-Virus Software Review — www.anti-virus-software-review.com/

CERT (Computer Emergency Readiness Team). "Browsing Safely: Understanding Active Content and Cookies." — www.us-cert.gov/cas/tips/ST04-012.html

CERT Coordination Center (Various publication documenting viruses and how they work) — www.cert.org/other_sources/viruses.html

Charter Communications — "Understanding E-mail message headers." FAQ by Andy Olds. — swins.com/support/online/faqs/email_headers.html

Common Vulnerabilities and Exposures (CVE) — www.cve.mitre.org

Cowan, Crispin, et al. "StackGuard: Automatic Adaptive Detection and Prevention of Buffer-Overflow Attacks." Department of Computer Science and Engineering, Oregon Graduate Institute of Science & Technolog — www.usenix.org/publications/library/proceedings/sec98/cowan.html

Definitive Solutions (Larry Leonard's Web site is subject to periods of unavailability owing to access limits set by his ISP) — www.definitivesolutions.com

Doxdesk (Andrew Clover's excellent, but eclectic site, which includes great spyware/adware information and pointers under the general heading of parasites, but no bulletins or alerts) — www.doxdesk.com

eEye Digital Security (This company shows up frequently in news reports when it breaks advisories or alerts on security threats and vulnerabilities) — www.eeye.com

International Computer Security Association (CSA, now part of TruSecure Corporation) — www.icsalabs.com/html/communities/antivirus/index.shtml

Internet Assigned Numbers Authority (IANA) — www.iana.org/assignments/port-numbers

Kaspersky. "Computer Virus Classification." — www.avp.ch/avpve/classes/classes.stm

Kaspersky Labs — www.kaspersky.com

Kawamoto, Dawn. "Security-appliance market sees gains." CNET, September 2003. — news.com.com/2100-7355-5079045.html

Meta, Cade. "Spam Blockers." *PC Magazine.* February 17, 2004. — www.pcmag.com/article2/0,1759,1615479,00.asp

Metz, Cade. "Spy Stoppers." *PC Magazine.* March 2, 2004. — www.pcmag.com/article2/0,1759,1524269,00.asp

Microsoft. Developer note. "Avoiding Buffer Overruns." — http://msdn.microsoft.com/library/en-us/secbp/security/avoiding_buffer_overruns.asp?frame=true

Microsoft. "How To Tell if a Microsoft Security-Related Message Is Genuine." — www.microsoft.com/security/incident/authenticate_mail.mspx

Microsoft. "Internet Connection Firewall Overview." — www.microsoft.com/WINDOWSXP/home/using/productdoc/en/hnw_understanding_firewall.asp

Microsoft. Protect Your PC home page. — www.microsoft.com/athome/security/protect/default.aspx

Microsoft. "What You Need To Know about Phishing." — www.microsoft.com/athome/security/spam/phishing.mspx

Microsoft. *Windows XP Professional Product Documentation.* "Nslookup." — www.microsoft.com/resources/documentation/windows/xp/all/proddocs/en-us/nslookup.mspx

Microsoft Boycott Campaign. "Replacements for Explorer." — www.msboycott.com/thealt/alts/internetexplorer.shtml

Microsoft security issues and information — www.microsoft.com/security/

OASIS (Organization for the Advancement of Structured Information Standards) — www.oasis-open.org

Ohio State University (Index of RFCs) — www.cis.ohio-state.edu/cs/Services/rfc/index.html

PC Magazine (Reviews of anti-virus and other software) — www.pcmag.com

Pisello, Tom. "The ROI for Antispam Initiatives." SearchSmallBizIT.com. — searchsmallbizit.techtarget.com/columnItem/0,294698,sid44_gci991440,00.html?track=NL-118&ad=487443&Offer=smb728

Registry Watch — www.easydesksoftware.com/regwatch.htm

RFC 3000 — www.cis.ohio-state.edu/cgi-bin/rfc/rfc3000.html

Rubenking, Neil J. "Can You Sniff Out Fraud?" *PC Magazine.* July 28, 2004. — www.pcmag.com/article2/0,1759,1628424,00.asp

SANS Institute (Newsletters *@Risk: The Consensus Vulnerability Alert* and *SANS NewsBites*) — http://portal.sans.org

Secunia (One of the most consistent breakers of early news and information on threats and vulnerabilities, especially for Windows platforms) — http://secunia.com

SecurityFocus (Not only runs a vulnerabilities database, reports on security news, and operates various interesting newsletters and mailing lists, but it's also home to Russ Cooper's BugTraq, which aggregates bug, threat, exploit, and vulnerability reports from all over the world) — www.securityfocus.com

Spybot-Search & Destroy (Operated by Patrick Kolla. You can find some news and articles there, plus lots of other interesting resources, but nothing like alerts or bulletins on these pages) — www.spybot.info and www.safer-networking.org/en/home/index.html

Spy Sweeper (Spyware information center provides access to all kinds of useful data) — www.webroot.com/wb/spywareinformation/

Spyware Info (Runs a set of well-used and moderated newsgroups and has a newsletter, *Spyware Weekly*) — http://forums.spywareinfo.com

Spyware Warrior (Pretty nice general spyware site, but unfiltered) — www.spywarewarrior.com/

StopSpam. "Reading EMail Headers: All About Email Headers." — www.stopspam.org/email/headers.html

SurferBeware (Covers all kinds of Web-related security topics, including spyware, viruses, cookies, pop-ups, spam, Web safety, and firewalls) — http://spyware.surferbeware.com/spyware-news.htm

Symantec. Virus Encyclopedia. — http://securityresponse.symantec.com/avcenter/vinfodb.html

Symantec. "What Is the Difference between Viruses, Worms, and Trojans?" — service1.symantec.com/SUPPORT/nav.nsf/docid/1999041209131106

Symantec Security Response Center (Latest virus threat information, updates, and security advisories) — securityresponse.symantec.com

TechTarget.com (Various security Web sites) — www.SearchSecurity.com, www.SearchWindowsSecurity.com, and www.SearchWin2000.com

Topix.net (Runs a thread on spyware that aggregates spyware-related stories from news feeds of all kinds; updated daily) — www.topix.net/tech/spyware

TopTenReviews. "Anti-Spyware Software Review." — www.anti-spyware-review.toptenreviews.com/

Trend Micro Technical Note. "Spyware — a Hidden Threat." — www.trendmicro.com/NR/rdonlyres/B942C2E4-16A1-4AC0-9D42-B208558AE187/11977/WP01Spyware_ForTMWebsite_070204US.pdf

Ulanoff, Lance. "Opting into Identity Theft." *PC Magazine*. July 21, 2004. — www.pcmag.com/article2/0,1759,1625608,00.asp

Virus Bulletin (Test results for more than 20 anti-virus applications in the June 2004 issue) — www.virusbtn.com/vb100/archives/tests.xml

Virus Bulletin tutorials — www.virusbtn.com/support/tutorials/

Wegert, Tessa. "Pop-Up Ads, Part 1: Good? Bad? Ugly?" March 14, 2002. — www.clickz.com/experts/media/media_buy/article.php/991121

Wegert, Tessa. "Pop-Up Ads, Part 2: Usage Guidelines for Legitimate Marketers." March 21, 2002. — www.clickz.com/experts/media/media_buy/article.php/995311

Zone Labs (Security advisories, technical notes, and technical support information, including anti-virus information, adware and spyware alerts, newsletters, and tutorials) — www.zonelabs.com/

Software

ActiveX Controls (Microsoft) — www.microsoft.com/com/tech/activex.asp

Norton Ghost (Symantec) — www.symantec.com/sabu/ghost/ghost_personal/

Firefox (Mozilla) — www.mozilla.org/products/firefox/download.html

InaQuick Rescue (IQR) — www.inasoft.com/products/products.asp

JavaScript — www.javascript.com/

Opera (Opera Software) — www.opera.com/download/?lng=en&ver=7.54

Sun Microsystems (Java) — java.sun.com/

Virus hoaxes

F-Secure Security Information Center — www.f-secure.com/virus-info/hoax/

Hoax Busters — www.hoaxbusters.org

HoaxKill — www.hoaxkill.com

Jeff Richards' Virus Hoaxes and Netlore Web page — hoaxinfo.com

Truth or Fiction — www.truthorfiction.org

U.S. Department of Energy's Computer Incident Advisory Capability (CIAC) Hoaxbusters page — hoaxbusters.ciac.org/

Vmyths — www.vmyths.com

Glossary

ABetterInternet — A relatively benign adware program that has been around for a while. To remove ABetterInternet from your system, see Chapter 4.

active content — Scripts that execute programs within a Web browser. Although much active content creates enhancements to Web pages, it can also be used to automatically display pop-up ads or allow an attacker to unleash malicious code on a computer.

Active Server Pages (ASP) — Microsoft's scripting environment that combines scripts, HTML, and ActiveX components to produce dynamic Web content.

ActiveX controls — A key Microsoft technology used for providing active Web content of all kinds, ActiveX is an extension to other Microsoft technologies — object linking and embedding (OLE) and the Component Object Model (COM).

Address Resolution Protocol (ARP) — A protocol that is used in translating numeric IP addresses to MAC addresses.

adware — Any mechanism used to deliver ads beyond a normal Web page ad; *see* malware and pop-up.

Application layer — The layer of the TCP/IP protocol stack where a protocol stack hooks up with applications or processes on a host machine. This layer deals with user interfaces and services capabilities and is where recognizable services such as e-mail, Web access, file transfer, and other activities operate; also known as the Process layer.

automatic invocation — The triggering of unrequested and probably unwanted material by a simple act such as a mouseover or moving something from a Web site to your desktop.

back door — An opening or break left in network or system security by design. Back doors are intended for debugging purposes, but can be exploited by worms, viruses, and other forms of malware; also known as a trap door.

BHO (Browser Helper Object) — An add-in or plug-in to some specific Web browser, designed to extend core functionality that runs as part of the overall Web browser process; can be benign or malign.

BHODemon — A program published by Definitive Solutions that can show all the Browser Helper Objects installed in a version of Internet Explorer and rate what it finds.

blacklisting — Maintaining a list of domains associated with known spammers from which no inbound e-mail will be accepted. *See also* whitelisting.

blended threat — Can refer to either a malware package that combines Trojans, worms, or viruses or a threat that seeks to exploit more than one system vulnerability.

buffer overflows (or buffer overruns) — A technique for stuffing input handling software with more data than it was intended to handle; when this occurs in improperly tested software, it's often possible to execute commands or programs a the same level of privilege as the program that's accepting input. This explains why it's the most common technique for unauthorized system penetration, and the most common type of software or system vulnerability.

Category 4 — A classification of malware, typically a mass-mailing worm, but may be any kind of malware. To meet the criteria for this classification, malware must have a high Wild metric for either Damage or Distribution.

CIDR (Classless Inter-domain Routing) — An Internet addressing system that allows one IP address to refer to multiple unique addresses. CIDR is also referred to as supernetting.

client — Anything running on your computer (also called the local machine) and accessing services on the Internet; for example, the Web browser or an FTP client; also called client side. *See also* server.

Common Vulnerabilities and Exposures (CVE) — A database of well-documented computer vulnerabilities and exposures maintained at `www.cve.mitre.org` as a service to software developers, security professionals, and the IT profession.

cookie — A small piece of text data that a Web server exchanges with your browser that gets stored on your machine. Each time you return to the site that originally provided the cookie, the cookie identifies you. For example, it is a cookie that allows the Amazon.com site to greet you by name each time you return.

DARPA (Defense Advanced Research Projects Agency) model — Another name for TCP/IP, named after the government agency that funded the original development of TCP/IP.

distribution — A measure of how quickly and how far a malware threat is able to spread.

distribution in the wild — Term that refers to the total number of documented infections, number of sites affected, geographical distribution of the infection, the amount of work involved in containing or blocking the threat, and the amount of work involved in cleanup or removal of assessing a particular malware threat.

DNS (domain name system) — The Internet database that maps domain names to IP addresses; that is, the DNS translates names of the form "mycat.com" to the numerical address that identifies that site to the computers that make up the Internet.

dotted decimal form—A kind of IP address made up of four decimal numbers, separated by dots or periods; also called dotted-quad notation. For example, 172.16.1.33 is the private IP address that my current desktop uses as I write this definition.

drive-by download—A download, often of spyware or adware, that occurs as an unadvertised consequence of visiting a Web page, sometimes associated with questionable, if not malign, motives.

dynamic port numbers (49,152–65,535)—Memory locations or addresses that are used only during a temporary, active connection between a sender and a receiver. Once closed, dynamic port numbers are discarded so they can be reused as needed.

executable process—Any program that runs in Windows (and in most operating system environments) operates within the context of a virtual machine that defines system variables and access, mediates input/output, and in general creates a stable, apparently independent runtime environment called an execution process. Thus, any program or code you run on Windows that adds an entry to the process table may be called an executable process, and you can find it easily using the Process tab in Task Manager. Individual processes run separately from one another in Windows, and provide additional protection against bugs or errors in any single process by protecting how processes interact, communicate, and share resources.

exploit—A threat made real; an actual, successful attack on an existing vulnerability.

file infectors—Any of a number of malware items, usually viruses, that are capable of insinuating themselves (particularly, the code they need to execute) inside another file in a computer's file system.

firewall—Software or hardware that sits between your computer and the Internet to screen traffic. It should deny transit to anything recognizably malign, unwanted, inappropriate, or even suspicious, while allowing at least some benign information.

FTP (File Transfer Protocol)—A commonly used file transfer service on the Internet, based on well-known TCP port addresses 20 and 21.

GUI (graphical user interface)—A front-end user interface, such as found in Windows and Apple Macintosh systems, that uses graphics and menus rather than commands. Used in contrast to a command-line interface like MS-DOS (the old disk operating system) or Linux.

hives—The hierarchical data structures into which Windows registry is divided: `HKEY_CLASSES_ROOT`, `HKEY_CURRENT_USER`, `HKEY_LOCAL_MACHINE`, `HKEY_USERS`, and `HKEY_CURRENT_CONFIG`. *See also* Windows registry.

hoax—An e-mail message warning of a new and especially virulent computer virus and asking the recipient to warn everyone else he or she knows. Several Web sites keep up-to-date lists of such hoaxes.

Host-to-Host layer—*See* Transport layer.

HTML (Hypertext Markup Language) — A descriptive computer language that underlies all content on the World Wide Web. Browsers interpret HTML to display most Web pages. Although HTML is not a programming language, languages such as JavaScript, PHP (Hypertext Preprocessor), and others can be embedded in HTML to add functionality not available in HTML itself.

HTTP (Hypertext Transfer Protocol) — The underlying communication mechanism for the Web that controls how Web pages are transmitted across the Internet.

HTTPS (Secure HTTP) — A version of the HTTP protocol that uses the Secure Sockets Layer (SSL) to conduct secure, encrypted transactions. Web addresses using this protocol begin with `https://`. When a Secure HTTP connection is established with a server, most Web browsers display a padlock in the status bar on the Web page.

hybrid virus — A virus that combines characteristics of multiple types of malware, so that a single item might include Trojan horse (by installing remote access client and back door software), worm (reproducing via e-mail), and spyware (capturing and disclosing sensitive user information) characteristics. *See also* blended threat.

Hypertext Preprocessor (PHP) — A server-based scripting language with syntax like that of Perl or C that is used in the creation of dynamic Web pages.

ICSA (International Computer Security Association) — A former information security association, now a commercial entity known as TrueSecure, Inc., that offers various well-respected security testing and certification labs and services to the industry.

IMAP (Internet Message Access Protocol) — Internet protocol, similar to POP, that is used in e-mail retrieval; in an IMAP environment, messages are stored on the server, though users can still organize them into folders as they see fit.

Internet layer — The layer of the TCP/IP protocol stack that handles addressing and routing among computers on the Internet. This layer also allows multiple networks to interconnect and supports global naming and addressing schemes of the public Internet.

IP (Internet Protocol) — The primary Internet protocol, IP provides the basis for communication across platforms and systems.

IRC (Internet Relay Chat) — An older system requiring a client program that allows live, real-time messaging over the Internet. More people today use instant messaging (IM).

Java — An object-oriented programming language developed by Sun Microsystems that is similar to C++. Java applets are ideally suited to the Web due to their small size and universal availability across platforms and browsers.

Java Server Pages (JSP) — An extension of Sun's Java language, JSP works in conjunction with HTML and allows users to do things such as query a database.

JavaScript — A scripting language developed by Netscape for the creation of interactive, dynamic Web sites.

JVM (Java Virtual Machine)—A runtime environment that operates on various types of computers and most known operating systems that lets Java programs operate more or less the same way in all of these situations.

keystroke logger—A type of unwanted software often associated with Trojan horse or spyware programs that captures all keyboard input on a computer into some hidden file, usually for transmission to another computer elsewhere so that the illicit recipient can comb the file for passwords, credit card numbers, or other sensitive or personal identity data.

LAN (local area network)—A small (fewer than 10 computers and other devices) to medium-sized (up to 1,000 computers and other devices) network operating in close physical proximity, usually on a collection of cabled and/or wireless network segments or address ranges.

LKGC (Last Known Good Configuration)—A last-ditch maneuver for fending off an attack. While Windows is first booting up, hit the F8 key to see a menu of options. Choose Last Known Good Configuration, and Windows should boot running the version of the registry that existed the last time your system booted.

Logical numeric (IP) address—For IPv4, this is a string of four numbers, separated by dots, for example, 10.6.120.78 or 172.16.1.33.

MAC (Media Access Control) address—*See* physical numeric address.

macro virus—A computer virus in the form of a macro embedded in a document, such as a Microsoft Word document. After it gets on your computer, a macro virus will infect any new documents you create in the same application.

malware—Short for *malicious software*, this is a general term for programs such as computer viruses and worms that can damage computer systems and content.

MBR (master boot record)—A program that executes when you boot up your computer. MBR viruses put new code in place of the MBR.

MIME (Multipurpose Internet Mail Extension)—The e-mail protocol that supports attachments to messages.

Network Access layer—The layer of the TCP/IP protocol stack in which cables, interfaces, and hardware connections to computers and other devices work; also known as Network Interface layer.

network address—Some special kind of name or numeric value used to uniquely identify a single network interface to a network. On a TCP/IP network, each network has a unique MAC layer numeric physical address as well as a unique numeric IP address (it's guaranteed to be unique globally if public IP addresses are used, but only locally if private IP addresses are used).

Network Address Translation (NAT)—Enables a LAN (local area network) to use two sets of IP addresses: one for internal communication and one for external, Internet communication.

Network Interface layer — *See* Network Access layer.

OASIS (Organization for the Advancement of Structured Information Standards) — A consortium of business, research, academic, and other interests that develops and promotes information standards and services that are industry- or market-focused and aim to help consolidate and unify how they define, transport, and exchange information.

payload — The part of a malware program that actually does the damage.

PHP — *See* Hypertext Preprocessor.

physical numeric address — A 6-byte numeric address, called a Media Access Control (MAC) layer address, that is assigned to a network interface during manufacturing.

POP (Post Office Protocol) — An e-mail client for retrieving e-mail; older than and similar to IMAP.

pop-up — An application that automatically displays — or "pops up" — advertising content while you are online or on a particular Web site. This is usually an uninvited or unsolicited browser window that shows up on your desktop.

port (or **port address**) — A term for a location or address in memory assigned to a specific function or protocol; specific ports are used in various attacks and should be protected by a firewall, ports are numbered from 0 to 65,535 and grouped in the following way:

- **0–1023** — Well-known ports, or service ports, are associated with public, well-known IP-based services.
- **1,024–49,151** — Registered port numbers may sometimes be associated with specific, registered applications or used for other purposes.
- **49,152–65,535** — Dynamic port numbers are always used for temporary, transient service connections.

Process layer — *See* Application layer.

protocol — A collection of rules that describe the kinds of communication that can occur between a sender and a receiver, specifies what order those messages should or must follow, and lays down rules to delineate the formats that such communications should use.

protocol stack — A group of a layered, interdependent set of software components that actually implement the protocols on a particular device or computer.

protocol suite — A group of related and interdependent network protocols, such as TCP/IP.

registered port numbers (1,024–49,151) — Memory locations that correspond to specific industry applications or processes; for example, port 1188 is associated with HP's Web administration services.

registry — *See* Windows registry.

Reverse ARP (RARP) — A protocol that translates MAC addresses to numeric IP addresses. RARP operates at the Network Access layer, because it identifies specific hardware components attached to a network.

RFC (Request for Comment) — Formal specifications for Internet and Web protocols and languages; RFCs describe and govern existing and proposed protocols and services. RFCs are notes and papers and although they do not constitute a set of standards, they are usually treated as standards.

server — A term used to describe a computer that provides some service to a client (an application running on your machine, like the browser). There are many kinds of servers; one machine may act as more than one kind of server; also called server side. *See also* client.

service — Some function you need that is provided to your client by a server; a Web server provides you with Web services through various TCP/IP-based protocols.

SMTP (Simple Mail Transfer Protocol) — A network protocol that describes how information is exchanged. SMTP is the Internet protocol for e-mail.

spam — The electronic form of junk mail — unwanted and unsolicited e-mail. Currently this is the biggest component of all e-mail Internet traffic.

spambot — Short for spam robot. Like the demon in the Bible who roams the world "seeking whom he may devour," spambots roam the Web looking for e-mail addresses to exploit.

spyware — Anything that takes up residence on a computer, usually uninvited, that can report on the activities and preferences of the computer's users, or disclose information about data stored on a computer.

SSL (Secure Sockets Layer) — A common protocol, developed by Netscape, for managing Internet messaging security.

startup group — A special folder in Windows that contains shortcuts to run applications as Windows starts up (see Start → All Programs → Startup). Sometimes used to load security software but malware sometimes runs from this folder as well.

symbolic names — Internet domain names in a human user-friendly form, such as `www.microsoft.com` or `etittel@lanw.com`. The DNS must translate these names to numeric IP addresses for use by computers over the Internet.

system or boot-record infectors — A type of malware, usually a virus, that infects the special innermost sectors on a hard drive or floppy disk that are read as a computer is starting up. This type of malware can infect other media (primarily floppies and hard disks) but since modern 32-bit Windows don't access this part of the disk after boot-up is complete, they're no longer as common as they once were (when operating systems routinely accessed these on-disk areas).

TCP (Transmission Control Protocol) — *See* TCP/IP.

TCP/IP (Transmission Control Protocol/Internet Protocol) — The basic data transmission protocol underlying all networks, including the Internet. *See also* DARPA model.

threat — A computer or network is under threat when it harbors persistent software vulnerabilities; the possibility (if not certainty) of a malicious attack.

Transport layer — The layer of the TCP/IP protocol stack that handles everything necessary to transfer data from one computer to another; also known as Host-to-Host layer.

Trojan horse — A form of malware; a program or file that a user allows or invites onto his or her system, believing that it is benign software. Trojans actually provide an entry point for intrusion from the outside.

UDP (User Datagram Protocol) — A network communications protocol alternative to TCP. Because UDP does not provide data packet sequencing, it is best used on networks that transmit small amounts of data at a time.

virus — A program, almost always malicious, that can automatically replicate itself. Virus programs usually have a trigger — such as opening an e-mail attachment — and a self-replicating component.

vulnerability — A design flaw, programming error, or some kind of inherent weakness in a software implementation, application, or operating system that malware can exploit.

well-known port numbers (0–1,023) — Port numbers that correspond to various TCP/IP core services; also known as "service port numbers" or "service ports." These numbers typically identify well-known services such as FTP (ports 20 for data transfer and 21 for command and control information), SMTP (port 25), HTTP (port 80), and POP3 (port 110).

white hat — Used to describe people who attempt to expose security vulnerabilities for good instead of evil.

whitelisting — The opposite of blacklisting, maintaining a list of e-mail addresses you will accept e-mail from. *See also* blacklisting.

Windows registry — The Windows registry is a database of most configuration settings of Windows and applications running under Windows. *See also* hives.

World Wide Web Consortium (W3C) — An international industry group for promoting Internet and interoperability standards specific to the World Wide Web.

worm — A form of malware that seeks to infect and replicate without targeting and infecting specific files. For example, the `W32.Randex.ATX` is a Category 2 worm discovered on June 28, 2004. To remove this worm from your system, see Chapter 4 for details.

Index

A

continued

B

C

I

J

K

L

M

N

O

P

continued

Q

R

S

continued

PC
MAGAZINE
www.pcmag.com

T

U

V

W

continued

X

Z